W9-BWD-910

COVER PHOTO CREDITS

The AFRICAN-AMERICAN Century

How Black Americans Have Shaped Our Country

HENRY LOUIS GATES, JR. *and* CORNEL WEST

A TOUCHSTONE BOOK
PUBLISHED BY SIMON & SCHUSTER
NEW YORK LONDON TORONTO SYDNEY SINGAPORE

TOUCHSTONE
Rockefeller Center
1230 Avenue of the Americas
New York, NY 10020

First Touchstone Edition 2002
TOUCHSTONE and colophon are registered trademarks
of Simon & Schuster, Inc.
For information about special discounts for bulk purchases,
please contact Simon & Schuster Special Sales:
1-800-456-6798 or business@simonandschuster.com
Designed by Bonni Leon-Berman
Manufactured in the United States of America
10 9 8 7 6 5 4 3

The Library of Congress has cataloged the Free Press edition as follows:

Gates, Henry Louis.
    The African-American century: how Black Americans have shaped our country /
    Henry Louis Gates, Jr. and Cornel West.
        p.   cm.
    Includes index.
    1. Afro-Americans—Biography.   2. Afro-Americans—Intellectual life—20th century.
3. United States—Civilization—Afro-American influences. 4. Afro-Americans—
History—20th century.   5. United States—Civilization—20th century.
    I. West, Cornel.   II. Title.

E185.96.G38   2000
920'.009296073'00904—dc21
[B]
                                                                                              00-063596

ISBN 0-684-86414-2
        0-684-86415-0 (Pbk)

TO OUR BELOVED MOTHERS

Pauline Augusta Coleman Gates

and

Irene Bias West

CONTENTS

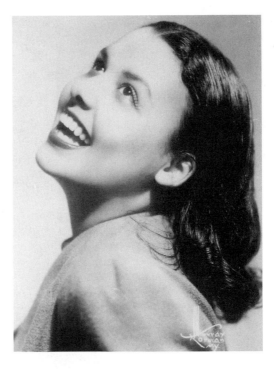

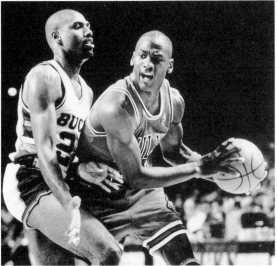

CONTENTS

The African-American Century Research Team

The scope of *The African-American Century* is both magnificent and daunting. We begin our chronicle with African Americans born into slavery and end it with those born after the assassination of Dr. King. We celebrate the achievements of black people working in fields as diverse as music, science, business, the military, sports, politics, literature, entertainment, and academia. In order to tell the stories of these one hundred lives we have relied heavily on the research skills of a wonderful team of writers.

First and foremost, we must give credit to the extensive work of Richard Newman of the Du Bois Institute for Afro-American Research at Harvard University. Newman's erudition and breadth of historical knowledge is evident in every biographical essay in this volume and in the appendices. We also want to acknowledge the administrative work of Nina Kollars and her predecessor, Miranda Pyne, who was instrumental in photographic research and organization. At the Free Press, Chad Conway, Alys Yablon, and intern Keisha Mason were indispensable. Celia Knight, David Frost, Iris Cohen, and designers Lisa Chovnick and Bonni Leon-Berman turned our rough pages into a beautiful book.

Each biographical essay was researched by a member of our research team as noted:

1930–1939

Marian Anderson	Miranda Pyne
Sterling A. Brown	Peter Hudson
Father Divine	Richard Newman
Charles H. Houston	Kate Tuttle
Zora Neale Hurston	Michael Train
Robert Johnson	Peter Hudson
Joe Louis	Miranda Pyne
Jesse Owens	Kate Tuttle
Paul Robeson	Miranda Pyne
Bojangles Robinson	Richard Newman

1940–1949

Charles R. Drew	Miranda Pyne
Katherine Dunham	Miranda Pyne
Duke Ellington	Miranda Pyne
Billie Holiday	Miranda Pyne
Lena Horne	Miranda Pyne
Jacob Lawrence	Miranda Pyne
Adam Clayton Powell, Jr.	Kate Tuttle
A. Philip Randolph	Kate Tuttle
Jackie Robinson	Miranda Pyne
Richard Wright	Adam F. Bradley

1950–1959

Ralph Bunche	Miranda Pyne
Nat King Cole	Kate Tuttle
Miles Davis	Peter Hudson
Ralph Ellison	Adam F. Bradley
Althea Gibson	Miranda Pyne
Lorraine Hansberry	Richard Newman
Willie Mays	Miranda Pyne
Rosa Parks	Kate Tuttle
Art Tatum	Miranda Pyne
Sarah Vaughan	Peter Hudson

1960–1969

Muhammad Ali	Miranda Pyne
James Baldwin	Michael Train
John Coltrane	Miranda Pyne
Angela Davis	Peter Hudson
Fannie Lou Hamer	Kate Tuttle
Jimi Hendrix	Miranda Pyne
Martin Luther King, Jr.	Elizabeth Herbin
Thurgood Marshall	Kate Tuttle
Sidney Poitier	Adam F. Bradley
Malcolm X	Adam F. Bradley

1970–1979

Hank Aaron	Miranda Pyne
Maya Angelou	Adam F. Bradley
Romare Bearden	Miranda Pyne
James Brown	Miranda Pyne
Marvin Gaye	Adam F. Bradley
Barbara Harris	Richard Newman
Dorothy Height	Miranda Pyne
Barbara Jordan	Miranda Pyne
Leontyne Price	Miranda Pyne
Richard Pryor	Miranda Pyne

1980–1989

Alvin Ailey	Peter Hudson
Bill Cosby	Kate Tuttle
John Hope Franklin	Kate Tuttle
Jesse Jackson	Kate Tuttle
Michael Jackson	Miranda Pyne
Carl Lewis	Adam F. Bradley
Jessye Norman	Miranda Pyne
Martin Puryear	Miranda Pyne
Alice Walker	Adam F. Bradley
August Wilson	Adam F. Bradley

1990–1999

Louis Farrakhan	Michael Train
Michael Jordan	Adam F. Bradley
Spike Lee	Adam F. Bradley
Wynton Marsalis	Adam F. Bradley
Toni Morrison	Richard Newman
Colin Powell	Michael Train
Tupac Shakur	Adam F. Bradley
Denzel Washington	Adam F. Bradley
Oprah Winfrey	Kate Tuttle
Tiger Woods	Adam F. Bradley & Kate Tuttle

ACKNOWLEDGMENTS

Introduction

"... whatever else the true American is,
he is also somehow black."

— *Ralph Ellison, "What America Would Be Like
Without Blacks" (1970)*

It was the century in which African-American life was transformed—and the century in which African Americans changed America. And yet,
when the twentieth century opened, African Americans had been "up from slavery,"
as Booker T. Washington would put it in his classic autobiography, for only thirty-
five years. Over the long and arduous course of the next hundred years, the achievements of our people would be nothing less than miraculous.

Remember: In 1900 blacks were systematically barred from full and equal par-
ticipation in the larger society. No African American could serve in a position of
authority over white soldiers, or fight by their sides; no black could participate in
professional baseball, the national pastime. The classic blues and jazz had not
emerged as the defining forms of American music. Black Americans were routinely lynched with impunity. "Separate but equal" was the institutional law of the
South and the de facto law of the land. Racist "Sambo" images of blacks proliferat-
ed in advertisements, postcards, games, tea cozies, and a thousand other sources. The
future of the race, at the turn of the century, looked rather bleak indeed.

At the dawn of the twenty-first century, by contrast, we cannot imagine a truly
American culture that has not, in profound ways, been shaped by the contributions
of African Americans. Who could imagine the American Century without the
African-American experience at its core? When we listen to that century, there
would be no Louis Armstrong. No Duke Ellington. No Billie Holiday or John
Coltrane. In fact there would be no jazz. No blues. No rock and roll. When we read

that century, there would be no Ralph Ellison. No James Baldwin. No Toni Morrison. When we think about what democracy means in such a century there would be no W. E. B. Du Bois. No Thurgood Marshall. No Martin Luther King, Jr. When we rent the movies of that century there would be no Bojangles Robinson. No Sidney Poitier. No Spike Lee. When we reminisce about the sports heroes of that century there would be no Jesse Owens. No Jackie Robinson or Althea Gibson. No Muhammad Ali. When we laughed about that century there would be no Bill Cosby. No Richard Pryor.

Such a century would not seem very American, would it?

Of course, the most fundamental significance of what is called the American Century was the unprecedented expansion of democratic sensibilities around the world. Nowhere were these sensibilities more apparent than in the extraordinary lives of those African Americans in this book. From American slaves to American citizens (most of whom are descendants of American slaves), these figures enact and embody the core of the democratic faith: the precious notion that ordinary individuals and everyday people possess the capacity to attain the highest levels of excellence and dignity. In this deep philosophic manner, the African-American Century sits at the center of the American Century just as black culture constitutes an essential element of American culture.

The song known as the "Negro National Anthem," penned by James Weldon Johnson and J. Rosamond Johnson in February 1900, expresses the essential principle of democracy: "Lift Every Voice." The *ethical* precondition for democracy is to allow every voice of the citizenry to be heard in the basic decisions that shape the destiny of its people. The *political* prerequisite for democracy is to secure the rights and liberties for every citizen, especially the most vulnerable ones. And the *economic* requirement for democracy is fair opportunity to every citizen. The African-American Century was first and foremost the black struggle for these ethical, political, and economic conditions of democracy in the face of vicious antidemocratic practices. This struggle is one of the great historical dramas of modern times. The people in this book are major agents in this unfinished struggle and incomplete drama.

We chose these particular persons because they represent the exemplary virtue of the black struggle for respect and liberty—namely, the courage to embody and live their respective truths in the face of overwhelming obstacles, including often the threat to their very lives. This courage was grounded in a profound commitment to enhance and elevate the deplorable plight of African Americans. As we probed into the remarkable lives of these figures we were struck by two recurrent features. First, we noticed the complex interplay of quiet despair and active hope in their diverse personalities. All of these individuals at some point in their lives were pushed to the edge of America's racist abyss. Each one of them experienced the absurd side of American life that reveals the lie of America as the land of liberty and justice for all. Second, we were brought to tears by these individuals' incredible efforts to affirm the full-fledged humanity of black people. These efforts took many forms, yet their common denominator was an unwavering self-confidence in their astonishing aspirations to achieve and excel. Be they artist, scholar, activist, scientist, or businessperson, of whatever political persuasion, these extraordinary persons who ushered forth from a hated and hunted folk never lost their belief in themselves in their quests for betterment.

Our selections were complicated by the dominant stereotypes of black people as born entertainers and natural athletes. Needless to say, some of the greatest entertainers and athletes of the twentieth century were black. So we had to walk a thin line in acknowledging this rich cultural heritage—owing to tremendous discipline and dedication to their crafts—while accenting the many spheres of life from which they were often excluded owing to their skin color. This balancing act is a tricky one because the undeniable achievements in black entertainment and sports in the eyes of many (of all colors) downplay black accomplishments in other areas of American society.

Needless to say, there are many towering figures who belong in this book yet do not appear as individual essays—Arthur Ashe, Harry Belafonte, Mary Frances Berry, Jim Brown, Johnnetta Cole, Marian Wright Edelman, John Johnson, Quincy Jones, Edwin Moses, and Gordon Parks, to name but a few. It could be said that each and every one of these people are part of the great story of the African-American Century. Our focus is less on individuals as isolated icons and more on individuals as part of a grand tradition that deepened democratic roots in an insufficiently democratic America. In this regard, the real heroes are the often overlooked anonymous foremothers and forefathers who loved, nurtured, and sacrificed for millions of black children.

One fundamental truth informs this book: American life is inconceivable without its black presence. The sheer intelligence and imagination of African Americans have disproportionately shaped American culture, produced wealth in the American economy, and refined notions of freedom and equality in American politics. And, on a deeper level, black reflections on the human condition in this land of sentimental aims and romantic dreams injected tragicomic sensibilities into the American experience. In other words, black people have always tried to remind America of its night side, of the barbarism lurking underneath its self-congratulatory rhetoric of universal freedom and equal opportunity. Black perceptions of American democracy are rooted in blue notes—the inescapable realities of pain, hurt, misery, and sorrow in human life and American society. In this sense, the response to white supremacy is not only the ultimate litmus test for American democracy, but wrestling with its tragicomic realities is the primary criterion of American maturity. Hence, the lives of these twentieth-century blues people constitute a major challenge to us all in the twenty-first century. This challenge takes the form of two basic questions: Will America continue to deny the pervasive impact of its ugly past on its evanescent present? Can America survive and thrive without coming to terms with its roots in slavery, its expansion in Jim Crow and conquest, and its prosperity alongside discrimination and devaluation of people of color? In this way, the distinct personalities in this book are not simply exemplary Americans to celebrate but also—and more importantly—grand moments of a great struggle for freedom with which America must contend if we are to preserve the precious liberties and opportunities in twenty-first-century America. How we view and understand the African-American Century deeply affects whether the next century will be another American Century or simply another hundred years in which history repeats itself not as tragic but as traumatic.

The lives of the African-American Century illuminate a central dilemma: How do we affirm black dignity and preserve black sanity in the face of the American denial of black humanity? All one hundred figures find themselves thrown in a whirlwind of white supremacy in American life and hence must discover and cultivate effective strategies to survive and thrive. They pursue their life passions under adverse circumstances—even after their relative success. They forge a courage to be with self-confidence and self-respect. They marshal a courage to love with self-regard and self-determination. They promote a courage to fight for justice against the grain of American institutional terrorism (Jim Crow and lynching) and/or individual insult (from racist fellow citizens). And the fruits they yield in every sphere of life are extraordinary—so extraordinary that we and the rest of the world must take notice. Their grand efforts and fruits are a crucial part of a great caravan of black love and achievement that creates a strong wind at our contemporary backs.

Yet they are who they are primarily because they preserved memories that put a premium on possibilities and promoted progeny whose hearts, minds, and souls were focused on accomplishments. Their incredible intelligence and imagination, creativity and ingenuity bespeak their unique fusions of talent, discipline, and energy. In short, their own distinctive forms of black genius make visible the pervasive black geniality—largeness of black heart, mind, and soul—among often everyday black folk.

So this book is a tribute to the world-historical contributions of people of African descent in the United States of America that have repercussions around the world. We want fellow human beings across the globe to know—and never forget—that here in this colossal American empire and past American century lived a great people who strived with much dignity and discernible effect to be true to themselves and their ideals of freedom against overwhelming odds and adverse circumstances. And we especially want our children—*all* children—to remember that more democracy is always a possibility if they are willing to carry on the precious heritage with vision, courage, and compassion.

Henry Louis Gates, Jr.
Cornel West
July 2000
Cambridge, Massachusetts

The
AFRICAN-
AMERICAN
Century

W. E. B. Du Bois

Black Public Intellectual
(1868–1963)

W. E. B. Du Bois was the greatest African-American intellectual figure of the twentieth century and one of the most influential black political thinkers before Martin Luther King, Jr. A man often known for elitist public stances and his haughty temperament in private, as a public intellectual, however, he was dedicated to the work of full citizenship for African Americans, and he fought against racial prejudice wherever it might be found. While his crusade eventually would take him across the globe, from Germany to Russia and, finally, to the new African state of Ghana (where he died a citizen in 1963), Du Bois was, above all, an American freedom fighter.

Du Bois was a black New England Victorian, a child of the Enlightenment, and a citizen entranced by the American dream. These three facets of his thought—his Enlightenment worldview, a certain Victorian sensibility, and an American optimism—came together to create a political philosophy for black America that was at once visionary and pragmatic.

In a life that spanned from the Reconstruction Era to the apex of the civil rights movement (he died on the eve of the historic 1963 March on Washington), Du Bois spent his intellectual life coming to grips with the past, addressing the present, and envisioning a future for American race relations. "[T]he problem of the Twentieth Century," he intoned famously and prophetically in his magisterial collection of essays *The Souls of Black Folk,* "is the problem of the color-line." Throughout his career Du Bois wrestled with a range of strategies to solve this problem, from socialism and communism to black cultural nationalism and Pan-Africanism, but always with a profound awareness of the undeniable fact of American cultural pluralism.

William Edward Burghardt Du Bois was born in Great Barrington, Massachusetts, on February 23, 1868. Within a year of his birth, his father, Alfred,

left town and never returned. Early on, it was clear both to those around him and apparently to Du Bois himself that he was destined for great things. Looking back on his childhood while a graduate student at Harvard, Du Bois wrote that "[m]y boyhood seems, if my memory serves me rightly, to have been filled with incidents of surprisingly little importance. . . . In early youth a great bitterness entered my life and kindled a great ambition. I wanted to go to college because others did. I came and graduated and am now in search of a Ph.D. and bread. I believe, foolishly perhaps but sincerely, that I have something to say to the world."

Unlike his political counterpart Booker T. Washington, who was born in slavery, Du Bois grew up with a sense of possibility that, if not exactly unfettered, offered him some flexibility in imagining how to traverse the color line. Great Barrington's black population was small, and Du Bois studied and worshiped mostly with white people. He distinguished himself among his white classmates in school, and was the first African American to graduate from his high school; he did so in 1884, with high honors. His mother died the next year, leaving Du Bois alone and penniless. But white leaders from local Congregational churches stepped in to furnish him with a scholarship. Du Bois initially wanted to attend Harvard, but bowed to his benefactors' wishes that he attend Fisk, one of the preeminent black institutions of higher education.

While Du Bois was disappointed not to be attending Harvard, he saw it as a chance to learn something of the South; Harvard could wait. "I was going into the South," he wrote in *Darkwater: Voices From Within the Veil* (1920), "the South of slavery, rebellion and black folk; above all, I was going to meet the colored people of my own age and education, of my own ambition." In the South Du Bois also became acquainted with the racial violence that had crippled the hopes of Reconstruction. Although during his time at Fisk (1885–1888) Jim Crow laws had not reached their full influence, the atmosphere of racial animus that spawned them was palpable. For the first time in his life, Du Bois found himself on intimate terms with black poverty and suffering.

Du Bois's newfound connection with southern black folk was most evident in the summers he spent teaching in the rural South while at Fisk. Chronicled in "Of the Black Belt" and other parts of *The Souls of Black Folk,* this was clearly a formative experience in Du Bois's developing social and cultural consciousness. And while he is criticized often for his lack of a sophisticated understanding of class tensions in his writing, his early writing in rural Tennessee suggests that he knew something of the economic basis of racism.

After graduating from Fisk in 1888, Du Bois realized his deferred dream of attending Harvard. Enrolled as a junior, he received his second bachelor's degree that next year before continuing his graduate study, in history, at Harvard. While Du Bois never was permitted into the social life of the institution, he was enmeshed quickly in the academic life. Among his mentors were some of the preeminent thinkers of the day: William James and George Santayana in philosophy, Albert Bushnell Hart in history, and Frank Taussig in economics. In 1892, funded through an experimental American fellowship program, Du Bois traveled to Berlin to study sociology and economics as a graduate student at Fredrich Wilhelm University. Beyond his work in the classroom (which included attending lectures by the sociologist Max Weber), Du Bois felt a new sense of freedom, unencumbered by constant racial questions. But this would prove to be short-lived. When his funding ran out, he was forced to return to Harvard, where he reluctantly completed graduate study.

While Du Bois certainly could have responded with despondency to this setback (he had some reason to believe that the rejection of his application to complete his doctoral thesis in Berlin was due to racism), he used it instead as a sign that he had been chosen to commence his assault on white supremacy in the United States through the life of the mind. It had come time for him, he writes in his journal on his twenty-fifth birthday, "to make a name in science, to make a name in literature and thus to raise my race." Upon his return from Berlin, he began this plan in earnest, securing a position teaching classics at Wilberforce University in 1894 and, a year later, becoming the first African American to earn a Ph.D., in history, from Harvard. His thesis, *The Suppression of the African Slave Trade to the United States of America, 1638–1870,* was the first work published in the Harvard Historical Monograph Series (1896). That same year he met and married Nina Gomer. After a year of research in Philadelphia, which resulted in *The Philadelphia Negro,* published in 1899—one of the seminal works in American sociology—he took a position at Atlanta University that offered security for himself and his new wife.

For the next twelve years, Du Bois taught at Atlanta. Between 1897 and 1903 he was among the most prolific authors in the nation, publishing essays in a range of periodicals from *Harper's Weekly* to *The Dial.* By the time of publication of his landmark *Souls of Black Folk* in 1903, the thirty-five-year-old Du Bois was one of the most widely read, broadly traveled, and impeccably educated men in the world. In the mold of Frederick Douglass, Du Bois had cemented his reputation as the voice of the black intellectual elite.

Du Bois is unprecedented as an African-American political figure in that he wrote himself into a position of power. Even his contemporaries were aware of this unusual road to prominence. William H. Ferris, black educator and Yale graduate, expressed this surprise in 1913 in the pages of *The African Abroad:* Du Bois, Ferris noted, was one of the few people in history who was hurled on the throne of leadership by the dynamic force of the written word. He was one of the few writers who became a leader and the head of a popular movement through impressing his personality upon society by means of a book.

That book, of course, was *The Souls of Black Folk,* and its publication stands as the high-water mark in Du Bois's career. In the process, the book established him as the second great public intellectual of black America, after Frederick Douglass a generation before. *Souls* is a curious and eclectic volume, a bold narrative declaration of the nationhood of a people, the Negro Americans. It is a series of fourteen essays framed by a lyrical "Forethought" and "Afterthought." Part sociology, part history, part polemic, and part creative literature, *Souls* proposed to give voice to the "nation-within-a-nation" that was the eight million black Americans. Through myth and metaphor, and in a lyrical yet polemical prose, the young Du Bois charted the contours of the civilization—the arts and sciences, the metaphysical and religious systems, the myths and music, the social and political institutions, the history both before and after Emancipation—that defined a truly African-American culture at the outset of the new century.

The governing tropes of *Souls* are double-consciousness and the "veil"—the curtain separating black and white life. By turns, Du Bois locates himself above, below, within, and without the veil, employing an imagery as old as the Bible. Allied with this is his concept of double-consciousness—a term with roots in contemporary thought, and certainly in that of earlier American thinkers such as Emerson and James, but which Du Bois makes uniquely his own. "One ever feels his two-ness—," Du Bois wrote in the signal passage defining double-consciousness, "an American, a Negro; two souls, two thoughts, two unreconciled strivings; two warring ideals in one dark body, whose dogged strength alone keeps it from being torn asunder." This metaphor would prove to be the governing trope of African-American literature from the publication of James Weldon Johnson's *The Autobiography of an Ex-Colored Man* (1913) through Ralph Ellison's *Invisible Man* (1952) to Toni Morrison's *Beloved* (1988)

But while Du Bois may have written himself into power, he did not limit himself to writing. In 1905, he collaborated with William Monroe Trotter, the militant editor of the *Boston Guardian,* to form the Niagara Movement—a short-lived organization dedicated to ensuring full civil and political rights for black Americans. But it was his role as a founding member of the National Association for the Advancement of Colored People (NAACP) that proved the most significant of his organizational efforts. As the only African American on the first executive board, his importance to the subsequent shape and success of the NAACP is inestimable. As director of publications and research, he founded *The Crisis*—the NAACP's official magazine—which, under his editorship between 1910 and 1934, published work by the preeminent black thinkers and artists of the day. James Weldon Johnson, Langston Hughes, Countee Cullen, to name a few, published in its pages. Du Bois was also a frequent editorial contributor, expressing his outrage at racial injustice while championing the role of the arts and education in the fight against racism.

> *I have loved my work, I have loved people and my play, but always I have been uplifted by the thought that what I have done well will live long and justify my life, that what I have done ill or never finished can now be handed on to others for endless days to be finished, perhaps better than I could have done.*
>
> —W. E. B. Du Bois

Looking at his editorials from 1910 to his resignation as editor of *The Crisis* in 1934, one can see the evolution of Du Bois's political thought toward a more international understanding of race relations. In 1919 he helped organize the second Pan-African Congress. His 1915 sociopolitical study, *The Negro,* reflects this new diasporic vision of America's racial crisis. The question, he wrote on his first visit to Africa, is whether "Negroes are to lead in the rise of Africa or whether they must always and everywhere follow the guidance of white folk." In addition, Du Bois's exploration of the potential utility of socialism in the Negro's struggle began at least as early as his visit to the Soviet Union in 1926. These newfound radical leanings put him in conflict with Walter White, the more conservative secretary of the NAACP, leading to Du Bois's resignation in 1934.

After leaving the NAACP, Du Bois tried in vain to publish *The Encyclopedia of the Negro,* and returned to Atlanta University, where he remained active, writing columns for black newspapers and publishing bold analyses such as *Black Reconstruction in America* (1934), *Black Folk:Then and Now* (1939), and *Dusk of Dawn: An Autobiography of a Concept of Race* (1940). Du Bois resigned from Atlanta University in 1944 and rejoined the NAACP—though not as editor of *The Crisis.* Now in his mid-seventies, Du Bois decided to dedicate "the remaining years of [his] active life" to fighting racism at home and colonialist imperialism abroad. In 1945 he was elected international president of the third Pan-African Congress in Manchester, England, attended by such future African leaders as Kwame Nkrumah, who would become the first president of Ghana (1952). Du Bois's writing reflects his newfound focus: He published *Color and Democracy: Colonies and Peace* in 1945 and *The World and Africa* in 1947.

In the fifties, Du Bois's sympathies for the Soviet Union became more strident precisely when the United States was in the grip of a manic cold war paranoia. In 1951 he was indicted under the Foreign Agents Registration Act of 1938 and, although he was acquitted, had his passport revoked until 1958. Once his travel ban was lifted, Du Bois left the country to travel throughout Europe, stopping as well in communist China and the Soviet Union. Finally, in 1961 Du Bois accepted Kwame Nkrumah's invitation to move to Ghana to live and work on the *Encyclopedia Africana,* a project he never completed. Six months after becoming a Ghanaian citizen, Du Bois died at the age of ninety-four, on the eve of the March on Washington.

Du Bois's legacy is so far-reaching that, in a sense, it would be true to claim that all black intellectuals and all of our civil rights leaders are, in some manner, his heirs. His influence is palpable in everything from the continuing influence of his literary works—most notably *The Souls of Black Folk*—to the completion in 1999 of his vision of an *Encyclopedia Africana.* More than anyone else, he was the father of the civil rights era, the theorist of the movement that Dr. King led so brilliantly. Du Bois is the brook of fire through which we all must pass in order to gain access to the intellectual and political weaponry we need to sustain the tradition of radical opposition to antiblack racism and economic exploitation in our time.

T. Thomas Fortune

Afro-American Agitator
(1856–1928)

T.Thomas Fortune was the preeminent black journalist of his age, and also the first to popularize the term "Afro-American." More than semantics are at stake with such an appellation. In conceiving of black Americans as both intimately tied to Africa and yet essential to America, Fortune was expressing something that, while commonly accepted today, ran counter to both the back-to-Africa movements of Marcus Garvey and others and to the ambiguity of origin implied by such terms as "Negro" and "colored." "As an American citizen," he wrote in *Black and White* (1884), "I feel it born in my nature to share in the fullest measure all that is American, feeling the full force of the fact that while we are classed as Africans, just as the Germans are classed as Germans, we are in all things American citizens, American freemen."

Fortune was the leading black editor and journalist of the late nineteenth and early twentieth centuries. While often eclipsed in historical memory by the mythic duality of W. E. B. Du Bois and Booker T. Washington, he is essential to a full understanding of black leadership after Reconstruction. He grappled, above all, with the fundamental question of what it meant for a black American to be an American citizen. He presages the words of Ralph Ellison almost a half century after Fortune's death that "whatever else the true American is, he is also somehow black."

Timothy Thomas Fortune was born a slave in Marianna, Florida, in 1856. In the years after Emancipation, Fortune was exposed to the violence of racial animus. Jackson County, his birthplace, was notorious as the site of many of the Ku Klux Klan's most brutal attacks. Fortune's father was an outspoken advocate for racial equality, and pressures from the Klan forced him to relocate his family to Jacksonville. Here Fortune began to cultivate his dual interests in politics and journalism. He served as a page in the state Senate and learned the printers' trade at various local newspapers. Fortune was largely an autodidact, although he briefly attended a school sponsored by the Freedmens Bureau, and spent a year in a preparatory program at Howard University in Washington, D.C.

Fortune left Florida in 1881 and settled in New York City, his home for the remainder of his life. After a brief stint working on a white-owned newspaper, Fortune launched out on his own to found what would later become the *New York Age.* Fortune retained control of the paper from 1887 until 1907, when he sold his interest. During that time, Fortune established the *Age* as the preeminent black newspaper in the country and himself as the most influential voice in black journalism. As an editorialist, Fortune excoriated everyone from local white politicians to racist representatives of the "New South" to the U.S. Supreme Court. Flying in the face of the powerful disenfranchisement movements in the South, he demanded that black Americans, as Americans, be entitled to all the rights that citizenship entails, particularly the right to vote. Fortune called for white Americans to deny the letter of the law and for black Americans to use their political rights to protect themselves and ensure their own futures. These ideological fundamentals made Fortune less wedded to partisan politics—politics, he felt, should be a pragmatic expedient for the Negro's larger goals.

Perhaps Fortune's most divisive stance from the perspective of fellow African Americans was his position on racial intermarriage. Black Americans, he pointed out, were already a mixed race. One need look no further than the fair-skinned Fortune to substantiate this. Other leaders, such as the dark-skinned Alexander Crummell, took issue with Fortune. In response, Fortune cautioned against forming a "color line within a color line." What made him most vilified among whites was his support of violence in the name of self-defense. "We do not counsel violence," he explained, "we counsel manly retaliation. We do not counsel a breach of the law, but in the absence of law we maintain that the individual has every right to protect himself." Force was one—not the only, but one—method by which blacks could assert their humanity and citizenship.

Fortune was an exact contemporary of another slave turned political leader, Booker T. Washington. It is essential to view Fortune's career in light of his connection to Washington. Fortune's life would prove intimately conjoined with Washington's. The two men first met sometime in the 1880s, well before Washington delivered his 1895 Atlanta Exposition address that would launch him into the national limelight as the preeminent black leader at the turn of the century. They became close friends in the succeeding decades, with Fortune often visiting Washington at Tuskegee on his trips to the South. The white press frequently presented them as counter forces, with Washington as the "sound" and "safe" voice of Negroes, and Fortune as the "agitator." As one Syracuse newspaper suggested: "According[ly] as the T. Thomas Fortune type, with its loud insistence upon rights, is forced to subside, and the Booker T. Washington type, with its earnest effort in the direction of quiet self-improvement, gains ascendancy, progress for the race may be expected."

Yet those in the black community often saw Fortune as a cipher for Washington, another wand for the wizard of Tuskegee. The truth, however, is far more complex. In an article entitled "The Quick and the Dead," written after Washington's death, Fortune reflects on their relationship. He acknowledges an affinity of purpose with Washington, particularly regarding the education and economic development of the race. And yet Fortune insists that he had "nothing in common with the policies of Dr. Washington, especially his personal and political ones." Like Du Bois, he questioned Washington's means, and he was uncomfortable with what he perceived to be Washington's conciliatory stance toward southern whites. In all, Fortune had the freedom, because of his reputation as a radical, to say things to which Washington would agree in private but never could utter in public. Indeed, Washington occasionally wrote unsigned pieces that were published in the *New York Age.* Fortune was ahead of his time, it would seem, in some of his organizational ambitions. In 1887, in the pages of the *Freeman,* he proposed the formation of the National Afro-American League to work against lynching, disenfranchisement, and other Jim Crow policies. Two years later, in December 1889, delegates from twenty-three states (including six from the South) met in Chicago to work for full citizenship and equality for black Americans.

While Fortune was the natural president of the organization (he was selected the temporary chairman), he ultimately was deemed too controversial a figure, and was made secretary instead. While Fortune exerted no small effort in galvanizing local chapters to support the national branch, the league failed to emerge as a major force. While it continued until 1902, it achieved only meager results. But its goals would be appropriated and realized by the Niagara Movement (1905) and, ultimately, by its successor, the NAACP.

Fortune's personal life, as well, took a turn for the worse. In 1907 he suffered a mental collapse, undoubtedly the culmination of the economic and psychological pressures that had beset him for years. He increasingly grew disillusioned with the prospect of racial uplift, resigning the presidency of the National Afro-American Council in 1904. "I have reached the conclusion that the Fates have the cards stacked against me," he wrote to a friend in 1905. "All the way I have shaken the trees and others have gathered the fruit." The following year he separated from his wife and turned to alcohol. Fortune's influence as a race leader was almost completely gone by the time he sold his interest in the *Age* to Fred R. Moore in 1907. Fortune lived for another two decades, but they were a bitter postscript to his vibrant public life of the decades before. The details of his life after 1907 are vague: He bounced from paper to paper working as a correspondent and editorial writer for several ephemeral publications. And while he continued to correspond on and off with Washington, their relationship was never as close as it had been.

We are African in origin and American in birth.

—T. Thomas Fortune

Fortune's last major work stands in rather jarring contrast to his past ideology; from 1923 until his death in 1928 he served as editor for the *Negro World,* the publication of Marcus Garvey's Universal Negro Improvement Association whose racial separatism and back-to-Africa program were antithetical to Fortune's long-held positions. But far from erasing his life's work, Fortune's decline amounts to something of a tragic postscript that points both toward and away from the life that preceded it. Nevertheless, Fortune will be recalled as the father of African-American journalism and one of the first proponents of political organizations that would create and realize the goals of the modern civil rights movement. His analysis of the colonial exploitation of Africa was prophetic:

Bloodshed and usurpations, the rum jug and the Bible—these will be the program of the white race in Africa, for, perhaps, a hundred years. . . . But, in the course of time, the people will become educated not only in the cruel and grasping nature of the white man, but in the knowledge of their power, their priority ownership in the soil, and in the desperation which tyranny and greed never fail to breed for their own destruction.

Matthew Henson

The Explorer
(1866–1955)

Matthew Alexander Henson was the codiscoverer of the North Pole in 1909 along with Admiral Robert E. Peary and three Inuit men. They were the first people to reach the Pole in the long and treacherous history of Arctic exploration. Henson's victory was a Pyrrhic one, however, diminished by racism in America. Henson was never mentioned at the time of the discovery, and only in 1948 were his achievements truly recognized.

Although Europeans dominated exploration in the late nineteenth century, at the turn of the twentieth century, with the closing of the American frontier, Americans turned their eyes to the rest of the world. It was a period of discovery and adventure, when the opening of the Panama Canal linked the Atlantic with the Pacific and the Wright brothers crossed distances by air. Of course, African Americans had been on the move since the Civil War. They traveled in search of family members sold during slavery, as well as for a place they could call home, which in some cases was not America. There were black western pioneers, but many also left America altogether, for Canada, Brazil, the West Indies, and Africa. Others found work near the docks so they could go to sea. Matthew Henson, who sailed around the world aboard the merchant vessel *Katie Hines,* was one such mariner.

Henson was born on August 6, 1866, on a farm that had been used as a slave market, in Najemay, Charles County, Maryland. He fled the farm after his parents died, and took to the road again at the age of eleven because of abuse by a cruel foster mother. He recalled that an uncle of his lived near Washington, D.C., and went in search of him. The uncle made arrangements to enroll Henson in school, but he could not afford to send him. His education stopped before it had begun, Henson found a job as a dishwasher in a restaurant in Baltimore. While working, he overheard dinner conversation talk of the sea, of the docks, and of distant lands. At thirteen he packed up what little he had and joined the *Katie Hines,* bound for Hong Kong.

For six years Henson traveled the world aboard the ship. Captain Childs became very fond of Henson and taught him navigation, mathematics, seamanship, and geography. Henson benefited immensely from this new attention showed him by his mentor, and he found the world a more fulfilling place than he had ever imagined. He became fluent in Russian on one trip, a feat that indicated his linguistic skills. In 1885, tragedy befell Henson when Captain Childs died; at the age of nineteen, stranded again, Henson dejectedly returned to Washington. He secured a temporary job in a hat store. In 1896, at the store, Henson was introduced to Lieutenant Robert Peary, a civil engineer with the U.S. Navy and an avid explorer at heart. Peary had just returned from Nicaragua, where he had been attempting to find a way across Central America to connect the Atlantic with the Pacific. Matthew Henson made such a strong impression that Peary offered him a job as his personal assistant on his next trip. In 1887, Henson was back on the road, traveling with Peary on a survey expedition to Nicaragua. This was the start of a fourteen-year friendship, during which Peary and Henson made seven polar expeditions together.

No one had yet reached the North Pole or the polar ice cap, one of the bleakest, most enigmatic places on earth. Despite the hundreds of voyages made by Scandinavian, Dutch, and English explorers, the vast polar sea, covering an expanse of nearly five million square miles, bordering Greenland, North America, and Asia, was still completely unknown at the turn of the century. After the fur hunters and whalers had flocked to the Arctic region in the nineteenth century, the focus of exploration shifted to the North Pole itself. Even pioneering Norwegian scientist Fridtjof Nansen could not survive the harsh, virtually impossible winters and died before returning home. Greenland, however, despite sub-zero temperatures, teemed with animal life, and it was and is still inhabited by the Inuit people as well as other ethnic groups. Henson lived with the Inuit on and off for over fourteen years. He learned to speak Inuit and how to survive in the Arctic climate. On one of Peary and Henson's missions, as their successive failed expeditions came to be called, the two explorers collected two of three meteorites that had landed in Greenland. They returned for the third one in 1897, which weighed seventy pounds and was said to be the largest meteorite in the world. All three are now on display at New York City's Museum of Natural History.

1900–1909

Their missions to the Arctic region, although grueling, were liberating for Henson and Peary. Henson nurtured those talents he had for exploration, which offered him opportunities vastly superior to what he would have encountered back home in early-twentieth-century America as a porter or janitor. His uncommon skills made him indispensable to Peary. First, Henson was the only one who was fluent in Inuit. He had learned it between 1897 and 1902, when both Henson and Peary remained in the Arctic for four uninterrupted years of exploration, during which time both created families with Inuit partners. Second, he was responsible for much of the material comfort during their missions: He built their headquarters, hunted, drove the dog sled that took them to the Pole, and never abandoned Peary,

> *When I reached the ship again and gazed into my little mirror, it was the pinched and wrinkled visage of an old man that peered out at me, but the eyes still twinkled and life was still entrancing. This wizening of our features was due to the strain of travel and lack of sleep; we had enough to eat, and I have only mentioned it to help impress the fact that the journey to the Pole and back is not to be regarded as a pleasure outing, and our so-called jaunt was by no means a cake-walk.*
> —Matthew Alexander Henson

even when others in the team did. Henson also disproved dominant turn-of-the-century race theories that claimed that black-skinned people could not survive Arctic weather.

The two men finally reached the North Pole on April 6, 1909. (Most scholars today think that they were really a few miles from the actual pole.) Henson, who typically broke the trail while pulling a sled, probably reached the Pole forty-five minutes before Peary. The "discovery" of the North Pole was until recently credited to Peary alone. Henson is mentioned as a man of African descent who was Peary's servant but not as his partner. This reduction of Henson's role belies the friendship, partnership, and collaboration that the two men enjoyed.

In 1912 Henson wrote *A Black Explorer at the North Pole*. In 1913, President William Howard Taft personally recommended Henson's appointment to the United States Customs House in New York City in recognition of his exploits in the Arctic. In 1944 Henson received a joint medal from Congress, honoring the Peary expedition. He also was honored by President Harry Truman in 1950 and admitted to the Explorers' Club. All the same, Henson died in obscurity in 1955 and was given a simple burial bereft of any fanfare. In 1986, Henson was commemorated on a postage stamp. And in 1988, thanks to the campaign of Professor Allen Counter at the Harvard Medical School, who had investigated Henson's life and gone to meet both his and Peary's descendants in Greenland, Henson was reburied in Arlington National Cemetery with full honors. Henson's mastery of the art of science and exploration, precisely at a time when America denied the innate intelligence and strength of African Americans, would be recounted as salient proof that only thirty years after the abolition of slavery, descendants of slaves possessed the requisite skills and drive to excel even in that most difficult and arduous profession: exploration and discovery.

1900–1909

Jack Johnson

The Boxer
(1878–1946)

Because of Jack Johnson, the idea of a Great White Hope had to be invented. More than any other sport, boxing provoked the deepest white anxiety about black manhood and black equality. Replete with social and cultural symbolism, the sport assumed a heightened racial aura throughout the twentieth century, from Johnson's day to the advent of Muhammad Ali. Highly ritualized, as well as an often sordid affair, boxing pits one man's wit and sheer strength against another's. Two muscled, almost naked men dance a grueling fight to a "knockout," an end that symbolically and purposefully imitates a form of death. In the early part of the century, whites feared that blacks would interpret any victory of black boxers over white boxers in fair public bouts as a sign of their inherent equality with white America. This anxiety was well grounded, of course—boxing victories *were* interpreted this way, by blacks and whites alike. And this is what happened when African-American John Arthur (Jack) Johnson took the world heavyweight title in 1908 from Tommy Burns with a mocking ease and then went on to defeat the greatest white boxers of his day, such as Jim Jeffries. For the rest of Johnson's career, the boxing establishment was in search of the Great White Hope, a boxer who would redeem the racial order.

Boxing has ancient roots in the gladiator spectacles of Greece and Rome. American boxing's direct antecedents are to be found in English bare-knuckle fighting, sometimes called the noble art. Before the Civil War it was a common, if barbaric, betting practice for white slave owners to force black slaves to fight to the death in a makeshift boxing ring. This "sport" was made more dreadful by the paraphernalia associated with the ring: dog collars around the boxers' necks, blindfolding of the eyes, shackles around their ankles. By the end of the nineteenth century, boxing gradually became popular entertainment, with fighters drawn from working-class backgrounds, often recent European immigrants to America. It was a taboo sport, alternately encouraged and supported, and often officially scorned and even prohibited at times, by the upper and middle classes.

It was clear from watching his monumental fight with Tommy Burns in 1908 that Jack Johnson brought a unique style to this crude sport. An excellent strategist, his approach was one of measured violence. He controlled the fight with his strength, height, and sophisticated technique. He toyed with his opponents by gently taunting them, even applauding when they hit him. Overall, he was defensive, one of the best counterpunchers of his day. Only at the end would he unleash a finishing blow that knocked his opponent out. He towered over Tommy Burns, whose punches, feebly drowning in Johnson's flesh, were futile in comparison. Amid racial insults from the spectators, Johnson, refusing to be unnerved, gave an excruciating lesson in the mauling of a human body. At the fight's end he knocked Burns out of the ring.

> *I know the bitterness of being accused and being harassed by prosecutors. I know the horror of being hunted and haunted. I have dashed across continents and oceans as a fugitive and have matched my wits with the police and secret agents seeking to deprive me of one of the greatest blessings man can have—liberty.*
>
> —Jack Johnson

In 1908, Johnson was not just another boxer; he embodied the ideal of black masculinity that whites feared most. As a result, his victories (in 113 fights, he lost only 8) sometimes caused race riots and even lynchings across America. Outside of the ring he was made into Public Enemy Number 1, because, although he slept with both black and white women—including society ladies and prostitutes with whom he had longstanding affairs—his wives were all white. All of it—Johnson's wives of different white ethnic backgrounds, his finely tailored suits, his penchant for race car driving, his successful business ventures, his broad, confident, and calm smile, and most of all the fact that he was entirely unafraid—was too much: his lifestyle so agitated his enemies outside the ring that they decided Johnson was too dangerous a symbol of racial equality to be allowed to thrive.

Jack Johnson came from an impoverished area of Galveston, Texas. He left school prematurely, soon after completing the fifth grade. He found work over the years as a painter, a baker, and a dockworker in the Galveston harbor. While a janitor at a local gymnasium, Johnson watched boxers practice and observed boxing matches. Intrigued, he studied the sport intensively. Johnson had his first professional fight in

1897. Although in his early years he suffered from malnutrition and fatigue, he was by 1903 the unofficial black heavyweight champion, having beaten the reigning black champion, "Denver Ed" Martin. Johnson railed against the American color barrier in the United States that prevented him from fighting the leading white heavyweights, John L. Sullivan and Jim Jeffries, in particular, who, in turn, flatly refused to fight him. His reputation in international boxing circles, nevertheless, eventually made evasion impossible, and a bout was scheduled for December 26, 1908, between Johnson and the international heavyweight, Australian Tommy Burns, in Sydney, Australia. Johnson won. So horrified was the world at the sight of a black man winning that the fight was etched into sports history as significantly as Jackie Robinson's first foray into baseball three decades later. During the next two years, Johnson defended his championship title against five more white contenders. The search for the "Great White Hope," the name given to any serious white challenger for the title, began in earnest. One possibility was the great but retired world heavy-

JAMES E. PEPPER WHISKY.
"BORN WITH THE REPUBLIC".

WORLD'S CHAMPIONSHIP BATTLE, JULY 4, 1910
ROUND 14

weight champion Jim Jeffries, who was living the placid life of a farmer. The novelist Jack London, in Australia and writing for the *New York Herald,* spoke on behalf of white fans everywhere when he urged Jim Jeffries, on the front page of the newspaper, to "wipe that smile off of Jack Johnson's face."

Bowing under the pressure, Jim Jeffries agreed to fight Jack Johnson in Reno, Nevada, on the most patriotic of America's holidays, July 4, in 1910. It was dubbed

"The Fight of the Century." It was an extremely tense day. The myth of white supremacy relied heavily on Johnson's defeat. To America's horror, Johnson beat Jeffries soundly. The country exploded in widespread race warfare and racially motivated class conflict. Across the nation there were vitriolic denunciations of boxing: Theodore Roosevelt, a longtime fan of the sport, turned angrily against it, while Christian groups in several cities attempted to ban the film that had been made of the contest. Johnson, apparently unperturbed by the racial conflict escalating in his honor, calmly married a white high-society woman named Etta Terry Duryea. He traveled to England with her in 1911, where they were received as celebrities. Not surprisingly, the marriage was a turbulent one. Etta, overwhelmed by the racism they encountered in public, as well as being married to a notorious playboy, committed suicide a year later. Her death outraged the public even more. In 1912, Johnson added fuel to the fire by falling in love with his white bookkeeper, the much younger Lucille Cameron, whom he married. White reporters added this to their ridicule of his new business venture—the highly successful Café de Champion saloon in Chicago.

In 1913 Johnson was arrested and convicted under the Mann Act, known as the White Slave Traffic Act, which prohibited men from transporting women across state borders for "immoral" purposes. Johnson had traveled with both of his wives, Duryea and Cameron, but the law was invoked to define interracial marriage as immoral. Johnson fled the United States for France to avoid serving a prison term. He lived there for two years, conducting boxing and wrestling exhibitions. In the spring of 1915 he returned to competitive boxing in Havana, Cuba, only to lose his heavyweight title to the white American boxer Jess Willard. In 1920, Johnson was forced to serve a year in prison upon his return to the United States. When he was released, he devoted the rest of his life to writing, appearing in boxing exhibitions, and managing a series of business enterprises. After eleven years of marriage, Johnson divorced Cameron for Irene Pineau. Jack Johnson lived until he was seventy years old. On June 10, 1946, he died in an automobile accident in Raleigh, North Carolina. He was not inducted into the International Boxing Hall of Fame until 1990. Inadvertently, Johnson unveiled the political symbolism of sports in an American society desperate to preserve the fiction of "natural" inequality between blacks and whites. He was, in his way, a germinal force in the nascent civil rights movement, a living symbol that blacks could prevail in fair competitions with whites, both in the ring and outside of it.

Scott Joplin

The King of Ragtime
(1868?–1917)

He changed the world's very concept of music. Scott Joplin is not the only creative African-American entertainer of whom this can be said, but his compelling ragtime piano carries cosmic significance as a harbinger of modernity. The social impact of ragtime is clearer, however, than its origins. With its strict two-four time and syncopated melody, ragtime was first played sometime before 1900 in low-down black sporting houses and dance halls. These are the places Scott Joplin found it and played it, as well as where he perceived ragtime's inherent beauty, complexity, and meaning, and set out to transform it into an art form that would give birth to jazz. Its earliest history will never be known, but there are some clues.

Visiting America, Ignacy Paderewski, the classical composer, reports being taken slumming by a *Post-Dispatch* reporter in the 1890s to Babe Connors's black St. Louis bordello. A blind pianist played for dancing "Creole" girls who wore only stockings, and a woman known as Mammy Lou sang "Ta-ra-ra-boom-de-ay" and other songs not yet known to white people. Ragtime was first heard outside of black circles in 1896 at Tony Pastor's Theater in New York, where Ben Harney, a black musician passing for white (or maybe he was a white musician passing as a black musician passing for white), played what was then called "jig piano." The word ragtime probably first appeared in print in Bert Williams's 1896 song "Oh, I Don't Know, You're Not So Warm." The next year a white Chicago bandleader, William Krell, copyrighted "Mississippi Rag," soon followed by "Harlem Rag" by Tom Turpin, the first ragtime tune published by an African American.

Scott Joplin, who came to be the master of the genre, was born in Texarkana, Texas, around 1868. He was one of six children of Giles Joplin, a former slave who worked on the railroad, and Florence Givens Joplin. His father, who played the fiddle, deserted the family, and his mother, who played banjo, was left to support the children as a domestic servant. But she recognized the boy's talent for improvisation and persuaded the white people whose homes she cleaned to allow him to practice on their pianos. Joplin started playing in churches and at social events, and then graduated to where the money was, pleasure houses. Whether or not he had early musical training is uncertain, but when he attended the George R. Smith College for Negroes in Sedalia, Missouri, he was admitted to advanced classes in composition and harmony.

Joplin became an itinerant musician. In 1885 he worked in St. Louis's red-light district at the Silver Dollar Saloon, which served as an employment office for piano players. A young woman would appear from one of the houses and announce that they had a customer and needed a "perfesser." He went to the World's Columbian Exposition in Chicago in 1893 and discovered that white people liked his music. The next year he was in Sedalia, playing at the Maple Leaf Club. In 1896 he toured with his Texas Melody Quartet (which had five members) and published his first piano compositions, "Please Say You Will" and "A Picture of Her Face." They were not rags, but Joplin was soon to change not only his own life but to bring to white America the first crossover black music. He wrote "Maple Leaf Rag," the music he knew best, and sold it in 1899 to John Stark, a white Sedalia music dealer.

Stark gave Joplin an unusual contract. He didn't buy the song outright for a few dollars, as was the usual practice, but offered royalties: one cent on every copy of sheet music that sold for fifty cents. In the first year Stark sold four hundred copies, and Joplin earned four dollars. But in 1900 "Maple Leaf Rag" became a national sensation. It sold one million copies, it made Stark rich and Joplin famous, and it changed American popular music forever. Publication also changed Scott Joplin. He had imagined ragtime as a kind of classical music both African and American in form and content, and success made it possible for him to give that vision concrete form. He continued to write great popular rags, such as "The Entertainer," "Cascades," and "The Gladiolus Rag," but he now devoted himself to legitimizing ragtime as high art.

Joplin wrote a ragtime opera, *A Guest of Honor*, which was performed in St. Louis in 1903, but the manuscript was never published and is now lost. He then obsessively set about creating what he conceived as his masterpiece, a 230-page ragtime grand opera, *Treemonisha,* in which the black heroine frees her people from ignorance. No one would publish it, no one would stage it, so Joplin published and staged *Treemonisha* himself in 1915 without sets, costumes, or even an orchestra at Harlem's Lincoln Theater. It was an economic disaster that left Joplin penniless, in bad health, and broken in spirit. He was haunted also by the fact that a popular song in 1910 was "Alexander's Ragtime Band" by Irving Berlin. *Variety* called it "the musical sensation of the decade" and it earned an astonishing thirty thousand dollars in royalties. Joplin knew that the tune was taken from the finale of *Treemonisha* and that Berlin had been working at Crown-Seminary-Snyder, the music publisher, when Joplin had submitted his opera there, where it had been rejected.

"Alexander's Ragtime Band" was a nonsyncopated caricature, but it was weak and homogenized enough to enter mainstream American music. It was just the vulgar imitation and cheap commercialization Joplin despised. Profoundly ill, he was committed to Manhattan State Hospital, where he died on April 1, 1917. Ragtime was absorbed into newly emerging jazz, and Joplin and his music essentially were transcended by the new medium. In 1970, however, pianist Joshua Rifkin rerecorded Joplin's rags. The irresistible syncopated sound made the same sensational impact it had seventy years earlier. George Roy Hill used Joplin's rags in his 1973 Academy Award–winning film *The Sting,* revitalizing Joplin's place in American musical history. *Treemonisha* was fully staged for the first time in Atlanta in 1973. Joplin's seminal place in music history was secured at last.

But he had made one serious error in judgment. He thought ragtime had to be formalized and elevated to achieve recognition and legitimization. Joplin did not understand that by perfecting the vernacular black music of Sedalia and St. Louis, he already had lifted up a uniquely American and distinctively African-American art form of the highest order. This dilemma about the relation of black vernacular art form and "art," which James Weldon Johnson made a central theme of his classical novel *The Autobiography of an Ex-Colored Man* (1912), would haunt black artists in many genres over the next few decades. But Joplin's genius was to realize that an experimental, playful, underground music was the nonverbal embodiment of the roots of American modernism itself.

Henry Ossawa Tanner

The Dean of Art
(1859–1937)

Henry Ossawa Tanner was the first African-American artist to receive international recognition. At the age of thirteen, upon seeing an artist at work—a landscape painter seated on a bench in Fairmont Park, Philadelphia—he experienced an epiphany. From that day in 1872, until his death in 1937, Tanner lived the life of a painter. "After seeing this artist at work, for an hour," he later said, "it was decided on the spot, by me at least, that I would be one, and I assure you it was no ordinary one I had in mind." By the 1900s he had won both the prestigious gold medal of the Paris Salon and the Lippincott Prize, and become a cultural icon of the black world. Even so, he resisted public attention and remained painfully shy.

Tanner attracted popular acclaim for his work in 1893, when he painted *The Banjo Player,* followed by *The Thankful Poor* in 1894. Remarkably beautiful, this series offered dignified depictions of the kind of everyday black domestic scenes that Americans had become accustomed to seeing portrayed as distorted racial caricatures. The dignity of Tanner's characters was groundbreaking. They refreshed and inspired white and black viewers alike conditioned by a century of racist stereotypes. From vaudeville acts and minstrel posters to paintings such as *"I's So Happy"* by white artists such as Thomas Howvenden (1885), images of shiftless, good-for-nothing blacks strumming the banjo circulated throughout the public market in abundance. Tanner's *The Banjo Player,* a masterpiece in simplicity, depicted an elderly black man seated in front of a fire, enveloping a small boy on his lap who, with great focus, struggles to learn the banjo. Tanner, already a master of the conventions of the European peasant genre he learned when studying in Paris in 1891, had applied his training in realism and astute observation to the rural black poor of North Carolina. It was the first time that a painter captured the light, rich tones, ochres, pinks, and browns that play on black skin. Neither *The Banjo Player* nor *The*

Thankful Poor earned prizes despite their entry in competitions. But Tanner was the first black artist to paint in a black genre, writing that it was his humble intention "to counter the comic stereotypes then common in American art and literature." His work had a strong influence on both the white and African-American artists who followed him.

Henry Ossawa Tanner was named for Osawatomie, the town in Kansas where, in 1856, the white militant John Brown launched his courageous antislavery campaign. Tanner's parents were "race" people, proud and upright. His father, Benjamin Tucker Tanner, was born of free black parents in Pittsburgh in 1835 and earned his way through Avery College as a barber before entering the Methodist ministry. The Reverend Benjamin Tucker Tanner studied at Western Theological Seminary for three years and eventually became a bishop in the African Methodist Episcopal Church, as well as one of its leading intellectuals. Tanner's mother, Sara Elizabeth Miller, born a slave, ran and taught in a small private school in their home. Despite his fragile constitution (as a child, his parents were unsure whether or not he would live) and pale skin that confused many a curious person, Tanner grew up believing that black people could accomplish the impossible and that race did not limit one's talents; society did.

Tanner first learned how to paint truthfully and competently on his own, starting with landscapes and maritime scenes and dabbling briefly in the depiction of animals. He saved fifty dollars to hire an instructor, and when none would take him on properly as a private student, he applied to the Pennsylvania Academy of Fine Art. Under Thomas Eakins's directorship and mentorship, Tanner was enrolled, amid protest, in 1880. Eakins, the foremost painter and proponent of realism in America, was responsible for bringing the nude figure into the American art classroom and encouraging his students to paint what they saw around them, rather than to adhere strictly to pseudoclassical scenes. Eakins, significantly, also believed that both women and blacks should be taken seriously as artists, at a time when professional careers in this field were closed to them.

Encouraged by his friend the painter C. J. Shearer, Tanner longed to go to Rome, where Edmonia Lewis, the African-American sculptor, had gained some notoriety. Needing money to finance his trip, Tanner moved to Atlanta to open a photography studio. The studio made very little money, however. Tanner fell back on a part-time teaching position at Clark College secured for him by Bishop Joseph

Hartzell. Together with Bishop Benjamin Payne, Hartzell assisted Tanner by purchasing his entire collection of art for three hundred dollars at his first unsuccessful exhibition, held in Cincinnati in 1890. This financed the young artist's emigration. But in 1891, en route to Rome, Tanner stopped in Paris and, falling in love with the city, decided to stay. Enrolling in the Académie Julien, one of Paris's best schools, Tanner was fortunate to be taught by Jean Joseph Benjamin Constant, who had taught the sculptor Auguste Rodin, and Jean-Paul Laurens. Tanner assimilated aspects of the Impressionist style, focusing on the effects of light and developing

techniques that he would apply to all of his paintings. He even developed a style using lights and blue paints that came to be known as "Tanner's Blues."

What was supposed to be a permanent move, however, was interrupted by illness, and Tanner returned to Philadelphia in 1893 to recover. Here he painted *The Banjo Lesson* and *The Thankful Poor.* The art world initially paid scant notice, and when they did they were more concerned with the import of his race than of his work. On the other hand, black America wanted him as a hero. Suddenly Tanner felt an intense claustrophobia: He wanted to paint African Americans, but the public emphasis on the aspect of race alone bewildered him. In addition, he was becoming attracted to religious themes, influenced by his strong Christian

background as a son of a bishop, and reflecting, by all accounts, a growing mysticism and belief in the universal brotherhood of man. He returned to France. Booker T. Washington followed close on his heels. Curiously, Washington met with Tanner to attempt to persuade him to produce more work like *The Banjo Lesson* and *The Thankful Poor.* Under great duress, Tanner explained that he was not running away from race, and that he could paint only what he was moved to paint.

In 1895 Tanner painted *Daniel in the Lion's Den,* his first work based overtly on religious themes, yet rooted in a Biblical story that was significant to African Americans. The painting received an honorable mention in the Paris Salon. He painted *The Raising of Lazarus* the next year, entered it in the Paris Salon and then left for a trip to the Middle East, where he hoped to sketch as much as possible to get authentic material for more paintings in this genre. It seems a great irony today that it was not the landscapes, animals, or maritime genre scenes, nor the few paintings of African-American subjects that garnered for Tanner the coveted prizes, but these deeply felt religious paintings. Success came to him at thirty-eight years old; in 1897 he won the prestigious gold medal for *Lazarus.* The French government purchased *Lazarus* for the Luxembourg Museum in Paris. Only a few Americans had won such attention. (James McNeill Whistler for his painting of his mother is one.) *The Raising of Lazarus* was later hung in the Louvre, and then placed in the Musée d'Art in Paris. In 1900 he received a Walter Lippincott prize at the Pennsylvania Academy of Fine Arts, and in 1905 his painting *Christ and Nicodemus* was awarded the Purchase Prize. This was followed by several paintings, but the most well known from this period are *The Two Disciples at the Tomb* (1906), *The Disciples of Emmaus* (1906), and *Flight in Egypt* (1916). At the age of forty, Tanner married the white American singer Jessie Macaulay Olsen, in London. They had one child, a son named Jesse Ossawa.

During World War I, Tanner contributed to the war effort through his work on an agricultural project at a Red Cross Camp near Paris, where wounded soldiers and refugee children grew vegetables. After the war, Tanner was extolled as the grandfather of black art. At the height of the Harlem Renaissance Alain Locke called him the "leading" artist of the "journeyman period" of black art in the nineteenth century. By the 1920s and 1930s he had reached the pinnacle of his work. The black journalist and satirist George Schuyler wrote that just as the dean of the black literati was W. E. B. Du Bois, Henry Ossawa Tanner was widely considered the dean of black American painters. Clearly he had come a long way from the young man who described in his autobiographical writings a "heartache" that emerged when trying to find *one* art teacher who would instruct him regardless of race. Tanner was no longer the fragile man who upon his acceptance to the Philadelphia Art School endured the humiliation of being strapped to his easel by racist colleagues and left outside on a freezing Philadelphia night. He had survived recurring and destabilizing bouts of illness, including typhoid, that had plagued his youth. However, like so many artists, Tanner suffered from finance-related stresses all his life, despite his solid reputation and fame.

Tanner was criticized by some African Americans who wished him to use his talents to develop an African-American style and aesthetic that would give rise to a "School of Negro Art." These critics charged that Tanner had never really attempted to do this. It is true that Tanner had painted few black subjects, but he was the first African-American artist to produce a black genre based on a black experience in the Americas, and to do it with a sophisticated style. Moreover, his religious paintings also make covert and rich reference to the experience of slaves. For his part, Tanner remained convinced that categorization of art by the artist's race led to a kind of "ghetto of isolation and neglect," even within his own community, a neglect from which black artists should escape if they are to gain artistic freedom and recognition. Whether he chose to paint black subjects or nonblack subjects, the black artist should be taken seriously on his technique alone, according to Tanner, not for the content or themes of his paintings.

Tanner, however, was a huge influence on African-American artists. For most of his adult life he lived in Paris, to be free from the oppressive racism of America and to be free to make the kind of art he wanted to make. Many black artists made pilgrimages to meet him; others studied with Tanner in the 1920s, including William Eduard Scott, William H. Johnson, Palmer Hayden, Elizabeth Catlett, and Hale Woodruff. James A. Porter, who became head of the art department of Howard University, called Tanner a "genuis." He was the first artist to be elected to membership within the National Academy as associate academician in 1909, a status extended to full academician in 1930. He was elected to full membership at the American National Academy of Design in 1927 and named chevalier of the French Legion of Honor in France in 1923. Tanner died in Paris on May 26, 1937; by then he finally had established the place of an African American as a master of the visual arts.

Madame C. J. Walker

The Hairdresser
(1867–1919)

Madame C. J. Walker, née Sarah Breedlove, made beauty her business. If we were to write a political history of African Americans based on changes in hairstyles, ranging from kinky and short to kinky and long, from greased and "pressed" (with a stocking cap) to straightened, waved, or jerry curled, Madame C. J. Walker would be the one for better or worse, who "made straight hair 'good hair'" and, in doing so, made a fortune for herself as well as a decent living for a workforce of agents that numbered twenty thousand in the United States and the Caribbean.

With the exception of Maggie Lena, "madame" of insurance and banking, no African-American woman other than Mme. C. J. Walker became a self-made millionaire in the first half of the century. Walker essentially invented the modern black hair-care and cosmetics industry. Hers is the quintessential American story: Owen and Minerva Breedlove were slaves who gave birth to Sarah Breedlove on a cotton plantation near Delta, Louisiana, in 1867; they died from yellow fever in 1874. Orphaned at age seven, she and her older sister survived by working in the cotton fields around Vicksburg, Mississippi. At fourteen she married Moses McWilliams, a Vicksburg laborer, to escape abuse from her cruel brother-in-law. McWilliams was killed in an accident six years later. Widowed at twenty with a daughter to take care of, she moved to St. Louis, Missouri, where she earned a subsistence living as a laundress. Seeking to supplement her income—and cure her own case of alopecia, or baldness, commonly suffered by black women at the time because of scalp diseases, poor diet, and stress—Breedlove became an agent for Annie Turnbo Pope Malone's Poro Company, selling its Wonderful Hair Grower. Realizing the potential of these

products, Breedlove took her daughter A'Lelia and $1.50 in savings to Denver, married her third husband, a newspaper sales agent named Charles Joseph Walker, and with him established a hair-care business. The Walkers made brilliant use of advertising in the growing number of black newspapers, such as those edited by T. Thomas Fortune.

Walker had invented her own "hair growing" product, she claimed, after "a big black man appeared to me [in a dream] and told me what to mix up for my hair." Some of the remedy was grown in Africa, she would recount, "but I sent for it, mixed it up, put it on my scalp, and in a few weeks my hair was coming in faster than it had even fallen out." Walker's grooming products, she insisted, did not "straighten" hair—even then, a politically controversial process—but she also sold a "hot comb," which did in fact straighten kinky hair, consciously tapping into a racial aesthetic that favored Caucasian over African physical characteristics. Throughout the century such celebrities as Nat King Cole, Sugar Ray Robinson, Sammy Davis, Jr., James Brown, and Michael Jackson became cases in point. Walker's products, aided by before-and-after ads that rivaled anything Madison Avenue would invent, made their way into virtually every black home.

In 1908, she temporarily moved her base to Pittsburgh where she opened Lelia College to train Walker "hair culturists." In 1910 she moved her business to Indianapolis, creating the Madam C. J. Walker Hair Culturists Union of America. Tirelessly she traveled the United States, giving lectures and demonstrations on this new and difficult art. Walker attracted the notice of the race's elite, despite the dubious regard in which they held women and hairdressers. She disrupted Booker T. Washington's National Negro Business League Convention in 1912 by demanding to be heard. "Surely you are not going to shut the door in my face," Walker shouted to Washington, who had ignored her for three days. "I have been trying to tell you what I am doing. I am a woman who came from the cotton fields of the South. I was promoted from there to the washtub. Then I was promoted to the cook kitchen. And from there I promoted myself into the business of manufacturing hair goods and preparations. I know how to grow hair as well as I know how to grow cotton. I have built my own factory on my own ground." Needless to say, she got Washington's attention.

Walker became a central figure in black leadership and one of the first black philanthropists: She funded the construction of a black YMCA in Indianapolis and financed the restoration of Frederick Douglass's home in Washington, D.C. In July 1917, when a white mob murdered more than three dozen blacks in East St. Louis, Illinois, she helped lead a protest against lynching, contributing five thou-

sand dollars to the NAACP antilynching movement and traveling to the White House with other leaders to present a petition to President Woodrow Wilson. Walker herself moved to New York in 1916, leaving the day-to-day operations of the Mme. C. J. Walker Manufacturing Company in Indianapolis to managers. She quickly became involved in Harlem's social and political life.

In 1918 she moved into the neo-palladian Villa Lewaro, an estate she built at Irvington-on-Hudson, New York, which was designed by the first registered black architect, Vertner Tandy, and situated near the estates of John D. Rockefeller and Jay Gould. At a time when unskilled white workers earned about eleven dollars a week, Walker's agents were making five to fifteen dollars a day, pioneering a system of multilevel marketing that Walker and her associates perfected for the black market. When Walker died of kidney disease in 1919, her fortune and business were left to her daughter, A'Lelia, who like her mother enjoyed entertaining and supporting causes. During the Harlem Renaissance of the 1920s she organized a literary salon in her townhouse at 108 West 136th Street. The salon was called "The Dark Tower" after Countee Cullen's column in *Opportunity* magazine. Its purpose was to provide a place for young African-American artists and writers to discuss and exhibit their work.

More than any other single businessperson, Madame C. J. Walker unveiled the vast economic potential of an African-American economy, even one suffocating under Jim Crow segregation in the South and less rigid but still pernicious forms of oppression in the North. She showed how black people could prosper by focusing on the particular needs and desires of their fellow African Americans.

1900–1909

Booker T. Washington

The Wizard of Tuskegee
(1856?–1915)

He was without doubt the most controversial African American of the century, and many of the issues that swirled around him are still with us. On September 9, 1895, in a fifteen-minute speech, Booker T. Washington addressed the Cotton States and International Exposition. Here, in his famous "Atlanta Compromise" address, Washington capitulated to the South's victory over Reconstruction and its promise of full black citizenship. He urged African Americans to eschew politics and to emphasize economic self-reliance instead. It had been a mere six months since the death of Frederick Douglass, the symbol of equality and civil rights, but the Atlanta speech gave a black blessing to the debasing era of segregation—"separate but equal"—that was to last for another eighty years. Yet on March 23, 1916, when the militant black nationalist Marcus Garvey landed in New York, it was Booker T. Washington he had come to see and to emulate. What is Washington's real place, influence, and legacy?

Washington was born, probably in 1856, enslaved to James Burroughs, a small planter near Hale's Ford, Virginia. His mother was a cook in the Burroughs's house. His father was an unknown white man, and it is often suggested that Washington's life is about his search for a father. As a child, Washington worked as a house servant. When Union victory brought freedom in 1865, his mother took him and his half-siblings to Malden, West Virginia, where her husband, Washington Ferguson, worked in salt and coal mines. Washington the boy worked with Ferguson and began to learn to read by puzzling over the numbers drawn on the barrels he and his stepfather loaded with salt. In 1872 Washington walked across the state to Hampton Normal and Agricultural Institute. Here he found a role model in Civil War general Samuel Chapman Armstrong, the white principal, who believed that what the freedpeople needed was practical education and character building.

Washington absorbed the New England general's virtues of hard work, serious-

ness of purpose, thrift, and personal morality. He already had
learned the gospel of cleanliness from the mine owner's wife
in West Virginia, for whom he had worked as a house servant.
He was an excellent student and public speaker who, after his

graduation, taught school back in Malden, briefly sampled the liberal arts at Wayland
Seminary in Washington, and returned to Hampton, where he was put in charge of
the Native American students. A decisive moment came in 1881 when Armstrong
recommended him, instead of a white person, as principal of a new black school to
be established in Tuskegee, Alabama. Starting with no buildings, no faculty, and no
students, but merely two thousand dollars to pay salaries, Washington's Tuskegee
became an unqualified success. By 1888, it embraced five hundred acres and enrolled
four hundred students. At Washington's death in 1915, its endowment stood at two
million dollars, with a staff of two hundred and two thousand enrolled students.

Washington's 1895 Atlanta speech brought him to national attention. He was
crowned by whites, and some blacks, North and South, as *the* Negro spokesperson.
Only months after the address, Harvard granted him an honorary master's degree,
the first awarded to an African American in its two-hundred-fifty-year history.
Washington used his prestige to raise money for Tuskegee, and to spread the doctrine of vocational training. In 1900 he founded the National Negro Business
League, a coalition dedicated to fostering the growth of African-American businesses. A genius at strategy, he insinuated himself into white power centers, such as
the Republican party, and black power centers, such as the African-American press.
"The Wizard of Tuskegee" certainly built and ran "The Tuskegee Machine."

But Washington was a complex person. He was inordinately optimistic, a subtle
master of self-promotion and public relations, often so conciliatory to whites that
he was willing to blame Negroes for their own limitations—and even throw in a
few minstrel jokes for good measure. On the other hand, though he undoubtedly
believed what he was preaching, he secretly funneled money into civil rights test
cases. His most articulate opponent over the proper role of education of the newly
freed Negro was W. E. B. Du Bois, the intellectual and activist who believed that
black Americans should use education as the route to full integration into American
society at every level.

Washington's battles with Du Bois were not merely a matter of training versus
education; behind them also stood Du Bois's idea of the elite Talented Tenth, and

1900-1909

Washington's concern for the poor black farmers of the South. But in order for Du Bois's brand of political activism to succeed, African Americans needed the kind of economic security advocated by Washington, as Reconstruction had demonstrated.

Perhaps most important, Washington's ideal of a self-reliant black community turned segregation upside down into separation; it was the celebration of "the nation within the nation" that will never be integrated, a vision that has inspired nationalists from Martin R. Delany and Marcus Garvey to Malcolm X.

Washington's heritage is ambiguous at best. He was secretive, power hungry, and an empire builder; his humility was simulated, yet his inspiring and classic autobiography, *Up from Slavery,* is a classic text of African-American literature. Washington could say: "Go out and be a center, a life-giving center, as it were, to a whole community, when the opportunity comes, when you may give life where there is no life, hope where there is no hope, power where there is no power. Begin in a humble way, and work to build up institutions that will put people on their feet." More than any other black leader of his day, Booker T. Washington understood the economic basis of antiblack racism and the necessity of building self-sustaining black social and educational institutions in an era when the full civil rights of blacks could scarcely be conceived. It is a tribute to his complexity—to his genius—that aspects of his political platform have been embraced both by black nationalists such as Malcolm X, black power advocates in the 1960s, and even the Nation of Islam, as well as black conservatives such as Thomas Sowell and U.S. Supreme Court Justice Clarence Thomas.

Washington died of arteriosclerosis at St. Luke's Hospital in New York on November 14, 1915. He was the first African American to have created a successful, self-perpetuating institution outside of fraternities and the church.

Ida B. Wells Barnett

The Reformer
(1862–1931)

Ida B. Wells Barnett was one of the great political reformers in the first quarter of the twentieth century. A fearless and outspoken activist and writer, she remains one of our most shamefully neglected crusaders. Through a fierce and relentless rhetoric, Wells Barnett attempted to persuade American society of the necessity of protecting its citizens, regardless of gender or race. No other black leader of her time was so vigilant or devoted as she to demystifying lynching. Utterly engaged with the political issues of the day, Barnett created her own newspaper, *Free Speech and Headlight,* until she was forced by a lynching mob to flee Memphis for her life. She began one of the first black feminist organizations, wrote books and columns for T. Thomas Fortune's *New York Age,* the *Detroit Plain Dealer,* the *Indianapolis Freeman,* the *Gate City Press,* the *Little Rock Sun,* the *Chicago Weekly,* and *The Conservator.* She was a cofounder of the NAACP, and still found time to work with newly migrated jobless and homeless black men and women in her adopted home of Chicago.

Her colleagues sometimes considered Wells Barnett "difficult." She was assertive, outspoken, and sometimes intolerant of the black male leaders of her day, even though she supported W. E. B. Du Bois against Booker T. Washington, whom she denounced in her newspaper column with some regularity. When the NAACP's executive leadership virtually excluded her for her radicalism, despite her foundational role in its creation, few came to her defense, not even Du Bois. As a result, after 1912, she became inactive in the NAACP. On the other hand, Frederick Douglass had anointed her when he wrote in 1895: "Brave woman! you have done your people and mine a service which can neither be weighed nor measured. If American conscience were only half alive, if the American church and clergy were only half christianized, if American moral sensibility were not hardened by persistent infliction of outrage and crime against colored people, a scream of horror, shame and indignation would rise to Heaven wherever your pamphlet (against lynching) shall be read." Revolted by brutality against black children and women, morally disgusted by the lynching that engulfed the South, and intolerant of an apolitical or tentative black middle class, Barnett nevertheless loved the arts. She especially loved the theater and knew many people in the entertainment world. She raised funds for actors and writers, financing in particular Chicago's historic Pekin Theatre, the first legitimate African-American theater in the United States.

Ida B. Barnett, née Wells, was born a slave during the Civil War in 1862, in Holly Springs, Mississippi, six months before the Emancipation Proclamation. She was orphaned by the 1878 yellow fever epidemic, and following her parents' deaths was forced to support herself and her siblings by working as a schoolteacher in rural Mississippi and Tennessee, a job she held until 1891. In 1884, she filed a civil rights lawsuit against the Chesapeake, Ohio, and Southwestern Railroad for forcing her to give up her seat, the second African American after Sojourner Truth to do so. Some money was awarded her initially by the local court, but eventually the ruling was overturned.

Her pastor at the Tabernacle Missionary Baptist Church invited her to contribute a story about her frustration with the courts to the *Living Way,* a religious weekly. Wells Barnett held regular literary gatherings with other teachers at Memphis's Vance Street Christian Church. The article was well received, and Wells Barnett began to write for the local black press under the pseudonym "Iola." In 1889, she was elected secretary of the Colored Press Association. That same year, she joined J. L. Fleming and the Reverend Taylor Nightingale, pastor of the Beale Street Baptist Church, as partner and editor of the militant journal *Free Speech and Headlight,* publishing between 1889 and 1892 articles and editorials about racist practices directed toward African Americans.

On March 9, 1892, three close friends—Thomas Moss, Calvin McDowell, and William Stewart—were hung from trees, their bodies mutilated, on the outskirts of

Memphis. Moss was killed for owning a prosperous grocery store that competed successfully with a white grocer directly across the street, revealing the economic tensions and rivalries in America as Reconstruction opened opportunities to African Americans. Iola instigated riots with her pen. She urged people to abandon Memphis and move west, where blacks still had a chance. Failing that, they should bring the city streetcars down through boycott. Over two thousand blacks left Memphis, while the streetcars were almost bankrupt by the end of the summer. In retaliation, local whites burned Wells Barnett's newspaper offices to the ground, forcing her to seek refuge in the North. The pioneering T. Thomas Fortune embraced her and gave her a job writing for his influential paper, the *New York Age*.

The impact of the Thomas Moss affair was far-reaching: Barnett began to research the background of hundreds of lynching cases. The book that resulted was entitled *A Red Record: Tabulated Statistics and Alleged Causes of Lynching in the United States, 1892-1893-1894*. It was the first statistical record on lynching. It demystifies the myth of the lascivious black male who raped virtuous white women, and confronts the white community about the psychological basis of their fear of black sexuality. *A Red Record* angered local whites so much that they responded in blind anger to the "man" who dared to write: "If the negroes themselves do not apply the remedy without delay it will be the duty of those whom he has attacked to tie the wretch who utters these calumnies to a stake at the intersection of Main and Madison Sts., brand him in the forehead with a hot iron and perform upon him a surgical operation with a pair of tailor's shears." This was the kind of danger and brutality that Ida B. Wells Barnett courageously confronted.

Barnett refused be silent and, with the help of Fortune, embarked on an antilynching crusade in England, Scotland, and Wales in 1893 and 1894. The aim was to inspire international moral outrage and to set up organizations in solidarity with the antilynching cause in America. Perhaps not since Frederick Douglass had taken his antislavery crusade to the United Kingdom in 1845 was a black leader so effective in swaying British public opinion toward condemnation of racism in America. In 1893 she edited a pamphlet protesting the exclusion of blacks at the World's Columbian Exposition in Chicago, and she urged every organization she could to help her with her fight. That same year, she organized a Negro Woman's Club in Chicago which eventually came under the Federation of Colored Women's Clubs. She went on to found the National Association of Colored Women (NACW) in 1896.

In 1895 she married Ferdinand Barnett, a lawyer and editor from Chicago, with whom she had four children. She founded the Negro Fellowship League, a social center with reading rooms and a dormitory for black men. From 1913 to 1916 she served as a probation officer for the Chicago Municipal Court. She traveled to the race riot in East St. Louis, Illinois, in 1918 to force the city to do something in the name of justice, and when new riots burned through Arkansas and Ohio, Wells Barnett was there.

Her work with women was both pioneering and enduring. She established the Alpha Suffrage Club in 1913 to agitate for African-American women's right to vote, and she marched in the famous suffrage parade of that same year, defying white suffragists who feared that black men would be enfranchised before women would be. Later she worked with Jane Addams to fight school segregation in Chicago. Politically engaged with the radical men of her generation, she became involved with Marcus Garvey's Universal Negro Improvement Association in 1916. She worked closely with William Monroe Trotter, the strident African-American journalist, who went to Paris to protest America's practice of de jure segregation at the Versailles Peace Conference in 1919.

Until she died in 1931, Wells Barnett promoted civil rights and justice for all African Americans, male and female. If one person can be said to stand as the creator of the black feminist movement in the United States in this century, surely it is Ida B. Wells Barnett.

Bert Williams

The Entertainer
(1874–1922)

He was arguably the most brilliant comedian America has produced. Bert Williams was once visiting a friend in a mental institution, where he noticed an inmate playing a game of cards by himself. A master of pantomime and the subtleties of parody, Williams used what he had seen in the hospital to craft an act for the stage. He silently took the roles of all four players in a card game. There was peeking at cards, suppressed emotion, hesitant gestures, quickly exchanged looks, delicate but revealing expressions. Night after night, Williams's performances sent audiences into gales of laughter. He was a mimic, a singer, a dancer (of sorts), a straight man to his partner George Walker, but most of all, he was a master of fluid physical movement. Even before the curtain opened, the exposed, slowly moving appearance of only Williams's spotlighted white-gloved hands was skilled—and funny—enough for the audience not merely to laugh but to understand they were being entertained by a master mimic and student of human behavior.

Egbert Austin Williams's origins are not entirely clear. He was born in Nassau, Bermuda, "an unnamed child of mixed race." He was the son of a white woman, Julia Monceur, and Franklin K. Williams, Jr., "a fair man with red hair." The mystery is the identity of Franklin Williams, Jr.'s father. He was a Dane, and Bert promised his father that he would never reveal his grandfather's real name. Bert Williams's grandmother is known, however. She was Emaline, or Emma, Armbrister, a West Indian, probably half African and half Spanish, and she and "Franklin Williams, Sr." were not married. Bert Williams, then, was probably fifteen-sixteenths white. The immediate family moved to California. Williams could not afford to study engineering at Stanford, as he had hoped, and he drifted into singing and playing the banjo along San Francisco's Barbary Coast.

In 1895, Williams's life changed, and the stage was set, both literally and figuratively, for a fundamental change in American popular entertainment. He met George Walker, a handsome, dark-skinned African-American singer and dancer from Kansas, and the two joined forces. Despite the virtual reenslavement of blacks in the South during the Jim Crow era of the 1890s, the urbanized North was becoming a sassier, more sophisticated place as it rejected the sentimentality of the

nineteenth century and became ready to move to a faster beat. That tempo was provided by two African-American art forms: ragtime music and the cakewalk, a high-stepping, exuberant black dance from plantation days. Black movement, pace, and style were being appropriated by white entertainers drifting away from outdated minstrelsy. Williams and Walker knew they could provide black entertainment better than white people pretending to be black, so they billed themselves "The Two Real Coons" and went on the road.

Williams and Walker's genius lay not only in their innate talent, but in their marriage of the cakewalk and ragtime. The combination of fast stepping and syncopated music caught the spirit of the times, the Gay Nineties, the Gilded Age, and before it was over, President Theodore Roosevelt was leading a cakewalk promenade down the East Room at a White House party. The first black music and the first black dance had "crossed over" and begun an unstoppable cultural process. Williams and Walker added black style and black humor to their repertoire, reappropriating racist stereotypes from the nineteenth-century minstrel stage. The shorter, dapper Walker was the sharp-dressing, fast-talking, girl-chasing Jim Dandy, while Bert Williams was the slow, confused, malaprop-speaking, unlucky Sambo whose pathos created humor, unique African-American humor, at a deeper level, the level where the acceptance of adversity triumphs over adversity itself. The "darky" stereotype was so foreign to Williams he had to observe, study, and master it, as well as take off his elegant clothes and put on rags and blackface every night.

Williams and Walker's great contribution was the creation of the ragtime musical, a series of Broadway revues that took the country by storm. It was a stud-

ied art, far more self-conscious than it ever appeared to be to white audiences. The acts included scenes set in Africa, but the effect depended upon jokes within jokes, as when Williams and Walker had a long humorous dialogue about "crackers." Their series of shows included "Sons of Ham," "In Dahomey," "Abyssinia," and "Bandanna Land." Williams's most memorable creation, perhaps, was a black preacher named Elder Eatmore, prefiguring the use of parody to comment on African-American social practices that would later characterize the work of other artists. Williams and Walker gave a command performance on the palace lawn in London for the Prince of Wales's birthday. It was widely rumored that Williams taught Edward VIII how to shoot craps, but it is a fact that the king gave Walker's beautiful, dark-complected wife, Aida Overton, a diamond bracelet.

Acceptance by British royalty meant little back in the States. Bert Williams once ordered a gin at a New York bar. The bartender looked him in the eye and said in a controlled voice, "That will be one hundred dollars." Williams quietly responded, "Then I'll have ten," and calmly pulled a thousand-dollar bill out of his vest pocket.

Bert Williams was a gentle, pipe-smoking, home-loving man who collected books, was an active Mason, and resignedly performed in hotels where he couldn't stay. When George Walker died, Williams continued on alone, and was invited by Florenz Ziegfeld to star in the *Follies,* the acme of American musical theater, a place no African American had ever performed before. Despite this breakthrough, his contract stipulated that he could not ever appear on stage at the same time as a white female cast member. Williams remained sad and depressed, the man who experienced absurdity on the stage and off, but who, like the blues, turned that suffering into humor and so transcended it.

On February 25, 1922, ill from pneumonia, Bert Williams collapsed onstage, in the middle of a performance in Chicago. Ten days later, on Saturday, March 4, 1922, at 11:30 P.M., Bert Williams died. The master of social parody, he was the godfather of the twentieth-century's greatest black comedians, such as Redd Foxx, Moms Mabley, Bill Cosby, Richard Pryor, and many many others.

1900–1909

Mary McLeod Bethune

The Black Rose
(1875–1955)

Mary McLeod Bethune was as much of an institution in African-American life as Eleanor Roosevelt, her good friend, was in mainstream America. If one person could embody a journey up from slavery, it was Bethune. The black woman in the White House, a fur coat draped around her shoulders, gray hair curling from under her hat, her face an array of kind features, became an exemplary black figure in the halls of white power. In the 1930s President Franklin D. Roosevelt named her director for Negro affairs of the National Youth Administration, the most influential position a black woman had ever held in the federal government. As president of the National Association of Colored Women (NACW), and later of the National Council of Negro Women (NCNW), she preached female solidarity and empowerment.

Bethune also reached out to women outside the United States and, in 1926, called for "a worldwide meeting of women of color" to chart a strategy for mutual progress. Power emanated from her, by virtue of her strength and influence when she was in the White House, but also by the fact that she was a school principal. She came from a rich tradition, and she viewed herself as both a representative and a symbol of black female achievement. Bethune was among those leaders such as Mary Church Terrell, Nannie Helen Burroughs, Lucy Laney, and Ida B. Wells Barnett who provided local self-help programs and a vision of black female self-sufficiency for African Americans before the dawn of the New Deal. She championed the cause of women and the underdog at each crossroad. She spoke with ease to poor and rich alike; many in the nation embraced her, as she embraced them.

Before Bethune opened her school for African-American girls, she planned to be a missionary in Africa, and this zeal lay at the root of her public work. Raised in Mayesville, South Carolina, she was the daughter of former slaves who had become hardworking farmers. She grew up at the height of African-American missionary fervor—Edward Wilmot Blyden had instructed African Americans to look to Africa—and she was not alone in hoping to be either a schoolteacher or a missionary. At ten years old she was enrolled in the Presbyterian Mission School. She attended Scotia Seminary in 1888, a missionary school in Concord, North Carolina, and then

I leave you hope. The Negro's growth will be great in the years to come. Yesterday, our ancestors endured the degradation of slavery, yet they retained their dignity. Today, we direct our economic and political strength toward winning a more abundant and secure life. Tomorrow, a new Negro, unhindered by race taboos and shackles, will benefit from more than 330 years of ceaseless striving and struggle. Theirs will be a better world. This I believe with all my heart.
—Mary McLeod Bethune

entered the missionary training school in Chicago now known as Moody Bible Institute. The Presbyterian Church, however, rejected her application to work in Africa. As an African-American missionary in the Congo later noted, black missionaries could be seen as dangerous and subversive by colonial higher-ups.

In 1896 a nineteen-year-old disheartened Bethune returned home, where she found a job teaching at Haines Normal and Industrial Institute in Augusta, Georgia. The African-American principal was Lucy Laney. A mentor to Bethune, Laney instructed her students to believe in themselves despite the history of their sexual exploitation under slavery, their limited education, and their restriction to domestic service. She insisted that black women were still moral, intelligent, and upright human beings. Inspired, Bethune went to teach at another school, the Kindell Institute in Sumter. In 1896, she and Laney attended one of Booker T. Washington's conferences for black educators at Tuskegee. Bethune was impressed by the way he raised money from wealthy benefactors, something she would emulate years later when she set up her own school.

In 1898 she married Albertus Bethune, a former teacher and menswear salesman. The couple relocated to Palatka, Florida, where they had their only child, Albert. In Palatka she opened a mission school, where she taught for five years until she separated from Albertus. She moved to Daytona, where the abundance of crime, prejudice, ignorance, and meager educational facilities ignited the missionary within her. With a reputed $1.50, commitment, and perseverance, she opened the doors of her Daytona Normal and Industrial Training School for Negro Girls in 1904. There were five young students. These young women were to be instructed in

1910–1919

Loving yours
Mary McLeod Bethune
1930.

Christian piety and personal self-reliance. In 1905 she campaigned to outlaw the local sale of liquor, launching an evangelical campaign for temperance among blacks who lived in the lumber companies' work camps near Daytona. Booker T. Washington visited the school in 1912.

In time, the school offered academic subjects and expanded to include a farm, high school, and nursing school. By its second year of enrollment, there were 250 students. Merging with the nearby Cookman Institute for boys, it became a fully accredited coeducational college in 1943. As founder and president of Bethune-Cookman, Bethune had carried out a remarkable achievement which won her, in 1935, the NAACP's prestigious Spingarn Medal.

Throughout her tenure as president of the school, Bethune also spent time working with and overseeing local women's organizations. That work culminated in her founding of the National Council of Negro Women (NCNW) in 1935. By the end of her presidency in 1949, the NCNW had coordinated the activities of many black women's organizations, presenting a unified voice to the federal government to secure greater equity for African Americans in social welfare programs. She was honored, throughout her life, with awards for her work as a civil rights and women's rights leader.

Bethune became the symbol of the race leader when she joined Franklin D. Roosevelt's New Deal administration. From 1936 to 1945, as part of FDR's informal "Black Cabinet," she advised the president on race matters. She was the Director of Negro Affairs for the National Youth Administration from 1939 to 1943. She fought to distribute funds to young black people and to secure state and local government positions for African Americans. She participated in the New Negro Alliance's picket line in 1939, and she worked with A. Philip Randolph in the March on Washington movement in 1941. Even when the U.S. House Committee on Un-American Activities labeled her a communist in the 1940s, Bethune remained fully committed to civil rights.

The daughter of former slaves, Bethune participated in four decades of immense change for African Americans. Her heroic commitment to racial uplift revolved around an African-American religious sensibility, a faith in values and ethics that was crowned by shrewd intelligence and framed by an indifference to the things that simply didn't matter. Bethune's vibrant soul seems, even today, alive and resplendent, overflowing with love for young black children, especially girls, but always at war with American racism and sexism. An elderly Bethune once visited a rose garden in France, where she noticed a black velvetlike rose growing among its fellow white and red ones. It affected her powerfully and, using the imagery of the garden, Bethune became transfixed by the beauty and independence of the black rose. She was herself a black rose in the midst of American racism—a beacon of hope in the darkness.

George Washington Carver

The Peanut Man
(1864–1943)

George Washington Carver, the wizard with plants, was a true American folk hero. Out of the simple peanut plant, Carver derived three hundred different products; from the sweet potato, he got 118. What other person performed such wizardry with crops, especially in impoverished southern soil? Carver is our most famous chemurgist, and certainly, when we were growing up in the sixties most small children, black and white, could name him by sight. Even today, on the roster of African-American scientists, of whom there are many far too unknown, Carver exceeds everyone else in popularity. He combined thrift and industry, faith and science to emerge as a kind of a black Horatio Alger figure. And to those who doubted the ability and intelligence of African Americans, Carver was the race's vindication. Though for years he was lauded as the one "token" black scientist, Carver's legacy is indisputable. As a proponent of scientific agriculture, Carver distinguished the study of farming while emphasizing the necessity of environmental conservation. He confronted an increasingly marginal southern economy devastated by war, poor farming, malnutrition, and ignorance, and he was able to improve the health and agricultural output of both black and white southern farmers, developing hundreds of uses for a mono-crop economy. He exemplifies the ability to make much out of little—a persistent theme in black history.

Carver fulfilled certain American folk hero mythologies, because his childhood was rural, and despite true hardship, it was Edenic. Growing up in post-Emancipation Missouri, Carver developed a lifelong love for a variety of wild plants and flowers from the forests surrounding his home. He not only collected and experimented with flora, but also sketched them. He was born in slavery in 1864 on Moses Carver's plantation in Diamond Grove, Missouri. Both of his parents were slaves; his father died in an accident before Carver's birth. When Carver was an infant, Confederate slave raiders kidnapped his mother. The raiders ransomed the infant back to slave owner Moses Carver for a horse. Orphaned, sickly, and frail, unable to do hard work, Carver was brought up by Moses and Susan Carver. He looked after the garden and all the plants around the plantation.

At only ten years of age, Carver decided to leave for school, in the nearby community of Neosho. He worked and lived with a black family and put himself through that school, through high school in Minneapolis, Kansas, and, later, when he moved, through one year at Simpson College in Iowa, followed by the Iowa State College of Agricultural and Mechanic Arts (now Iowa State University). He was the first African American to attend Iowa State. Carver graduated in 1894 with a B.S. degree in botany and agriculture, and he spent two additional years there to complete a master's degree, studying agricultural chemistry, geometry, bacteriology, zoology, and entomology. As an undergraduate, Carver became passionate about botany and managed the university's greenhouse, where he quietly conducted experiments on plants and taught other undergraduate students.

Carver's energies went in many directions: He was a leader in the YMCA and the debate club; he worked in the dining rooms; he was a trainer for the athletic teams; he was captain of the campus military regiment. His poetry was published in the student newspaper, and two of his paintings were exhibited at the 1893 World's Fair in Chicago. Because of his proficiency in plant breeding, Carver was appointed to the faculty, becoming Iowa State's first African-American faculty member. As assistant botanist for the College Experiment Station, Carver quickly developed scientific skills in plant pathology and mycology, the branch of botany that deals with fungi. He published a few articles on his work and gained national attention.

Carver's life changed dramatically in 1896, when Booker T. Washington invited him to head the agricultural department at the Tuskegee Normal and Industrial Institute in Alabama. Facilities and funds for the agricultural department, in particular, were woefully lacking. Carver literally and symbolically transformed the department: He assembled a small group of students to collect materials that could be used to construct laboratory equipment—pots, pans, tubes, wire—and created the devices necessary to conduct experiments. Tuskegee's first proper laboratory was built with bottles, old fruit jars, and other found objects. He began to instruct his students in the disciplines of botany, chemistry, and soil study, making scientific agriculture increasingly attractive.

Carver is famous, however, not because he built the first laboratory at Tuskegee, but because of the way he responded to the problems around him. He immediately perceived the degraded environment, the widespread poverty and malnutrition endemic among the farmers, and the ill-considered ecological practices. Year after year, farmers planted cotton on the same plots of land, exhausting the topsoil's nutrients. When Carver tested the soil he found it starved of nitrogen, which accounted for consistently low harvests. Back at Iowa State, Carver already had explored certain plants in the pea family, such as the peanut plant, which extracted nitrogen from the air and deposited it in the soil, enabling it to retain its nutrients.

Traveling once a month to rural Alabama to instruct farmers in new techniques, Carver advised them first to alternate the planting of cotton with peanuts. Peanuts, little known then, are a valuable source of protein. Carver had figured out that farmers could improve their diets and health by using this underused crop in tasty and well-balanced meals. To that end, Carver taught many housewives just how to do this, including in his repertoire the tomato plant, which many blacks deemed poisonous. Carver explained its nutritional value and demonstrated several recipes in which families might make optimum use of them.

But there were disadvantages in emphasizing the peanut alone. Once a highly insignificant crop, it now flooded the market, dropping the price of peanuts substantially and making it less attractive, say, than cotton to farmers desperate to pull themselves out of debt. So Carver began to explore the potential of diversification of the peanut with other crops, such as sweet potatoes. He found literally hundreds of alternative uses and ways in which the peanut crop could be used, thereby increasing its market value. Along with peanut butter, Carver was able to make adhesives, axle grease, bleach, buttermilk, chili sauce, fuel briquettes, ink, instant coffee, linoleum, mayonnaise, meat tenderizer, metal polish, paper, plastic, pavement, shaving cream, shoe polish, synthetic rubber, talcum powder, and wood stain. He went even further to protect the southern economy: In 1921 he helped the United Peanuts Growers Association persuade Congress to pass a bill calling for a protective tariff on imported peanuts. By 1938, one year after the film of his life, called *The Life of George Washington Carver,* opened in Hollywood, peanuts were a two-hundred-million-dollar industry and the number one product in Alabama.

Carver had a solid and distinguished reputation across the world, receiving invitations, honors, and accolades. Selma University and the University of Rochester awarded him honorary doctorates, Henry Ford dedicated the Carver Museum, and he received the Roosevelt medal for Outstanding Contribution to Southern Agriculture. He was asked to teach at many other higher-paying schools. But because he lived frugally on a small portion of his modest monthly salary of $125, he declined. When he died in 1946 he donated his entire savings (thirty thousand dollars) for the study of soil fertility and continued creation of useful products from waste materials. In his entire working life, Carver only patented three of his five hundred agriculture-based inventions.

In 1916 Carver was appointed to the Royal Society of Arts in London, England. In 1923 he was awarded the Spingarn Medal by the NAACP for his contributions to agriculture. In 1947 a stamp was issued with his image, and his profile appeared on a fifty-cent piece in 1951. He was elected to the Kansas City, Kansas, Agricultural Hall of Fame of Great Americans in 1977 and into the National Inventors Hall of Fame in 1990. The ingenuity and resourcefulness of Carver

1910–1919

can be seen today in the excellent research that continues at Tuskegee Institute. New scientists clearly influenced by George Washington Carver develop new ways to deal with poverty, famine, and malnutrition and do research on how to sustain healthy and environmentally friendly local economies in the United States and Africa. This humble scientist of quiet dignity left an indelible mark on American society and black culture.

Benjamin O. Davis, Sr.

The General
(1880–1970)

A career military officer, Benjamin O. Davis, Sr., was the first African American to reach the rank of general in the U.S. Army. He was a quiet and determined trailblazer, working his way up through the ranks with hard work and dignity, and serving as an example to those who sought to integrate the long-segregated American armed forces. He was an American soldier and patriot who longed to be treated as a full-fledged American citizen.

Davis was born on May 28, 1880, in Washington, D.C., to middle-class parents: His father was a civil servant, his mother a nurse, and many of his ancestors had been free southern blacks. Growing up with black middle-class aspirations, Davis felt the pressure to succeed from his father, a remote and serious man. His mother cared about his education and hoped her son would become a minister. A good student and standout athlete at the famous black M Street School in Washington, Davis had his eye on a different career. As a boy, he already had been schooled in close order drill and arms presentation by a friend's father—a Civil War veteran—and when the all-black Ninth Cavalry was stationed across the river in Virginia, Davis and his friends would watch the black soldiers for hours. "I always longed for the day, when I too would be a cavalry soldier and ride a beautiful horse," he wrote later.

Davis followed his dream to the M Street School's Cadet Corps, where he distinguished himself enough to win a District of Columbia National Guard commission his senior year in high school. It was 1898, the Spanish-Cuban-American war was heating up, and there were rumors the National Guard would be sent into active duty. When the government determined it could not afford to lose the many government employees in the Guard, however, the plan was dropped. Still, Davis had seen his future: He would be a soldier. That summer, just after Davis received his diploma, he was made first lieutenant of the newly formed, all-black, Eighth United States Volunteer Infantry, Company G.

Stationed in Chickamauga Park, Georgia, Davis had his first taste of Deep South Jim Crow, along with the racist segregation of the U.S. Army. He would later comment that the racism he encountered in his early postings had "a most depressive effect" on him. Mustered out of the Eighth in 1899, Davis enlisted as a clerk in Troop I, Ninth Cavalry, and was sent to Fort Duchesne, Utah. In the isolation, Davis grew close to his men, teaching illiterate veteran soldiers to read and write. He used his time off to continue seeking an officer's commission in the regular (nonvolunteer) army. It was a long shot: At the time, the only black officer in the entire regular army was Davis's own lieutenant, Charles Young. In March 1901 Davis completed the grueling officer's test, which contained written sections on constitutional law, history, mathematics, and other subjects, along with physical and military drill demonstrations. He was one of two black soldiers to pass the test that year. The next month Davis

was discharged as an enlisted man and took his oath as a second lieutenant with the Tenth Cavalry.

Following a brief stint in the Philippines (during which Davis learned basic Spanish and Visayan), his unit was sent to Fort Washakie, Wyoming. Once again stationed in the remote and empty West, Davis took the opportunity of his first leave to come home to Washington and marry Elnora Dickerson. They traveled with Davis's assignments, which included duty in Arizona, Liberia, and Wilberforce University, the black school in Ohio, where Davis taught military science. In 1917, now a lieutenant colonel (temporary) and a widower—Elnora had died in 1916 after the birth of their third child—Davis was sent to the Philippines as a supply officer for the Ninth Cavalry.

In letters home to the woman who would become his second wife, Davis wrote of his frustration with the racism that continued to block his progress. "I am getting to the point where I am beginning to believe that I've been kept as far in the background as possible," he wrote, after being denied yet another chance to join active duty in Europe. He spent World War I in the Philippines, far from action. Davis's analysis was absolutely correct. Despite the need for experienced officers in France, he was put on the shelf to avoid a racial situation where he might have to command white troops, or even more serious, where he might outrank a white officer. Davis's isolation reflected War Department policy. This is why we place Davis in this decade and see him as a person of the 1910s: The rejection of his capacity and commitment by a racist America symbolizes the decade.

Davis continued to study and lecture along with his regular duties. Davis returned to his children in 1920 with a new wife, the former Sadie Overton, and a new rank: captain. For the next twenty years, Davis continued to serve an army that didn't want him to command troops. At a time when African-American veterans of World War I, back from making the world safe for democracy, questioned their government's commitment to democracy at home, Davis simply kept on plugging. He taught at Tuskegee Institute, where he stood up to Ku Klux Klan intimidation over a new black-run hospital. He taught soldiers throughout the state of Ohio. He was promoted to lieutenant colonel, then colonel. But not until 1937 was he put in charge of troops—the legendary 369th Infantry.

Perhaps Davis's most important assignment, however, came in 1940, when

Just have patience, concentrate all you have got and, who knows, you may lead your class . . . if you do that you have the world waiting for you. Remember twelve million people [the African-American population at the time] will be pulling for you with all we have . . . save your letter of acceptance. Somebody, someday may wish to write something about us.

—Benjamin O. Davis, Sr., to his son at his admission to West Point, 1932

President Franklin D. Roosevelt—hoping to allay black mistrust of his administration and its military—promoted Davis to brigadier general. In 1941 he was put to work for the inspector general, investigating race relations in the armed forces. The War Department itself was a hostile environment from which to expose racism, but Davis quickly began taking testimony from soldiers about their experiences in the segregated army. He heard tales of unfairness, harassment, and violence, and reported his findings to the president and Congress. From 1942 to 1944, Davis toured the battlegrounds of Europe, continuing to document inequality among soldiers. He recommended integration of the forces, along with training for white soldiers unused to viewing African Americans as their equals, but some felt Davis's report did not go far enough. Still, his work was clearly instrumental in the executive order signed by Harry S. Truman three years after World War II ended, finally desegregating the American armed forces.

Davis retired in 1948 after fifty years of service. He was awarded the Distinguished Service Medal for his work on the race question, the citation praising his "initiative, intelligence and sympathetic understanding" and his "wise advice and counsel." In addition, Davis earned the Bronze Star Medal, the Croix de Guerre with Palm from France, and the Grade of Commander of the Order of the Star of Africa from Liberia. His son, Benjamin O. Davis, Jr., followed in his footsteps, graduating from West Point, flying with the Tuskegee Airmen, and becoming the first African-American general in the U.S. Air Force. Davis died in 1970, but not before easing the way for countless future black soldiers. How ironic it is that black progress in the military now exceeds that of any other sphere of American life—or is it troubling that the military forces that protect the American way of life provide so many opportunities for those often excluded from advancement in the civilian sphere?

1910–1919

Thomas A. Dorsey

The Father of Gospel Music
(1899–1993)

Although now remembered as "The Father of Gospel Music," Thomas Andrew Dorsey in fact had two careers: one as a creative composer of religious music based on African-American traditions, the other in a parallel realm, as a major composer and performer of low-down blues. Dorsey was born in 1899 in Villa Rica, Georgia, and grew up steeped in the musical wealth of the black church, where his father was a preacher. In 1908 the Dorseys moved from the country to the nearest big city, Atlanta, where young Thomas was exposed to secular music, including the urban blues of Bessie Smith and Ma Rainey. At twelve he was a competent pianist; by his late teens he had left for the freedom and promise of the North, moving to Chicago in 1916.

Dorsey studied music at Chicago's College of Composition and Arranging and began to make music. He registered his first blues composition, "If You Don't Believe I'm Leaving, You Can Count the Days I'm Gone," in 1920, and his first gospel song, "If I Don't Get There," in 1922. But the money was in the blues, so despite an early 1920s revelation that he should write religious music, Dorsey continued as a composer of secular songs. In 1920, he began working with a band, the Whispering Syncopators. In 1923 Chicago's top jazz musician, King Oliver, recorded Dorsey's composition "Riverside Blues," which became his first hit song. Before long, Dorsey was in demand as a pianist, and the next year he joined Ma Rainey's Wild Cat Jazz Band, where Dorsey worked for the next two years.

Dorsey continued to vacillate between the religious and secular realms, dropping out of professional music in the late 1920s but returning to work with guitarist Hudson "Tampa Red" Whittaker, with whom he recorded dozens of songs between 1928 and 1932. As Georgia Tom, Dorsey wrote and recorded dozens of popular and sexually suggestive blues songs, including "Pat My Bread" and his classic "It's Tight

1910–1919

Like That," which sold seven million copies. In 1932 Dorsey was converted both religiously and musically. Inspired by the death of his wife and infant child, Dorsey, who had been touring, returned home and sat at the piano and composed his most famous gospel song, "Precious Lord, Take My Hand." The song reached national prominence when Mahalia Jackson sang it, at King's request, at the funeral of Martin Luther King, Jr., in 1968.

"Precious Lord" became one of the standards of American music and launched Dorsey into a new career, wholly gospel. In 1933 Dorsey cofounded the National Convention of Gospel Choirs and Choruses, and for the rest of his life he composed only religious music. He was instrumental in other gospel ventures, including establishing the publishing company Dorsey House and touring with a band with Sallie Martin ("The Mother of Gospel Music") and the greatest of the gospel singers, Mahalia Jackson. Born in New Orleans, Jackson's untrained but vibrant voice, combined with the depths of true religious sincerity, made her unique.

Dorsey would marry again and father another child, but the religious conversion he experienced at his first wife's death would stick; he never again composed or played the blues. The remaining sixty years of his life were spent writing and promoting gospel music. Based at Chicago's Pilgrim Baptist Church, Dorsey composed such classics as "When the Gates Swing Open" and "Peace in the Valley," providing hit songs for artists ranging from Sister Rosetta Tharpe to Elvis Presley.

Although he had penned some of the most well-known gospel songs ever recorded, including "Never Turn Back," "Rock Me," and "Standing Here Wondering Which Way to Go," Dorsey fell into relative obscurity until the 1980 release of a documentary film titled *Say Amen, Somebody,* which highlighted gospel music and Dorsey's influence. He died in 1993 at the age of ninety-three, leaving behind a legacy of music that brought together religious devotion combined with the rhythmic urgency of the blues. His work reveals the way in which the "blue note" black people have injected into modern music and American culture is not confined to the blues, but is also heard every Sunday morning in black churches throughout the country.

W. C. Handy

The Father of the Blues
(1873–1958)

W.C. Handy, "The Father of the Blues," knew something about the "man farthest down." Born in a log cabin only a few years after Emancipation, Handy knew something of Jim Crow race hatred, and something of trouble. But, like the music that would prove to be his trademark, he found a way to transform his experience into art. This transformation of a cry into a song and pain into an art form was achieved by a highly disciplined sense of craft and technique, a knowledge of earlier religious music, and the joy of improvisational freedom.

While Handy certainly did not invent the blues—blues-inflected tones had been part of black music for years—he was instrumental in developing it as an idiom. His first blues composition, "Memphis Blues" (1912), was the first published composition to include the word "blues" in its title, and the first to employ "blue notes"—the flattened thirds and sevenths that are the stuff of the blues sound. He published some sixty compositions in all, including the classic "St. Louis Blues," "Beale Street Blues," and "Careless Love" that have since become jazz standards. As a bandleader, songwriter, teacher, and publisher Handy's name became synonymous with the blues, at the same time as his own relationship with the music often was conflicted.

Having received some formal training in the particulars of the European musical tradition, Handy often expressed his feeling that the blues are a "primitive" form. And yet, he felt that the blues were the form of pure American culture. This ambivalence suggests something of the complexity of Handy's life and art.

William Christopher Handy was born in Florence, Alabama, on November 16, 1873. The son and grandson of African Methodist Episcopal preachers, he was steeped in the church. Throughout his life, he would imbue his music with the rich harmonies and dissonances of the sacred and profane of black culture. As Albert Murray wrote in his landmark study *Stomping the Blues,* "[M]any of the elements of blues music seem to have been derived from the downhome church in the first place." And so Handy would later describe his compositions as evoking "the sound of a sinner on revival day."

Handy's career in music began in opposition to his father's wishes. Handy would recall in his autobiography, *Father of the Blues* (1941), that his father took him aside and said, "Son, Id rather see you in a hearse, I'd rather follow you to the graveyard than to hear that you had become a musician." Even against such stringent opposition, Handy left home at the age of fifteen to join Mahara's Minstrels, a traveling review. He took on the musical directorship of the troupe in 1896 and performed light classical pieces, popular dance numbers, and rags throughout the Mississippi Delta. After leaving the group, Handy moved to Teachers Agricultural and Mechanical College in Huntsville, Alabama, where he worked as a teacher and bandmaster. In 1893, during an economic depression, he formed a quartet to perform at the World's Columbian Exposition in Chicago. After bouncing around at odd jobs for several years, he finally settled in Memphis, Tennessee.

In 1908 Handy was asked by the leading mayoral candidate of Memphis, E. H. "Boss" Crump, to compose a campaign song. The song, originally entitled "Mr. Crump," became a hit, and took on the new name of the "Memphis Blues." The song is said to be the first blues ever copyrighted, and while some debate whether it is blues proper—it does not, for instance, follow the usual AAB rhyme pattern, nor does it, in Murray's words, have "mournful lyrics"—it nonetheless inspired a spate of blues publications.

Regardless of its precise musical provenance, "Memphis Blues" and Handy's other early publications mark a key transitional moment in American music, where ragtime, blues, and jazz all converge. In composing his music and lyrics, Handy drew from spirituals, work songs, and folk ballads to create a mélange of musical idioms. Most radically, perhaps, he established the blues as a framework within which it was possible to improvise, thus leading to the jazz "breaks" that would mark the later innovations on the traditional blues form.

While Handy was nowhere as talented an instrumentalist as his contemporary Jelly Roll Morton, his work as a cornet player and band-leader proved influential. Perry Bradford, only one of the songwriters inspired by Handy's work, composed "Crazy Blues" for Mamie Smith, who made it the first ever recorded blues in 1920, ushering in the century's classic period of the blues.

> I think that America concedes that [true American music] has sprung from the Negro. When we take these things that are our own, and develop them until they are finer things, that's pure culture. You've got to appreciate the things that come from the art of the Negro and from the heart of the man farthest down.
> —W. C. Handy

Handy himself saw the lucrative possibilities in blues publication. He published "St. Louis Blues" and "Yellow Dog Blues" in 1914 and "Beale Street Blues" in 1916. In 1917 he moved to New York, where he recorded with his own band until 1923. Handy did much to codify the blues form. Beyond writing and publishing his own blues songs, he edited two volumes of blues lyrics, including *A Treasury of the Blues* (1926), which included illustrations by the acclaimed Jazz Age artist Miguel Covarrubias.

Handy faded from the music scene in the 1940s as a revival of early New Orleans jazz began to take precedence over the blues. But the blues lived on in several forms. In the Delta, where the blues were born, pickers and singers such as Robert Johnson continued to play in the pure country style, while others spilled over to influence new musical forms such as R&B and rock 'n' roll. There would have been no Elvis Presley if he had not heard Arthur Crudup sing "That's All Right Mama." Likewise, the pure urban blues of Bessie Smith remained caught in time, unequaled as the performance of a unique African-American genre. Urban blues, too, exerted permanent influences—through Ethel Waters to Billie Holiday, Ella Fitzgerald, and Sarah Vaughan.

Reflecting upon his life in his autobiography, Handy called to mind the words of his devout father—the same man who forbade him to follow a career in music: "If, as my father often said, 'You are trotting down to Hell on a fast horse in a porcupine saddle,' I rode with a song on my lips and its echo in my heart." Handy's hell may well have been Jim Crow America, but his songs and their echoes now resound everywhere.

1910-1919

James Weldon Johnson

The Renaissance Man
(1871–1938)

James Weldon Johnson was a Renaissance man—an "alchemist who turns baser metals into gold," as Charles Van Doren, historian and literary critic, said about his friend and colleague. Johnson's career was a combination of high literary achievement, most notably his novel *The Autobiography of an Ex-Colored Man* and his collection of poems *God's Trombones,* with an active political life; he was fundamental to the early successes of the NAACP and he served as U.S. consul in Venezuela and Nicaragua. In the words of one of the chroniclers of his career, Sondra K. Wilson, Johnson was "a songwriter, poet, novelist, diplomat, playwright, journalist, and champion of human rights." His curiosity was inexhaustible; his courage, incredible; his commitment, unflinching.

One would be hard-pressed to name someone who could rival Johnson's versatility, perhaps only the towering W. E. B. Du Bois comes close for the sheer multifariousness of his work. Over the course of a life that spanned Reconstruction and its demise, and those initial inroads that would lead to the successes of the civil rights movement, Johnson's influence is undeniable. As a songwriter, along with his brother J. Rosamond Johnson, he penned a Broadway hit, "Under the Bamboo Tree," and what would soon be adopted as the Negro national anthem, "Lift Every Voice and Sing." As a literary figure, he published one of the most influential and accomplished novels written by a black American between the Civil War and the Harlem Renaissance, and he acted as one of the handmaidens of that same cultural movement that sprang up in Harlem in the 1920s.

James Weldon Johnson was born on June 17, 1871, in Jacksonville, Florida. He was raised in a middle-class household; his father was a headwaiter in a luxury hotel and his mother was an elementary school teacher. He received exceptional educational opportunities for the time and place. In 1887 Johnson enrolled at Atlanta

University, where he emerged as a scholar-athlete, and delivered the commencement address in 1894. After a brief stint as principal of his former school in Jacksonville, Johnson formed a legal partnership, becoming, in the process, the first black lawyer admitted to the bar in Duval County, Florida.

By 1904 Johnson had become involved in Republican party politics, writing two songs for Theodore Roosevelt's presidential campaign and serving as treasurer of the Colored Republican Club. In 1906, at the recommendation of Booker T. Washington, Johnson was named U.S. consul to Venezuela (1906–1909) and Nicaragua (1909–1912). After the election of Democrat Woodrow Wilson it became clear to Johnson that his political future was limited. He returned to the States in 1912 to publish anonymously *The Autobiography of an Ex-Colored Man,* written while in Nicaragua, and to take on the editorship, in 1914, of the *New York Age,* the preeminent black newspaper in the country.

But it was Johnson's appointment as field organizer for the nascent National Association for the Advancement of Colored People (NAACP) in December of 1916 that proved to be of the greatest consequence. He oversaw the expansion of the organization, increasing its number of regional branches from 68 in 1917 to 310 in 1920. That same year he became secretary of the NAACP, an office he would hold for the next decade and use as a platform for his political thought. In his later years, he became Adam K. Spence Professor of Creative Literature and Writing at Fisk University.

Johnson is perhaps most widely known today as one of the key figures in the African-American literary tradition. Few books before the Harlem Renaissance had

O black and unknown bards of long ago. How came your lips to touch the sacred fire?
—James Weldon Johnson

a greater impact on the shape of the tradition than Johnson's *The Autobiography of an Ex-Colored Man.* Johnson helped create the first-person black novel, transferring the classic nineteenth-century slave narrative into the fictional autobiography "as a way of rendering in fiction the range of sensibility and consciousness of a black character his ambitions and dreams, his weakness and fears, his aspirations and anxieties about racial relations in American society even more fully than the slaves and ex-slaves had done in their popular slave narratives."

Like Du Bois in *The Souls of Black Folk,* Johnson proposed to take his reader behind the veil to offer a "view of the inner life of the Negro in America, . . . into the freemasonry, as it were, of the race." He crafted an unnamed narrator with the fluidity of racial identity to slip back and forth between the calcified racial divides. In doing so, he created a character not only representative of a race, but representative of the very alienation of modernity to which all, white and black, have fallen prey.

In 1927 Johnson published *God's Trombones: Seven Sermons in Verse,* a collection of poetry that attempts a mimetic capturing of the black church sermon. Johnson attempted to give voice to this sacred speech without making recourse to the misspellings and orthographic tricks often employed in representing black vernacular speech.

In addition to these signal contributions, Johnson edited three significant anthologies, *The Book of American Negro Poetry* (1922), *The Book of American Negro Spirituals* (1925), and *The Second Book of American Negro Spirituals* (1926). In the anthology of black poetry, he makes the claim that it is literary achievement that marks the stature of a race.

Johnson served as a conduit between the past and a contemporary age of African-American leadership and letters. Bridging Booker T. Washington with the civil rights leaders of the fifties and sixties, leading the literary tradition from Chesnutt to Toomer, Johnson was a true racial and cultural alchemist. He refused to separate the personal from the political, the existential from the economic, the spiritual from the social in his broad vision of black freedom.

Jelly Roll Morton

Mr. Jelly Lord
(1885?–1941)

He hated Negroes. Ferdinand Joseph La Menthe was a fair-skinned New Orleans Creole who claimed, perhaps accurately, that his family originated in France. He believed he was white, and he passed across the color line whenever he could. But the pianist who became Jelly Roll Morton was honest enough as a musician to understand that jazz, the music that marked the twentieth century, was born of the blending of African and European traditions, the very amalgamation he denied in himself. Jelly even asserted that he "invented" jazz himself in 1902, when he first played four beats to the bar instead of ragtime's two. Given what we know of jazz musician Buddy Bolden, this is probably not true. What is sure, however, is that Jelly was not only a brilliant pianist, able to play anything in any style, he was jazz's first composer as well. This was his greatest contribution: the ability to put jazz's improvisation together with arrangement and rehearsal—without sacrificing spontaneity. This complex and conflicted black genius who wrestled with self-hatred yet produced profound art is a kind of enigma.

Jelly was orphaned early and raised by his grandmother, Eulalie Echo. She once lent the child to a friend who wound up in jail, and Jelly claimed his first musical inspiration came from hearing the prisoners sing to stop his crying. Another influence was his Aunt Lalie, a vodun practitioner who kept glasses of holy water around his bed. Like many other Creoles, Jelly's family was musical, and he tried several instruments before deciding on the piano. As an adolescent, he was earning three dollars a week as a barrel maker when he got a job playing in a high-class sporting house. He made twenty dollars in tips the first night. Storyville, New Orleans's wild and wide-open red-light district, ran twenty-four hours a day on alcohol, drugs, gambling, prostitution, fights, and murder—and was probably the greatest constellation of musical genius ever concentrated in one place. Jelly had found his world.

When his grandmother found out where the money was coming from, though, she threw him out of the house.

Thus Jelly began an itinerant career as an urban pool hustler, card shark, con man, gambler, pimp, but always the piano player. He played ragtime, popular songs, French quadrilles, blues, a bit of opera, hymns, minstrel tunes (all spiced with what Jelly called "the Spanish tinge") that were blending and synthesizing into jazz. His greatest musical influence was Tony Jackson. Jackson was the dark-skinned New Orleans piano player who composed "The Naked Dance" for the high point of the expensive sporting houses' evening entertainment, as well as the still-popular "Pretty Baby," which he wrote for his gay lover. Jelly sometimes even imitated the way Jackson sat on the piano bench, casually sideways, but intently looking down at the keyboard. Somewhere along the way, Jelly picked up his nickname. Jelly Roll was slang for sex in general, and female genitalia in particular. It is unclear whether it stood for his own prowess or was related to the string of hookers who traveled with him.

The nickname entered history when Jelly published "Jelly Roll Blues" in 1915, the first printed jazz orchestration. He began recording in 1923, and his discography runs to twenty-two pages. The tunes he wrote, arranged, recorded solo, and most important of all, recorded with the Red Hot Peppers, are classics: "Milneberg Joys," "The Pearls," "Grandpa's Spells," "Kansas City Stomp," "Frog-i-More Rag," "King Porter Stomp," "Smokehouse Blues," "Black Bottom Stomp." They retain the same freshness and originality today as when they were cut, and their genius is as evident as the impact and influence they had on everyone who played and everything that was recorded afterward. There is a direct and traceable line from Jelly's "King Porter Stomp" to Fletcher Henderson to Benny Goodman to Duke Ellington. Jelly's hand is always evident, characterized by what critic Gunther Schuller calls "a triumphant fusion of composition and improvisation."

Unfortunately, Jelly's work is now sometimes overshadowed by his personality and reputation. He was a braggart, perhaps because he needed to affirm himself, caught as he was in the lonely space between the black world, which he rejected, and the white world, which rejected him. He carried around a trunk full of money and was so flashy he not only had a diamond stickpin, but diamonds on his socks and a diamond set in the center of one of his prominent gold teeth. He was slightly built, but he was a scrapper. He didn't know fear, and he could be tough. Kid Ory tells about a 1923 Chicago record date for the Okeh label when Zue Robertson was on trombone and wouldn't play a melody the way Jelly wanted it played. As Ory recalls, "Jelly took a big pistol out of his pocket and put it on the piano, and Robertson played the melody note for note." In the rough-and-tumble world of early jazz, this was a true artist at work.

Jelly was also jazz's first, and best, historian. Alan Lomax, the folklorist, found him in 1939 and invited him to the Library of Congress for hours of recording.

Recognized and vindicated at last, Jelly described "the district," Storyville, and its music so vividly that in his recordings we can see the balconies built for the bands—so that their instruments wouldn't get damaged in the brawling. Best of all, we can hear the music, because Jelly plays everything—and in the style of whatever "professor" Lomax inquires about! Jelly sings in a surprisingly sweet voice, and as he gets to trust Lomax he adds the verses that are still unprintable. If we discount Jelly's megalomania, this is the closest we will ever come to knowing the world that produced Louis Armstrong and Sidney Bechet, King Oliver and Baby Dodds. In the end, though, Jelly was crucially important because he was a great composer and a great artist. He was even, as he himself liked to claim, "Mr. Jelly Lord." He died in Los Angeles on July 10, 1941. Jelly was quintessentially American—often denying his past yet ingeniously creating something new and novel out of that past.

Charles Henry Turner

The Entomologist
(1867–1923)

Charles Henry Turner was fascinated by ants. As a child, he watched their lives, otherwise unnoticed, beneath the hard pavements and in abandoned lots, swarming from one destination to another. He was equally curious about all small creatures that crawled or flew. As an adult he wrote nature studies for children and composed a book of poems. But, first and foremost, Turner became one of the most respected entomologists of his day through his observations of the behaviors of the smaller insects, particularly bees.

During the first two decades of the twentieth century, Turner made major, even phenomenal, contributions to the scientific understanding of insects. His work in fact helped lay the groundwork for the contemporary field of animal behavior psychology. A prolific writer and creative researcher, he proved that insects can hear and can distinguish pitch. He discovered that the common cockroach learns by trial and error. In 1910 he found out that the honey bee can distinguish color and is drawn to flowers not just by odor but by sight as well. Conversely, he noticed that ants found their way back to the colony by light rays, not by odor, and that wasps use visual landmarks to find their way home and not, as it was commonly thought, from an instinctual sixth sense. He also investigated tropisms, movement caused by stimulus, and demonstrated that when stimulated by light or sensory excitation, invertebrates displayed turning behaviors. That behavior is now known as "Turner's Circling."

Turner was born in Cincinnati, Ohio, two years after the end of the Civil War. His father, Thomas Turner, from Alberta, Canada, was a church custodian; his mother, Addie Campbell Turner, from Lexington, Kentucky, was a practical nurse. In 1891 Turner earned a B.S. degree and in 1892 an M.S. degree, both in biology from the University of Cincinnati. From 1892 to 1893 he served as an assistant instructor in the biology laboratory at the University of Cincinnati. Like most other bright young graduates of the 1920s who were committed to teaching black students, he moved South.

Turner's first job was professor of biology at Clark College in Atlanta, Georgia. From 1893 to 1905, Turner was in charge of the science department. In 1895 his wife, Leontine Troy Turner, the mother of his five children, died. He went on to teach in Indiana, Tennessee, and Georgia, where he held several positions in education, including high school teacher, high school principal, and college professor. He carried out original scientific experiments on all the common insects people take for granted, from ants to cockroaches. During these years, Turner carefully recorded everything he saw and did. His observations of minute details, such as whether an ant moved left or right, were accompanied by exact times, weather, and nesting conditions as well as hand-drawn diagrams. He enrolled at the University of Chicago and resumed his study of biology while still teaching. He amazed his professors and colleagues with his pioneering dissertation. For his discoveries and contributions to knowledge of the field of animal behavior, the University of Chicago awarded Turner the degree of doctor of philosophy, summa cum laude, in 1907.

Turner was invited to stay at the University of Chicago, but in 1908 he moved to St. Louis, Missouri, where he accepted a position as a biology teacher at Sumner High School, a position he held until his death in 1923. Turner believed he was more useful teaching biology and psychology in a black high school in St. Louis than holding a prestigious professorship at the University of Chicago. He repeatedly refused jobs that would have allowed him to devote all his time to scientific research. During the 1920s there was a hungry desire for knowledge in the black community and he wanted to work "among his people," as he expressed it in a letter to Booker T.

Washington in 1923. His teaching ensured that he would be forever a respected and inspiring member of the black community.

Turner was an unusually gifted human being, one of those rare people who hold the magnifying glass to nature and deal only with the most humble and small things in life. His publication in journals as varied as the *Biological Bulletin,* the *Journal of Comparative Neurology,* the *Zoological Bulletin,* the *Journal of Animal Behavior,* and the *Psychological Bulletin* made him well known and respected among American and international scientists. His animal behavior research resulted in more than fifty research papers published on neurology, invertebrate ecology, and animal behavior. For more than seven consecutive years he reviewed the current literature on the behavior of spiders and insects other than ants. His studies include "Psychological Notes on the Gallery Spider," "Habits of Mound-Building Ants," "Experiments on the Color Vision of the Honey Bee," "Behavior of a Parasitic Bee," "Hunting Habits of an American Sand Wasp," and "Do Ants Form Practical Judgments?" He was quoted in most of the important science books of the time, such as *The Animal Mind* (1908), *The Psychic Life of Insects* (1922), and *Wheeler's Ant Book* (1926). In 1915 Turner was elected to the St. Louis Academy of Sciences and he was also made an honorary member of the Illinois Academy of Science and the Entomological Society of America.

In 1923 Charles Turner died. After his death the St. Louis Board of Education named a recently built school for physically disabled children the Charles H. Turner School. It became the Turner Middle School in 1954. This humble scholar, equiped with the raw stuff of achievement—talent, discipline, and energy—who quietly studied ants, spiders, and insects, made the world a wiser place for humanity.

Jimmy Winkfield

The Jockey
(1883–1974)

Jimmy Winkfield was the last of America's great black jockeys. Only three other jockeys, white or black, have ever won back-to-back Kentucky Derbies: Ike Murphy, the black jockey, in 1890 and 1891; Ron Turcotte in 1972 and 1973; Eddie Delahoussaye in 1982 and 1983. Jimmy Winkfield twice captured the title riding His Eminence in 1901 and Alan-a Dale in 1902. He was the last black equestrian of the twentieth century to win the Derby, although Jess "Longshot" Conley in 1911 was the last black jockey actually to compete. But Winkfield was still at the top of the game as late as 1923, when he took the Prix du Président de la République du State at St. Cloud, France, on a striking thoroughbred named Bahadur. Like much of black history in America, however, Winkfield's grand achievements have been rendered invisible.

Winkfield's story ended the fascinating history of African-American jockeys who dominated American racing before the Civil War. Professional jockeys were most often slaves who had grown up in the rural South looking after horses. In the inaugural Derby on May 17, 1875, fourteen of the fifteen jockeys in the race were black. Oliver Lewis, an African American, won riding Aristides. After the Civil War, some African-American jockeys were among the wealthiest jockeys of the period. Willie Simms, for example, who taught the English how to ride American style, crouched down low, made up to twenty thousand dollars by the time he died in 1927.

As early as 1884, when Winkfield was one year old, Isaac "Ike" Murphy was the only American jockey to have won the Derby, the Kentucky Oaks, and the Clark Stakes. Three of his Derby wins were unequaled for thirty-nine years, and he was the first jockey to be voted into the Jockey Hall of Fame (1955) at the National Museum of Racing in Saratoga Springs, New York. Winkfield, who looked up to Murphy, followed him into Derby history when he won two as well.

Winkfield left racing in the United States because of his adventurous sense of possibility, his need to make more money, and increasing white racist resentment of black success. He made a name for himself in Europe, particularly Russia and France, earning at the height of his career in 1916 something like one hundred thousand dollars a year. In America, on the other hand, he would, by that time, have been barred from the sport's lucrative earnings because of his race. "Money changes everything," he said once.

Born in 1883, he grew up poor in Chilesburg, Kentucky, the heartland of horse country. Winkfield went as often as he could to the local racetrack. He was good with horses and had a splendid constellation of black jockey stars for role models and heroes. In the spring of 1897 he began to work as a stable hand and was hired a year later by the horse racer Bub May. In 1899 Winkfield rode Evans Stock at the Hawthorne racetrack in Chicago, and followed with thirty-nine victories at a small racetrack in Indiana. May gave Winkfield a three-year contract that guaranteed twenty-five dollars a month plus room and board. In 1900 he was the number three jockey at the New Orleans Fairgrounds. He came in third at the 1900 Kentucky Derby. That August at Chicago's Harlem tracks, jealous white fans resenting the success of black jockeys crowded him against a fence, causing what was described by the local press as a minor race riot. Both Winkfield and his horse were injured.

In 1901, May sold Winkfield's contract to a horse breeder named Patrick Dunne. At the Kentucky Derby that year, Winkfield won riding His Eminence, the best horse of the day, and he became one of the top riders in

the country. Thomas Clay McDowell of Kentucky, great-grandson of Henry Clay, asked him to come and work for him. Winkfield rode his Allan-a-Dale at the Kentucky Derby in 1902, becoming the second jockey, black or white, in history, after Isaac Murphy, to win back-to-back Derbies. He earned a one-thousand-dollar bonus and was placed fourteenth on the national list at the end of 1902. In 1903 he lost the Derby, his defeat mourned by a large and disbelieving crowd. Nevertheless, he set his sights on one of the richest races in the country, the Futurity at Sheepshead Bay which was worth thirty-six thousand dollars to the winner, more than seven times the purse of the Kentucky Derby. Things went wrong. Winkfield agreed to ride Minute Man for John Madden, but he jumped his contract for three thousand dollars to ride High Ball for Bub May at the last minute. Winkfield and High Ball came in sixth, Minute Man, third. Afterward Madden threatened the twenty-year-old Winkfield with the loss of his career for double-crossing him. "So that winter, when I got a chance to go to Russia, I went," chuckled Winkfield in an interview he gave to *Sports Illustrated* years later.

According to Edward Hotaling, the NBC sportswriter who has studied black jockeys in the first decade of the century, both white and black jockeys were migrating to Europe, especially England, France, Poland, and Russia. Some left because they were overweight and weight restrictions in Europe were more relaxed; others because their techniques and mastery made them in greater demand than the local European racers. Black jockeys were being pushed out of the sport in the United States, as Winkfield was, for being "too smart for his pants." Winkfield settled first in Poland with other expatriate racers so that he could exploit the northeast circuit, which stretched from Warsaw to Moscow to St. Petersburg and then back again. Michael Lazarieff, an Armenian oil tycoon and the leading horse owner in Poland, hired him because of his excellent reputation.

Winkfield did not disappoint. He won the 1904 Russian National Riding Championship over white American Joe Piggot. Racing for the czar, he won all of Russia's big derbies, becoming one of the top national riders. In 1909 he went to Austria and Germany to ride for a Polish prince and a German baron. There he won

1910–1919

the Grossier Preis von Baden worth one hundred thousand marks. Four years later he returned to Russia to work for another Armenian, Leon Matacheff, for a reputed salary of twenty-five thousand rubles a year, plus ten percent of all the prizes he won. Winkfield lived royally at Russia's National Hotel in Moscow, eating caviar for breakfast. But as Europe exploded into war and the communists took over Russia, Winkfield, on the wrong side, began losing money.

In April of 1919, the Moscow Jockey Club, of which he was a principal member, fled with two hundred thoroughbreds to Odessa on the Black Sea. Chased by the communists, who wanted the horses and income tax, Winkfield and a Polish nobleman led the horses to Rumania. In Bucharest, they put women and children onto trains bound for Warsaw. Then, in what seems a surreal act of love for racing, they led the horses past the Transylvanian Alps, across a desperately cold Hungary and Czechoslovakia. Some of the horses starved to death and the small band of jockeys were forced to eat the others. They made it to France in 1920, where Winkfield built up a life racing again. He won the Prix Eugene Adam on a horse named Bahadhur and the Prix du Président de la République in 1923.

In Paris, he met and married the daughter of a Russian aristocrat. They had a son, Robert, and a daughter, Lillian. Winkfield rode until 1930, when he was forty-eight years old, then settled down at his newly bought, elegant property surrounded by forest. Maison Lafitte, a dozen miles northwest of Paris, became a stable where Winkfield trained thoroughbreds. But the respite from running did not last. In the late 1930s, Winkfield would have to flee again, this time from Nazis as they occupied France. He returned to America with his family, where he found work with the prominent Peter Bostwick stable in Aiken, South Carolina. But his wife, always more comfortable in France, urged him to return to Paris, which he did in 1953.

The last time Winkfield visited America was in 1960. He had been ill and was recovering at his daughter's house when he decided to see the 1961 Kentucky Derby. Word got out, and the National Turf Writers Association honored Winkfield with a banquet at the Brown Hotel in Louisville. After all that Winkfield had experienced, however, the old man was barred from entering the front of the hotel. Until Derby officials arrived and escorted him inside, Jim Crow customs forced him to wait outdoors. Winkfield returned to France and died there at the age of ninety-two.

Carter G. Woodson

The Historian
(1875–1950)

He pioneered the historical study of black America. He was not the first historian, nor was he the greatest, but Woodson established institutions and provided the intellectual discursive space for young historians moving into this new field. Were it not for this idiosyncratic, driven, meticulous, and sometimes didactic man, we would not have had the Association for the Study of Negro Life and History (1915) nor the Associated Publishers (1920) publishing books about black people when others would not; nor would we have that masterpiece of scholarly endeavor, the *Journal of Negro History* (1916). Carter G. Woodson also wrote over nineteen important books. Scholarly studies included *The Negro Church* (1921), the first attempt to study in depth the oldest African-American institution. *The Miseducation of the Negro* (1933), his classic book of essays, was a radical discourse geared toward "ahistorical" blacks who, following the country's general trend, were ignorant about our own contributions. It admonished institutionalized racism in educational institutions.

Woodson was one of the few black scholars to grapple with slavery—attempting to understand it from the slaves' perspective, noting its different forms in South America, and acknowledging the cultural influences brought from Africa. Along with other young and brilliant scholars—Charles H. Wesley, Rayford W. Logan, Monroe Nathan Work, and John Hope Franklin—Woodson steered African-American history toward becoming a recognized and respected academic discipline. He encouraged historians to reinterpret standard American history critically and to draw upon the discoveries and revelations of archaeologists and anthropologists. For Woodson, such reevaluations proved that prejudice was a learned phenomenon, the culmination of uninformed teaching and poor research. Scholarship by being accurate could be subversive.

Like his contemporary W. E. B. Du Bois, Woodson believed that Americans labored under the impression that "black history was but a negligible factor in the thought of our world." Unlike Du Bois, Woodson was solemn and introverted, lacking close friends, and living a spartan and lonely life. As Du Bois would have it, Woodson had "no conception of women in the place of creation, [and was] not a genius, but [possessed] a steady, sound mind," if not "mechanical." Criticism of that

sort was not foreign to Woodson. Although he complained about the lack of scientific objectivity in the field, he was far more of a propagandist than he admitted—some of his more popular work was likened to "compendiums of facts" designed to agitate the "race problem."

However, like Du Bois, Woodson possessed a certain intellectual arrogance, a rage ignited by the slovenly thought of others' persistence in distorting African-American history. Writing about African history, he said, "Unfortunately most of our information about African history comes from missionaries, travelers, and public functionaries who are not reliable sources." The same rang true for African-American history. Despite his covert message of affirmation for African Americans, he fulfilled his own rigid criterion for producing "good," "objective" history in place of historical ambiguity. The 1918 *Times Literary Supplement* said about *A Century of Negro Migration:* "There is no exuberance of statement, no fervid inaccuracy, no frothy declamation," clearly not something one would say about his more polemical *The Miseducation of the Negro.* The *New York Times* said about *Negro Orators and Orations, 1800–1860* (1921) that it "presents such an insight into the mentality of the Negro during the period of slavery as can hardly be found anywhere else." The level of academic scholarship Woodson achieved was undisputed.

Because Woodson was a consummate scholar in his later life, it is remarkable to think he entered Frederick Douglass High School when he was already twenty years old. One of nine children, Woodson grew up in New Canton, Virginia, poor and uneducated. If it were not for his mother who, as a former slave, secretly had learned to read and write as a child, a skill she passed on to her children, he would have been illiterate as well. But Woodson spent his evening hours immersed in self-instruction and his days working at the Fayette Coal Mines, in Huntington, West Virginia, where old black Civil War veterans told him stories that were unrecorded gems of historical detail.

When Frederick Douglass High School did accept him, to make up for what must have seemed true deprivation Woodson completed a four-year high school curriculum in two years, by 1896. He attended Berea College in Kentucky and received his bachelor's degree in 1903. After teaching for several years in West Virginia, serving for three years as supervisor of schools in the Philippines (1903–1906) during the Spanish-American War, and visiting Europe, Africa, and Asia, Woodson returned to the United States in 1906. During the summer of 1902, Woodson began studying for his B.A. in European history through correspondence classes at the University of Chicago. In the spring of 1908, he received the B.A., and in the late summer of that same year, he earned his M.A. By 1908, Woodson could relish a journey that had begun in the coal mines, and could look forward with pride to obtaining a Ph.D. in history from Harvard in 1912. After W. E. B. Du Bois, he was the second African American to earn a Harvard doctorate in history.

Woodson moved to Washington, D.C., one year before he handed in his dissertation, making use of the integrated Library of Congress. When strapped for cash, he taught French, English, Spanish, and American history at the M Street High School, a position that lasted until 1917. But in 1915, along with the publication of a second book, *The Negro Prior to 1861,* Woodson cofounded and headed a new organization called the Association for the Study of Negro Life and History (ASNLH) in Washington, D.C., later the Association for the Study of Afro-American Life and History. It was established with the aim to encourage, publish, and raise funds to support research and writing about the black experience.

Woodson's meager teaching salary—obtained from his work as a principal at the Armstrong Manual Training School in D.C., and his later work at Howard, where he served as the dean of the school of liberal arts, the head of the graduate faculty, and as professor of history—was put toward the venture. The first substantial financial support for the *Journal* came from Julius Rosenwald, who for years gave one hundred dollars a quarter for the support of the association and its publication. When the Carnegie Corporation appropriated twenty-five thousand dollars to the association, and the Laura Spelman Rockefeller Memorial gave a like sum, Woodson was able to give up teaching school and become full-time director of the association.

Woodson increasingly devoted his time to his own scholarly work as well as the mission of popularizing little-known black historical facts. He set up Associated Publishers to handle the publication and sale of books. It issued, in its first twenty-five years, over thirty volumes, and by 1940, the Association was directing studies of African-American history in clubs and schools. The Association became very successful: Under Woodson's direction it set up a home-study program, produced textbooks, subsidized young scholars, and sent investigators to work in international archives. Woodson continued to do his own research and wrote numerous articles and books, including *Negro Orators and Orations* (1925); *The Mind of the Negro as Reflected in Letters Written during the Crisis, 1800–1860* (1926); *Negro Makers of History* (1928); *African Myths, Together with Proverbs, A Supplementary Reader Composed of Folk Tales from Various Parts of Africa* (1928); *The Works of Francis J. Grimke* (four volumes, 1942); and *African Heroes and Heroines* (1944).

The ASNLH was truly a center of intellectual strength and inspiration for aspiring historians. Through the Association's quarterly publication, the *Journal of Negro History,* and its editorial board, boasting the best-known names in the field, historians were encouraged to submit their best articles and book reviews. Between 1932 and 1950 several prizes were awarded to papers that focused on some aspect of black history. Woodson's own doctoral students made their debut in its pages. During its first year, the journal circulated on all five continents, and it began its second year with a circulation of four thousand.

Marking the birthdays of Frederick Douglass and Abraham Lincoln, in February 1926 Woodson also launched Negro History Week, intended to commemorate black achievement. Originally an effort begun by the national black fraternity, Omega Psi Phi, Woodson, an honorary member, convinced its leaders that he could make the celebration more effective by sponsoring it. He was right. That short week was to become Black History Month in 1976. Woodson distributed kits containing pictures of and stories about notable African Americans to children, who had never known such a public or official gesture. He wrote later in *The Miseducation of the Negro* (1933): "Looking over the courses of study of the public schools, one finds little to show that the Negro figures in these curricula. . . ." He continues, "Even in Black schools one finds invariably that they give courses in ancient, medieval and modern Europe. Yet Africa, according to recent discoveries, has contributed about as much to the progress of mankind as Europe has, and the early civilization of the Mediterranean world was decidedly influenced by Africa." Woodson's *The Negro in Our History* (1922) went through nineteen editions and was the best textbook in its field until John Hope Franklin's *From Slavery to Freedom* in 1947. Educators, social workers, and even businesspersons supported wholeheartedly Woodson's popular work, his several fact books, bulletins, and textbooks, such as the *Negro History Bulletin* (1937), that popularized black history.

Carter Woodson died in 1950. His enormous efforts bore much fruit—from national observances of Black History Month to departments of African-American Studies in colleges and universities around the country. The nation has yet to come to terms with his powerful indictment of its racist past and present.

Louis Armstrong

"Satchmo"
(1901–1971)

He didn't know precisely when he had been born, so he picked July 4, 1900, thereby proclaiming himself a true American for a new century. The recent discovery of a birth record changes his birth date to August 1, 1901, but his true American status remains: More than any other single person, Armstrong made jazz America's music—and America's greatest aesthetic gift to the world. Armstrong's way with a cornet or trumpet was unique. Here was purity and clarity of sound, perfection of tone, exquisite timing, mastery of improvisation, an unsurpassed depth of feeling, unlimited range, wholeness of body, and seemingly unlimited power. Satchmo's creative genius makes him not only the greatest American musician of the century, but perhaps the most innovative and influential twentieth-century musician in the world. Listen to only a few bars of any of his recordings. You will understand the awe with which Duke Ellington remarked that musicians had "never heard anything else like it," or the reason Quincy Jones has said, "Everything comes from Louis."

Armstrong was born, of course, in New Orleans, the cradle of African-American music, where African, European, and Caribbean cultures mingled and changed. He was not a light-skinned, overconfident, musically educated, middle-class Creole. Armstrong brought to the table the black half of the jazz equation, and he summoned his gifts from the most impoverished depths of the black community. He was born in a neighborhood so rough that, in the midst of other poor, crime- and disease-ridden neighborhoods, it was called "The Battlefield." His unmarried mother was a fifteen-year-old washerwoman and part-time prostitute. Armstrong lived with her on the corner of Liberty and Perdito Streets, where the lowest-class black hookers plied their trade. On occasion, young Louis was forced to eat food out of garbage cans. After an arrest for delinquency, a judge sent him to the Colored

Waif's Home. The home boasted a brass band that, critic James Lincoln Collier suggests, "undoubtedly had a certain vitality and rhythmic courage." When the band director handed the twelve-year-old Armstrong a cornet, it had something else.

After his release, Armstrong began to play in the streets when he wasn't at his job delivering coal to the "cribs" of the fifty-cent prostitutes. He was too young to be admitted to Pete Lala's Cabaret, which showcased the hottest jazz bands. But the street women liked him, and if they were between customers they would let him stop and listen to the music inside the cabaret. Armstrong was an extraordinary musician from the very beginning. Edward "Kid" Ory let him sit in, when he was only sixteen, for his cornet player, the fabled Joseph "King" Oliver. Like many New Orleans jazzmen, Armstrong could not read music—though it is unclear whether he believed, with many, that it would spoil his playing. But Armstrong was forced to learn how to read musical scores when he got a job with the more sophisticated Fate Marable's Kentucky Jazz Band, which played on the *Dixie Belle,* a Mississippi River paddleboat. So many of Marable's sidemen became famous that his band was called "the floating conservatoire." While playing on the *Dixie Belle,* whose passengers were all white, Armstrong also learned the critical lesson of how to tailor jazz to white audiences.

July 8, 1922, was a momentous day that changed the course of history. With the closing of New Orleans's red-light district by the U.S. Navy, King Oliver and his Creole Jazz Band followed the momentum of the great migration and moved north to Al Capone's Lincoln Gardens Café in Chicago's black South Side. On that day, at Oliver's request, Armstrong arrived in Chicago to play second cornet in Oliver's band. "We never had to look at each other when we played," Armstrong said of Oliver. "[We were] both thinking the same thing." Still, the talented young horn player was a country bumpkin, who sported a box suit and an unfashionable hairdo. But he had left behind his hometown wife, and Oliver now introduced him to the world. Lil Hardin, Oliver's pianist, had a music degree from Fisk, and immediately saw Armstrong's potential. She bought him new clothes, changed his hair, taught him how to act, talked him into leaving Oliver, and married him. The rest, as they say, is jazz history.

Armstrong became known as the best player of the new "hot" music when he broke with Oliver and moved to New York to join the Fletcher Henderson Orchestra. In 1925, however, he returned to Chicago to lead a series of spectacular

recordings. His sessions with the pickup bands that came to be known as the Hot Five and the Hot Seven changed jazz history. In recordings such as "Muggles," "Cornet Chop Suey," "Potato Head Blues," and "Muskrat Ramble," Armstrong revolutionized the role of the soloist, making it the focal point of any jazz performance or recording. According to legend, in a February 1926 recording session Armstrong dropped the lyric sheet to "Heebie Jeebies" and was forced to improvise his lines without words. Naturally, he imitated the sounds of a horn, and scat singing was born. Although many consider the story to be more myth than fact, Armstrong is credited with inventing the technique that remains central to all jazz vocalists today.

By the end of the 1920s, recordings such as "(What Did I Do To Be So) Black and Blue" and "I Can't Give You Anything But Love" gained Armstrong more popular recognition than had the influential Hot Five and Hot Seven recordings. After singing "Ain't Misbehavin'" from the orchestra pit of the Broadway show *Hot Chocolates,* he was catapulted onto the stage and into the public eye. Although he continued to perform in serious jazz concerts with fellow musicians like Sidney Bechet, his work as a vocalist and entertainer became more commercial in the 1930s and 1940s. He appeared in over fifty films, including *Rhapsody in Black and Blue* and *Pennies from Heaven,* and became the first African American to have a major sponsored radio show. Louis Armstrong was a star.

Man, if you gotta ask, you'll never know.
—Louis Armstrong, when asked to define jazz

Much later, in the 1960s, he recorded such popular tunes as "Hello, Dolly" (which pushed the Beatles off the charts), "Mack the Knife," "Blueberry Hill," and "What a Wonderful World." The public loved Armstrong, but some music critics believed he sacrificed his art for popular acclaim. Those in between said there never could be enough applause to compensate for a deprived childhood. Not unrelated was the criticism that he grinned and fawned and played the fool for white people. Amid all the controversy, Armstrong's music survives and prevails. He still occupies the spotlight, a handkerchief in his right hand, blowing those clear round notes nobody had ever heard before, or has since. Always at ease in the idiom of popular song, Armstrong has had a profound impact on vocalists from Bing Crosby to Billie Holiday to Ella Fitzgerald to Frank Sinatra.

After struggling with ill health, Armstrong died of heart failure on July 6, 1971. His fourth wife, Lucille Wilson, to whom he was married for nearly thirty years, continued to live in the modest home she and her husband bought in the Corona neighborhood of Queens, New York. Since her death the house has been maintained as a historic archive by Queens College of the City of New York.

Armstrong knew he came from a tradition. "Before my time," he once said, "the name was levee camp music, then in New Orleans we called it ragtime. The fantastic music you hear on radio today, used to hear it way back in the old sanctified churches." Despite his modesty, he was not unaware that he was contributing to that tradition. "We all do 'do, re, mi,'" he said, "but you have to find the other notes yourself." After Armstrong, the art of finding it yourself—improvisation—has remained at the heart of jazz and all American music.

1920-1929

Junius C. Austin

The Dancing Political Preacher
(1887–1968)

Before Gardner Taylor, Sandy Ray, Samuel Proctor, J. H. Jackson, and Martin Luther King, Jr.—all twentieth-century preachers of enormous influence—there was Junius C. Austin. As pastor for forty-two years of the third-largest Baptist church in black America, Austin was the most respected orator of his day. He was also an activist and pragmatic preacher who worked closely with Garvey's UNIA, Du Bois's NAACP, A. Philip Randolph's Brotherhood of Sleeping Car Porters, Mme. C. J. Walker's Business Enterprises, Bill Thompson's Republican political machine in Chicago, Carter G. Woodson's Association for the Study of Negro Life and History, along with the Elks, Masons, the Knights of Pythias, and the Independent Order of St. Luke. Because his style was so smooth and his movements so syncopated, he was called "The Dancing Preacher."

The only child of Carey Austin and Mary Austin of New Canton, Virginia, Austin was called to the ministry at the age of eleven. He was educated at Virginia Seminary and College at Lynchburg, where he received his A.B. (1905), B.A. (1908), and D.D. (1910). He was awarded a B. Th. degree from Temple University. After serving several Virginia churches over a total of five years, he was called to Ebenezer Baptist Church in Pittsburgh. For eleven dynamic years, during which he was closely associated with Marcus Garvey's militant and nationalist Pan-African movement, the Universal Negro Improvement Association, Austin mesmerized his congregation, promoted black economic development, and focused on African missions. He often said, "The Negro in America will never be free until Africa gets her clothes on." Widely regarded as "that young intellectual giant from Pittsburgh" and "America's Greatest Pulpit Orator," Austin was the leading Christian figure in the black nationalist movement. In an acclaimed speech at the Universal Negro Improvement Association international convention in 1922, he told his audience,

---

"The idea of the one true and living God came from Abraham. The only thing the white man has done is to put it in such a way that it has often proved to be a curse to the world." Austin and Garvey also established a close personal friendship. In a famous photograph of Marcus Garvey seated in an open touring car, Austin is the handsome and elegantly dressed man on Garvey's right.

In 1926, Austin moved to Pilgrim Baptist Church in Chicago. For the next forty-two years, he pursued his social gospel with vigor and verve. When he arrived at the church, its debt stood at one hundred fifty thousand dollars. Within ten years—during the Depression—he liquidated the debt, set up new missions in Africa, built a huge community center, and constructed a gymnasium and housing project. For Austin, the church could not afford to ignore the interlocking evils of racism and economic irregularity. "Slavery! Slavery!" he thundered. "Economic slavery, peonage, and race injustice in general must go." Austin regarded American laissez-faire capitalism as a "relic of 1776" and derided the hypocrisy of a capitalist social order that "clings to the moribund platitude that all men have equal opportunity to acquire and achieve."

People often traveled two hours to fill the twenty-five hundred seats in his church—two and three services every Sunday. His sermons had the intellectual depth of David Walker, the bodily grace of the Nicholas Brothers, and the political passion of the prophet Amos. His music ministry was guided by the gospel legend Thomas Dorsey. His social ministry included support from local Chicago branches of the NAACP, the Urban League, and the Sleeping Car Porters. He also formed one of the first organizations of black aviators in America at his church. He played a crucial role in electing Oscar DePriest to the U.S. Congress—the first black congressman since Reconstruction. Austin's Cooperative Business League, established soon after his arrival in Chicago, was a gallant attempt to galvanize and politicize black class-consciousness.

Austin was a towering figure in the largest institutional presence in the black community—the black church. As Randall K. Burkett rightly notes, his life and work exemplified an "independent, Pan-Africanist and black religious nationalist spirit." He was a visionary and courageous leader—at the grassroots and national levels—and was one of the first black ministers to demonstrate both the economic and political potential of the church.

Josephine Baker

The Cleopatra of Jazz
(1906–1975)

How she danced! When Josephine Baker and *La Revue Nègre* stunned the opening-night audience at the Théâtre des Champs-Elysées on October 2, 1925, the dazzling young African-American dancer and comic was a long way from home. Born in the slums of East St. Louis in 1906, Baker entered show business at fourteen, when she abandoned her job as a domestic to enter the black vaudeville circuit. With extraordinary energy and a boundless desire to please the audience, she enlivened every show with her crazy antics and frantic dancing: She played the part of the goofy novice on the end of the chorus line, who constantly forgets her steps and messes up the routine. With these early successes, Baker, like many other chorus girls, dreamed of dancing on Broadway.

She first appeared in a traveling road show edition of *Shuffle Along,* featuring Eubie Blake's music and Noble Sissle's lyrics, which became one of the most successful musical comedies in American theater. Two years later, in 1924, Sissle and Blake gave Baker star billing as "the highest paid chorus girl in the world" in their next show, *The Chocolate Dandies.* Although Baker appeared in blackface in the comic role of Topsy Anna, she discarded her comic persona in the musical's "Wedding Finale." As a "deserted female" Baker appeared in a glamorous white satin gown slit alluringly up the left leg. It was this image—the very image of an elegant, composed, polished performer—that Baker would use to conquer the French.

Baker's ticket to Paris came from Caroline Dudley Reagan, a white society woman who wanted to show Parisians "real" Negro music and dance. Reagan assembled what would become known as *La Revue Nègre,* which included composer Spencer Williams and clarinetist Sidney Bechet. Josephine Baker joined the troupe as lead dancer, singer, and comic. When the troupe reached Paris, opening night was ten days away. During that brief time the revue became more "African,"

placing less emphasis on tap dancing and spirituals and more on Josephine Baker and her suggestive dancing.

On opening night at the Théâtre des Champs-Elysées in 1925 the house was packed. When audience excitement and anticipation climaxed, Josephine Baker entered the stage in blackface lips and plaid dungarees, with knees bent, feet spread apart, buttocks thrust out, stomach sucked in, cheeks puffed out, eyes crossed. She appeared to be part animal—some people saw a kangaroo, others a giraffe—part human. Her movements were just as astonishing: shaking, shimmying, writhing like a snake, contorting her torso, all this while emitting strange, high-pitched noises. Then, almost before the audience could comprehend what this apparition might possibly be, she burst off-stage on all fours, stiff-legged, derrière extended into the air, hands spanking the boards as she scuttled into the wings.

When Josephine Baker reappeared for the spectacular finale, set in a Harlem night-club, the stage belonged to her and her partner, Joe Alex, and their *Danse sauvage*. Their entrance was astonishing, Janet Flanners wrote in *The New Yorker* several years later:

She made her entry entirely nude except for a pink flamingo feather between her limbs; she was being carried upside down and doing the split on the shoulder of a black giant. Midstage, he paused, and with his long fingers holding her basket-wise around the waist, swung her in a slow cartwheel to the stage floor, where she stood like his magnificent discarded burden, in an instant of complete silence. She was an unforgettable female ebony statue.

While the French dance critic André Levinson was seduced along with every-one else by the "black Venus," he also commented on the inseparability of the music and Baker's dance movements:

There seemed to emanate from her violently shuddering body, her bold dislocations, her spring-ing movements, a gushing stream of rhythm. It was she who led the spellbound drummer and the fascinated saxophonist in the harsh rhythm of the "blues." It was as though the jazz, catching on the wing the vibrations of this body, was interpreting word by word its fantastic monologue. The music is born from the dance, and what a dance!

When the curtain fell, some applauded wildly, others booed in derision, just as had the first audience to hear Igor Stravinsky's *Le Sacre du Printemps* performed in the same theater in 1913. But defenders and detractors alike shared one reaction: shock. No one had ever witnessed such unbridled sexuality on a stage.

Exactly what Baker's allure meant to French culture was the subject of fervent debate both in cafés and in the press. For some, Josephine Baker and *La Revue Nègre* represented a transfusion of new blood and energy for a France stultified by tradition and sorely in need of renewal. For others, who held that the future of civilization itself lay in protecting an untainted French culture from jungle invaders, *La Revue Nègre* foretold the disintegration of centuries of classical cultural attainment, achievements of the mind over the body. Predictably, all this talk boosted box office receipts at the Théâtre des Champs-Elysées and guaranteed that the revue would be a success—the irresistible *succès de scandale* that it quickly turned out to be.

Josephine Baker's personal success was as formidable as her exotic stage presence. With her well-oiled skull-hugging coif and her Paul Poiret dresses, she was a model of Parisian chic. Often escorted by artist Paul Colin, who sketched her in his studio as frequently as possible, Baker was invited to all the best parties in the city. Soon, she received an offer from the Folies-Bergère to be the star of their new show, *La Folie du Jour* (Madness of the Day). Within a year, there would be Josephine Baker dolls, costumes, perfumes, and even a hairdressing called "Bakerfix."

When *la Joséphine* opened at the Folies-Bergère in April 1926, she appeared in a venerable French institution. First of the French music halls, the Folies was founded in 1869. Its premier reputation rested on its first-rate, popular artists (such as Yvette Guilbert, Maurice Chevalier, and Mistinguett), its elaborate sets and costumes, and since 1894, its stage nudity—which presented women bare from the waist up standing, like statues, in tableaux. The contrast between their alabaster immobility and Baker's wild dynamism on opening night was as dramatic as Picasso's use of African masks in *Les demoiselles d'Avignon* had been exactly twenty years earlier.

Once again, Baker's entrance was arresting. Baker appeared onstage as the young savage Fatou, in an African jungle with a French explorer asleep at the base of the palm tree and quasinaked black men singing and drumming softly nearby. There she stood, laughing, in the witty, scandalous costume that would make people snicker and nudge each other for years after: a girdle of drooping bananas just waiting to be aroused. And arouse them *la Joséphine* did, while exuding bemused innuendo. Baker seemed to be a goddess of vitality, Eros itself in blackface. "This girl," wrote critic André Rouverge for the *Mercure de France,* "has the genius to let the body make fun of itself."

Over the next span of years, *la Joséphine* captured the imagination of Paris as few others had done. But an American tour with the Ziegfeld Follies in 1936 did not generate the enthusiastic reception that Baker enjoyed among the French, and when she returned to Paris she took as her second husband a French sugar broker named Jean Lion. Though she soon divorced Lion, she became a French citizen in 1937. During the Second World War Baker was active in the service of the Red Cross and the French Resistance: doing undercover work, entertaining troops in Morocco, and even driving an ambulance. She married orchestra leader Jo Bouillon after the end of the war, when she also received the Croix de Guerre and the Legion of Honor.

During the late forties and fifties Baker made several tours of the United States. Her refusal to play to segregated audiences or stay in segregated hotels, and her vocal support for the civil rights movement, won her renewed admiration in America. Through the early sixties she crossed the Atlantic to give benefit concerts for American civil rights groups and, ultimately, to participate in the 1963 March on Washington. At home in France, Baker's other great passion was her "Rainbow Tribe"—the ten sons and two daughters of different races and nationalities she adopted as an "experiment in brotherhood." However, financial difficulties and poor health made it difficult for her to support the tribe and her lifestyle at her beloved château in the Southwest of France, Les Milandes. Though she benefited from the largesse of friends such as Princess Grace of Monaco and married American artist Robert Brady in 1973, Baker spent years struggling with private poverty that belied her glamorous public persona. Four days after the April 8, 1975, Paris opening of *Josephine,* a show based on her life, she died of a fatal cerebral hemorrhage—fifty years after she arrived in Paris and took it by storm. She was one of the few performers ever to be given a state funeral in France.

Baker embodied both the energy of *le jazz hot* and the elegance of the black Venus. The tension between these two impulses created the spellbinding effect that Josephine Baker exercised in her youth and in her mature years. The ultimate African-American expatriate, she found in France what she was denied in the U.S.: the freedom to be at once erotic and comic, suggestive and playful, intense and insouciant, primitive and civilized.

Bessie Coleman

Aviator
(1892–1926)

Bessie Coleman, known as "Brownskin Bess" and "Bess the Brave," was the first black woman aviator. Every April, on the anniversary of her death, black men and women pilots from the Chicago area and the Negro Airmen International fly over Lincoln Cemetery in Chicago to drop flowers on her grave. Coleman flew when only men and a handful of women—all white and mostly upper class—had access to planes and pilot licenses. White American women such as Blanche Scott began to fly as early as 1910, and the famous Amelia Earhart began her career in 1921, the same year Coleman received her license. Coleman, a poor manicurist, wanted to open a flying school for blacks and women, to turn "Uncle Tom's cabin into a flying hangar," as she quipped to the press.

Coleman was born in Atlanta, Texas, in 1892 to Susan and George Coleman. The family moved to Waxahachie, Texas, to sharecrop cotton. When Coleman was six, George Coleman abandoned the family, returning to his Choctaw reservation in Oklahoma, and she and her siblings made ends meet by picking cotton. Susan Coleman excused Bess, who appeared to be "different" at an early age and who was an inefficient daydreamer in the cotton fields. Her mother made sure that Bess was stocked with books from the traveling library that came through their town twice a year, and permitted her to save what little earnings she made helping out with white people's laundry. For a while, Bess attended the elementary division of the Colored Agricultural and Normal University in Langston, Oklahoma. But when money ran out, Bess was forced to withdraw.

In 1917, Coleman migrated to Chicago to board with her older brothers. One brother worked as a Pullman porter, a prestigious job in those days; the other, Johnny Coleman, cooked for the gangster Al Capone. Johnny Coleman was also a recent veteran of World War I and he shared with Coleman stories of the war abroad, and the bitterness he felt upon his return, as well as anecdotes about fighter planes. Before Bessie Coleman took to the skies, however, she, like Madame C. J. Walker, sought employment in beauty culture, a profession that welcomed young black women looking for an alternative to domestic work. After training at Burnham's School of Beauty Culture, Coleman found a job as a manicurist in the White Sox men's barbershop, located at the center of Chicago's exciting club land. Her clientele was reputedly "fancy men of the streets"—racketeers, entertainers, businessmen, soldiers, and pimps—men who had time and money on their hands. Situated in the South Side, Coleman sometimes relaxed with musicians and actors. The young Josephine Baker was among her friends.

Coleman, often bored, eavesdropped on World War I veterans chatting in the masculine environment of the barbershop. Women in France flew planes, she heard. She studied extended weekly reports of the little-known exploits of black pilots and soldiers, poring over their photographs, especially those of the segregated New York Fifteenth and Illinois Eighth regiments—two black regiments that had fought in France—soldiers to whom she would later pay tribute in her acrobatic stunt shows. With a fascination that turned into an obsession, Coleman quit her job and began to inquire about possible schools that offered aviation lessons to blacks and/or women. Of course, none would in America, but in France, they did. Aware of the financial reality of aviation training, Coleman began a small business to increase her income, establishing a chili parlor at Thirty-fifth Street and Indiana Avenue. She also sought investors, namely African Americans Robert Abbott, founder and editor of the *Chicago Defender,* and Jesse Binga, founder of the Binga State Bank, to help with her education in France. She learned French, and then sailed to Le Crotoy Somme, France, in November 1920, where at twenty-four years old she was accepted by the Condrau School of Aviation.

In June 1921 she received her international pilot's license, the first awarded to any American woman or any African American, from the Federation Aeronautique Internationale. Afterward, she moved briefly to Paris for instruction from an ace pilot who had shot down thirty-one German fighter planes. Before leaving France, she ordered a 130 horsepower Neuport de Chasse plane, which was to be sent to her in America, in case she was denied the right to purchase a plane in the States. In fact, finding safe planes would be a perennial problem for Coleman for the rest of her life. On September 29, 1921, Coleman sailed back to New York and was met by reporters from all the largest African-American newspapers, including the cast from the black musical *Shuffle Along*. The cast presented her with a silver cup to show Coleman the community's admiration and respect, and she in turn announced her intention to begin barnstorming to raise money for an aviation school. However, Coleman could not find employment in commercial aviation, without which she could not afford to pay for the plane she had ordered. Without the plane, she could not finance her aviators' school. So, unemployed, Coleman returned to Europe.

Her second period in Europe proved to be very exciting: Throughout 1921, Coleman received advanced flight instruction in Germany, Holland, and Switzerland, where she studied with a famous German pilot, Captain Keller, and test-piloted airplanes for the "Flying Dutchman," Anthony Fokker, the world-famous acrobatic stunt performer. In Germany, Coleman piloted a 220 horsepower Benz motoring plane—the largest plane ever flown by a woman at that time—for Pathé News photographers, permitting photographs of the kaiser's palace from the air. She test-piloted the Dornier seaplane for the newly founded Dornier company, manufacturers of large "flying boats." After studying and working in France, Germany, and the Netherlands, where she gained a stellar reputation as an ace pilot, she decided to barnstorm. Barnstorming, a term usually applied to traveling actors who entertained from town to town sleeping in barns, meant that Coleman was a stunt pilot, performing figure eights, truck climbs, twists and turns, and nosedives. Film reels captured the beauty of Coleman's flying skills. When she returned to America in 1922, these newsreels had arrived before her. This time, reporters from the *New York Times* and the *Chicago Tribune* greeted her arrival.

Her first aerobatic performance occurred soon after her return. In 1922, she exhibited at the Curtis Airfield in Garden City, Long Island. The program consisting of stunts and a parachute leap by Herbert Fauntleroy Julian, honoring the Fifteenth Black Regiment. Near the end, she took black bystanders up in the air for five dollars a ride. At her second show in Chicago in October 1922, she paid tribute to the Eighth Regiment of Illinois. As she twisted through the air, the Eighth Regiment Band, once led by James Reese Europe, entertained the crowd with jazz and marching tunes, and to the crowds' utter delight, during intermission, Colonel Otis B. Duncan, commander of the Eighth Illinois Infantry, escorted Coleman to her plane, got in, and took off with her at the wheel. Coleman decided to barn-

storm the South, to the dismay of her African-American manager, who promptly resigned after only a few months—believing that the South was no place for a black woman in planes. Coleman persisted, and at her first stop in her hometown of Waxachachie, she refused to perform at the airport unless African Americans were allowed entry, which turned out to be a successful gamble. Her southern trip turned out to be full of thrills as well: In Wharton, Texas, Coleman hired a white female fellow pilot to parachute from the plane. During the exhibition, the pilot, Eliza Delworth—seized with fear—refused to jump, so Coleman parachuted—impromptu—instead. Coleman continued with her tributes to pilots who had gone before her, and in 1923 she flew a memorial flight in Boston in honor of the white pilot Harriet Quimby (1884–1912), who had crashed and died over the Charles River. Coleman herself crashed in 1924—but survived with facial lacerations, three broken ribs, and two double fractures of her left leg. While recuperating, the Dahomean prince Kojo Touvalou Houenou courted her, to no avail.

Coleman endeared herself to black communities through numerous lectures and talks at theaters, churches, and school halls, and of course she gave numerous flying exhibitions to black audiences. In 1926, the Negro Welfare League invited Coleman to Jacksonville, Florida, to perform for their May Day holiday. She readily agreed, despite her family's pleas for her not to do so, so soon after her crash. She had trouble locating a plane in Florida, because southern dealers would not sell, rent, or loan an airplane to an African American. She contacted her white mechanic, William D. Wells, in Dallas, Texas, and asked him if he would bring her a veteran surplus plane, which was all she could afford. It was the last plane she flew. The day before the May Day event, practicing in the air with her mechanic, Coleman's plane spiraled out of control. Coleman, sitting in the back seat with her belt unfastened, was catapulted out of her seat, falling five hundred feet to the ground. Her mechanic managed to right the plane, but crash-landed. A wrench used to service the engine had slid into the gearbox and jammed it.

Coleman had three funerals: Her body was carried by train to Jacksonville, Orlando, and Chicago, where thousands of African-American mourners came out to pay their respects. The Reverend Junius C. Austin officiated at the funeral. He said Coleman was one hundred years ahead of the race she loved well. He rebuked the community, however, for not supporting her, allowing her to fly old, inferior planes because of a lack of money. In Chicago, where Austin, pastor of Pilgrim Baptist Church, and the Reverend C. M. Tanner, pastor of Greater Bethel Church, officiated, ten thousand people gathered for the service. Ida B. Wells Barnett, a fan and a friend, was mistress of ceremonies.

Flight would remain a veritable last frontier for African Americans until the Tuskegee Airmen demonstrated the Negro's capacity to fly in combat during World War II. Both Richard Wright and Ralph Ellison would depict in their fiction the frustration of African Americans with the racism of aviation. But Bessie Coleman's pioneering example—as a black person and as a woman—made it impossible to claim that only white males possessed the requisite intelligence and skill to master the art of flying.

Marcus Garvey

The Black Moses
(1887–1940)

Marcus Garvey was the Moses of twentieth-century black folk. His was a bold revolutionary vision of a "United States of Africa," a homeland for all the children of the diaspora. To repatriate its dispersed daughters and sons back to Africa, Garvey incorporated a shipping company, the Black Star Line. He created the largest black political movement in history, establishing hundreds of branches of his Universal Negro Improvement Association (UNIA) throughout the United States, the Caribbean, and Africa. News of relevance to black people was aired in the pages of his internationally circulated newspaper, the *Negro World*.

For all of Garvey's efforts, his movement failed. The United States of Africa has never materialized. The Black Star Line eventually would collapse in acrimony and financial disarray. With only a handful of branches remaining, the UNIA today has nothing of its former strength and glory. Yet Garvey ignited the imagination of a black proletariat disappointed by the promises of urban immigration and frustrated by racial injustice in America. A principal hallmark of Garvey's legacy is that so many of the symbols he invented to rally black people to his cause have become commonplace today, canonical features of contemporary African-American culture. The logic of black pride and economic self-reliance that was such a central part of Garvey's platform has become the collective property of black people at home and abroad.

Marcus Mosiah Garvey was born in St. Ann's Bay, Jamaica, in 1887. His father was a stonemason, a well-read but distant man of Maroon descent whose library formed the foundation of his son's education. His mother has been described as a soft-spoken, modest, devout Christian. Garvey was the last of seven children, all of whom died during birth except his sister, Indiana. After apprenticing as a printer during his teens, he moved to Kingston, where he worked as a printer and journalist and became involved in politics. By 1910, at age twenty-three, he decided to test his fortunes off the island, spending the next few years traveling and working as a journalist, printer, publisher, and timekeeper on the banana plantations of the Caribbean and Latin America.

What he saw in his journeys horrified him. Everywhere he went he saw that the conditions of black people were uniformly oppressive. By 1912, he had abandoned work on the plantations, but he was fueled with a desire to improve the lot of black people. He went to England where, some believe, he attended classes at Birbeck College. He lectured on a Hyde Park corner on the conditions of West Indians, and began writing for Duse Mohammed Ali's Pan-African and Pan-Asian journal, the

African Times and Orient Review. While in London he read Booker T. Washington's *Up from Slavery.* Inspired, he decided to return to Jamaica; on the long passage home, he realized his mission. "Where is the Black man's government," he asked himself. "Where is his King and Kingdom? Where is his president, his country, and his ambassador, his army, his navy, his men of big affairs? I could not find them and then I declared I will help to make them."

Upon his return to Jamaica in 1914, Garvey founded the Universal Negro Improvement Association and African Communities League. Its motto was "One God! One Aim! One Destiny!" Its original mandate, however, was slightly more modest. The UNIA would act as a benevolent association with the goal of building a technical college in Jamaica similar to Booker T. Washington's Tuskegee Institute. But Garvey found that the level of "race consciousness" among Jamaica's black population was low, and they did not see the need for such an organization. He decided to leave Jamaica, hoping to meet Washington and interest him in supporting his organization. But Washington had died in 1915, a year before Garvey arrived in the United States.

Garvey came to in New York in 1916, staying briefly in Harlem before embarking on a five-month, thirty-eight-state speaking tour. He had planned to return to Jamaica soon after, but black America, and particularly Harlem, excited him. At first, Garvey was but one of many street corner speakers selling spiritual or secular salvation in a range of packages. But Garvey's message of race pride and self-determination, and his powerful oratory, soon distinguished him from the others. In 1918, he established a Harlem branch of the UNIA. Over the next few years, driven by Garvey, it would thrive. In addition to the Black Star Line and the *Negro World,* the UNIA's Negro Factories Corporation, which operated a chain of businesses in Harlem, would employ over a thousand Harlemites in the early 1920s.

In August 1920, Garvey staged his first convention. It attracted some twenty-five hundred delegates from around the world to Madison Square Garden and the UNIA's Liberty Hall. Its spectacular parade caused thousands of onlookers to fill with pride: The delegates were dressed in military regalia, appearing to be statesmen of an African government in exile. Other members carried placards proclaiming "Africa for the Africans" and "All men are created Equal." The UNIA unveiled a flag with three bars, of red, black, and green, that has now become a ubiquitous sym-

1920–1929

bol in black popular culture for black cultural nationalism. For a moment, even though Garvey and the UNIA had no developed plan or politics, his proposed United States of Africa seemed at least imaginable.

The dream would not last, however. Garvey was indicted on charges of mail fraud stemming from his dealings on behalf of the Black Star Line. Before his trial, a "Garvey Must Go" campaign was led by rivals both inside and outside the UNIA. He was convicted and incarcerated in Atlanta in 1925. While Garvey was imprisoned, his second wife, Amy Jacques Garvey, managed to maintain the organization through tireless devotion. His sentence was commuted two years later, but authorities deported him upon release. But even after his release, the UNIA could not regain its former strength. Garvey would never again enjoy the status of an international black statesman. After he left the United States, he tried to rebuild the organization. He held UNIA conventions in Canada, and would later try his hand, unsuccessfully, at party politics in Jamaica. He migrated to England in the late thirties, where, as one of his final acts of international diplomacy, he criticized Ethiopian emperor Haile Selassie during Mussolini's invasion of that country. In the process, Garvey alienated many blacks in America, the Caribbean, and in Europe and Africa, who were passionately rallying around Selassie's cause.

In 1940, he had a stroke that left him partially paralyzed. He died a few months later from another stroke, reportedly caused by the shock of reading his own obituary, written by a malicious reporter. Garvey did not leave behind established institutions—libraries, research centers, journals—that continue to play a viable part in black politics. What he did leave was his vision of a republic based on a common skin color, a powerful legacy of black cultural nationalism.

Langston Hughes

The Poet
(1902–1967)

With a career that extended from the Harlem Renaissance of the 1920s to the Black Arts movement of the 1960s, Langston Hughes was the most prolific black writer of his era. Between 1926, when he published his first pioneering poems, *The Weary Blues,* until 1967, the year of his death, when he published *The Panther and the Lash,* Hughes wrote sixteen books of poems, five works of nonfiction, and nine children's books; he also edited nine anthologies of poetry, folklore, short fiction, and humor. He translated Jacques Roumain, Nicholas Guillen, Gabriela Mistral, and Federico García Lorca, and wrote at least thirty plays. It is not surprising that Hughes was known as "Shakespeare in Harlem" and "The Poet Laureate of the Negro Race."

Hughes was born in Joplin, Missouri, in 1902. His father, James Nathaniel, was a black businessman, a victim of his own internalized racism, and his mother was Carrie Langston Mercer, a descendent of black abolitionists. Hughes attended Columbia University in New York from 1921 to 1922, and received his B.A. from Lincoln University in Pennsylvania in 1929. His unorthodox career included stints as a laundry boy, assistant cook, and busboy; he also worked as a seaman on voyages to Europe and Africa. Fluent in French and Spanish, he lived for periods in Mexico, France, Italy, Spain, and the Soviet Union. But it was in New York, as one of the earliest participants in the Harlem Renaissance, that Hughes's genius was discovered and developed. The Renaissance was a spectacular flowering of African-American culture during the 1920s, an era of exciting creativity in literature, art, music, and dance. Originally called the New Negro movement, the renaissance was an era of black pride, positive self-consciousness, and cultural affirmation. It was a golden movement.

Langston Hughes's writing is deceptively simple, and his life also is often enigmatic, even disingenuous. Hughes's biographer, Arnold Rampersad, writes that Hughes's own autobiography, *The Big Sea,* "is a study in formal sleight of hand, in which deeper meaning is deliberately concealed." In fact, Hughes was a mask-wearing man who worked to protect his vulnerability by constructing a facade of personal compliance, asexuality, and political moderation.

Hughes endured a series of betrayals: from his racist father; from "godmother," the wealthy white patron who smothered his freedom; from Zora Neale Hurston, whom he believed stole his work; from the political left, which used him; from publishers and a public that pushed him from artistry toward commercialism; from an America that patronized and ignored him. After forays into these worlds, Hughes built a wall of geniality. But he knew where the real basis of his creativity lay.

He returned constantly to the life-affirming folk tradition of the black masses: "After all the deceptions and disappointments, there was always the undertow of black music with its rhythms that never betray you, its strength like the beat of the human heart." Hughes's genius lay in expressing black consciousness, interpreting to the people the beauty within themselves, and in raising the racial folk form to literary art. He used the incredibly creative poetry of black language, blues, and jazz to construct an Afro-American aesthetic that rarely has been surpassed. He learned the hard way that his strength was in loyalty to black culture and identification with "my people." "I don't study the black man," Hughes said. "I 'feel' him." Rampersad writes that Hughes discovered "in his chronic loneliness, true satisfaction came only from the love and regard of the black race, which he earned by placing his finest gift, his skill with language, in its service."

Hughes's work was reviewed in mainstream journals by mainstream writers, where few fully appreciated his experiments with the blues, jazz, and black talk. His experiments in these forms was expressed most directly by his popular newspaper columnist alter ego, Jesse B. Semple (a.k.a. "Simple"), whose musings Hughes published in the *Chicago Defender.* Simple's discussion of issues such as the complexities of bebop were remarkably rich; when we juxtapose them with Hughes's comments about the ways jazz informed his poetry, we understand that we must read Hughes both as a product *of* and a reaction *to* the African-American vernacular.

Others would soon pick up on his techniques. As Leopold Sedar Senghor has remarked, Hughes's style was "analogical, melodious, and rhythmical," rife with "assonance and alliteration." Senghor notes, "You will find this rhythm in French poetry; you will find it in Claudel; you will find [it] in St. John Perse. . . . And it is this that Langston Hughes has left us with, this model of the perfect work of art." In these and other respects, Hughes's best work was probably his vernacular poetry, cast "in the idiom of the black folk " and found, especially, in *The Weary Blues, Fine Clothes to the Jew,* and *Ask Your Mama.*

1920–1929

Hughes spent his life creating; he was perhaps the first black author to earn a living, however modest, from writing. He went on many reading tours to black colleges and other organizations, selling and signing books. He was briefly on the teaching staff at Atlanta University and the Laboratory School of the University of Chicago. In the 1950s he appeared before Senator Joseph McCarthy in the government's witch-hunt for communists. He was reconciled enough to lecture in 1965 in Europe for the U.S. Information Agency. He went to Dakar to the First World Festival of Negro Art. Hughes died in New York of congestive heart failure on May 22, 1967.

Before his peers Sterling Brown and Zora Neale Hurston, Hughes demonstrated how to use black language and music as a poetic diction—at a moment when other black writers thought the task fruitless at best, detrimental at worst. Indeed, so much of the best of the African-American literary tradition—Brown, Hurston, Ellison, Morrison—grows out of his elevating the vernacular into literature. Hughes, in other words, undertook the project of constructing an entire literary tradition from the common language. This was the very language, ironically, that the growing and mobile black middle class shunned as the embarrassing legacy of slavery. We may fail to recognize the boldness of Hughes's innovation because of his triumph: Adopted, accepted, and naturalized by his successors, black vernacular is now everywhere in American speech and literature. Even without his other contributions, this achievement alone ensures his permanent place in American letters.

Ernest Everett Just

The Biologist
(1883–1941)

Ernest Everett Just was a brilliant biologist who sought freedom from racism in the objective truth of science. A professor of biology at Howard University for more than thirty years, Just was the first great modern African-American scientist. He was awarded the NAACP Spingarn Medal in 1915 for his work on the embryology of marine invertebrates, and again in 1939. He published *The Biology of the Cell Surface* (1939), a groundbreaking text based on research at the Marine Biology Center at Woods Hole, Massachusetts, in the 1920s and in Europe in the 1930s. Just's research concentrated on the process of fertilization, as well as on parthenogenesis, the development of unfertilized eggs. He discovered the fundamental role played by protoplasm (the substance that lies outside of the nucleus of the cell) in cell development, including its influence on heredity.

E. E. Just was born on August 14, 1883, in the old decaying southern city of Charleston, South Carolina. As a child, he moved to James Island, a Gullah community just off the coast, when his father, a dock builder, died. His mother, a schoolteacher, supervised his education. As a widow, Mary Cooper Just was forced to find work where she could and took a job in the Jamestown phosphate mines. Undeterred by the obstacles she faced with her four children, she sent Just to the Colored Normal, Industrial, Agricultural and Mechanical College in South Carolina, which prepared him, however inadequately, for college. She later sent him to Kimball Union Academy in Meridien, New Hampshire, which offered Just a more thorough education. The family arranged for Just to sail to New York—he paid for his way by working on the ship—and once he got to New York, he worked to pay his expenses. Just graduated from Kimball in 1903, the same year his mother died. That fall he enrolled at Dartmouth College, where he was the only black freshman. Receiving degrees in zoology and history, Just was the only student to graduate magna cum laude.

After graduation, Just was appointed professor of zoology and physiology at Howard University Medical School. Just's popularity as a teacher was legendary, and his support of students extended beyond the classroom. In 1911, he helped Howard students establish Omega Psi Phi, a national black fraternity. He began his graduate training at the Marine Biological Laboratory (MBL) at Woods Hole in 1909. The MBL gathered eminent biologists to work with marine organisms and attracted its share of Nobel prize winners over the years. Yet, Woods Hole also practiced the racism widespread in the wider society. One summer, Just's wife, Ethel Highwarden, joined him at Woods Hole, a common practice among the other scientists. But the Justs were ostracized by the other families. Mrs. Just—who was more darkly complected than her husband—was left to wander Woods Hole alone each day for the entire summer. Although his wife never again set foot in Woods Hole, Ernest Just would return every summer for twenty years. The world's preeminent center for marine biology research offered him a much needed respite from a busy teaching load at Howard.

Just became a research assistant to the noted scientist Frank R. Lillie in 1911. Head of the zoology department at the University of Chicago, Lillie worked on the fertilization process of the sandworm *Nereis*. In 1912, Just published his first paper describing the results. His paper was discussed widely in domestic and foreign journals. Nobel laureate T. H. Morgan called it the fundamental and authoritative study on the subject. In 1916, after four years of long-distance study and the publication of several papers, Just received his Ph.D. in zoology from the University of Chicago. Over the course of his highly productive career, Just would publish fifty scientific papers, as well as his famous textbook, *Biology of the Cell Surface.*

> We feel the beauty of nature because we are a part of nature and because we know that however much in our separate domains we abstract from the unity of Nature, this unity remains. Although we may deal with particulars, we return finally to the whole pattern woven out of these.
> —Ernest Everett Just

Beginning in 1929, Just regularly traveled to Italy, Germany, and France for scientific conferences and study. He felt that he was treated as a human being in Europe and grew increasingly embittered about the lack of career opportunities in the United States, despite his scientific achievements. Just continued to travel back and forth to Europe until 1940, when he and his second wife, a German—he and his first wife had divorced—were held briefly in a concentration camp in Nazi-occupied France before they could return to the United States. After he was released and had returned to America, Just learned that he had pancreatic cancer. His health worsened, and he died in 1941.

Although Just was consulted frequently on selections to the National Academy of Sciences, he himself was never elected to this prestigious body. He was elected vice president of the American Society of Zoologists, however, and held membership in many European and American scientific bodies. In 1983 the Twenty-sixth Southeastern Conference on Developmental Biology held a symposium on the cellular and molecular biology of invertebrate development at the Bell W. Branch Institute for the Marine Biology and Coastal Research in South Carolina. The conference was dedicated to E. E. Just. The scientist Richard Sawyer declared that "Just laid a part of the foundation on which we [cellular biologists] stand today." It is difficult for us to appreciate how crucial Just's scientific achievements were in refuting racist stereotypes about black mental capacity. For his pathbreaking biological research and his courage, it is fitting that today we regard Ernest Just as the father of black scientists.

Oscar Micheaux

Cinematographer
(1885–1951)

Oscar Micheaux captured on film the "colored heart." At least that's what he intended to do. Not only did he run his own production company, he also wrote, directed, filmed, and edited his own films. He transported these black-and-white reels from colored-only cinemas to Negro church halls by bus, car, and on foot, and even persuaded white southern theater owners and urban northern cinema managers to show his "race" films at their segregated theaters. His goal was to convince a suspicious African-American audience that fully developed, non-stereotypical, black characters could exist on the screen. With the latest technology in his hands, Micheaux released over forty-three dramas—twenty-seven silent movies and sixteen sound films, only ten of which have survived. In these films he sought not only to counter the cruel stereotypes of the day, but to dramatize his generation's aspirations of social acceptance and assimilation. Fraught with unresolved racial tensions, these films often depicted an uncritical black bourgeoisie as well as light-complexioned actors. Nevertheless, Micheaux's films were responsible for critiquing the nascent cinema industry's pervasive images of shuffling, black servants. Moreover, Micheaux dealt with real and frightening themes, filming ideas that other filmmakers refused to touch. For instance, *Lynching Within Our Gates* (1919) dealt with the cruel and barbaric American "sport" that had been celebrated in D. W. Griffith's classic film *Birth of a Nation,* released in 1915, a film applauded by President Woodrow Wilson.

Oscar Micheaux was a "New Negro" artist long before that movement came into vogue in the 1920s. He was a self-made pioneer emboldened by his acute awareness of the enormous potential of the new medium of film. The fifth of thirteen children, he was born in 1884 in Metropolis, Illinois. Before becoming an artist, he worked as a coal miner, docker, and Pullman porter. It was after eking out an existence in Chicago in the early 1900s that Micheaux decided to move to Gregory, South Dakota, in 1915 to homestead. Later, Micheaux would represent in his novels and films the positive effects of black migration to the Great West. Even when the Micheaux Film Production Company was based temporarily in Chicago, he believed that urban economies depended upon poor, unskilled, and dispirited blacks accepting ridiculously low wages. Micheaux, influenced no doubt by Booker T. Washington's ideologies of self-reliance and thrift, obtained several acres of prairie land in Gregory County on the Rosebud Indian Reservation, where he built a house and barn. At age twenty-four and something of a precocious romantic, he wrote his first book, *The Conquest: The Story of a Negro Pioneer* (1913). Micheaux published this novel himself, and subsequent ones, through the Western Book Supply Company. Selling door-to-door, he eventually sold about twenty-five hundred copies of his first novel.

During the teens, Micheaux became interested in the few black films in circulation and determined to see blacks portraying blacks in the cinema. Images of blacks had appeared first on the screen as early as 1898, only months after Lumière's first theatrical projection of moving images, in the form of black soldiers departing to fight in the Spanish-American War. In 1903 a fourteen-minute adaptation of *Uncle Tom's Cabin* appeared. By 1905, the year in which the Niagara Movement was founded, the *Wooing and Wedding of a Coon,* described as a "genuine Ethiopian comedy," was released, typically racist and demeaning. In 1918, however, George P. Johnson and his brother, Noble, founded their own Lincoln Motion Picture Company in California, the first black-owned production company. Lincoln approached Micheaux to adapt his novel *The Conquest* for film. By 1920, the Lincoln Company had completed five films, two pictorials, and three dramatic subjects, including a five-reel feature titled *A Man's Duty.* Micheaux gradually developed reservations about a contract he had signed, which would not allow him to direct and to exercise control over his work. Though the Lincoln Film Company was managed by blacks, the direction and cinematography of their productions was entrusted to white cameramen, particularly Harry Gant, who later produced and directed low-budget westerns. Micheaux resisted any hint of black stereotype on film, and with absolutely no experience he took the bold decision of filming his novel himself. In 1919 he founded the Micheaux Film Company in Sioux City and Chicago. It was financed by both black and white farmers from South Dakota. Reworking the plot of *The Conquest,* Micheaux released his first feature film, *The Homesteader,* later that year.

Micheaux produced films with enormous gusto and style. The Micheaux Film Company spawned black stars who were cast to play gangsters, preachers, detectives, kings, and queens. Perhaps the most significant film Micheaux made was *Body and Soul* (1924), starring the celebrated singer and activist Paul Robeson in his first movie. Robeson starred doubly as a troubled, dishonest preacher and his honest twin brother. Micheaux survived the demise of the silent era: *The Exile,* in 1931, was the first black talking picture, and it made its debut at Harlem's Lafayette Theatre. *The Girl from Chicago* (1932) and *Swing* (1938) would follow. In 1948 he made his last film, *The Betrayal,* based on his book *The Wind from Nowhere.* Three years later, on one of his whirlwind promotional tours in North Carolina, Micheaux died. An annual Oscar Micheaux Award, presented by the Black Filmmaker's Hall of Fame to promising young black filmmakers, underscores Micheaux's pioneering role in the history of African-American cinematography. He was the first black person to realize the enormous potential of the film medium to both entertain and inform society.

Bessie Smith

The Empress of the Blues
(1894?–1937)

"The greatest blues singer in the world will never stop singing." So reads the tombstone Janis Joplin and Juanita Green erected on Bessie Smith's grave in Philadelphia's Mount Lawn Cemetery in 1970, a grave that had been left unmarked for over thirty years. Both statements on the tombstone are true. Bessie Smith will never stop singing because she cut 150 sides for Columbia and they are available in every record store. There is no question that she was the greatest of all the urban women blues singers. Louis Armstrong, one of a handful of her peers in twentieth-century American music, said, "She used to thrill me at all times, the way she could phrase a note with a certain something in her voice no other blues singer could get." But that is not the essence of her story. It is not simply that Bessie Smith was a singer, like a few others, of extraordinary talent. Another of those peers, the jazz clarinetist and bandleader Sidney Bechet, understood her at a deeper level. "She was the best blues singer there was," he said, "but that trouble was inside her and it wouldn't let her rest."

If some restive internalized "trouble" is the sine qua non for real blues singing, Smith met the qualifications. She was born on an uncertain date to a desperately poor family living in a one-room shack in Chattanooga, Tennessee. She was one of seven children of William Smith, an unskilled laborer and itinerant Baptist preacher, and Laura Smith. They both died during Bessie's childhood. The oldest sister, Viola, supported her siblings by taking in white people's laundry. As a small child, Smith sang and danced on the streets for pennies, and then, like Josephine Baker, she found a way out of poverty by finding a way out of town. As a young teenager, she joined tent shows, traveling through the segregated South in groups with names such as Florida Cotton Blossom Minstrel Show and Fat Chappelle's Rabbit Foot Minstrels. Smith, at this point, was primarily a dancer, an aspect of her career about which little is known. Graduating to black theaters and clubs, and moving further afield, she played the Dixie in Atlanta, the Paradise in Atlantic City, Horan's Madhouse in Philadelphia, and the 81 Theater in Atlanta, the last of which became her headquarters.

It is not known when and how Bessie Smith evolved as a singer. She may have traveled with Ma Rainey, "The Mother of the Blues," and they may have been lovers. During World War I she put together her own show, *Liberty Belles,* where she sang, danced, and appeared in drag. Audiences loved it, but managers wouldn't book *Liberty Belles,* presumably because the chorus line was dark and heavyset, like Bessie, but just as likely because the show was too raucous even for low-down theaters. But it was the great migration that made Bessie Smith, as thousands of displaced southerners hungered for the sounds of home. They went to hear her sing, and when Columbia recorded her, on separately catalogued "race records," people bought so many it made both Columbia and Bessie rich. They loved her back in the South too, where her records were sold off trains by Pullman porters hitting one southern town after another. Poor people put together a dollar to buy a Bessie Smith record, and so by themselves supported

from below the industry that produced some of the greatest music ever created.

Smith almost didn't get to record. When Mamie Smith's *Crazy Blues* was a sensational hit among African Americans for Okeh Records's race list, the companies went looking for female blues singers. Smith was at first rejected by all the labels'

white executives because they found her voice too "rough," her accent too southern, and her personality too crude. Thomas Edison personally evaluated her "NG"
for "no good." But on February 6, 1923, the Columbia
Gramophone Company cut two sides, "Downhearted Blues" and
"Gulf Coast Blues." She was scared and her voice is in fact a little uncertain, but the purity and feeling are there from the outset. "Downhearted Blues" runs three minutes and twenty-five
seconds; it sold over 750,000 copies in the first six months; Bessie
was paid a flat $125, with no royalties. Every song she recorded

is a gem: "Empty Bed Blues," "Cake Walking Babies from Home," "Gimme a
Pigfoot," "Nobody in Town Can Bake a Sweet Jelly Roll Like Mine," "Ticket Agent,
Ease Your Window Down." What is her greatest? Probably W. C. Handy's "St. Louis
Blues," which she did in one take with a twenty-four-year-old Louis Armstrong
playing background on muted cornet.

Bessie Smith was a big-boned, two hundred-pound woman who drank hard,
talked tough, and lived large. She could be volatile and violent. In one of the frequent knockdown fights with Jack Gee, her second husband, a rough security
guard who claimed to be a policeman, she gave as good as she got. Bessie would
walk into a black honky-tonk, throw a hundred-dollar bill down on the bar, and
yell, "Lock the door! Don't let nobody in, don't let nobody out!" She was barely
literate and had to memorize lyrics because she couldn't read the words. She didn't
like white people, or even light-skinned Negroes, and she never sang before a
white audience. Except for a tiny coterie of aficionados, white people neither
heard her nor heard of her. Because of that, her singing was never modified for a
white audience, and it retains the honesty and authenticity of her own experience,
the "trouble" that Sidney Bechet heard and understood, the trouble inside her
which would never let her rest. Bessie Smith died as the result of an automobile
accident on September 26, 1937.

Bessie Smith preserved the southern black oral folk tradition. She sang as no one
else of human despair, of a sadness, as Langston Hughes described her, "not softened
with tears, but hardened with laughter, the absurd, incongruous laughter of a sadness without even a god to appeal to." She will be remembered as the most accomplished female blues singer of the twentieth century, and she will never stop singing.

1920–1929

Jean Toomer

A New Negro
(1894–1967)

Jean Toomer's *Cane* (1922) was the boldest experimental novel of the Harlem Renaissance. Yet soon after the novel's publication, the aesthetically restless author began searching for new forms to express his developing vision of racial transcendence. Alienating many in the black literary world, Toomer's work fell into obscurity for decades. Toomer was rediscovered in the midst of the black power and black arts movements in the 1960s. Ironically, he denied that he was black for almost forty years.

Born in 1894 in Washington, D.C., into a prominent racially mixed family headed by Reconstruction statesman P. B. S. Pinchback, Toomer was abandoned by his father and lived with his mother until her death in 1909. His grandparents cared for him until he left for college. He studied agriculture at the universities of Wisconsin and Massachusetts. He spent time in New York City, moved back to Washington for a year, and spent another in Sparta, Georgia, where he taught high school—an experience which later served as the basis for *Cane. Cane* is a curious book. It is not a novel, but a farrago of stories, sketches, and poems, culminating in a one-act play. The book is unexpectedly "modern," with seemingly discontinuous sections, an element of surrealism, and a fragmentation and apparent meaninglessness that makes the reader think of *Waiting for Godot*. The word "cane" refers to roots, and the book is about the complex ambiguous realities of black experience in America.

In his travels, Toomer came across the teachings of George Ivanovich Gurdjieff, the Russian-born spiritual teacher. In 1924 he took his first trip to France to study with the great mystic. Toomer arranged to have his next book, *Essentials: Definitions and Aphorisms,* privately published in 1931. He also married Margery Latimer, who died a year later giving birth to their daughter. Toomer married again in 1934; he eventually settled down in Doylestown, Pennsylvania, with his second wife, Marjorie Content, to live a life of peaceful obscurity. He spent the next thirty years, until his death in 1967, searching for a philosophy of mystical transcendence.

Two years after Toomer's death, Robert Bone published a reappraisal of *Cane* in the *New York Times Book Review*. This posthumous renaissance probably would not have surprised Toomer; after all, few writers have been so enthusiastically promoted by such a wide assortment of reviewers. Not only had Max Eastman and Claude McKay published his work in the *Liberator,* but Alan Tate and William Stanley Braithwaite considered *Cane* a seminal modernist text. Tate wrote that sections of *Cane* "challenged some of the best modern writing" and that the book was "highly important for literature." Braithwaite praised him as the Negro writer "most surely touched with genius," the first black writer to write "about the Negro without the surrender or compromise of the artist's vision."

The irony is that Toomer was never successful in articulating an artistic vision after *Cane*. Soon after its publication, he decided to stop being "a negro" in order to become "just American." He even started going by the sobriquet "The First American." It was a complicated shift that took him a decade to complete. In a letter of June 1922, he wrote, "As near as I can tell, there are seven race bloods within this body of mine. French, Dutch, Welsh, Negro, German, Jewish, and Indian. . . . One half of my family is definitely colored. For my own part I have lived equally amid the two groups. And I alone, as far as I know, have striven for a spiritual fusion analogous to the fact of racial intermingling. . . . Viewed from the world of race distinctions, I take the color of whatever group I at the time am sojourning in."

Rather than transcending race, Toomer had immersed himself completely in race—all races. In 1930, Toomer passed for good from the black literary world when he denied James Weldon Johnson the rights to reprint his work in the *Book of American Negro Poetry*. Refusing Johnson, the dean of black arts and letters, was as clear a statement of intent as any black writer could make.

As Toomer knew, the attempt to be racially indeterminate changed his voice: "Since *[Cane]* I have become more psychological, to include even more of that labyrinth—and this is the simplest explanation I can give to those who expect poetry from me, get psychology, morality, and something of religion, and are puzzled. . . . I count it good that any poet stops writing his own small verse, that any man stops doing his own small work, and becomes a student of the Great Work."

Many readers saw an artistic death in this attempt "to pass," rather than the liberating assumption of a new identity. "He never wrote another *Cane*," is the refrain of much Toomer criticism, "after he passed." But for Toomer, passing was not suicide; rather, it was a step toward more universal possibilities.

The problem for Toomer was not just racial, it was also aesthetic: how to move past the integrating lyricism of *Cane* toward a more accurate representation of the fragmentation he felt. He treated this as a structural problem: "The reality of man's life, as I perceive and understand it, is complex beyond the possibility of formulation. How represent in sequence that which exists simultaneously? Where begin, where end? Yet a book about man must be written in sequence, and it must begin and end."

Toomer wanted all possibilities in play at once, in parallel, not in sequence—a schematic permitted only the mystic, or perhaps the ideal mythic American. No longer could the repetitions of *Cane* imply such an eternal moment. Toomer wanted nothing less than to develop a language that conveyed the colorless and the transcendental perfectly to the reader. In his art, he had passed not only beyond race, but beyond the earthly.

We have been reading Toomer again for three decades now, determined, it seems, to go back to the beginning to derive our own understanding of his work. He may have moved beyond race, but we are still unsure of how to get there, or even if we want to. The questions are unresolved, the conflicts of *Cane* too fertile to let lie fallow. We are still struck by the cleft between the force of his original language about race and his desire to annul race. It is this rift between personal lyricism and disinterested philosophy that we must straddle, if possible, in an attempt to celebrate difference even as we avoid it. Toomer may have come up short, but the attempt compels us back to him again and again in our attempts to move forward.

Marian Anderson

The Baby Contralto
(1897–1993)

Marian Anderson sang at the Lincoln Memorial and made most people standing there weep. As a child, the opera star Jessye Norman heard a recording of Marian Anderson's exquisite contralto and it too brought tears to her eyes. Norman thought, "This can't *just* be a voice, so rich and so beautiful." To a generation of African-American opera singers, classical musicians, and concert recitalists, Anderson had a voice that conveyed more than technical artistry. Her voice at once contained the beauty of the German lieder, the aria, and the African-American spiritual, her signature finale. Her singing transcended Jim Crow laws and racial discrimination; black listeners were humanized and uplifted. "Yours is a voice such as one hears once in a hundred years," the conductor Arturo Toscanini once told her. She sang with her mind set on excellence and her heart set on freedom.

Who can ever forget the story of that April day in 1939 when Marian Anderson stood alone on the steps of Lincoln Memorial. She sang for over seventy-five thousand people in a nationally broadcast concert supported by Eleanor Roosevelt. With this single act she made opera both beautiful *and* political, democratizing the great art form that America believed was for Europeans alone. Marian Anderson was supposed to perform at Constitution Hall in Washington, D.C., but the blue-blooded Daughters of the American Revolution (DAR) refused to reconcile her blackness with her talent. The principled Mrs. Roosevelt resigned her membership in the DAR in response. She rebuked them: "I am in complete disagreement with the attitude taken in refusing Constitution Hall to a great artist. You have set an example, which seems to me unfortunate, and I feel obliged to send in to you my resignation. You had an opportunity to lead in an enlightened way, and it seems that your organization has failed." Four years later the DAR invited Anderson to sing at

115

Constitution Hall to raise money for relief programs in China and she gracefully accepted.

It was the example that Marian Anderson set, not just at the Lincoln Memorial, but in her life that made her admired and beloved. Although she claimed that she was not a fighter, she performed publicly and boldly in the operatic world that barred blacks, with notable exceptions such as Paul Robeson. More than just an opera star, she was a symbol of inspiration and courage.

Born in South Philadelphia, Pennsylvania, to an intelligent, humble, working-class family, Marian Anderson always knew she was destined to sing. "I don't feel that I had to decide," she said. "It was something that just had to be done. I don't think I had much say in choosing it. I think music chose me." At the age of six she joined the junior choir at Union Baptist, the church to which her father belonged. Nicknamed "Baby Contralto," Marian Anderson made a profession out of her childhood passion for song after her mother's poverty, which worsened after the death of her father, necessitated that she work.

Anderson sang professionally during high school with a black ensemble called the Philadelphia Choral Society. Her voice attracted the attention of the celebrated black

tenor Roland Hayes, who suggested professional coaching. Members of the Philadelphia black community started to save money for the "Fund For Marian's Future." This generous gesture allowed Anderson to study with the local contralto Agnes Reifsnyder from 1916 to 1918. During the summer of 1919, she studied with Oscar Sanger at the Chicago Conservatory of Music. After graduating from South Philadelphia High School for Girls in 1921, she applied to music college, but was refused entrance on the basis of race. She continued her studies with Giuseppe Boghetti, who taught her classical songs and arias.

In 1925, she appeared at Lewissohn Stadium with the New York Philharmonic Orchestra. After her Carnegie Hall debut in 1928, Anderson toured extensively in Europe. During this time she gave some of the most technically masterful performances of the era and sang to full houses in the major opera houses of London, Oslo, Berlin, Copenhagen, and Helsinki. She also was accompanied by the some of the best classical music conductors and composers of the era, including Kosti Vehanen and Jean Sibelius, Finland's greatest composer. Her repertoire expanded to comprise over two hundred songs in nine languages.

Ironically, the same year that Anderson was invited to sing for England's King George VI at the White House and became the first black person to perform for Japan's Imperial Court, she was barred from one of America's great performance halls. The offense provoked a national debate on the depth of American racism and the cruelty of segregation. Anderson had protested segregated conditions in the artistic community and championed racial equality, but after the DAR fiasco in 1939 she was propelled to the forefront of the civil rights struggle. The NAACP

1930-1939

awarded Marian Anderson their Spingarn Medal for high achievement by a member of her race, and Eleanor Roosevelt presented the medal.

In 1955 Anderson, now world famous for over twenty years and past her prime, became the first black woman to perform at the Metropolitan Opera in New York City. She sang the role of Ulrica, the tragic heroine, in Verdi's *Un Ballo in Maschera* (A Masked Ball) to standing ovation and full houses. Three years later President Dwight D. Eisenhower asked Anderson if she would accept a post with the American mission to the United Nations, where she served as cultural ambassador. She sang at President John F. Kennedy's inauguration in 1961 and received the Presidential Medal of Freedom in 1963. Between 1964 and 1965 she conducted a worldwide farewell tour, knowing that she wished to retire from singing to settle down with her new husband, Orpheus Hodge Fisher, who lived in Danbury, Connecticut. In 1977 President Jimmy Carter presented her with a congressional gold medal bearing her profile; in 1991 she received a Grammy award for lifetime achievement.

On her eighty-third birthday Anderson was serenaded by Shirley Verrett and Grace Bumbry, the two opera singers who had both won Marian Anderson scholarships for study. Her legacy to the black classical world is apparent in all the singers who come after her, in such towering talents as Leontyne Price, Jessye Norman, and Kathleen Battle. Her genius, dignity, and determination will live forever.

Sterling A. Brown

The Vernacular Poet
(1901–1989)

Sterling Brown wrote in the language of real black country people. *Southern Road,* Brown's masterful first collection of poetry, not only announced the arrival of an up-and-coming literary talent, it also broke with the aesthetics of the Harlem Renaissance and the New Negro. In *Southern Road,* Brown resuscitated dialect poetry, a genre that had been confined to what one critic called "the waste-bins of minstrelsy" and dismissed by Renaissance writers who found its attempts to replicate African-American speech patterns and vernacular culture demeaning. James Weldon Johnson himself quit writing it, famously declaring that it was only capable of humor and pathos and thus confined African Americans to a one-dimensional plane. But after reading *Southern Road,* Johnson did an about-face, praising the work for its "delicious, ironical humour," finding in it evidence of a capable talent that could forge his own, unique poetic voice from African-American tradition. Sterling Brown was the first great black poet to circumvent the white normative gaze and freely display black humanity as he saw fit.

But it was not only as a poet that Brown would create a legacy during the 1930s. Over the decade, Brown would create a legacy as a cultural critic and anthologist that remains unsurpassed today. Brown was born into the privileged enclave of Washington, D.C.'s middle-class black community. His father, an ex-slave, was the pastor of Lincoln Temple Congregational Church and taught in Howard University's School of Religion; he counted Booker T. Washington and Frederick Douglass among his acquaintances. His mother was valedictorian of her graduating class at Fisk University. Brown attended Dunbar High School and was taught by the writers Jessie Fauset and Angelina Weld Grimke. Graduating with honors in 1918, he won a scholarship to Williams College. He graduated cum laude in 1922 and went on to Harvard University, where he completed a master's degree in English in 1923.

Brown had begun writing poetry at Williams, but it was when he accepted a teaching position at Virginia Seminary after graduating from Harvard that he found the subject matter that interested him. During the three years he spent in Lynchburg, he wandered among rural black communities, listening to their blues and spirituals, their mythologies and aphorisms. He would admit later that these rural black folk were his greatest teachers. And indeed, the complex, essential humanity of these people entered Brown's writing, often acting as a humorous counterpoint to the aristocratic pretensions of his peers.

In 1929, Brown returned to Washington and began teaching at Howard, where he stayed until his retirement in 1969. Over the next decade he would produce a body of work that still serves as a cornerstone of African-American letters. First, *Southern Road* appeared in 1932. This was followed by two important works, *The Negro in American Fiction* (1937) and *Negro Poetry and Drama* (1937), which argued for the black folk tradition as the foundation of any African-American literary aesthetic. Brown had an acute understanding of the formal qualities of art and of the influence of black folk traditions on it. His studies were generous but nuanced, critical, and unafraid to cast judgment. He refused to celebrate the work without asking whether or not—and how—it functioned formally as art.

Meanwhile, Brown contributed a steady output of poetry, reviews, and essays to *Opportunity,* the *New Republic, The Nation,* the *Journal of Negro Education, Phylon,* and *Crisis,* on a range of subjects, as well as coediting the seminal anthology *The Negro Caravan* (1941). In the 1930s he also held the position of editor of Negro affairs for Roosevelt's Federal Writers Project where, according to scholar Paula Giddings, "he created a model for humanizing the representation of black subjects." In this position, too, he supervised all FWP projects on blacks, contributed the essay "The Negro in Washington" to the massive *Washington, City and Capital* (1937), and initiated studies such as *The Negro in Virginia* (1940).

Brown's publisher refused to reprint *Southern Road,* however, despite its positive reviews, and around the same time rejected his second manuscript. Brown became deeply despondent at the lack of attention and recognition his work was receiving.

Southern Road finally was republished in 1975, the same year that his second book of poetry, *The Last Ride of Wild Bill and Eleven Narratives,* appeared. By then Brown had been hailed by many of the alumni of the black arts movement—a number of whom he had taught at Howard—as a progenitor for their own innovative work on African-American art and culture. Indeed, it was their lobbying that prompted Howard to offer an honorary doctorate.

He combined "high" art and "low": A man with Ivy League training, he wrote in the idiom of plain people. He was the first to go beyond the dialect poetry of Paul Lawrence Dunbar in articulating the voice of black folks, and he surpassed James Weldon Johnson in the attempt. He struggled against culture that comes from the top down, knowing that a blues sensibility originates from below. In their framework he was the first major intellectual to discern and defend a democratic mode of the tragicomic.

Sterling A. Brown died of leukemia in 1989. He created a legacy and a standard of intellectual inquiry and poetic excellence that stands today. Crucially, he understood the importance of creating an archive of African-American letters, a tradition that would be accessible to future generations of poets and scholars and a larger reading public and that demonstrated the strength, richness, depth, and élan of our culture. Notwithstanding his grand accomplishments, his personal struggles with insanity and invisibility reveal the costs of his courageous witness.

Father Divine

God in a Body
(1879–1965)

Father Divine is God. Or so thousands of followers believed in his heyday, the 1920s and '30s, when the short, stocky, bald-headed man who called himself Rev. M. J. (for Major Jealous) Divine was establishing his kingdom on earth. Cynics quickly rejected him as yet another religious con man whose devotion was limited to collecting money and wooing female disciples. But more recent scholars have begun to see Father Divine both as an early leader in the civil rights movement and as the creator of a social institution that, as he claimed with some accuracy, fed, housed, and clothed more New Yorkers during the Great Depression than the city's relief agencies. Divine's Peace Mission Movement also captured a large number of self-identified Pan-Africanists at the decline of Garvey's Universal Negro Improvement Association. Father Divine's movement was a unique phenomenon in black life, led by a fascinating figure with his mind set, in part, on black freedom.

Perhaps appropriately, Father's earthly origins are a little difficult to pinpoint. He himself claimed he was not born but "combusted" on Seventh Avenue. At his death (or, when he sacrificed his precious body, to use the terminology of the movement), no relatives showed up with inheritance claims, an argument his wife, Mother Divine, uses to prove that they didn't exist. Father's (unofficial) biographer, Jill Watts, comes closest to historical documentation, claiming on the basis of census records that he actually was born George Baker in Rockville, Maryland, in 1879. This very thought is of course anathema to movement members. They have refused even to say the name (substituting "G.B." instead) and persuaded the Library of Congress to change its cataloging rules, eliminating "Baker, George, self-named Father Divine" as an official subject heading.

> *Condescendingly I came as an existing spirit unembodied, until condescendingly inputting Myself in a Bodily form in the likeness of men, I come, that I might speak to them in their own language, coming to a country that is supposed to be the Country of the Free.*
> —Father Divine

Father started out as a Baltimore gardener and an itinerant Baptist preacher. Calling himself The Messenger, he apparently became a follower of Samuel Morris, a religious prophet known as Father Jehovia. They met up with John A. Hickerson, a gaunt, light-skinned man wearing a crown and robes who was described once as the exact image of Jesus Christ. Hickerson called himself St. John the Vine. The three delved into the religious movement New Thought, with its positive thinking of self-actualization and its powerful notion of the indwelling God. When pushed, the theory of God within easily leads to "Every Man a God." Hickerson later claimed The Messenger stole the idea of his divinity from him in 1912. The trio split up when, as one scholar suggests, they realized that several deities in such a small group was more than sufficient.

Now on his own, Father Divine conceived the idea of bringing his few disciples together to live in one house, where he would manage an employment agency for domestics and gardeners. Their pooled resources meant they could live quite comfortably. Father's charisma was the centerpiece. It manifested itself in the group's nightly gathering for dinner, a lengthy and elaborate meal of great quantities of good food combined with singing and testimonies, all presided over by Father, who preached to ecstatic response. It was not a major step to perceive this as the Lord's Supper, Holy Communion, God's people celebrating the marriage supper of the Lamb with God himself in their midst. God had been, to borrow another of Father's terms, "tangibilated" in the flesh. The dining room rocked with enthusiastic renditions of "God in a Body," sung to the tune of "Roll Out the Barrel." The kingdom had come!

With this good news, the movement spread. A number of white people, many with substantial funds, joined, in order to be close to God. The hard work and clean living produced profits with which to buy real estate, especially restaurants, stores, and hotels. There is no evidence any of the money went to Father, especially after he learned that no assets should be recorded legally in his name. Father's divinity inspired the down-and-out to get off alcohol and drugs, clean up, get a job, and live respectably in a financially secure community. The idea of cooperative and communal living was hardly new to America, but it has probably never worked so successfully before or since. And of course it was of particular benefit to poor people of color, who desperately needed an economic alternative to the intertwined oppression of racism and capitalism.

God's Kingdom was not only economically prosperous, it was integrated racially. Father drew upon his New Thought background to fight segregation by making the ideal come true by speaking and acting as if it were true. He eliminated the prejudicial words n-e-g-r-o and b-l-a-c-k and replaced them with the value-free descriptors "light-complected" and "dark-complected." At the famous nightly banquets, diners "enacted the bill," which meant dark and light people intentionally sat in alternate seats: The Bill of Rights that guaranteed equality was made real by literally acting it out. This may sound odd, even dotty, but the truth is that the Peace Mission Movement was probably the most thoroughly integrated institution up to that time in American history, an achievement that ought to be considered with a good deal more seriousness than it has been.

The Peace Mission Movement began to decline at Father's death on September 10, 1965. He was succeeded by Edna Mae Ritchings, a young, white Canadian woman whose name in the movement was Sweet Angel, whom he had married a short time before his death. The marriage was spiritual, that is, not physical, and was meant to symbolize the international and interracial character of the Peace Mission. Sexual relationships of any kind were strictly forbidden by Father from the very outset in "The International Modest Code." Followers said there was no sex in Heaven, where they believed they were, and sociologists said any hint of black-white relationships would have allowed critics to destroy the movement. Mother Divine presides over a dwindling, geriatric community outside Philadelphia, and has said she knows the group will go the way of the celibate Shakers.

Father Divine often is dismissed as a bizarre cult leader whose appeal was to the culturally displaced southerners who came north in the great migration. But he leaves his mark on the twentieth century as one who created extraordinary and untried new ways to deal with racism and poverty. His movement exemplifies the creative ways in which black people used religious imagination and business ingenuity to promote interracial harmony and human solidarity in the midst of a racially divided civilization.

Charles Hamilton Houston

The Lawyer
(1895–1950)

Charles Hamilton Houston remains behind the veil—known to a few insiders, unknown to outsiders—a stalwart figure for justice hidden by neglect. He is one of the giants of the legal fight for racial equality. He is less well known than his protégé Thurgood Marshall, or the victories he pioneered, including the 1954 *Brown* v. *Board of Education* Supreme Court decision that ended legalized segregation in public education. Lack of public acclaim never seemed to concern Houston, who went about his work and life with a quiet energy and brilliance, drawing attention to his legal arguments, not himself. "Lose your temper," he often told his students at Howard University Law School, "lose your case." As the first chief legal counsel for the NAACP, Houston was called "the Moses of our journey," and although he died before seeing the final vindication of his leadership, he was the architect who crafted the strategy responsible for *Brown* and trained an entire generation of civil rights lawyers. He was a militant in moderate clothing, a radical whose subversive spirit was dampened by his visible strategies.

Houston was born September 3, 1895, and raised in Washington, D.C., the only son in a family that valued education. After excelling at the prestigious M Street School in 1911, he enrolled in Amherst College, an overwhelmingly white school. He was the only black student in his class, but social isolation did not hurt his studies; he graduated in 1915 and was elected to Phi Beta Kappa. Houston then taught part-time at Howard University, but in 1917, as America entered World War I, Houston had to decide, as an African American, how to approach the war. The segregated army offered only servile jobs to blacks. Houston decided to set aside his principled opposition to segregation and advocate a separate officer's training program. It was the only way to contribute his talent to the country at war.

Others agreed with him, and Houston trained at a newly established all-black officers' school in Iowa. He was then shipped to France in 1918 as a second lieutenant in the segregated army. "The hate and scorn showered on us Negro officers by our fellow Americans convinced

me that there was no sense in my dying for a world ruled by them," Houston wrote. "I made up my mind that if I got through this war I would study law and use my time fighting for men who could not strike back." He made good on the promise, entering Harvard Law School in 1919. The first black student to edit the law review at Harvard, Houston graduated in 1922, then traveled to Madrid, Spain, for further legal study.

He returned in 1924 and worked for a time for his father's law firm in Washington, but in 1929 the young lawyer joined the law school at Howard University as its vice dean. Mordecai W. Johnson, Howard's first black president, was determined to bring the underfunded, unaccredited institution up to a new standard. Under Houston's care Howard Law School not only earned accreditation, it became a training ground for lawyers interested, as Houston said, in "litigation against racism." But Howard was not the only arena for Houston's civil rights work; in the early 1930s he met the NAACP's energetic secretary, Walter F. White, and the two crisscrossed the American South, documenting racial inequality and planning the legal fight against it.

In 1935 White convinced Houston to join the NAACP as its first chief counsel. Houston's NAACP work would come to focus on educational equality, but he also represented criminal defendants and successfully argued against the exclusion of African Americans from juries (*Hollins* v. *Oklahoma,* 1935) before the Supreme Court. White and Houston agreed, though, that the heart of racial inequality in America was its segregated educational system. An NAACP-commissioned plan called the Margold Report laid out a strategy for ending school segregation by aiming straight at elementary schools, but Houston crafted a subtler approach. Assembling a team of lawyers and law students—including Thurgood Marshall, recently graduated from Howard Law—Houston worked around the edges of the educational system, winning case after case to build precedents that eventually would leave the Court no choice but to overturn 1896's notorious *Plessy* v. *Ferguson* decision, which had established the legal basis for the states's practice of separate but equal institutions.

1930–1939

Houston's strategy targeted graduate education, reasoning that the area was least likely to alarm white racists who feared social equality and most likely to yield victories when segregated systems could not meet the *Plessy* burden of "separate but equal." By demanding that states provide equal accommodations—an impossibility—Houston called into question not the morality but the feasibility of maintaining separate schools. Though he expressed his strong belief in the moral value of his work (he told his students that "a lawyer's either a social engineer or he's a para-

site"), Houston's legal strategy was dispassionate and technically brilliant, exposing the logical weakness of segregation.

Victory in 1938's *Gaines* v. *Canada* case illustrates Houston's strategy. Lloyd Gaines, a resident of Missouri, was rejected by the University of Missouri Law School, even though he met the qualifications, because he was black. The NAACP entered the legal case and, on the basis of *Plessy,* the Supreme Court told Missouri it must either admit Gaines to the university or provide him a "separate but equal" education. Incredibly, the state decided to open a separate school and rented space in a downtown St. Louis building. Gaines mysteriously disappeared before he could attend his own law school, but the Court had cracked open the closed door to southern graduate schools.

Houston's health was failing, and he retired from the NAACP job, leaving it in Thurgood Marshall's hands. Houston returned to his father's firm, representing two unions in labor cases that reached the Supreme Court. In 1944 he joined the Fair Employment Practices Commission, a body that arose from 1941's March on Washington movement, A. Philip Randolph's threat to innundate Washington with black people demanding jobs in the war industry. In 1948 he argued his last case before the Supreme Court, which issued an opinion striking down the legal enforcement of racially restrictive real estate covenants (*Shelley* v. *Kraemer*). Later that year he suffered a heart attack from which he never fully recovered. He died in 1950.

The year of Houston's death also saw rulings in two cases he had helped bring about: *McLaurin* v. *Oklahoma* and *Sweatt* v. *Painter,* both of which tied educational inequality (both cases involved segregation in graduate schools) to violation of the Constitution's Fourteenth Amendment equal protection clause. Four years later, the court would issue its unanimous ruling in *Brown* v. *Board of Education,* which at long last declared unconstitutional state-sponsored segregation in schools.

Thurgood Marshall eulogized Houston as "the engineer of it all." Howard University Law School renamed its main building after Houston in 1958, and law schools around the country have established chairs and scholarships in his name, tribute to a man who said in a 1934 speech that "the problem before the Negro today is not the depths from which he has come but the heights to which he aspires." His workaholic habits and impatience with injustice are but the surfaces of a soul on fire for freedom—a fire in no way extinguished in our time.

Zora Neale Hurston

The Anthropologist
(1891–1960)

Now, she is read and loved by students of all colors, everywhere. But there was a time, not much more than twenty years ago, that Zora Neale Hurston's work was largely out of print, her literary legacy alive only to a tiny, devoted band of readers often forced to photocopy her works in order to teach them. The black arts poet and critic Larry Neal saw to it that *Jonah's Gourd Vine* was reprinted in 1971, just as the scholar Darwin Turner had *Mules and Men* reprinted a year before. But those pioneering gestures were rare.

Today Hurston's works are central to the canon of African-American, American, and women's literatures. Recently, at Yale alone, seventeen courses taught *Their Eyes Were Watching God*. An extreme example perhaps, but it gives pause to those who would argue for the timelessness of literary judgment and taste. Which is not to say that her genius went unappreciated by her peers. The prodigious author of four novels—*Jonah's Gourd Vine* (1934), *Their Eyes Were Watching God* (1937), *Moses, Man of the Mountain* (1939), and *Seraph on the Suwanee* (1948)—two books of folklore— *Mules and Men* (1935) and *Tell My Horse* (1938)—an autobiography (*Dust Tracks on a Road,* 1942), and over fifty short stories, essays, and plays, Hurston was one of the more widely acclaimed black authors for the two decades between 1925 and 1945.

Zora Neale Hurston was born on January 7, 1891, in Notasulga, Alabama. (Hurston herself gave varying dates ranging from 1898 to 1903.) Parents Lucy Ann and John Hurston raised her and her seven brothers and sisters in Eatonville, Florida, an African-American community. Her experiences in Eatonville later would serve as the background that shaped the views of her writing. After the death of her mother, John Hurston remarried, and Zora was forced to relocate from relative to relative. Eventually she moved to Baltimore, Maryland, where she attended prep school at Morgan College until 1918. From 1919 until 1924 Hurston studied writing under Lorenzo Dow Turner and Alain Locke at Howard University. Turner and Locke greatly affected the development of her writing style.

In May 1925, she won second prize at the annual *Opportunity* magazine awards ceremony for her short story "Spunk" that had appeared in Alain Locke's germinal anthology *The New Negro,* which announced the birth of both the New Negro movement and the Harlem Renaissance of black expressive culture. At the age of thirty-four, the wind at her back, Hurston attended Barnard College to study anthropology, earning a B.A. in 1928.

Hurston then enrolled in Columbia's graduate program in anthropology and began to collect black folklore throughout the South between 1927 and 1931; in Jamaica, Haiti, and Bermuda in 1937 and 1938; and in Florida in 1938 and 1939. Hurston seems to have loved listening to and transcribing Negro folktales and myths. As late as 1946, when her own powers of storytelling were on the wane, Hurston was drawn to Honduras to gather more folklore. But despite the publication of two widely heralded collections of folklore, it was as a writer of fiction that Zora Neale Hurston excelled.

With the exception of her last novel, *Seraph on the Suwanee,* Hurston's fiction was well received by mainstream American reviewers. On the other hand, some prominent black male writers thought her work problematic for reasons that would convince few readers now.

No, I do not weep at the world—I am too busy sharpening my oyster knife.
—Zora Neale Hurston

Alain Locke, Richard Wright, and Ralph Ellison, for example, were dismissive of what they took to be the ideological posture inherent to her fiction—her "Afro-Americanization" of modernism. In the 1930s, at least, both Wright and Ellison were more interested in the resources of naturalism as a literary mode than they were in the sort of lyrical symbolism that Hurston developed.

In later years, however, Ellison himself would embrace the modalities of modernism in a way that would reinforce the counter tradition associated with Hurston. In general, Hurston's black male critics wrote against the majority opinion; Hurston was the most widely acclaimed black woman writer since Phillis Wheatley. When she appeared on the cover of the *Saturday Review of Literature* in 1943 and after winning the Anisfield-Wolf Book Award for *Dust Tracks,* she became the first black author to be honored in this way. Unfortunately, Hurston's career had reached its zenith with this event. By 1950 she was working as a maid; at her death in 1960 she had fallen into almost total obscurity.

Thirty years later, however, Zora Neale Hurston is the most widely taught black woman writer in the canon of American literature. Why is this so? While a significant portion of her readership is sustained by her image as a questioning, independent woman, her more lasting claim is staked on her command of a narrative voice that imitates the storytelling structures of the black vernacular tradition. Indeed, no writer in the African-American literary tradition has been more successful than she in registering the range and timbres of spoken black voices in writing. The language of her characters dances; her texts seem to come alive as veritable "talking books."

Hurston also succeeds in shaping a language where so many of her predecessors failed, and in creating a point of view directed at her black readers rather than to an imagined white readership. Almost never do we feel Hurston's hand on our shoulder as we read her texts. Given the historical prominence that propaganda has, necessarily, been accorded in the black formal arts, this is no mean achievement. Hurston was the first novelist to demonstrate the potential of the African-American vernacular to serve as a complex language of narration, but she was also the first novelist to depict a black woman's successful quest to find a voice and to overcome male oppression.

Robert Johnson

King of the Delta Blues
(1911–1938)

Some say he frothed at the mouth and howled like a dog, crawling on his hands and knees before dying. Another said he was slipped a "douche tablet" that caused the blood in his veins to dry up. Closer to the facts, most scholars believe that he was poisoned by a jealous husband whose wife he had courted: strychnine-diffused whiskey his final toast and the last note of the despair that marked his music. When his death certificate was located some three decades subsequently, no cause of death was listed and no doctor had signed it. Furthermore, it was annotated with the hearsay, gossip, and rumors that have helped to give substance to the twentieth-century American myth surrounding the life and death of Robert Johnson.

We do know that during the twenty-seven years that marked his stay in this world, Johnson created the most harrowing recordings of Mississippi Delta blues; his unique tunings and intricate guitar playing created a moody, richly textured backdrop to the desperation evidenced by his vocalizing. His lyrics hold more existential agony than a Richard Wright novel: The gothic romance of the rural South—where slavery still existed under other names and a black person's worth was measured by his or her strength as labor—infused his music like a haint.

Robert Johnson was born in Hazelhurst, Mississippi, in 1911. Of his mother's twelve children, he was the last—and born out of wedlock. He did not learn the identity of his biological father until he was in his late teens. He received the rudiments of a rural education in Tunica County, Mississippi, but left school to marry his first wife, Virginia Travis, who died at the age of sixteen during childbirth.

The shadow of this grief likely pushed Johnson further into music. As a youth he had begun playing the Jew's harp and harmonica. In the mid 1920s, he began playing guitar, influenced by Willie Brown, Son House, and Charley Patton.

133

However, after his wife's death, he appears to have become committed to music. Following the paths of his blues heroes, he became an itinerant musician. He began playing jook joints and roadhouses in Mississippi. Hopping trains, he traveled all over the state and later as far north as Canada, supporting himself through performing and by attaching himself to women. Johnson's legend began to emerge.

According to the myth, at some point in the early 1930s, Johnson went to a crossroads, the purported nexus of the spiritual and material worlds, and made a Faustian pact with Satan: his soul in return for musical talent. As evidence of this arrangement, blues ingenues point to "Cross Road Blues," one of his best-known compositions. (The lyrics to this song belie such proof; he falls down on his knees

and asks the Lord for mercy!) What is known is that a man with no previous skill became a master guitarist in about a year and a half.

Along with his other compositions, "Cross Road Blues" was reborn as "Crossroads" during the blues revival of the 1960s, when rock bands including the Rolling Stones, Cream, Captain Beefheart, and of course Jimi Hendrix, returned to classic blues material. This blues revival, however, was only one part of the ongoing process of Johnson's rediscovery. As one blues historian has described it, the literature on Johnson reads "like an ongoing detective novel, with Johnson . . . as the missing person whose trail leads everywhere but to himself." Johnson had recording sessions with the American Record Company in 1936 and 1937, but only a dozen records were released during his lifetime. *Terraplane Blues,* his "hit," logged a mere five thousand sales, mainly in the rural South. In 1938, talent scout and record producer John Hammond sent for Johnson. He wanted him to perform at his now legendary "From Spirituals to Swing" concert of black music at Carnegie Hall. He was unable to locate him, and learned only shortly before the event that Johnson had died under mysterious circumstances. Later blues historians searched throughout the Mississippi Delta for information about Johnson, recording Willie Brown, Son House, and Muddy Waters in the process. Photographs of Johnson surfaced for the first time in the 1980s.

To call Johnson the king of the Delta blues singers or to name him as the most influential blues musician of all time, as many fans and critics are wont to do, is a somewhat controversial assertion. His creativity and influence are undeniable. But his influence was only minimal during his lifetime and for thirty years after. Johnson was among the last of a dying breed. He played acoustic country blues at a time when the music was being transformed through rapid urbanization and increasing electrification. What characterizes Johnson, however, is his deeply personal embellishment of the most original of blues compositions that are set firmly within the stylistic limits of the genre. He was able to convey through the intensity of the vocalization of his lyrics the paradoxes of the joy and terror of being a black man in the South between the wars. Perhaps too, in his music, we can hear something of the shift from a rural to an urban mind-set in black folk life and its resonance of desire and loss.

Aside from the fact that Robert Johnson's musical creations constitute a watermark in black American musical culture, Robert Johnson's music is set apart in its inherent absence of hope. The essence of the blues is the triumph over sadness and despair, their transcendence through the music. Johnson's songs focus on raw pain and tragedy and offer no resolution. There is no hope, only emotional intensity, a direct impact, and bedeviled blackness in "Hell Hound on My Trail," "Love in Vain Blues," "I Believe I'll Dust My Broom," "Stop Breakin' Down Blues," and "Come on in My Kitchen." In the title line of one of his most austere compositions, Robert Johnson sings, "If I had possession over Judgment Day: the little woman I'm lovin' wouldn't have no right to pray."

There is a marble obelisk monument to Robert Johnson in the churchyard of the Mt. Zion Baptist Church near Morgan City, Mississippi, and there is a headstone with his name on it in the Payne Chapel graveyard in Quito, Mississippi, yet Robert Johnson's actual grave remains unmarked. His legacy is his music, an enduring American legend and a shadowy enigma that refuses to be resolved.

I have a bird to whistle
and I have a bird to sing:
Have a bird to whistle
and I have a bird to sing:
I got a woman that I'm lovin', boy,
But she don't mean a thing.
—Robert Johnson

1930–1939

Joe Louis

The Brown Bomber
(1914–1981)

Joe Louis was the first *really* famous black man in America. He was the first black man who became a mainstream cultural idol when he knocked out the German boxer Max Schmelling in 1938, delivering a massive symbolic blow to white supremacy in Nazi Germany and in America. For this, Louis was idealized in print, lionized on the screen, and immortalized in the painting *The Brown Bomber* (1939), by Robert Riggs. Louis held the heavyweight boxing title for eleven years, longer than anyone else, and defended the title more times and in more ways than any other fighter.

Joseph Louis Barrow was born on May 13, 1914, in a sharecropper's shack in the hills of Alabama. He had seven full siblings and five half-siblings from his stepfather. His birth father was committed to a psychiatric hospital for the colored insane, but everyone imagined him to be dead. Until 1926, when the family moved north to Detroit, they chopped cotton on rented land.

In Detroit, Louis hauled coal and delivered ice, but he began to box without his mother's knowledge. He found a trainer, discarded the "Barrow" from his name (as most boxers did in order to keep their profession a secret from their families), and paid the trainer the little sum he was supposed to use for violin lessons. Louis became a sought-after amateur light-heavyweight boxer by age nineteen, breezing through fifty fights, forty-three by knockout. John Roxborough, an African American who sold real estate and operated illegal lotteries in Detroit, spied Louis and arranged to manage the young boxer. Through Roxborough, Louis was introduced to Jack Blackburn, an African-American trainer who had sparred with Jack Johnson—and served time for murder. Roxborough and Blackburn would be hugely influential in Louis's development at a time when career black managers were virtually unheard of. Hypersensitive to the legacy of Jack Johnson, the two men shaped a safe public persona for Louis. He was to be the antithesis of Jack Johnson. Technically, he was to use compact quick punches and a flat-footed shuffle. The quiet, modest, and naive Louis was also warned, and coached, not to pander to racial stereotypes, to avoid drinking, smoking, and especially being seen alone with white women in public. Instead, he was to compose himself like a black man with dignity. Ironically, Louis was just as hedonistic as Johnson and discreetly enjoyed the company of women of all races.

On July 4, 1934, twenty-four years after the Independence Day that Jack Johnson had fought Jim Jeffries, Louis fought Jack Kracken in his first professional fight. The bout was a nonstarter: Kracken went down within two minutes of the first round. Louis continued to win all twenty-two of his professional fights. He was ready for Madison Square Garden but, because of race, could not get a fight. Roxborough signed over a percentage of Louis's monies in future fights to promoter Mike Jacobs, who would become boxing's most dominant figure. Jacobs had connections with sports writers, and media access for Louis became easier than ever.

From 1935 onward, some of Louis's fights had furious political subtexts: In the summer of 1935 Louis fought Primo Carnera of Italy at Yankee Stadium. For many Carnera represented Benito Mussolini's Italy, a country ruthlessly invading Ethiopia, one of Africa's few independent countries. African Americans, as a result, crowded that stadium to see Louis knock Carnera out in the sixth round. In Chicago, he fought Max Baer. Because it was his second victory over a white former heavyweight champion, black Chicago's response was a terrifically joyous one. Richard Wright wrote:

Something had popped loose all right. And it had come from deep down. Four centuries of oppression, of frustrated hopes, of black bitterness, felt even in the bones of the bewildered young, were rising to the surface. . . . From the symbol of Joe's strength they took strength, and in that moment all fear, all obstacles were wiped out, drowned.

Fighting German Max Schmelling in 1936, the third former champion, transformed Louis into a potential symbol of democracy versus Nazism. He lost that fight. It was his first defeat, and it was to a German! If it wasn't for Jesse Owens, who four weeks later came home with four gold medals from the Olympics in Munich, black American sports fans would have been devastated. Moreover, Schmelling was

1930–1939

> *Every Negro boy old enough to walk*
> *wanted to be the Brown Bomber.*
> *—Malcolm X*

not a Nazi, which is why Hitler had not touted him as the super Aryan. Schmelling had lost to Max Baer, an American Jewish fighter, in a fight in 1935. But the dictator would have been more embarrassed if Schmelling had compounded that defeat by losing to a black man. After Schmelling's victory over Louis, Hitler removed Schmelling's Jewish trainer, and the Reich embraced the boxer. A reporter in Germany even proposed that the boxing match had somehow proved white intelligence. On the other hand, it was Louis's first hard loss. Congressman Adam Clayton Powell, Jr., wrote rather dramatically in the weekly New York *Amsterdam News:* "Along came the Brown Bomber, Death in the evening, and our racial morale took a sky high leap. . . . Gone today is the jauntiness, the careless abandon, the spring in our stride—we're just shufflin' along."

Nevertheless, on June 22, 1937, in Chicago's Comiskey Park, Joe Louis fought Lou Braddock, the heavyweight champion, and knocked him to the canvas with a sharp punch. At just twenty-three years old, Louis became heavyweight champion of the world, the first African American since Jack Johnson. The fight was followed, one year to the day later, with a rematch against Schmelling. This fight was more nerve-racking and gut-wrenching than the first. War loomed. Franklin Roosevelt told Louis that America needed his victory. The Bomber himself was worked up about his mission. When asked by a reporter if he was scared, an intense Louis said he was liable to kill his opponent. In the first round, Louis knocked Schmelling out. Instantly, he was one of the most popular athletes in America, indeed, in the whole of the Allied world, not to mention the black world. He had crossed the line from being a boxing champion to a black American idol.

Despite the fanfare America made of him, Louis soon had to answer to financial challenges as well as athletic ones. For most of 1940 and 1941, he entered the ring every month to pay off his debts. The number of contenders he took on during that period was unheard of among boxing champions. He defeated them all, and his opponents were satirized in the media as members of the "Bum of the Month Club." He followed this grueling program with nearly one hundred exhibition matches when he joined the army during the war. Controversy surrounded a 1947 split-decision match from which Louis emerged victorious after Jersey Joe Walcott had leveled him twice. A rematch ensued; Louis knocked Walcott out. He retired for the first time in 1949, with only one loss.

Louis was forced back into the ring in 1950 to pay back taxes of more than one million dollars. He lost twice, to Ezzard Charles and Rocky Marciano. His final record was sixty-eight wins, fifty-four by knockout, and three losses.

Louis's final two decades were a sad nightmare. Overwhelmed by his debts, he became a professional wrestler until he was injured. In the late 1970s, he signed an agreement with Caesar's Palace in Las Vegas, which paid him fifty thousand dollars a year merely to greet guests. By 1977, a cerebral hemorrhage confined him to a wheelchair and destroyed his speech. But the legend remains—Joe Louis established the role of the black athlete as both a model of physical prowess and as a symbol of the undaunted power of American democracy.

Jesse Owens

Olympic Hero
(1935–1980)

Jesse Owens struck a blow against the Aryan racism of Hitler's Germany at the 1936 Berlin Olympics by winning gold medals in four events. Yet the life of the "world's fastest human" before and after Olympic fame was one of struggle and reversals that reveal the obstacles even ordinary African Americans faced in the first half of the twentieth century. Owens's battle against German racism was paralleled by his efforts to overcome American racism at home.

Born into an Alabama sharecropping family in 1913, Jesse Owens was the seventh of eight living children raised by Emma and Henry Owens. He was a sickly child, often suffering from pneumonia and other ailments, a situation exacerbated by the family's poverty. When Owens was nine his parents sold their most valuable possession—a mule—and moved to Cleveland, Ohio, part of the great migration of southern blacks seeking a better life. When he entered school in Cleveland a teacher misunderstood his nickname, J.C., and called him Jesse, the name he would use the rest of his life. While most sources record his full name as James Cleveland Owens, his father at times told reporters he'd named his son simply J.C.

It was at Fairmount Junior High School that Owens's talents as an athlete were first spotted by a teacher and coach named Charles Riley. Riley recruited Owens after timing him sprinting down a street near the school and began cultivating him as a runner. Owens could jump, too, setting a new junior high world record in the broad jump and high jump. In high school, still coached by Riley, he set a broad jump record his sophomore year and was among the top finishers in the 100- and 200-yard dash events at the 1931 state scholastic meet. By his junior year Owens dominated the state meet, tying the record for the 100-yard dash and winning the broad jump and 220-yard low hurdles. As a senior he entered his first national scholastic track meet and broke world scholastic records for the 100- and 220-yard dashes and the broad jump. Owens returned to Cleveland a hero.

After dominating the state meet his junior year Owens had told the crowd, "When I run in college it will be for you." But his choice of Ohio State University—among the dozens that recruited him—dismayed some in the black community, who pointed to the school's tradition of segregation. Owens struggled academically at OSU but excelled athletically, electrifying the Big Ten championship meet in 1935 by setting new world records in five events. He was elected captain of the OSU track team, the first African American to captain any team at the school. The next year he won a spot on the U.S. Olympic Team.

Set in Berlin, Germany, the 1936 Olympics were controversial before they began, with many groups threatening not to take part in a competition set in Nazi Germany. The Nazi philosophy already had infected sports, and tension over racist theories and athletic superiority was in the air. Owens arrived on contested grounds and proceeded to dominate it, winning gold in the 100- and 200-meter dash events (setting a new world record in the 200), and the 400-meter relay. His gold-medal broad jump, at 25 feet, 10¼ inches, set a world record that stood for a quarter-century.

Returning to the United States, Owens found that the equality he had proven in Berlin was harder to find back home. It is often commented that Hitler refused to shake hands with him. Owens pointed out that neither did President Roosevelt. The Olympic Committee suspended his amateur status because he had elected to come back and work for pay rather than stay and compete in European meets. But the pay rarely materialized, and when it did it came from humiliating performances, including racing against a horse. Owens had left OSU without graduating, and the only steady work he could get was menial. Occasional speaking engagements kept him in the public eye, though, and by the 1940s he was able to support himself on the lecture circuit.

As the civil rights movement emerged in the 1950s and 1960s, Owens increasingly found himself out of step with many in the black community. Asked to mediate between U.S. officials and the sprinters Tommie Smith and John Carlos, who gave the black power salute on the medals podium at the 1968 Mexico City Olympics, Owens angered the young athletes and began to attract criticism as an Uncle Tom. A Republican, he wrote in 1970 that "[i]f the Negro doesn't succeed in today's America, it is because he has chosen to fail."

In 1972 Owens moved from Chicago to Phoenix, Arizona, partly for his health and partly for the renowned golf courses, where he became a familiar figure when not on a speaking tour. In Phoenix Owens became a philanthropist, giving his money and his name to the Jesse Owens Memorial Medical Center and Jesse Owens Memorial Track Club. He served on the boards of the Boy Scouts of America, the National Council of Christians and Jews, and other organizations. Perhaps most gratifying to Owens, OSU awarded him an honorary degree in 1972. When he died in 1980, Arizona governor Bruce Babbitt arranged for his body to lie in state in the capitol building before being returned to Chicago for burial. Despite his often contentious relations with mainstream black leaders, Owens is remembered for his amazing grace under pressure in 1936, when he showed the world that Hitler was wrong. In the process, Jesse Owens also revealed the depth of how America was wrong about his fellow black human beings.

Paul Robeson

Citizen of the World
(1898–1976)

One of the most gifted men to rise to prominence in the twentieth century was Paul Robeson. He was a world-renowned thespian, a highly talented singer, a scholar, a linguist, and a courageous political activist. He stands as one of the first black artists to use his eminence in the worldwide struggle against bigotry and injustice. By the 1940s, he was so widely recognized as a prominent activist that the United States government mounted a sinister attack on his career and reputation. His career did not survive, but his reputation has only increased in luster.

Robeson was born the son of a slave, William Drew Robeson, a remarkable man who escaped from bondage in North Carolina at the age of fifteen. He graduated from college and became a Presbyterian minister in Princeton, New Jersey. The youngest of five children, each of whom was expected to be a high achiever, Paul Robeson was sent to school in a neighboring town in Somerville, New Jersey, because of a segregated school system in Princeton that did not offer secondary education for black children. In 1915, he won a scholarship to Rutgers, where he excelled both academically and in sports. He was twice named an All-American in football and was a member of his college team in baseball, basketball, and track. Not only known for being a champion debater, he was elected to Phi Beta Kappa during his junior year and chosen to be his class valedictorian. In 1919, Robeson attended Columbia Law School. In 1921, he married Eslanda Goode. Their only child, Paul Robeson, Jr., was born in 1927. During his time in law school, Robeson was drawn to the stage.

After playing a lead in the short-lived Broadway play *Taboo,* which traveled to London in 1922, he became a replacement cast member in *Shuffle Along,* the history-making musical created by Eubie Blake and Noble Sissle. In 1923, Robeson decided not to pursue law after all, selecting the stage indeed. His big break came when he was invited to join the Provincetown Players, the influential Greenwich Village theater company that included playwright Eugene O'Neill among its three associate directors. In 1924, Robeson appeared in the revival of O'Neill's *The Emperor Jones* and premiered in the playwright's *All God's Chillun Got Wings,* a play embroiled in controversy because of a scene involving an interracial kiss. Robeson's acting career gathered pace with his 1930 London performance of *Othello*. Not since Ira Aldridge in the 1860s had a black man played this role. Robeson excelled in a 1932 Broadway revival of Hammerstein and Kern's musical *Showboat,* which featured his dramatic rendition of "Ol' Man River"; it was followed by a long-running and critically acclaimed production of *Othello* on Broadway in 1943.

Robeson is perhaps best known for the instrumental role he played in bringing African-American spirituals into classical music repertory. A scene in *Emperor Jones* called for whistling, which Robeson could not do, and so instead he sang a spiritual. He was praised for his vocal talent even more than for his acting ability. In 1925, he and his longtime pianist and arranger, Lawrence Brown, who also played with the African-American tenor Roland Hayes, staged a recital at the Greenwich Village Theatre. This was the first time in which a black soloist sang an entire program of spirituals before the white public. For the rest of his life, although he would sing a wide range of material—including popular tunes, work songs, political ballads, and folk music from all over the world—Robeson was admired as an interpreter of spirituals.

Robeson also developed a career in films, making his debut in 1924 in *Body and Soul* by the black filmmaker Oscar Micheaux. His most fruitful screen years were between 1933 and 1942, when he was featured prominently in *The Emperor Jones* (1933), *Show Boat* (1936), *Tales of Manhattan* (1942), and several British films. He became disillusioned with his work in films, however, coming to believe that with few exceptions, such as *Song of Freedom* (1936) and *The Proud Valley* (1940), his characters were little more than racial stereotypes, comics, or "primitives." His subservient role in the film *Sanders of the River* (1936), which extolled British imperialism, plagued him as his interest in the African heritage grew. In 1926 he wrote, "There can be no greater tragedy than to forget one's origins and finish despised and hated by the people among whom one grew up. To have that happen would be the sort of thing to make me rise from my grave." Robeson eventually became the first black person in film history to win the right to exercise final approval of his films. He also refused to perform in front of segregated audiences.

Robeson's decision to settle in London in the early 1930s opened up new cultural and political arenas. Socializing with a cosmopolitan community of blacks from England, Africa, Asia, and the Caribbean, he would declare with some humor that it was in London that he discovered Africa. Studying at the School of Oriental and African Studies at the University of London, Robeson learned two African languages and plunged into the heated world of anticolonial and antifascist

thought. He also wrote a series of essays that became a blueprint for the Negritude movement that emerged in Paris in 1934. He contributed to the study of music by analyzing the similarities in Chinese and African music based on the pentatonic scale. He met future African leaders Jomo Kenyatta of Kenya and Nnamdi Azikiwe of Nigeria, and he was influenced deeply by such political activists as C. L. R. James, the radical Caribbean theorist; William Patterson, the black American trade unionist; and American anarchist Emma Goldman. He developed a profound awareness of his relationship as a black American to residents of the Third World. He participated with some regularity at labor and peace marches in England. He protested British colonialism in Jamaica, spoke at a London rally for Jawaharlal Nehru, the father of Indian independence, performed at benefit concerts for the Spanish Republic, and in 1938 traveled to Spain to sing for Republican troops. He first visited the Soviet Union in 1934 to meet the Russian film director Sergei Eisenstein. Although Robeson was never a member of the Communist party, and was often misguided about the Soviet Union's own racist and anti-Semitic agenda toward its own colonized peoples, he had close ties to many of the party's leaders and would continue to defend the Soviet Union until his death.

1930–1939

After more than a decade of living in London Robeson returned home in 1939. As soon as he arrived, he gave his support to the labor union movement and sang on radio the now famous egalitarian song "Ballad for Americans," the first lines of which are "Man in white skin can never be free, while his black brother is in slavery." Robeson served on the board of many black cultural, political, and civil rights organizations, including the Council on African Affairs, an American-based organization that distributed information on African struggles for freedom, where he shared the chairmanship with W. E. B. Du Bois. During World War II he fully supported the war effort but did not refrain from protesting against the poll tax, the segregation of American armed forces, and overt racism. He worked for a federal antilynching law and consistently protested the inequality and disparity of class lines in America. "It means so little when a man like me wins some success," Robeson once said. "Where is the benefit when a small class of Negroes makes money and can live well? It may all be encouraging, but it has no deeper significance. I feel this way because I have cousins who can neither read nor write. I have had a chance. They have not. That is the difference." After the war, Robeson, W. E. B. Du Bois, and Bartley Crum, a liberal white lawyer, called for a national conference to secure a federal antilynching law. Robeson also protested the antilabor Taft-Hartley Act and campaigned for Henry Wallace's liberal Progressive party in the 1948 election.

As the Cold War intensified, Robeson found himself severely attacked and isolated in the United States. As early as 1941 the FBI placed him under surveillance, the beginning of years of harassment and denigration, not only because of his alleged communism, but also for his militancy on civil rights. A statement Robeson made at a peace conference in 1949 enraged them: "It is unthinkable that American Negroes would go to war on behalf of those who have oppressed us for generations against a country [the Soviet Union] which in one generation has raised our people to the full dignity of mankind." Deep in the throes of anti-communist hysteria, the House Committee on Un-American Activities (HUAC) announced in 1949 its intention to hold investigative hearings on Robeson and on the loyalty of African Americans. White liberals and black liberals alike, fearful of the taint of communism, ostracized him. In 1949, Robeson was supposed to perform at Peekskill, New York, but the concert was disrupted by mobs, which viciously attacked concertgoers. A rescheduled event, guarded by members of several left-wing CIO unions, passed without incident, only because over two thousand people formed a human shield

> *Every artist, every scientist, must decide now where he stands. He has no alternative. There is no standing above the conflict on Olympian heights. There are no impartial observers. Through the destruction, in certain countries, of the greatest of man's literary heritage, through the propagation of false ideas of racial and national superiority, the artist, the scientist, the writer is challenged. The struggle invades the formerly cloistered halls of our universities and other seats of learning. The battlefront is everywhere. There is no sheltered rear.*
> —Paul Robeson

around Robeson. On leaving, the audience was attacked by enraged rock-throwing locals. Eleanor Roosevelt issued a statement of outrage. State and local police were reported to have joined the mobs, and a grand jury investigation said that the violence had been provoked by Robeson's previous "unpatriotic" remarks.

Few can withstand such tremendous efforts to secure their silence. This campaign culminated in the withdrawal of Robeson's passport in 1950, preventing him from traveling or performing abroad. Blacklisted by Broadway and Hollywood, by concert halls and record companies, radio and television, his theatrical career was ruined. In 1956, Robeson spoke out against continuing racial injustice and refused to condemn the Soviet Union or answer questions about his membership in the Communist party. Robeson suffered for his beliefs at great personal cost. In 1961, he suffered a nervous breakdown, attempted suicide, and for the rest of his life he experienced severe depression. Despite obtaining his passport again, starring in another production of *Othello,* and publishing *Here I Stand,* an outspoken autobiography written with Lloyd Brown, he seemed to vanish from public life. Young student leaders of the Student Nonviolent Coordinating Committee (SNCC) proclaimed at a sixty-seventh birthday celebration for Robeson that "we of SNCC are Paul Robeson's spiritual children. We too have rejected gradualism and moderation." Other civil rights leaders ignored him. Indeed, Paul Robeson's last public appearance was at a benefit dinner for SNCC in 1966.

Paul Robeson was one of the most broadly talented African Americans in the twentieth century. He was a polymath, a scholar, an actor, and a singer. He was the first black male film star, and he was the first African-American intellectual or performer whose career would be destroyed because of his political beliefs. More than any other single performer, however, he made the spirituals—the music that slaves created and that his friend W. E. B. Du Bois called "The Sorrow Songs"—a central part of the canon of American music.

Bill Bojangles Robinson

The Tap Dancer
(1878?–1949)

On his sixty-fifth birthday, he tap-danced sixty-five blocks up Broadway, a block for each year. Bill "Bojangles" Robinson was the premier African-American dancer of the day. Like many other black artists, he is remembered not only for his own extraordinary talent, but because he was able to "cross over." Not unlike other key figures, he moved across the line separating the black world from the white, bringing with him the genius of black culture, but modified in ways that made it comprehensible and appealing to white people. Alain Locke believed Robinson's tapping to be a "symphonic composition of sounds" in which he heard the African heritage. Robinson turned those sounds into a percussive syncopation that made it part of that most American form of music, jazz. He was democracy in action—improvisational, flexible, fluid, protean, and experimental with and on his feet.

Luther Robinson was born, probably in 1878, perhaps on May 28, in Richmond, Virginia, thirteen years after the abolition of slavery. His working-class parents, Maxwell and Maria, died early, leaving him an orphan at about the age of seven. He stole the name Bill from his brother, and although there is uncertainty about the meaning of "Bojangles," it most likely signifies a scrappy fighter, which tells us something about his young life. Robinson ran away to Washington, where he worked as a stable hand and somehow found his way into minstrelsy. He got a job as a "pick" (short for pickaninny), with Mayme Remington, one of the many white female vaudeville stars who guaranteed success for her solo act by adding a finale with clever, black, dancing children. Robinson earned fifty cents a night.

Early in the 1890s, Robinson landed a bit part in *The South Before the War,* a large pageant that was one of the immediate precursors of the first golden age of black Broadway. The show featured Eddie Leonard, a master of the Virginia Essence, and

Robinson may have picked up dance steps from him. He teamed up with George W. Cooper when the vaudeville circuits accepted few African-American entertainers, and then only in pairs. But they were allowed to perform without blackface. When it became possible, Robinson appeared solo, billed as "The Dark Cloud of Joy." He developed his own style, wearing full dress, top hat, and carrying a cane, and leaving the stage with his signature exit, the Camel Walk, a black dance that Michael Jackson was to adapt much later as the Moon Walk. There were successes in London and at New York's Palace, vaudeville's summit, where he was one of the first blacks to headline.

It is often noted that, despite Robinson's enormous talent, he was not "discovered" until he was fifty years old. Lew Leslie had found international success in London with singer-dancer Florence Mills in *Blackbirds of 1927*. Mills died unexpectedly later that year, and Leslie supplemented the next edition, *Blackbirds of 1928,* with Bojangles Robinson performing "Doin' the New Low Down," tap-dancing up and down a five-step set of stairs. The critics and the audiences loved it, and Robinson was invited to appear in the first of what would be fourteen films. It is these for which he is best remembered, especially the series in which he was teamed with Shirley Temple, such hits as *The Little Colonel, The Littlest Rebel,* and *Rebecca of Sunnybrook Farm.* He later performed in *The Hot Mikado,* a jazz variation of Gilbert and Sullivan, as well as the all-black classic *Stormy Weather.*

Many blacks criticized Robinson for "tomming": his smiling, childlike, fawning behavior to whites, particularly his assigning credit to white people as originators of his dances. In fact, Robinson did emulate George Primrose, a white Irish-Canadian originally named Delaney, who was an elegant dance stylist in minstrelsy, especially with the soft shoe, a refinement of the black Virginia Essence. Perhaps the greatest influence on Robinson and others was a black man, King Rastus Brown, a buck dancer so expert Robinson refused ever to meet him in a cutting contest. Brown's dancing was flat-footed and shuffling, but Robinson, perhaps borrowing from Primrose's styling, was what Marshall Stearns calls "upright and swinging." Whatever the interwoven origins, Bojangles's dance was controlled, light, perfectly timed, tapping out a rhythm as clear as a Louis Armstrong note, and it opened a public window on black vernacular dance. Robinson was a complex person, a fighter and gambler who always carried a gold-plated pistol and had a reputation for

being, on occasion, a moody, volatile troublemaker. He had an obsession with police work and identified with police officers. He ate a quart of vanilla ice cream every day. He claimed he could run backward faster than anyone else could run forward.

He broke social and racial barriers. He was generous to a fault, and gave away most of his considerable income. The Negro Actors Guild made him their honorary president. He was so popular he was called the Honorary Mayor of Harlem, and Harlem's public schools were closed the day of his funeral. He invented a word, "copasetic," which means better than alright, really good, wonderful. It applies to Robinson himself, who may have been the greatest tap dancer America has produced. He moved with an incredible grace and speed. Black people hoped the country would move as quickly to rid itself of its racism.

1930–1939

Charles R. Drew

The Blood Man
(1904–1950)

As a surgeon, teacher, and researcher, Charles Richard Drew saved lives. In 1942, he became the director of the Red Cross's effort to collect and store blood on a large scale. He founded two of the world's largest blood banks, and his research on the storage and shipment of blood plasma (blood without the red blood cells) prevented millions of deaths. After World War II, he practiced surgery at Howard University and became the first African-American surgeon to serve as an examiner on the national medical examination board.

Drew grew up in a middle-class family in the racially mixed neighborhood known as Foggy Bottom in Washington, D.C. His family, active in their church, was industrious and conventional. The young Charles attracted attention by excelling in academics and sports. By the time he was eight years old he had won four swimming medals. He graduated from Dunbar High School, where his fellow students voted him "best athlete," "most popular student," and the "student who has done the most for the school."

He became interested in biology and chemistry after graduating from Amherst College on an athletic scholarship in 1926. To save enough money for medical school, Drew studied on his own, taught, and worked for two years. He was accepted by McGill University Medical School in Montreal. At McGill he began research on blood groupings. The four blood types had been discovered recently, but blood could only be stored for seven days before it began to spoil. Developing blood preservation and storage techniques for later use in surgery posed a major challenge to medicine. Drew's initial research was to continue and lead him to a major medical discovery.

Drew graduated from McGill and completed both his internship and residency at Montreal General Hospital. When his father died in 1935, Drew returned to

Washington and accepted a post at Howard University teaching pathology. He was made an instructor in surgery and an assistant surgeon at Howard's Freedmen's Hospital. He also held a postdoctoral fellowship at Columbia Presbyterian Hospital in New York, where he researched fluid balance, blood chemistry, and blood transfusion with John Scudder.

At Columbia Presbyterian Drew set up the first successful experimental blood bank. He described his research in a thesis entitled "Banked Blood: A Study in Blood Preservation," which earned him a doctorate of science in medicine from Columbia University in 1940. The Rockefeller Foundation funded the continuation of his blood research, which now focused on how to administer blood to patients during an emergency. At that time surgeons needed to have a blood bank nearby, as well as know patients' blood types, to perform blood transfusions. Drew began to experiment with plasma, or blood without red blood cells, and discovered that plasma could substitute for whole blood. He created techniques for processing and preserving plasma so that it could be stored and shipped great distances, including the development of dehydrated plasma that could be reconstituted by adding water.

This was a phenomenal discovery and it came at a fortunate time. England was suffering badly at the beginning of the World War II against Hitler's Germany. There were thousands of casualties, and the beleaguered Royal Air Force could not maintain banked blood near the battlefront. They turned to the United States for help. Drew was selected by his colleagues in the Blood Transfusion Association to be medical supervisor of the Blood for Britain program. He arranged to fly large amounts of plasma to England, and he set up several blood banks. After the success of his blood preservation and transfusion efforts in Europe, Drew was enlisted by the

American Red Cross in 1941 to establish a blood bank program in the United States. He initiated the use of refrigerated bloodmobiles, which the Red Cross continues to use to this day. The American Red Cross headquarters in Washington, D.C., was renamed the Charles R. Drew Center in the 1970s.

In 1941, the U.S. War Department ordered that blood be segregated by race. The department declared that "it is not advisable to collect and mix Caucasian and Negro blood indiscriminately for later administration to members of the military forces." Drew was furious and deeply upset. He resigned his position as director of the Red Cross Blood Bank Program in protest, saying, "In the laboratory I have found that you and I share a common blood; but will we ever share a common brotherhood? As repugnant as this scientific fact may appear to some, their quarrel is not with the Giver of Life whose wisdom made it so." Although War Department officials knew that, scientifically, blood could not be typed according to race, they refused to surrender their position, and it was not until 1949 that the U.S. military stopped segregating blood.

When the war was over, Drew returned to Howard, where he was promoted to professor of surgery and chief surgeon at Freedmen's Hospital. He had married Minnie Lenore Robbins in 1941 and received numerous honorary degrees and awards in the years before his early death. The NAACP awarded him the Spingarn Medal in 1944. In 1946 he was elected to the International College of Surgeons. In 1950, on his way to a conference at Tuskegee, Drew accidentally fell asleep while driving. His car overturned and he was killed. A handsome portrait of Charles Richard Drew joined the portrait gallery of distinguished physicians at the National Institutes of Health in 1976. He was the first African American to be accorded this honor.

Charles R. Drew was a scientist, but he was also a physician. He believed the advances of the sciences were not only theoretical achievements, but should contribute to human betterment. What better symbol of humanity than the blood Richard Drew made possible to share.

Katherine Dunham

The Dancing Anthropologist
(1909–)

Scholar, choreographer, dancer, and teacher Katherine Dunham brought Pan-African dance to the world's stage. At a time when black dancers were restricted largely to jazz and tap dancing and practically excluded from ballet, Dunham studied, recorded, and wrote about black dance and musical forms from across the Atlantic world and choreographed them for the concert stage. Talking about her anthropological fieldwork, Dunham explained that people often said of black dancers, "'Oh, their bodies are different. They are made different, and they can't do technical ballet.' Of course, that was an absurdity. So I came to try and find if there were not dance movements and forms that were more associated with people of color, black people—and of course, the Caribbean was full of them." An accomplished dancer in her own right, Dunham immersed herself in the traditions of the African diaspora. Her performances were almost always accompanied by brilliant lighting, stage settings, and costumes.

The Katherine Dunham Dance Company, founded in 1940, paved the way for later black dance companies. Long before Alvin Ailey or Arthur Mitchell, Katherine Dunham assembled a renowned dance company that showcased brilliant black dancers who could perform and articulate a wide range of dances from the black Atlantic world. Her method, the "Dunham technique," is still studied today by aspiring modern dancers throughout the world. But Dunham is also a scholar, and perhaps therein lies the appeal of her unique approach to dance. Whether her research took her to the Jamaican countryside, to southern jook joints, or to fishing villages in Martinique, Dunham was also the consummate anthropologist, recording her research in numerous books and even lighter magazine articles about the Caribbean under the pseudonym of K. Dunn.

Dunham was born on June 22, 1909, near Chicago's South Side to Albert

Dunham and Fanny June Taylor. Her mother died when she was very young, and the family moved to Joliet, Illinois, where Dunham developed a passion for dance. While studying for her doctorate in cultural anthropology at the University of Chicago, her interest in the black ethnic dance heritage, particularly of the Caribbean region, increased, even as her family hoped it might disappear. She continued with dance training throughout her graduate career, becoming a pupil of

Ludmilla Speranzeva, formerly of the Moscow Theater; Mark Turbyfill, a ballet dancer; and Ruth Page. Ruth Page was the ballet mistress at the Chicago Civic Opera and it was in her ballet called *La Guiblesse,* based on West Indian themes, that Dunham made her debut in 1933. Three years later, she received a fellowship from the Julius Rosenwald Foundation, which funded her dissertation research on the cultural and social dimensions of African-based dance forms.

Dunham set out for the Caribbean in 1936. Traveling in Martinique, Jamaica, Trinidad, and Haiti, she observed at firsthand some of the dances that African slaves brought to the New World. In the field of Haitian studies, she joined the small community of anthropologists such as Melville Herskovits, Alfred Metraux, and Jean Price Mars, whose interests ranged from Haitian peasantry religious rituals to their art and psychology. Dunham became one of the first African Americans to appreciate the aesthetic beauty of vodou and its implications for dance anthropology. Eventually she was initiated into its mysteries. *Journey to Accompong* (1946), Dunham's book based on her fieldwork on the Free Maroon Settlement in the Jamaican mountains, examined the koromontee, a sacred, secret war dance, and the myal dance, or dance of the dead. This intellectually formative period also influenced her choreography in such numbers as *l'Ag ya* (1938), *Tropics* (1939), *Tropical Revue* (1943), *Shango* (1945), and *Bal Nègre* (1946).

> *I wasn't concerned about the hardships because I always felt I was doing what I had to do, what I wanted to do, and what I was destined to do.*
> —Katherine Dunham

In 1937, Dunham returned to America. She was invited to serve as dance director for the Chicago branch of the Federal Theater Project, an extraordinary experiment in public art funded by the New Deal's Works Progress Administration. When the project ended in 1939, she established her own dance company and began performing at Chicago's Sherman Hotel, where Duke Ellington's orchestra took part in the floor show. Dunham incorporated historic African-American dances, such as the barrelhouse and the cakewalk, into her cabaret-style choreography, and even managed to include several so-called "primitive barefoot dances" in her repertoire. She also went to New York to coach the dancers in the Labor Stage production of *Pins and Needles* and, on the side, presented a series of Sunday afternoon concerts. In 1940, Dunham was booked at the Windsor Theater for the performance of two pieces she had choreographed herself, *Tropics* and *Le Jazz Hot*. *Le Jazz Hot,* featured the Florida swamp shimmy, a dance popular in black drinking dens. *Tropics* showcased Dunham herself, who performed while smoking a cigar. Few before had seen such spectacular, theatrically vital dance rooted in black cultural forms. Dunham was now established as a lasting black choreographer and a creative voice in the dance world.

Dunham was fortunate to be active in the late 1930s and 1940s, when "serious" choreographers from the "artistic" dance world, such as Martha Graham, began shaping the future of the Broadway stage. Replacing jazz and tap-dancing acts and female chorus lines, this new breed of innovators combined the choreographic techniques of ballet, modern, and ethnic dance with jazz and folk dance movements to produce what would become known as theatrical jazz dance. During these years Katherine Dunham's star rose not just as a choreographer but as a performer of monumental talent. She was rivaled only by the Trinidadian Pearl Primus, who brought West African dance to the stage and began her own dance school in New York.

In October 1940, Dunham received critical acclaim for her role as Georgia Brown in the Broadway musical *Cabin in the Sky,* which she also choreographed with George Balanchine. In a wave of creative momentum she appeared in *Stormy*

1940–1949

Weather (1943) and *Star-Spangled Rhythm* (1942); toured the United States and Canada in the *Tropical Revue* (1943–1944); codirected and danced in *Carib Song* at the Adelphi Theater in New York in 1945; and produced, directed, and starred in *Bal Nègre* at New York's Belasco Theater in 1946. In June 1948, she and her company made their European debut at London's Prince of Wales Theatre with *Caribbean Rhapsody,* which had already received accolades in the United States. Many Europeans were familiar with Josephine Baker but the European stage had never before seen black dance as a high art form. The effect was electrifying.

In 1943, the veteran scholar, choreographer, and performer established the Katherine Dunham School of Arts and Research in New York, which offered classes in dance, theater, and world cultures until 1954. Her classes were accompanied by conga drumming and involved step patterns with isolated movements of the shoulder and hips. She trained all the dancers who appeared in her works in the "Dunham technique," which combined classical ballet with Central European, Caribbean, and African forms. Many of her students went on to achieve fame in their own right, including Marlon Brando, James Dean, Eartha Kitt, and Archie Savage.

In 1959, President William Tubman of Liberia, an Americo-Liberian, appointed Dunham director of the National Dance Company of Liberia and head of the African Performing Arts Center in Monrovia. Dunham represented the United States at the Festival of Black Arts in Senegal, where she became cultural advisor to the Senegalese government, and helped train the National Ballet of Senegal. After a seven-year absence, Dunham continued to dance, choreograph, and direct on Broadway in such productions as *Katharine Dunham and Her Company* and *Bamboche* in 1962. With the 1963 production of *Aida* in 1963, Dunham became the first black person to choreograph for the Metropolitan Opera. She also choreographed and directed Scott Joplin's opera *Treemonisha* in 1972 and founded the Katherine Dunham Museum and Children's School, which are still main attractions in East St. Louis, Illinois. She has received many honorary degrees and awards, including the *Dance* magazine award in 1968, the University of Chicago Alumni Professional Achievement Award, the Albert Schweitzer Music Award, and the distinguished service award of the American Anthropological Society.

Katherine Dunham brought Pan-Africanism to dance, and modern dance to the Pan-African world, without succumbing to primitivist pandering. It is impossible to imagine the world of later black dancers, from Alvin Ailey to Bill T. Jones, without her.

Duke Ellington

The Duke
(1899–1971)

Duke Ellington was the king of swing, at a time when a radio program could prosper on a good collection of swing classics and the rambling of a disk jockey who would introduce the latest swing release. Swing fans listened repeatedly to the newest ten-inch 78 rpm records, living vicariously through the glamorous big bands. Touring bands crisscrossed America, and wherever they went they introduced dance crazes such as the lindy hop, named after Charles Lindbergh's solo flight, and the Suzie-Q or big apple—all black dances. From the ballroom dance floors to casinos, white teenagers crossed racial lines to do the black-inspired dance of the day at places such as the famous Harlem Savoy Ballroom on 140th Street at Lenox Avenue. Here, Ella Fitzgerald sang with Chick Webb's band and there, in the dimmed lights, white kids would watch young black couples spiraling, flipping, and defying gravity on the dance floor. As Duke Ellington would later title one of his tracks, "It don't mean a thing if it ain't got that swing."

Although Edward Kennedy "Duke" Ellington was surrounded by big bands like that of his black predecessor Fletcher Henderson, his band was not just the typical swing band: It was the preeminent orchestra of his day. For this reason, among others, Ellington is widely considered one of the first black jazz composers, as well as the foremost orchestra conductor of swing. Always uneasy about being too narrowly classified as a swing or jazz artist, Ellington was a master of ingenious creativity with his band; he was incredibly creative, producing more than three hundred songs and composing somewhere between one thousand and two thousand orchestral pieces throughout his lifetime.

Elegant, vivacious, and dapper, Ellington radiated a kind of self-composure, a self-assuredness and joie de vivre. He was the first performer to wear white tails onstage, and the first to wear ballet slippers with a tuxedo. Yet, for all his outwardly debonair ways, Ellington was an unknowable and inscrutable man. He possessed an element of mystery that undoubtedly played into the "Ellington Effect," as his long-time musical collaborator and friend Billy Strayhorn called it. The Duke had a melodic sensibility that wed, without anxiety or tension, the early forms of blues and ragtime, influenced by the antiphony of slave music, to Euro-American classical forms of music. Similar to Zora Neale Hurston, Katherine Dunham, and other artists of the time, his project was to excavate the past for the true vernacular of southern black folk, and this resulted in the broad recognition of black cultural forms as serious art. He succeeded in this endeavor, regardless of the pretensions and artifice that accompanied the process.

Duke Ellington grew up in the middle-class African-American community of Washington, D.C., which, during the 1930s and '40s was especially preoccupied with bourgeoisie pretensions and color distinctions. The young Ellington gave up the formal composition studies he had been afforded as a child, to make a Dante-like journey into the "black" music culture of the dimly lit poolrooms and the after-hours clubs. Here he listened to the major figures of the stride piano style, particularly James P. Johnson and Willie "the Lion" Smith. In 1923, Ellington moved to Harlem to work with Elmer Snowden, and in 1924 he formed the Washingtonians, his first real band. They auditioned at Harlem's Cotton Club and were hired. Already the Duke's work was being discussed by those who understood his compositions as full of "compositional ingenuity, harmonic adventurousness, sophistication, and professionalism."

The Cotton Club was lush. In fact, it was a segregated drinking spot, run by gangster Owen Madden and "Big Frenchy" De Mange, who kept all but the most affluent blacks off the premises. Lena Horne was a Cotton Club chorus girl at one time. She tried to leave once, but the bosses had her father beaten up. Protected by the mob, they strong-armed him from signing another contract at a Philadelphia theater. The name Cotton Club, moreover, like its rival, the Plantation Club, evoked images of the mythical "good old days." Partially to be consistent with its primitive theme, Ellington initiated his so-called "jungle music," the signature music of the Cotton Club. It also was named after the growling, plunger-muted solos of "Bubber" Miley, who defined the orchestra's so-called jungle style. At the same time, Ellington composed more serious pieces, including the early masterpieces "East St. Louis Toodle-oo" (1926), "Black and Tan Fantasy" (1927), and "Black Beauty" (1928). And he came to detest the confining categories of swing and jazz.

The 1930s signaled Ellington's emergence as a composer of extended orchestral works. After the death of his mother in 1935, he wrote and recorded a tribute, *Reminiscing in Tempo,* that stood apart from the jazz sounds of his peers. Yet in the same period he continued to demonstrate great range and versatility through his shorter pieces, four of which have remained timely for generations: "Mood Indigo" (1930), "It Don't Mean a Thing If It Ain't Got That Swing" (1932), "Sophisticated Lady" (1933), and "In a Sentimental Mood" (1935).

In this era the image of the bandleader was highly significant. The leader was responsible for public relations and band management as well as being the conductor and arranger. The sidemen he chose were invaluable to his image. Ellington managed his band as if he were painting a haphazard but beautiful picture. Notoriously chaotic in rehearsals, the band played as one person during performance and recording. He wrote directly for each of his sidemen, and as it is often said, he played a whole band rather than just the piano. And although his sidemen changed frequently, there were the few that became legendary: "Bubber" Miley, the exponent of the growl trumpet; Sidney Bechet, the brilliant New Orleans soprano saxophonist and clarinetist; Joe "Tricky Sam" Nanton, a trombonist; Johnny Hodges, the alto saxophonist; and Otto Hardwick, a reed player.

Billy Strayhorn, of course, Ellington's close collaborator as a pianist, composer, and lyricist who wrote "Take the A-Train," joined him in 1939 and stayed with him until his own death in 1967. "What little fame I have achieved is the result of my special orchestrations, and especially of the cooperation of the boys in the band, I cannot speak too highly of their loyalty and initiative," Duke wrote.

The band's popularity was ensured by weekly radio broadcasts from the Cotton Club, but it was cemented by their several Hollywood cameo appearances. Throughout the 1940s, they were fixtures in films such as *Black and Tan Fantasy,* the Ziegfeld revue *Show Girl, Check and Double Check, Belle of the Nineties,* and *Murder at the Vanities,* plus the Marx Brothers' film *A Day at the Races,* in which Ivie Anderson, the singer of the band, appeared. The Duke also composed sound tracks for films later revered as classics. *Cabin in the Sky* was one such venture, in which Lena Horne also was featured. His 1943 composition *Black, Brown and Beige: The History of the Negro,* which followed African Americans from Africa to Dixie, was predicated on his interpretation of the "natural feelings of a people." It embodies his gift to orchestral jazz: the discovery that bands can have an unmistakable sound and can play as a unified unit, a distinctive sound. His first complete film score, performed by the orchestra, was for *Anatomy of a Murder.* In 1960 he recorded music for *Paris Blues.*

By the 1940s the Duke was widely considered one of America's finest composers. Each new Ellington work was showcased at Carnegie Hall. But in the fifties, bebop began to eclipse the big bands, which now seemed outdated and clumsy, with too many musicians and instruments. Bebop was a new sound, that enabled small, inexpensive, and intimate groups to move in a new musical direction. Ellington made the cover of *Time* magazine in 1956, however, because of an exciting comeback performance at the Newport Jazz Festival. The "oldies" were rediscovered suddenly. Ellington collaborated with Billy Strayhorn on *Royal Ancestry,* a musical portrait of Ella Fitzgerald. He also recorded with the Count Basie Orchestra and the Louis Armstrong All Stars in the 1960s. He collaborated with the younger generation, making two recordings with the tenor saxophonists Coleman Hawkins and John Coltrane. He made a trio album with drummer Max Roach and double bass player Charlie Mingus in 1962.

The elder, more established Ellington was criticized in the 1960s by young black activists for not being sufficiently involved in the civil rights struggle. He replied, "I

Lovers have come and gone, but only my mistress stays. She is beautiful and gentle. She waits on me hand and foot. She is a swinger. She has grace. To hear her speak, you can't believe your ears. She is ten thousand years old. She is as modern as tomorrow, a brand new woman every day, and as endless as time mathematics. Living with her is a labyrinth of ramifications. I look forward to her every gesture. Music is my mistress, and she plays second fiddle to no one.
—Duke Ellington

wrote 'Black Beauty' in 1927. . . . We have been talking for a long time about what it is to be black in this country." Certainly *Deep South Suite* (1947) was based on black political aspirations and ambitions.

His creative energies found full expression in *Harlem,* an extended work that premiered at a fundraiser for the National Association for the Advancement of Colored People in 1951. In a letter addressed to Harry S. Truman, Ellington predicted that the concert would benefit "your civil rights program—to stamp out segregation, discrimination, [and] bigotry."

By 1963, he had written *My People,* an extended choral and orchestral work celebrating the Emancipation Proclamation of 1863, which challenged the demeaning stereotypes of African Americans in Hollywood films and throughout American popular culture. He also wrote *Jump for Joy,* which had a buoyant sense of political irony that is suggested in such numbers as "Uncle Tom's Cabin Is a Drive-In Now."

Ellington was a deeply religious man, and at the end of his life he wrote *Three Sacred Concerts* that were performed in Grace Cathedral in San Francisco and the Cathedral of St. John the Divine in New York City in the 1960s. His last concert, performed at Westminster Abbey in 1974, was for solo voices, choir, and Ellington's piano alone. In 1966, President Lyndon Johnson awarded him the Gold Medal of Honor, and he performed at President Richard Nixon's birthday in 1969, when he was awarded the Medal of Freedom. Between these awards and tours to South America and Europe, his dearest friend and collaborator Billy Strayhorn died. In 1974 Ellington died of cancer.

Duke Ellington was famous for creating what Francis Newton called the sound that was "New Orleans colors, the liquid Creole clarinet . . . the blue sound of muted brass . . . and a well mixed reed sound." He also established jazz as composed art form, mastering the art of composing those most fundamentally improvised mediums, to our eternal joy and delight.

1940–1949

Billie Holiday

Lady Day
(1915–1959)

Lady Day had her *own* way of singing. Saxophonist Lester "Prez" Young, the dear friend with whom Holiday shared the most profound musical empathy, used to shout out to musicians during jam sessions, "Tell your own story. Man, you can't join the throng 'til you play your own goddamn song." Ralph Ellison once described improvisational jazz movement as an art of individual assertion that occurred within and against the group. Billie Holiday's particular mode of assertion was to mimic the sounds of the band instruments in a sort of rasping, melodious voice that sometimes bordered on the mystical.

Holiday triumphed as a profound interpreter of lyrics. She could take the American popular song, the Tin Pan Alley rag, and convey an entirely new meaning. By infusing lyrics with an existential importance and simplicity, she replaced empty technical gestures in the cadence of her voice with the rich experiences of violence and pain, along with the love of living. She could reinvent the most banal of tunes by shifting its rhythm, varying her pitch.

Still, it's difficult to get past the caricature of Holiday as the tormented torch singer, the beautiful young woman with the white gladiolus behind her ear who succumbed to the ravages of heroin and alcohol addiction. What is clear is that Holiday evoked beauty in her music even when she became haggard, aged, and hardened by drugs and alcohol, even when her voice faltered and her sound was as barely recognizable as her body. She had what we might think of as a blues sensibility, though strictly speaking she was not a blues singer. Her work expressed the pathos of humor and the joy of despair. Early on, Holiday demonstrated extraordinary improvisational skill and proved that she could perform in the male world of jazz. As a result, she collaborated with and earned the respect of some of the finest names in the field. In her later years she made famous the antilynching anthem

"Strange Fruit," the first blues number with overtly political content. She had the ability to take us to the soul's deepest places, paradoxically expressing the most unspeakable black angst. Her art transcended the usual categorizations of style, content, and technique, able to reach a realm described by the musicologist Gunther Schuller as not only beyond criticism, but in the deepest sense, inexplicable. Though her career ended ignominiously, Billie Holiday ranks among the small number of women who are really jazz or blues legends.

She was born Eleanora Fagan on April 7, 1915, but like many performers Holiday renamed herself in young adulthood. Her father, an itinerant musician named Clarence Holiday who later played with the Fletcher Henderson band, left her mother, Sadie Fagan, before the baby's birth. Fagan raised her daughter in Baltimore, and before she was thirteen young Holiday was participating in jam sessions in the city's jook joints and nightclubs. Relatives and friends who cared for Holiday after her mother left to work in New York recalled that she often listened to the radio and sang along with it. She devoured Bessie Smith and Louis Armstrong records on the Victrola that she first heard in the brothel next door to her flat. While the vibrant musical tradition forged in whorehouses and gin joints shaped her musical gifts, the surroundings led her into prostitution. By age ten she had been raped and sent to a Catholic reformatory for wayward girls. Her mother promptly took Holiday back to New York with her.

In New York, Sadie Fagan found her daughter a temporary job as a maid in Long Branch, New Jersey, and unwittingly boarded the eleven-year-old with a woman in Harlem who turned out to be yet another madam. While she practiced her singing, young Billie worked as a prostitute for three years, until she was arrested for soliciting. At the age of fourteen, she spent four months in an adult correctional institution on the East River.

When she was fifteen, Holiday found her first professional singing job with saxophonist Kenneth Hollon at a venue called Grey Dawn, in Brooklyn. She was an immediate success. Holiday was soon hired to sing at an uptown favorite, Pod and Jerry's (also known as the Log Cabin), where she jammed with Bobby Henderson— among other piano greats—and joined a floor show organized by George "Pops"

Foster. Audiences were entranced by her. News spread quickly about this young woman, who had taken to wearing a gladiolus behind her ear and fixed the crowd with a mature, unwavering stare.

In the 1930s, Holiday was one of the most sought after vocalists in Harlem's clubs. In 1933, white record producer John Hammond—who would help launch the careers of Benny Goodman, Count Basie, Bob Dylan, and Aretha Franklin—heard Holiday sing "Wouldja for a Big Red Apple" at a club called Monettes. Hammond had convinced Columbia Records' Brunswick label to do black covers of popular white songs to meet the burgeoning jukebox market in black neighborhoods. Believing he had just heard the greatest living jazz vocalist, Hammond immediately organized recording sessions for Holiday. The musicians who played in these sessions over the next few years boasted some of the finest names in the field: jazz pianist Teddy Wilson, trumpeter Roy Eldridge, Ben Webster on tenor sax, drummer Cozy Cole, bassist John Kirby, John Truehart on guitar, Benny Goodman on clarinet, and, of course, Lester Young, Holiday's platonic soulmate, on saxophone. Holiday also appeared at the Apollo Theater, where critics roared that she tore the house down with "Them There Eyes." In 1935, when only twenty years old, she appeared in Duke Ellington's *Symphony in Black,* a short film designed to run with newsreels. Ellington later referred to her singing as the essence of cool.

By the mid-thirties, Holiday was a star, but she attained her mature style in the late thirties and early forties. She played regularly at the artsy, politically left-of-center and racially integrated club Café Society, opened by Barney Josephson in Sheridan Square in 1938. Here, night after night, she sang "Strange Fruit" tearfully at the closing of each performance to hushed and respectful audiences. Composed by Abel Meeropol, a New York schoolteacher, the ballad was unusually straightforward in describing the bitter results of southern race bigotry. Holiday used her tenderness and her knowledge of America's dark side to transform the lyrics of "Strange Fruit" into a political anthem. As performed by Holiday, "Strange Fruit" also became the expression of feminist horror of male brutality and public indifference. She recorded it with Milt Gabbler at Commodore Rare Jazz Records because Columbia refused to release such a political piece. Critic Gunther Schuller wrote that "Strange Fruit" was a powerfully moving monument to Billie's artistry—and courage. "It is also a fine unpretentious composition in B-flat minor, a key Chopin and other composers knew how to use well for their more sombre pieces. . . . It is a mark of the depth and breadth of her artistry that, without any drastic modifications, her basic style embraced this sombre opus too."

Through the early forties, Holiday headlined with the era's major swing bands, playing with Count Basie, Lionel Hampton, the all-white Artie Shaw ensemble, and her hero, Louis Armstrong. Some of her best-known tunes were recorded during this period, such as the original "God Bless the Child," "Lover Man," and "Good Morning Heartache." Angela Davis has discerned something utopian in Holiday's love songs, the affirmation of eros as a transformative force. The ability to love deeply, if tragically, was an essential part of Holiday's phrasing.

At the peak of her vocal powers, the year 1947 marked the beginning of Holiday's personal decline. After an unsuccessful stint in a drug rehabilitation clinic, she was arrested soon after for heroin possession. In a devastating blow, New York City authorities revoked her cabaret license. Making matters worse, Decca Records, which had signed Holiday in 1944, refused to renew her contract in 1950. But Holiday kept on. Without a license she could only play concert halls and theaters. Booked into Carnegie Hall, she sang to an audience so large and enthusiastic that extra chairs had to be put behind her on the stage. From 1952 to 1957, she recorded over a hundred new songs with the Verve label. Near the end of her life, in 1957, she performed on *The Sound of Jazz,* a television special with Lester Young. Their performance of "Fine and Mellow" is truly memorable, and the movie has been heralded as one of the most thoughtful jazz films ever made. By the fall of 1958, alcoholism and drug addiction had overtaken her.

Since the early days of her career, Holiday had participated in jazz's reefer culture. When she was in her mid-twenties, trumpeter Joe Guy introduced her to heroin. Married twice, her husbands only encouraged her narcotics dependency. When Lester Young died in 1959, Young's wife, who disapproved of Young's jazz friends, refused to let Holiday sing at his funeral. Brokenhearted, she fell into a deep depression. Four months later, she died, forty-four years of age, leaving behind a life as tragic as her music. When Holiday collapsed into a coma, track marks were found all over her body.

Billie Holiday's ability to convey so very deeply the tragedy at the heart of the blues, while managing to appeal successfully to a broad audience, was an extraordinary testament to the integrity of her artistry. She lives today, not in the myriad of stories, films, and myths around her, but in her music.

Lena Horne

Lena
(1917–)

Lena Horne was the first black female star. Thousands of black soldiers pinned her image to the walls of their barracks during World War II. Black women accustomed to seeing only mammies and maids on the screen were proud of Lena Horne, seeing her as the symbol of their collective poise and beauty. As time progressed and Lena's politics emerged, she became more than just a beautiful face; she became an activist, one of the most visible performer–civil rights activists in America, along with her friend Harry Belafonte.

Carving out a space for fair representation of black women in the music and film industry constituted a "peculiar kind of pioneering," as she describes it in her autobiography. Count Basie once remarked to her that Americans "have never been given a chance to see the Negro woman as a woman." Although she hates the phrase, Lena Horne became, in effect, our first "Negro sex symbol." With each seemingly effortless appearance in such highly successful films as *Cabin in the Sky* and *Stormy Weather,* Horne ameliorated, in her own way, the indignity of prevalent black female film imagery, while affirming that black women were "womanly" and feminine. Horne also demanded that Metro-Goldwyn-Mayer not cast her in subservient roles—unprecedented in Hollywood—and that the studio stop cutting her scenes when films were shown in the South. The NAACP supported her. She became a symbol of fair hiring practices for black performers.

Horne grew up in a world of black middle-class propriety and decorum, but she was also exposed to the fights for social equality and justice. An October 1919 issue of the NAACP *Branch Bulletin* includes a picture of a stern, chubby two-year-old Lena Horne holding a wilted rose. Horne's politically active and suffragist grandmother, Cora Calhoun Horne, had just enrolled her granddaughter as the youngest member of the NAACP. Horne lived with her grandmother when her mother,

The African-American Century

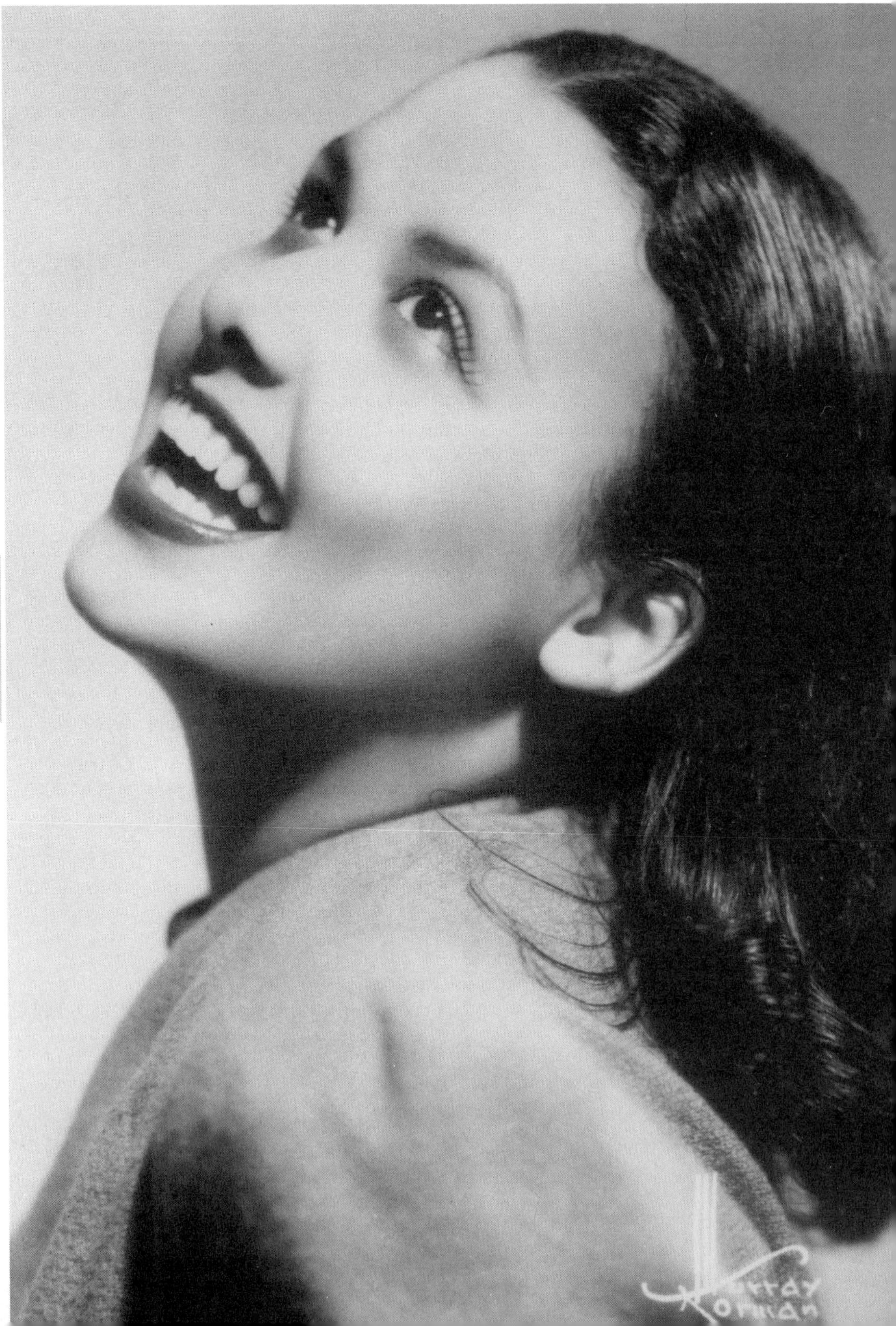

Edna Scottron, was abandoned by her husband and she was briefly trying her hand at an unsuccessful acting career. Her mother retrieved her when Lena was seven, and she spent the rest of her childhood moving from place to place. For a brief period Horne was enrolled in schools in Florida, Georgia, and Ohio. At fourteen, she left school, and by sixteen she was a chorus dancer at Harlem's Cotton Club, a notoriously exhausting job that was neither glamorous nor well paid. Hired for her good looks, Horne, nonetheless, pursued her singular passion, and took singing lessons on her own time. The sultry voice that is now so famous began to take shape. She was encouraged by Duke Ellington, and especially by Billy Strayhorn, who later became a very close friend. At nineteen, she married Louis Jones, with whom she had two children. They divorced in 1941.

Horne left the Cotton Club in the mid-1930s to sing and tour with Noble Sissle's Society Orchestra, which was based in Philadelphia. In 1934, she performed in her first Broadway show, the unsuccessful all-black musical *Dance with Your Gods,* in which she played a "Quadroon Girl" in a voodoo ceremony. She also appeared in an equally forgettable first movie role, *The Duke Is Tops.* Fortunately, better work came along. In 1939, she was cast in Lew Leslie's *Blackbirds,* and shortly after that saxophonist Charlie Barnett's all-white band hired her to sing as their lead.

She made her first record a few months before the outbreak of World War II, with clarinetist Artie Shaw and a band that included jazz greats such as trumpeter Henry Allen. She was just twenty-four years old. Suddenly, Horne became a sought after singer as well as a movie star. She became a favorite "pinup girl" among American GIs who loved her dusky voice as much as her sex appeal. Horne also recorded her first hit record, "Good-for-Nothin' Joe," in 1941, one of many recorded for Bluebird with Barnett. She was now featured on the radio and rerecorded a reprise of her first Cotton Club piece, "As Long As I Live." Around the same time, Barney Josephson featured Lena at his Café Society in New York. There she became acquainted with singer and civil rights activist Paul Robeson, and with Billie Holiday, both of whom were significant influences.

In 1942, she played a lead role in *Cabin in the Sky.* In 1943, she appeared in three films: *I Dood It, As Thousands Cheer,* and *Stormy Weather;* the title song of the last film became her trademark. On the set of *Stormy Weather,* Horne met Lennie Hayton, a white pianist, arranger, and conductor who had worked in the 1920s and '30s with many of the top names in jazz, such as Bix Beiderbecke, Frank Trumbauer, and Bing

> *I sometimes think the pattern of my life was established since the day I was born . . . being exhibited, as I was that first day, as an oddity of color—a Negro woman, a Negro entertainer who didn't fit the picture of personality and performing style the white majority used to expect. How I hated those awful phrases they used to trot out to describe me! Who the hell wants to be a chocolate chanteuse?*
> —Lena Horne

Crosby. Although the couple married in 1947, they waited until 1950 to publicly announce their controversial interracial marriage. During those years Horne continued to appear in such film musicals as *Two Girls and a Sailor* (1944), *Broadway Rhythm* (1944), *Ziegfeld Follies* (1945 and 1946), and *The Duchess of Idaho* (1950). In *Meet Me in Las Vegas* (1956), she was given her first speaking part. She also starred in the movie *Jamaica* in 1957 and appeared on several television shows throughout the 1950s.

Horne is outspoken about the role of her light-skinned beauty in her career. She recounts how studio executives and production managers asked her to apply dark makeup so she would appear darker than she was. Others advised her to "pass" as Latin so she could get more mainstream roles. She refused. Perhaps more than any other performer, Horne often was described by café au lait epithets, including "sepia songstress" or "coffee chaunteuse." She was an exoticized other among exotic others.

When her husband and manager, Lennie Hayton, died in 1971, Lena temporarily withdrew from show business, making a brief appearance in *The Wiz,* an all-black version of *The Wizard of Oz,* featuring Diana Ross and Michael Jackson. In 1981 she returned to Broadway in the Grammy-winning autobiographical play *Lena Horne: The Lady and Her Music,* which became the longest-running one-woman show in Broadway history, and won eight awards. In 1984, she repeated the show with equal success in London. In 1984 she received the Kennedy Center Award for Lifetime Achievement in the Arts as well as an honorary doctorate from Howard University, an Image Award, and the Spingarn Medal from the NAACP.

What Josephine Baker was to France, Lena Horne was to the United States: an embodiment of the racial zeitgeist, an object of sophistication and desire that crossed and united color lines, a thoughtful, intelligent, enormously talented singer and actress who utilized her popularity for larger political ends.

Jacob Lawrence

The Painter
(1917–2000)

Jacob Lawrence brought the history of black life to life in paint. He managed to render rich and brilliant color from the limited medium of flat tempera, and to transform formless designs into living, moving shapes. Devoid of propaganda, his art sensitively captures the social changes of the great migration as African Americans moved to industrialized urban centers in the North. Registering this monumental change in the visual realm was his great achievement. Often accompanied by text, his paintings are epic, sweeping narratives of the everyday experiences of forgotten and ordinary folk. His paintings memorialize the tragedy, the aspirations, the perseverance, and the joy of everyday African Americans.

Lawrence's artistry was forged in Depression-battered Harlem. The frivolity and eroticism that characterized the hedonistic twenties—the Jazz Age—had given way to a more somber and disenchanted decade, one characterized by deprivation. Black artists of the 1930s embraced leftist and working-class themes. Lawrence admired the images evoked by artists as varied as the Mexican muralist Clemente Orozco; the European social realist artists such as Käthe Kollowitz, William Gropper, and George Grosz; and the Chinese woodcut artists. Lawrence integrated his hard-won mastery of technique with his thematic passion for creating a visual narrative of black history.

"During the war there was a great migration by southern Negroes," reads Lawrence's first caption of the *Migration* series, and he had been part of it. Lawrence's parents, Rose Lee Lawrence from Virginia and Jacob Armstead Lawrence from South Carolina, are portrayed in the nameless, faceless shadows of these paintings. As the panels in the *Migration* series dramatically unfold, the poetry of the text recalls the movement of the railway train: "And still they came," as black migrants arrived in New York, Chicago, St. Louis, Philadelphia, and other northern cities, fled southern poverty and racism, with its poverty, inflation, boll weevil infestations, insecurity, and racial violence. The Lawrences had moved to New Jersey where Jacob was born on September 7, 1917. But they separated when they moved from Easton, Pennsylvania, to Philadelphia. Eventually Rose Lee Lawrence and her children went alone to Harlem.

Mrs. Lawrence, a hardworking single mother, enrolled Jacob in WPA-sponsored, after-school art classes at Utopia House, where the painter Charles Alston was teaching, and in crafts classes held at the 135th Street branch of the New York Public Library. By 1935, the nineteen-year-old Lawrence began to study at Alston's Harlem Workshop and the American Artists School, where he was given a two-year tuition scholarship. There he studied with Anton Refregier, Sol Wilson, Philip Reisman, and Eugene Morely. Among the older African-American artists, the sculptor Augusta Savage, who had just returned from Paris, took an interest in Lawrence's work and arranged for his employment at the Federal Arts Project.

The thirties and forties were a unique period in the production of American art. For the first time, the government actively supported the arts through President Franklin Roosevelt's Federal Arts Project (FAP), part of the Works Progress Administration (WPA). Black artists were given the opportunity to practice their art full-time. They were assigned teaching, restoration, and manual work in the cultural centers developing in neighborhoods such as Harlem. Charles Alston's experience was typical: He was commissioned to work on the Harlem Hospital murals; he was an active member of the Harlem Artists Guild, a group founded in 1935 to ensure black representation in artists' relief agencies; and he taught at Utopia Settlement House, which provided after-school programs for children. Lawrence, too, matured as an artist while working in the easel division of an FAP program. While working together in these projects, white and black artists, on the verge of success, met regularly to exchange ideas in an atmosphere crackling with creative electricity. Lawrence often said that this period was formative for him and that it fertilized his aesthetic vision.

In 1937, Lawrence started to work on a series based on the life of Toussaint L'Ouverture, the liberator of Haiti. "I've always been interested in history," Lawrence once said, "but they never taught Negro history in the public schools. . . . It was never studied seriously like regular subjects." Lawrence's love of history, stoked by the black history clubs that flourished in Harlem, would result in several paintings dedicated to black historical themes. After a New York showing at the De Porres

If I have achieved a degree of success as a creative artist it is mainly due to the black experience which is our heritage—an experience which gives inspiration, motivation, and stimulation. I was inspired by the black esthetic by which we are surrounded; motivated to manipulate form, color, space, line, and texture to depict our life; and stimulated by the beauty, and poignancy of our environment.
—Jacob Lawrence

Interracial Center, his *Toussaint Series* traveled to the Baltimore Museum of Art in 1939 for the exhibition *Contemporary Negro Art*. During this period he also painted the *Harlem Series,* sixty vignettes of urban life. The Harlem scenes were included in a 1937 group exhibition of the Harlem Artists Guild, and later featured in his first solo exhibition, held the next year at the Harlem YMCA.

No artist before Jacob Lawrence had developed themes from African-American history. Each painting in Lawrence's series is framed by text. Because these pictorial narratives required a great deal of historical research, Lawrence was a frequent visitor to the Schomburg Collection of the New York Public Library. In addition to the *Toussaint* and *Harlem Series* collections, Lawrence completed the *John Brown Series* (1941–1942), twenty-two paintings detailing the life of the militant white abolitionist, and the *Great Migration Series* (1940–1941). Other narrative depictions begun in that period and carried out to completion were *Frederick Douglass* (1938–1939), a series of 32 paintings, and *Harriet Tubman* (1939–1949), a series of 31 paintings. He pursued his work on both projects with backing from the Harmon Foundation.

But Lawrence's career really took off when Alain Locke, who had included Lawrence in his influential book *The Negro in Art* (1940), recommended him to the prominent New York art dealer Edith Halpert. She was so impressed with Lawrence she decided to give him a show at her Downtown Gallery. *Fortune* magazine reproduced twenty-six pictures from the *Migration Series* in its November 1941 issue, which brought the artist national acclaim. In the same year, Lawrence married a fellow artist whom he had met during his Harlem Workshop days, the talented Gwendolyn Knight.

During World War II, Lawrence was inducted into the U.S. Coast Guard in 1943 as a captain's steward aboard a segregated ship. Finding little time to paint, he requested a transfer. His captain assigned Lawrence to the USS *Sea Cloud,* the first integrated ship in the service, where he was promoted to public relations petty officer third class. In this position he had more time for his art and produced the stir-

1940–1949

ring fourteen-panel *War Series*. After the war, in 1946, Joseph Albers persuaded him to join the faculty of the Summer Institute of his experimental arts school at Black Mountain College, in Asheville, North Carolina. In 1947, *Fortune* commissioned his series on rural life in the postwar South, and a year later he illustrated the book *One Way Ticket* by Langston Hughes.

Despite these successes, his mental health suffered. Lawrence spent a year of voluntary confinement at Hillside Hospital in Queens for psychiatric treatment in 1949. He experienced depression, the result of the constant struggle to remain sane in a racist America. He used the opportunity to paint a *Hospital Series* of eleven panels, which was exhibited at the Downtown Gallery the next year. Fully recovered, he painted his *Theater* series in 1952. Influenced by his childhood experiences at the Apollo Theater, this series curiously included the most abstract compositions of his entire oeuvre.

In the summer of 1954, Lawrence taught at the Skowhegan School of Painting and Sculpture in Maine. From 1955 to 1970, he taught at Pratt Institute in Brooklyn. In 1971, Lawrence was awarded a full professorship at the University of Washington in Seattle, a position that he held until his retirement in 1986. More important, Lawrence continued to produce magnificent works of art. During the civil rights movement, he painted thirty panels of a projected sixty-panel series entitled *Struggle: From the History of the American People*. He and his wife lived in Nigeria, where he painted local market scenes.

Throughout the 1970s, Lawrence was busier than ever: He completed the *George Washington Bush Series* for the state of Washington in 1973, celebrating a black pioneer in the West. He began work on the *Builders Series,* paintings showing themes of the strength and perseverance of African-American communities. He designed *Time* magazine covers of Jesse Jackson and Colonel Ojukwu, the military governor of Biafra. He also designed a poster for the 1972 Olympic Games. His murals on the themes of sports and work can be found throughout America.

Before his death in Seattle on June 6, 2000, Jacob Lawrence had received a number of honors for a lifetime of artistic contributions. In 1990 he received the National Medal of Arts. In 1994, he was inducted into the American Academy of Arts and Letters. He is admired for being the first black visual artist to make African-American historical traditions the subject matter of his art. A master craftsman and practitioner of form, he has borne aesthetic witness to the great black past.

THE
INSTITUTE OF MODERN ART
138 NEWBURY STREET, BOSTON 16

FOUR MODERN
AMERICAN
PAINTERS

Peter Blume
"Vision Realist"

Stuart Davis
"Pure American Abstractions"

Marsden Hartley
"Intellectual Experiment..."

Jacob Lawrence
"Narrator of Negro Life"

2 Until APRIL 1, 1945

Adam Clayton Powell, Jr.

King of Harlem
(1908–1972)

Adam Clayton Powell, Jr. brought Harlem to Congress. Minister, politician, and public figure, Powell forced the city, state, and federal governments to make room for African Americans and their representatives. He was born on November 29, 1908, in New Haven, Connecticut, where his father was a student at the Yale Divinity School. When the younger Powell was just a baby, Adam Clayton Powell, Sr., was called to lead the Abyssinian Baptist Church, then located in midtown Manhattan's tenderloin district. Powell, Sr., energized his congregation and soon moved it to Harlem, where real estate was less expensive and where Harlem rapidly was becoming the heart and soul of black America.

Blond as a child, Adam Clayton Powell, Jr., grew up aware that he could pass for white. Both his parents had fair complexions, and outside of Harlem young Powell was often assumed to be white. He grew into a tall and handsome youth, very much interested in girls and considered a bit wild for a minister's son. After excelling at Townsend Harris Hall, a private high school, Powell enrolled at New York's City College in the fall of 1925. But the lure of nightlife and women derailed his studies, and after two semesters the senior Powell pressured his son to start over in less distracting circumstances. Powell entered Colgate University, an overwhelmingly white school in rural Hamilton, New York, in 1926. There, he weathered an awkward first year. His classmates were not sure of his race, and he nearly faced disaster for dating white women, but he went on to befriend his fellow black students and to win both academic and social acclaim.

After graduating in 1930—and taking a tour to Africa and the Near East, courtesy of his father—Powell returned to Harlem, planning to study at Union Theological Seminary and eventually to assume his father's Abyssinian pulpit. But politics intervened; Powell joined in local protests against alleged underfunding and

racism at Harlem Hospital and soon established himself as a formidable negotiator. Tapped to lead an insurgent New York mayoral campaign against Tammany Hall cronyism, Powell distinguished himself as a shrewd political strategist. He became an activist minister, establishing food banks for a growing constituency of weary Harlemites then struggling against the Great Depression. He succeeded his father as Abyssinian's senior minister in 1937 and launched a campaign of picketing and boycotts against white-owned Harlem businesses which would not hire blacks.

I am the product of the sustained indignation of a branded grandfather, the militant protest of my grandmother, the disciplined resentment of my father and mother, and the power of the mass action of the church.
—Adam Clayton Powell, Jr.

Elected to the New York City Council in 1941, Powell immediately began campaigning for an office that did not yet exist: a proposed congressional district that finally would give Harlem residents a chance at representation. Powell established himself as the leading candidate almost three years before the new district's first election in 1944. Powell also launched the *People's Voice,* a newspaper he published and edited, raiding the *Amsterdam News* for reporters and columnists. Against tepid Democratic and Republican opposition, Powell notched a decisive win, not only helping integrate the mostly lily-white Congress but also signaling the beginning of the end of white ethnic domination in New York politics.

Powell arrived in Washington a celebrity. He and second wife, Hazel Scott, the gifted pianist, were seen as black royalty: gorgeous, sophisticated, and effortlessly charming. But conquering the byzantine, tradition-bound world of the House of Representatives was not so easy. Still, Powell made his presence known by writing an amendment, which could be attached to nearly any spending bill, that would deprive federal monies to any state that continued to practice racial discrimination. The Powell Amendment was representative of its author's political savvy, and of the weakness of his position: The bill tended to expose liberal hypocrisy, but at the same time made some valuable bills vulnerable to quick defeat by the ruling Dixiecrats, right-wing segregationist southern Democrats who ruled Congress.

Throughout the 1940s and 1950s Powell climbed in seniority, voting his conscience but also playing tough politics. Cognizant of his power to deliver black votes, he held national candidates' feet to the fire over racial issues, punishing fellow Democrats such as Adlai Stevenson for their apparent weakness on civil rights. Despite some unease, he supported Kennedy's presidential campaign in 1960, the same election that found him gaining the chairmanship of the powerful House Education and Labor Committee. Powell soon became known as a brilliant, powerful chair, helping push through legislation increasing the minimum wage, establishing Head Start and other social programs, and creating the Office of Economic Opportunity, a Great Society jobs program.

At the same time, Powell attracted enormous controversy. His outsized romantic life—he left his second wife for a third but continued to have affairs—drew criticism, as did his personal dandyism and self-promotion. More important, Powell's arrogance offended civil rights leaders: Those he hadn't upstaged, he often criticized publicly. "The time has come for the Negro to close ranks," Powell had declared while speaking at his alma mater in 1938. By 1963, however, he found himself so distrusted by the mainstream black leadership that he was not invited to speak at the March on Washington organized by Bayard Rustin and A. Philip Randolph. In 1966, Powell found himself removed from the House for a constellation of alleged improprieties—including a longstanding warrant for his arrest in Manhattan over nonpayment of a libel suit settlement, along with allegations of misuse of government funds to bankroll pleasure trips. Powell may or may not have been as guilty of such charges as white members of Congress, but they were determined to punish him for refusing to keep his "place."

Powell had been in trouble before, successfully quashing persecution for tax charges in the 1950s, but this battle was dire. Friends and associates were called before a congressional committee investigating the charges, while Powell remained in seclusion on the island of Bimini. Here he held court with visiting members of the new guard, young black power leaders, who admired his courage and independence. In absentia, he won the special election to fill his seat in 1967; campaigning little, he won the regular election in 1968. But he returned to Congress stripped of his seniority and facing a hefty fine for his supposed misdeeds. Appealing to the U.S. Supreme Court, Powell won a decision that a duly elected representative could not be removed from his seat, but he did not regain his committee chairmanship, which was what congressional conservatives wanted.

Ailing and increasingly left behind by a changing Harlem, Powell lost in the Democratic primary of 1970 to Charles Rangel, who went on to win the general election and has held the seat ever since. Powell stepped down from the Abyssinian pulpit in 1971 and returned to Bimini, where he fished and sailed, drinking nights at a bar called The End of the World. He died April 4, 1972. They brought him back to Harlem, where more than one hundred thousand people filed past his coffin in to pay final respects to the man who had put Harlem—and black Americans—on the political map.

A. Philip Randolph

Union Man
(1889–1979)

Asa Philip Randolph has been called the prophet of the civil rights movement. As a union leader, magazine editor, and grassroots activist, he campaigned for decades for economic equality. A master strategist when it came to collective bargaining and the power of nonviolent protest, his influence extended from the Pullman porters in the 1930s to the 1963 March on Washington.

Born in 1889, Randolph grew up in Florida, the son of a preacher. After graduating as class valedictorian in 1907 from Cookman Institute, a segregated high school, he worked a string of menial jobs. In 1911 he moved to New York. Good jobs were hard to find there as well, and he worked as an elevator operator while continuing his education at City College and pursuing his first career dream: acting. In the end, his rich, deep voice would grace not theater stages but union halls and political rallies.

Randolph's political education began in Harlem, which was bursting with new migrants from the Carribean and the rural South. He joined the Socialist party, and in 1914 met Chandler Owen, a student at Columbia University whose politics mirrored his own. At first, the two spread their message by means of street-corner oratory. In 1917 they founded the *Messenger*, a radical magazine whose editorials took unpopular stands on a variety of topics, such as urging African Americans to oppose America's entry into World War I.

Economic justice was at the heart of Randolph's philosophy, and the year 1925 saw the start of his struggle for it. His opposition was the Pullman Company, which ran the dining and sleeping cars on railroads across the nation. Pullman prided itself on its elegant black porters, some of them college men and leaders in their communities, who performed acts of menial servitude for white customers. For years Pullman had ignored the porters' efforts to improve their working conditions, rectify a racist pay scale, and obtain the opportunity for career advancement. An official Pullman "union," founded by the company, effectively squelched real change.

Attracted by Randolph's political views, his reputation as a fighter, his formidable skills as a speaker, and his independence from Pullman (and therefore his freedom from direct economic reprisals), a group of porters asked him to represent them in their efforts. The Brotherhood of Sleeping Car Porters (BSCP) was launched in August 1925 and faced immediate opposition not only from Pullman brass, who spied on meetings

> *Salvation for a race, nation, or class must come from within. Freedom is never granted; it is won. Justice is never given; it is exacted. Freedom and justice must be struggled for by the oppressed of all lands and races, and the struggle must be continuous.*
> —A. Philip Randolph

and threatened and fired workers, but from many established African-American leaders. Black anti-BSCP sentiments stemmed from various sources: the bitter history of racist white unions, which had convinced some that management was a better friend than labor; the position of Pullman, in the dismal context of the times, as the largest and best employer of black men; and Randolph's own political background, which sparked fears of communist co-optation of black politics and activism.

Randolph waged a ten-year campaign to win official recognition of the BSCP, which in 1937 negotiated its first contract with Pullman. His growing influence as a labor leader carried him into his next arena, fighting for increased opportunities for black workers nationwide. After a stint as president of the National Negro Congress, Randolph took on the White House. Together with Walter White of the NAACP and T. Arnold Hill of the National Urban League, he pressured President Franklin D. Roosevelt to integrate both the growing defense industry, which was gearing up in advance of U.S. entry into World War II, and the nation's military. When Roosevelt waffled, Randolph threatened a march on Washington in the summer of 1941, a mass demonstration in support of equal opportunity. The threat worked in part; Roosevelt did not desegregate the armed forces, but he did sign Executive Order 8002, which integrated jobs within the war industry and established a Fair Employment Practices Committee.

Randolph continued pressuring government to integrate the military. In 1947 he established the Committee Against Jim Crow in Military Service and Training, which asked blacks to refuse to register for the draft or to refuse to report if draft-

1940–1949

ed. The committee's campaign of nonviolent civil disobedience, along with Randolph's persistent pressure, finally met with success when President Harry S. Truman signed Executive Order 9981 in July 1948, which desegregated the armed forces. Randolph continued his union work, agitating against racism within the American Federation of Labor, the BSCP's parent union. When the AFL merged with the Council of Industrial Organizations to form the AFL-CIO in 1955, Randolph became the federation's vice president, a post he held until 1968.

Serving as a bridge between black leaders of different and sometimes contentious camps, in 1963 Randolph revived his March on Washington movement. He asked Bayard Rustin to assist him in organizing a massive demonstration of African Americans seeking equality and freedom in both the political and economic arenas. Coming after a decade of battling for civil rights, the 1963 March on Washington focused on political issues—mainly segregation and voting—but Randolph saw to it that its official name included the phrase "jobs and freedom." The two were inextricably tied together, in his view. On August 28, 1963, Randolph saw his vision realized: the largest demonstration of the civil rights movement featured Martin Luther King, Jr., delivering his "I Have a Dream" speech to a peaceful crowd of 250,000 and ended with a visit to the White House. Within the next two years President Lyndon B. Johnson signed the 1964 Civil Rights Act and the 1965 Voting Rights Act.

His advancing years slowed but did not stop Randolph, who founded the A. Philip Randolph Institute, a training and employment organization based in Harlem. He was awarded the Presidential Medal of Freedom in 1964. He died in 1979. Many who came of age after the civil rights movement have forgotten his influence and his legacy—but we honor the memory of this "messenger" of economic and racial justice. Randolph saw that civil and economic rights were

inseparable. He left us a powerful message: "Salvation for a race, nation, or class must come from within. Freedom is never granted; it is won. Justice is never given; it is exacted. Freedom and justice must be struggled for by the oppressed of all lands and races, and the struggle must be continuous."

Jackie Robinson

The Chosen One
(1919–1972)

Jackie Robinson broke the color line in baseball. To tell that story again is to relive one of the greatest moral achievements of this country, but Robinson was, in a way, sacrificed. Branch Rickey, who signed him into the all-white Brooklyn Dodgers, sacrificed Robinson to his noble experiment, and he was ultimately a sacrifice for the race. Blacks had always played baseball. We had our own Negro Baseball Leagues from the end of the 1880s to the early 1960s. And those Negro Leagues are the stuff of legend and romance among black writers and the folk who witnessed the great heroes play. From the fertile ground of our own microcosmic baseball world came the truly great, such as Satchel Paige and, of course, Jackie Robinson. The paradox of integration was that so many integral black social and cultural institutions would be condemned to disappear. In baseball, for instance, when blacks entered the major leagues the inevitable happened: the old Negro League lost money and its fans because sooner or later the better players were being siphoned off to the majors. Roy Campanella joined Jackie Robinson in Brooklyn, and Satchel Paige, the Negro League pitcher, was hired by the Cleveland Indians. The Negro National League shut down in 1948, and the remaining clubs joined the new Negro American League, which at that time had two divisions, but which was also destined to fail.

For all the romance about the leagues, though, they were arduous for players and fans alike. The leagues were poor, and their players were forced to work for meager salaries. Jackie Robinson, who was with the Kansas City Monarchs, could not wait to get out. There was also the political and social reality that any national sport, such as American baseball, must recognize its team players as citizens. The Negro Leagues reminded us that we were not. Making matters worse, blacks and whites once played together as equals, after the Civil War. Among many others, infielder Bud Fowler, who played with an all-white team at New Castle, Pennsylvania, in 1873, and Moses "Fleetwood" Walker, who caught forty-one games for the Ohio Metropolis, were legendary among black baseball fans.

Robinson had been an athletic star since high school in Pasadena's John Muir High School in California, where he moved with his mother and siblings from Georgia. In 1940, Robinson entered the University of California–Los Angeles (UCLA), where he was the first man in the school's history to earn varsity letters in four sports: football, track and field, broad jump, and basketball. In 1941, he had become the assistant athletic director of the National Youth Administration Camp in Atascadero, California, playing semiprofessional football with the Los Angeles Bulldogs throughout the year. After an unhappy military experience fighting the racism of the U.S. Army, Robinson returned home looking for a job. By chance the Kansas City Monarchs of the Negro National League were looking for players. Robinson found himself in the world of professional baseball.

In the same decade, national baseball was changing. A Kentucky politician named Albert Benjamin "Happy" Chandler finally replaced Kenesaw Mountain Landis, the most racist commissioner that baseball had ever seen. Landis had refused consistently and vigorously to allow club owners to scout for black baseball players, even though, ultimately, that was what most wished to do. Branch Rickey, the president, part owner, and general manager of the Brooklyn Dodgers, believed that the greatest untapped reservoir of raw material in the history of the game lay in its potential black players. Rickey's economic motives for integration were supplemented by his religious background as a former Methodist lay preacher.

Rickey set out to find the player who could be the chosen one to break the color barrier. He found a young army private from Cairo, Georgia, recently discharged, and once court-martialed for refusing to sit in the back of an army bus. Robinson was also the star player with the Kansas City Monarchs. When he finally met Branch Rickey, the coach reenacted the insults and abuse Robinson would be exposed to if he were hired. Robinson listened patiently, and at the end inquired whether what Rickey wanted so desperately was a timid black ballplayer, one who was afraid to fight back. Rickey answered, "I *want* a ballplayer with enough guts *not* to fight back." Robinson accepted the challenge. He knew that this was an old civil rights strategy used by black protesters since the beginning of the century. It was an approach that presaged the Gandhian techniques of Martin Luther King's nonviolence campaign. Not every person could do it. But Robinson could and did. It was agreed that he would first be signed to the Montreal Royals, the Dodgers' AAA farm club. If he did well with them, he would be signed by the Brooklyn Dodgers.

In his first game for Montreal on April 18, 1946, Robinson endured slights, taunts, slurs, and ridicule. He also got four hits, including a three-run homer, stole two bases, and scored twice by provoking the pitcher to balk. The whole season was painfully difficult, and by the season's end Robinson had severe stomach pains and was on the brink of a nervous breakdown. But Robinson's record in batting and runs scored was at the head of the Class AAA International League. He led the Royals to the league championship and then to victory in the Little World Series with utter dignity. Through it all, Robinson, with the support of his wife, Rachel, valiantly kept his promise not to strike back against his tormentors.

The following year, on April 9, 1947, Branch Rickey announced that Robinson had officially been signed to play first base for the Brooklyn Dodgers. Robinson's entry into the white major leagues immediately drew a storm of controversy. Some coaches and fellow players vehemently opposed it—as did many white fans of the national pastime. Within the Dodger organization several players objected, circulating a petition to exclude him. In response, the manager, Leo Durocher, told the protesting players that they could leave. They didn't.

Nobody on the team left. In fact, they got tired of all the racial invective themselves, and after one vicious game against the St. Louis Cardinals, when player Enos Slaughter deliberately jumped in the air and sliced open Robinson's thigh with his spikes, they began to rally around and support him. Robinson went on to earn the Rookie of the Year award in 1947, with a .297 batting average and a league-leading twenty-nine stolen bases. In 1949 he won the Most Valuable Player award. During his ten seasons with the Dodgers, Robinson batted .311, led the team to six pennants and one World Series Championship. By so doing, he helped bring down racial barriers in other team sports as well. For his outstanding performance and lasting example, he was inducted into the National Baseball Hall of Fame in 1962.

After he retired, he refused to attend games or play in old-timers' games because of the dearth of blacks in nonplaying roles. Robinson became extremely vocal and fully engaged in the struggle for integration and black self-improvement, supporting mostly conservative means for improving the conditions of African Americans. He was a staunch Republican who supported Richard Nixon in his unsuccessful 1960 presidential race against John F. Kennedy.

Change came slowly to baseball, but it did come: In 1950, only five major league teams had black players: the Dodgers, the Giants, the St. Louis Browns, the Indians, and the Braves. But by 1959, when the Boston Red Sox added Elijah "Pumpsie" Green to their club, total integration was complete. Times had indeed changed. And surely the year that Jackie Robinson opened the season at first base for the Brooklyn Dodgers opened up a whole new world for black ballplayers in America, as well as for African Americans in their long march toward civil rights. Robinson died of a heart attack on October 24, 1972, his final request, forever striving for advancement, broadcast from the World Series to viewers across the nation nine days earlier: "I'd like to live to see a black manager."

> I don't know anyone who could have stuck all the abuse Jackie had to take in breaking into baseball and stuck it out to become the great player he was. When you know the true nature of Jackie . . . what a fighter he was and how he had to keep it inside of him . . . it's just unbelievable. Thinking back on it, I'm just glad I got to play alongside Jackie and be part of a history.
> —Pee Wee Reese

1940–1949

Richard Wright

Inside-Outsider
(1908–1960)

He gave a voice to the voiceless. Richard Wright was the first commercially successful black novelist, and the first to unveil the terrors of ghetto life. Richard Wright's life and work are marked both by success and excess. Consider the strange case of the filming of his most influential book, *Native Son,* first published in 1940. After seeing his novel climb the best-seller list, and after fielding offers for the film rights to the book, notably from Orson Welles, Wright decided that not only would he make the film himself, but he would play the central role of Bigger Thomas. Wright was then in his thirties, and having led the often sedentary life of a writer, he had few of the physical qualities, not to mention the acting skill, for the role of the young, virile, and violent Bigger. The film was a grand failure both financially and aesthetically, and Wright did not live to see his novel produced again for the screen.

This incident captures both the tragedy and the triumph that marked Richard Wright's life. For all the troubles he encountered—whether from racist whites as a boy growing up in the South or narrow-minded ideologues in the Communist party— much of Wright's conflict was internal. His greatest desire was to be considered among the most accomplished writers of his time, and yet political expression sometimes limited his craft. His preoccupation, until his death, was the life of blacks in America, and yet he spent his last years in a kind of self-imposed exile in France. Throughout his life he remained a kind of inside-outsider, at once intimately associated with his fellow African Americans and guardedly isolated in many other ways. To understand Wright is to understand these contradictions in black American life itself.

Richard Nathaniel Wright was born in Roxie, Mississippi, a rural outskirt of Natchez, on September 4, 1908. His father, a sharecropper who drank heavily, left his mother, a former schoolteacher, when Wright was only six years old. Wright recounts the early troubles of his youth in *Black Boy* and *American Hunger,* as his mother moved from job to job and town to town in order to support her two boys. After his mother suffered a stroke in 1919, Wright was sent to live with his grandmother, a sternly religious woman who was disapproving of Wright's literary inclinations. This childhood of want, hunger, and restriction molded Wright's aesthetic. One can see throughout his work a marked wariness of religion and an overall bareness of possibility in interpersonal connection. Rarely in Wright's work does one see love, between man and woman, father and son.

Wright attended school until the ninth grade before leaving for Memphis, Tennessee. As a boy, in 1924, he published his first piece of fiction, "The Voodoo of Hell's Half-Acre," in the Jackson *Southern Register,* the local black newspaper. Wright soon began to read widely, after discovering H. L. Mencken, Fyodor Dostoyevsky, Sinclair Lewis, Sherwood Anderson, and Theodore Dreiser. These realistic writers later would form something of Wright's literary pantheon of influences; they have a palpable presence in his work.

From Memphis, Wright moved north to Chicago in 1927, following the path of the great migration. He soon found a job as a postal clerk and continued his self-education in the craft of fiction. At this same time, Wright became intrigued by the Communist party, which he joined in 1933 and from which he resigned in disillusionment in 1944. As an active participant in the John Reed Club, an organization of leftist writers, Wright began to create in earnest. In 1935 he finished the manuscript *Cesspool,* a novel inspired by the modernist innovations of James Joyce. It portrays a day in the life of a Chicago postal employee; it appeared posthumously as *Lawd Today* (1963). In that same year, he began to work for the Federal Writers Project, writing travel guides and collecting folklore in Chicago and Harlem.

Wright emerged on the national literary scene in 1938 with the publication of *Uncle Tom's Children,* a collection of novellas detailing experiences of racial oppression in the South. And while he would later look back critically at this collection—he never wanted to write, he said, a book that a white woman could have a good cry over and then forget—pieces like "Long Black Song" remain among the most emotionally evocative prose in his entire oeuvre.

Wright's grandest popular success came in 1940. *Native Son* was chosen by the

Book-of-the-Month Club as a main selection, the first-ever such distinction for an African-American author. It sold a quarter of a million copies in the first year and would remain a best-seller for months. The novel centers on Bigger Thomas, a young black man from the South Side of Chicago who is trapped within the constraints of an oppressive white social structure and is caught within the limitations of his own nihilist vision of possibility. The bleakness of the novel, its violence and lack of feeling, stands in clear and deliberate contrast to Wright's previous work. He wanted to write a character that no one could find cathartic, he would say. Inspired by the naturalism of writers such as Dreiser, Wright's novel takes up the fictive challenge of creating protest fiction that avoids sympathy and banal sentimentality. While critics, notably Ralph Ellison and James Baldwin, decried the limitations of Wright's expression, the novel retains a force that has solidified its place in the African-American literary tradition and in the American literary canon.

Wright saw his composition of *Native Son* as, above all, a radical work of truth telling. "Just as a man rises in the mornings to dig ditches for his bread, so I'd work daily," Wright recalled. "I'd think of some abstract principle of Bigger's conduct and at once my mind would turn it into some act I'd seen Bigger perform, some act which I hoped would be familiar enough to the American reader to gain his credence. But in the writing of scene after scene I was guided by but one criterion: to tell the truth as I saw it and felt it." Wright offered in prose a vision of experience that had never quite been expressed to date in African-American literature. He offered something that was not the only truth, but rather a single unvarnished truth of the experience of racial oppression and the black nihilism that grows up in the face of it.

Wright followed *Native Son* in 1945 with another best-seller, *Black Boy,* a semi-autobiographical account of his youth in the South, another Book-of-the-Month Club selection. The commercial success of these early works afforded him the luxury of traveling to Europe, and in 1947 he migrated with his family, his daughters and his second white wife, Ellen, to France, where he remained for the rest of his life. The migration amounted to a renunciation of American racism and a profound pessimism about America's potential for change. In France he explored a range of philosophical and ideological stances, from existentialism to psychoanalysis to Pan-Africanism.

While in Paris, Wright struck up an acquaintance with Jean-Paul Sartre and Simone de Beauvoir and began a correspondence with Frantz Fanon. These philosophical explorations are apparent in the three novels Wright produced there: *The Outsider* (1953), *Savage Holiday* (1954), and *The Long Dream* (1958). While these novels failed to receive the popular acclaim of his early works, they nonetheless display an expansion of Wright's craft in a number of directions. Along with his nonfiction publications, *The Color Curtain* (1956), *Pagan Spain* (1957), and *White Man, Listen!* (1957), Wright displays a sense of urgency about the crises of racism, fascism, and colonialism.

Perhaps Ralph Ellison, Wright's part-time adversary and full-time friend, offers the best summation of Wright's career in his moving essay "Remembering Richard Wright":

Richard Wright was trying to add to our consciousness the dimension of being a black boy who grew up and who achieved through his reading a sense of what was possible out there in the wider world. A boy who grew up and achieved and accepted his own individual responsibility for seeing to it that America became conscious of itself. He insisted that this country recognize the interconnectedness between its places and its personalities, its acts and its ideals. This was the burden of Richard Wright, and, as I see it, the driving passion of Richard Wright.

1940–1949

While Wright's success with naturalism generated a school of writers directly descended from *Native Son,* only Ann Petry's *The Street* rivaled its power and effect, as if Wright's achievement had exhausted the potentiality of the form. Nevertheless, so great was Wright's literary triumph that the period in African-American literary history between 1940 and 1960 can be thought of as the age of Richard Wright.

Ralph Bunche

The International Diplomat
(1904–1971)

The first African American to win the Nobel Peace Prize, Ralph Bunche was a man of, and for, the world. Throughout his life Bunche was concerned with social justice and moral engagement in the international and national arenas. Some criticized his diplomatic political style as too naïve, given the entrenchment of racial antipathy in America. But this was a man who sat with Israelis and Palestinians, with Egyptians and Cypriots, brokering agreements between warring factions where peace was thought impossible.

A charismatic figure, often seen with a cigarette hanging from his mouth, his brow knit in deep concentration, Bunche seemed to glide over boundaries with tremendous ease. He managed to accomplish several firsts in his lifetime, but his role in three initiatives tower above the rest: He negotiated the Israeli–Palestinian armistice of 1949, for which he was awarded the Nobel Peace Prize. He designed United Nations international peacekeeping strategies during the turbulent Cold War years of the fifties and sixties. And at home, he worked tirelessly for black civil rights, where he always urged peaceful strategies in the pursuit of justice.

Bunche always worked through mainstream mechanisms and always opposed separatism in any form, applying democratic and inclusive principles to his work with the United Nations, as well as to his political activities in the United States. Peace, more than any other ideal, inspired his sense of duty to mankind. During the sixties, Malcom X, Stokely Carmichael, and Adam Clayton Powell sometimes called into question Bunche's commitment to civil rights, believing that his international stature compromised his passion for the plight of African Americans. But far from abandoning his people, Bunche served as advisor to several civil rights organizations. More visibly he joined Martin Luther King, Jr., in the 1965 Selma-to-Montgomery

Voting Rights March. At heart, however, Bunche was an international statesman who devoted himself to the skillful grace of diplomacy and negotiation, and it was on the world stage that he made his presence most felt.

Bunche was born in Detroit, Michigan, on August 7, 1904, but his earliest years were divided between Detroit and Albuquerque, New Mexico. Orphaned at thir-

teen years old, when his mother died of tuberculosis and his father abandoned the family, Bunche spent his later youth living in Los Angeles with his maternal grandmother, Lucy Johnson. Graduating from Jefferson High School in 1922, he attended the University of California at Los Angeles, where he wrote for the campus newspaper and graduated valedictorian of his class in 1927. Bunche promptly entered Harvard University, where, in 1936, he became the first black American to earn a Ph.D. degree in government from an American university. While still pursuing his doctoral research, Bunche taught at Howard, where he founded and chaired the university's political science department.

The African-American Century

Bunche was an unusually productive scholar. While teaching political science at Howard, he conducted postdoctoral research on African colonialism, and at one point worked closely with anthropologist Melville Herskowitz at Northwestern University. He also studied at the London School of Economics and at the University of Cape Town, under the harsh conditions of South Africa's apartheid regime. Reputedly he spent much of his time in Cape Town, giving encouragement to Africans.

Bunche immersed himself in issues of racial equality, civil rights, and decolonization—radical causes he closely identified with throughout his career. He also established the National Negro Congress, a forum for debate between young black scholars and older faculty about the stereotypes and representations of race. In 1944 Bunche collaborated with W. E. B. Du Bois, Allison Davis, St. Clair Drake, E. Franklin Frazier, Charles S. Johnson, and Kenneth Clark on Swedish sociologist Gunnar Myrdal's *An American Dilemma: The Negro Problem and Modern Democracy* (1944), a seminal work that framed intellectual debates about race relations for the next twenty years. For the study, Bunche conducted fieldwork in the South and wrote four monographs, the last of which was published in 1973 as *The Political Status of the Negro in the Age of FDR*.

Unable to fight during World War II due to a football injury, Bunche joined the Office of Strategic Services (OSS), the predecessor of today's Central Intelligence Agency (CIA), as a senior analyst. In 1947 he became chief of the Africa section in the U. S. State Department. He participated in the Dumbarton Oaks Conference, which laid the groundwork for the UN Charter. At this conference, Bunche put into practice the principle of trusteeship, which created a schedule for African colonial independence. Africans viewed it as a compromise that served only the interests of the established system. Bunche, a pragmatist, successfully argued that a gradual movement toward independence was the most feasible available option. Impressed by Bunche's negotiating skills and diplomatic finesse, the first secretary general, Trygve Lie, asked him to work permanently for the United Nations. Bunche served as the principal director of the Department of Trusteeship and Information for the Non-Self-Governing Territories from 1947 to 1954, a post that enabled him to assist more fully with the process of decolonization.

In 1948, Bunche was sent to Jerusalem to assist UN mediator Count Folke Bernadotte, in the attempt to find a peaceful resolution of the Arab-Israeli conflict over the legitimacy of the new Israeli state. The inexperienced Bunche was thrust suddenly to the center stage in 1949, when Bernadotte was assassinated by Israeli terrorists. He rose to the challenge and worked almost single-handedly to bring Israel and the Arab states to a truce.

At the height of the Cold War in 1955, Bunche was appointed UN Under-secretary for Special Political Affairs, a post from which he supervised UN peace-keeping operations in some of the most heated conflicts around the world. In Egypt, during the Suez Canal Crisis of 1956, he was responsible for mobilizing six thousand UN emergency troops to supervise the Egypt-Israeli border for eleven years. For his role in creating the unprecedented United Nations Emergency Force, Sir Brian Urquhart, Bunche's successor and biographer, called him the "original principal architect" of the concept of international peacekeeping. Bunche also represented the UN during crises in the Republic of the Congo, Cyprus, India, Pakistan, and Yemen.

Bunche received several honors in his lifetime. Before he was awarded the Nobel Peace Prize in 1950, he was awarded the Spingarn medal in 1949 and elected the first black president of the American Political Science Association in 1953. The following year he received the Theodore Roosevelt Association Medal. In 1963, President John F. Kennedy awarded Bunche the nation's highest civilian honor, the Medal of Freedom. Just one year after retiring, Bunche died in New York in 1971. A man who was able to affect more profound change on foreign soil than at home, Bunche remained a fervent believer in the possibility of racial equality in the United States. His academic and diplomatic career is one of the most distinguished in the history of this country.

Nat King Cole

The Suave Mellow Crooner
(1919–1965)

A virtuoso jazz pianist and trio leader, he sang his way into American living rooms in those white Eisenhower years. For years Nat "King" Cole was known mostly for his silky ballads, elegant style, and precise sense of melodic articulation. And he was magic—pure magic—in his ability to communicate the soul of a popular tune in his own distinctive way. Long after his death, Cole has been recognized as a great jazz and rhythm & blues artist. In 2000, he was inducted into the Rock and Roll Hall of Fame.

Cole was born Nathaniel Adams Coles (he later dropped the "s") in 1919 in Montgomery, Alabama. Like so many others, his family moved from the South to Chicago in the 1920s. By age twelve he was singing and playing the organ for his father, the minister of the True Light Baptist Church, and he soon began playing piano for his brother Eddie's jazz band, the Rogues of Rhythm. Cole broke into Chicago's jazz establishment at just sixteen, playing against his hero, Earl "Fatha" Hines, in a 1935 battle of the bands at the Savoy Ballroom. Hines was a touchstone and a lasting influence. As a result of the challenge posed by Hines's work, according to one critic, Cole became "the pianist who in the late thirties and early forties creat[ed] the link between the Golden Age of Jazz and the bebop era."

In 1936 Cole hit the road as band director on a touring revival of Noble Sissle and Eubie Blake's *Shuffle Along.* His great innovation came the next year, and it came by accident. Staying in Los Angeles when the tour ended, Cole took a nightclub gig. The club owner could pay for a small combo—piano, guitar, bass, and drum— but the drummer dropped out. With his guitarist, Oscar Moore, and bassist, Wesley Prince, Cole crafted his trio into a tight, exciting band that managed to swing rhythmically without a drum.

Along the way Cole, who at that point had done vocals only on novelty songs, began singing seriously. His vocal talents were highlighted most notably in the 1940 song "Sweet Lorraine." The band's first hit came in 1943 with "Straighten Up and Fly Right," followed by Cole's first R & B hit "(Get Your Kicks On) Route 66" in 1946, which music historians view as an important precursor to rock and roll. *Down Beat* magazine named the trio the best small combo every year from 1944 to 1947; Cole won an *Esquire* magazine award for best jazz artist in 1946.

By the mid-1940s, Cole also had won the admiration and friendship of some of the biggest names in jazz, and played with such luminaries as Art Tatum, Oscar Peterson, Lester Young, and Illinois Jacquet. In 1944, he launched "Jazz at the Philharmonic," an influential touring concert series. In the same year, Cole began appearing on a weekly radio series, foreshadowing his later celebrity on television. Based in Hollywood but touring relentlessly, Cole had built a stellar jazz career by 1950.

That year, the recording of a song he initially had not liked, "Mona Lisa," made Cole famous far beyond the world of jazz. The song reached number one on the pop charts and sold three million copies. It thrust Cole into his second career as a pop balladeer, "the man with the velvet voice." Songs such as "Unforgettable" and "The Christmas Song" became trademark numbers. Elegant and urbane, capable of appealing to white as well as black audiences, Cole became the first black artist to break into network television. *The Nat "King" Cole Show* debuted in 1956; it featured white and black guest artists, including rare nationwide appearances in that era by such genre-shaping musicians as Mahalia Jackson and Count Basie. But always fearful of offending white people, no white corporate sponsor would support the show, and it was canceled after sixty-four weeks.

Cole continued to tour widely, although audiences now requested his famous ballads more often than the innovative jazz he had pioneered in the 1930s. A long-time smoker, Cole died of lung cancer in 1965. But his influence lives: Musicians from Quincy Jones to vocalist Diana Krall count him among their heroes, and music historians point out that without Cole, a trailblazer, later black artists would have had much greater difficulty gaining access to the world of white acceptance and fame. "Nat told me there were two kinds of career paths for musicians," Quincy Jones wrote in an appreciation. "There was one that took you straight up to the top very quickly and burned you out just as fast. And there was another way, in which you just grew and studied and made your music better and better. . . . Nat always emphasized professionalism and longevity."

Cole really had two careers: as jazz pianist and pop vocalist. In the former he made real contributions, combining, as critic Bill Dabbius points out, Fatha Hines's intricate right hand with Count Basie's spare rhythmic left hand. Cole's career as mellow crooner, however, made him the most popular black entertainer following World War II, and most people will remember him best for this. Cole lived in a transitional time: His records sold millions, but nobody would sponsor his television show. He had thousands of fans everywhere, but he was beaten up by white supremacists on a Birmingham, Alabama, stage in 1956, performing for a whites-only audience. He contributed generously to the civil rights movement, but performed for segregated audiences. With the current rerelease of many of the Nat "King" Cole Trio records, and the "recording" of a magical virtual duet with his daughter Natalie in 1991, his gifts burn as brightly as when we first heard that jazz piano and that suave, smooth voice.

The African-American Century

Miles Davis

The Birth of the Cool
(1926–1992)

He gave birth to the cool, and to a whole new sound. The impact of Miles Davis on postwar jazz is unsurpassed. No other musician, besides Louis Armstrong and Duke Ellington, has had such an influence on the development of jazz as an art form or contributed so much to its evolution. For three decades Davis was not only an outstanding figure in nearly every major jazz movement, he also directed the changes: driving innovations in tone and texture, nurturing—in his own gruff way—the development of younger players, and constantly reinventing himself to avoid becoming part of the ossified, anachronistic, and sentimental museum. But his passion for unending invention was matched by a penchant for self-destruction. His genius may have been both fed and undone by his arrogance and lifestyle. In the end, it was perhaps these tensions that helped create his enduring body of work.

Miles Dewey Davis was born in Alton, Illinois, in 1926, but his family soon moved to the east side of St. Louis. Davis's father was a dentist and ranch owner who loved jazz. His mother was an exceptionally good, classically trained pianist who reportedly played a fierce blues—though she kept this a secret from her son until he was older. Davis was given a trumpet for his thirteenth birthday and began private lessons while playing in his high school band. Clearly superior to the white students he played with, he became embittered when the judges of school contests continually awarded prizes to them instead of him.

St. Louis trumpeter Clarke Terry was an early influence. Davis admired Terry's broad, warm tone. When he realized that the tone was created through a Heim mouthpiece, he began using one himself and kept using it throughout his career. As he listened to early recordings of Charlie Parker and Dizzy Gillespie, Davis realized that something was fomenting in New York City—a sound that couldn't be

matched by the laid-back style of St. Louis. When Bird and Diz came to St. Louis with Billy Eckstine's band, Davis got an opportunity that was a kind of epiphany. The band's trumpeter had become ill, and Davis offered to stand in for him. With this experience, he realized that he would never fulfill his parents' dream of joining the medical profession. In 1945 he moved to New York and began studying at the Juilliard School of Music.

Juilliard played only a minor role in his musical education, however. Initially devoted to his studies there, he began remedial classes at the jazz clubs of Manhattan, following Parker, his idol, from one club to the next. Though his playing was still tentative and immature, he performed with Bird on his early, classic recordings. His youthful idealization of Bird, however, led to disenchantment. Bird's heroin addiction made Parker callous, self-serving, and unreliable. Aware that his own aura in the jazz public was growing, Davis soon broke from Parker to pursue his own sound and style.

In many ways, Davis was ill-suited to the hard-driving sound of bebop. He teamed up with Canadian composer Gil Evans in what would become an enduring collaboration. Evans wanted to create a lush, multilayered sound, with less overt emphasis on rhythm and with impressionistic, sonic washes that would support, enhance, and provide counterpoint to a player's solo. *The Birth of the Cool,* a session recorded for Capitol, would emerge from this. Though now a classic, it was a commercial disaster. Audiences accustomed to the power of bebop found its atmospheric and moody landscapes unbearable. Davis was uncertain of the direction of his career, and financially unstable as well. Aware that white West Coast musicians had turned "the cool" into a commercially viable, if pallid and soulless, genre, he spent the next few years working to support his heroin habit.

In 1954, at the age of twenty-eight, Davis went cold turkey and became clean through an enormous power of will. The most productive period of his career now began with his 1955 performance of Thelonious Monk's "Round Midnight" at the Newport Jazz Festival. He hired the serious young saxophonist John Coltrane for his quartet, as well as the stellar young pianist Bill Evans and saxophonist Cannonball Adderley. He collaborated again with Gil Evans, producing *Miles Ahead, Porgy and Bess,* and *Sketches of Spain.* On the album *Milestones* he began experimenting with the space-inducing language of modal chord progressions. This style of playing would be perfected on the classic *Kind of Blue.* With one of the most cel-

1950–1959

ebrated groups of musicians in the history of jazz, Davis developed a whole new kind of modal improvisation that used scales rather than chord progressions as the starting point for solos. Improvising from only a skeletal architecture of the songs, the players created a masterpiece in one take. *Kind of Blue* became the best-selling jazz album of all time, and a critical success as well.

During this period, Davis became the best-known face of jazz, a vision of the artist turned pop star. He made the cover of *Time* and posed for *GQ*. His penchant for women, clothes, and fast cars turned the obtuse jazz musician into a new genre of celebrity sex object. He also developed a reputation for arrogance, partly because he refused to pander to the stereotypes and grotesque forms of showmanship that earlier black musicians were forced to perform. He invariably walked offstage after completing his solo. Coltrane left the Davis quartet in the 1960s to indulge in the radical experiments of free jazz, or the New Thing. Fearing his own obsolescence in the wake of these trends, and despising the antiformalist conceptualism of the New Thing, Davis sought a new direction. He adopted a more muscular, less minimalist sound that was influenced by the current group of younger players he assembled around him: Tony Williams, Ron Carter, Wayne Shorter, and Herbie Hancock. Shorter, with his brilliant compositional skills, was especially inspiring. The classic albums *Miles Smiles, Nefertiti,* and *ESP* were recorded by this group.

By the end of the 1960s Davis was ready for another new direction. Influenced by James Brown's funk and the acid-drenched electric blues of Jimi Hendrix, he turned increasingly to black pop formalism and embraced electric instruments. The albums from this period, both loved and hated, include *In A Silent Way, Down on the Corner, Bitches Brew,* and *Live/Evil*. Edgy, chaotic works, they became the foundational texts of jazz fusion. Some critics decried them as examples of Davis's restless entrepreneurism; others praised them as the future of the music. Supported by players such as Chick Corea and Joe Zawinul, they mapped out the landscape of jazz through the 1970s.

The era of jazz innovation that Davis had presided over came to an end with his experiments in jazz fusion. In the late 1970s he began using drugs again and became a recluse within the walls of his own home. Only a handful of friends visited him, and he rarely ever talked to them. By the mid-eighties, Davis reemerged from this isolation and tried to regain his former stature. He died in 1992—though his haunting sound still keeps us cool today.

Ralph Ellison

The True Native Son
(1914–1994)

Ralph Ellison wrote the novel that opened our eyes. At a Bard College symposium in 1953, Ralph Ellison, fresh from the publication of his debut novel *Invisible Man* (1952), sat at the seat of culture—dining with a distinguished group of novelists. One of the guests, the prolific mystery writer George Simenon, turned to the younger Ellison. "To be a novelist," he declared, "one must produce many novels. Ergo, you are not a novelist." Ellison's art proves this claim to be a lie.

By Simenon's reckoning, after forty years of articles, lectures, short stories, and countless manuscript pages, Ralph Ellison is still not a novelist. But at his death in 1994 he left a literary legacy that could well be sustained on the force of his single published novel alone. In an oft-cited writers poll, *Invisible Man* was named the most distinguished novel of the past twenty-five years. Add to that his rich essay collections, *Shadow and Act* and *Going to the Territory,* and Ellison is without question one of the towering figures of African-American—or American—letters.

More tantalizing was the prospect that his long-awaited second novel, *Juneteenth,* might bear still richer fruit. Ellison began work on the project before he completed *Invisible Man* and worked on it until the final days of his life. Ellison's second novel became the kind of complex mixture of chaos and order that he was so wont to remark upon in American culture. Multivocal and grandly conceived, it came to symbolize Ellison's view of America's unfinished quest for democratic expression. For many, Ellison's inability to finish the novel also exemplified the paralysis of black talent in the American context. John Callahan, Ellison's friend and literary executor, edited and published a version of *Juneteenth* in 1998, as well as posthumous collections of essays and short stories.

Ralph Waldo Ellison was born in Oklahoma City in 1914. Just a few years after becoming a state, Oklahoma still retained an air of possibility for a young, gifted black boy. We know a great deal about this period in Ellison's life because he himself wrote about it on numerous occasions.

His early life was set to the music of the time. Jazz was in the air, blues was in the soil. Charlie Christian and Jimmy Rushing both grew up near Ellison's childhood home. Most of the touring African-American jazz ensembles would find their way to Oklahoma City. Not surprisingly, Ellison's earliest aspirations were musical. As a boy he learned to play the trumpet, and by high school he was playing in the classical orchestra.

After graduation, Ellison was accepted to Booker T. Washington's Tuskegee Institute in 1933. The Tuskegee Institute had started out as a trade school, but now offered a liberal arts curriculum. Like his *Invisible Man,* Ellison received a scholarship from the town's leading white men in order to attend college. Train-hopping to Alabama—what Ellison calls in an unpublished memoir "the above-ground underground railroad"—he arrived at Tuskegee in time for fall classes. His interest in music deepened, particularly in classical composition. He set the goal of writing a symphony by the age of twenty-five. At Tuskegee, Ellison also became acquainted with the works of great literary modernists such as T. S. Eliot, James Joyce, and Ezra Pound. Ellison heard in Eliot's "Wasteland" something of the rhythms of the blues, something of the free-wheeling improvisation of jazz. It was an experience, he would later recall, that profoundly influenced his own aesthetic sense.

With his school funding running low, Ellison left Tuskegee to look for work in New York in the summer of 1936. There he met the writers Langston Hughes and Alain Locke, who put him in touch with a number of people in the fields of music and sculpture, his primary interests. Swept away by his work and his new circle of influence, Ellison never returned to Tuskegee. Through his growing circle of acquaintances, he met Richard Wright, with whom he formed the most significant—and stormy—literary friendship of his life. The fraternity took shape quickly. Wright was six years older than Ellison and a far more established writer, who helped introduce the younger man to the craft of fiction. He recognized in the countrified Oklahoman an uncommon aesthetic sensitivity, particularly rare among the Marxist writers with whom he was most closely associated. Wright convinced Ellison to try his hand at fiction. It was at Wright's insistence that Ellison wrote his first piece, which he then published in his journal, *New Challenge.* Ellison's early work—especially his manuscript *Slick*—is particularly heavily influenced by

Wright's naturalism and Marxist ideology. But Ellison would soon grow tired of the limitation ideology placed on art. His response, remarkably, magnificently, was *Invisible Man*.

Written over an intensive period of eight years, Ellison conceived of *Invisible Man* as a "raft of hope, perception and entertainment that might help keep us afloat as we tried to negotiate the snags and whirlpools that mark our nation's vacillating course toward and away from the democratic ideal." *Invisible Man* follows its nameless protagonist from South to North, from rural to urban, from innocence to experience. Framed by a masterful prologue and epilogue, the interior chapters tell the story of a man who has been driven to live his life underground by a world in which he feels he fits nowhere. By the end of the novel, Invisible Man is poised to move aboveground, to return to the place of social action, and to embrace the "beautiful absurdity" of American identity. "I am an invisible man," the protagonist intones in the opening lines of the novel. Together with W. E. B. Du Bois's double-consciousness, this invisiblity has been the enduring theme of black identity in America. Its potency lies in the tragicomic irony of it—that a people so highly visible could possibly be invisible. And while the novel is certainly written from the black experience, it challenges the limitations of narrow racial provincialism. Insisting that the baseline of our Americanness is our *humanity,* Ellison defied readers—black and white—who would read his novel as simply another work of protest fiction, a "race" novel.

Invisible Man articulated many of the themes that would preoccupy the rest of Ellison's career. Again and again, he would explore the contradictions of American

> *I don't recognize any white culture. I recognize no American culture which is not the partial creation of black people. I recognize no American style and literature, and dance, and music, even in any assembly-line processes, which does not bear the mark of the American Negro.*
> —Ralph Ellison

democracy. While some have portrayed him, simplistically, as a bland patriot, he really belongs in the tradition of American civil disobedience. As black American political thought shifted from the multiracial democratic vision of Martin Luther King, Jr., to the black nationalist and separatist ideologies of the Black Muslims, the Panthers, and the black arts movement, Ellison found himself more and more removed from the dominant racial discourses. His insistence on African Americans' place at the center of American society was equaled by his faith in the "sacred principles" of the nation's founding. "Whatever else the true American is, he is also somehow black," Ellison wrote in a 1970 piece for *Time* magazine, entitled "What America Would Be Like Without Blacks." His answer was "very little, indeed."

Invisible Man was well received, earning Ellison the National Book Award in 1953. And in the years following, Ellison settled comfortably into a relatively private public life. He sat on a number of national cultural boards and taught at numerous colleges and universities. He was Albert Schweitzer Professor of the Humanities at New York University throughout the 1970s and '80s. And yet he remained intensely private about his work. Even close friends knew little about the particulars of his novel in progress.

After fighting a losing battle with pancreatic cancer, Ellson died on April 16, 1994. After his death, when all the manuscript pages, typescripts, and computer disks had been assembled, it was clear that *Juneteenth* was broader in scope than *Invisible Man*. It was a multivocal jazz symphony, bearing the intonations of black, white, and Native American characters, men and women. Ellison never wrote out a table of contents, never told anyone in what sequence his various episodes should be placed. What he left amounts to something of a high literary jigsaw puzzle, a richly rendered collection of fragments—some leading to other fragments, others leading to nothing at all, but everything leading to a complex, beguiling final testament to the life of a *novelist.*. With the grand exception of Toni Morrison, there has been no greater novelist in African-American letters.

Althea Gibson

The Tennis Player
(1927–)

Althea Gibson was a pioneer in a sport reserved for wealthy whites and often disparaged by blacks as a "white sport." Unlike the black trailblazers in baseball and basketball, she had to overcome these two obstacles and break through the barrier of gender as well.

Until the 1950s, aspiring young African-American tennis players were excluded from the private tennis country clubs. They were not invited to the major international tournaments, such as the U.S. championships and Wimbledon, and they were barred from entering major tournaments in America. Then, along came Althea Gibson. Like Satchel Paige, Jackie Robinson, and Jesse Owens, she was an extraordinary athlete who had to bear the additional burden of smashing racial barriers erected to keep black athletes from competing with whites.

During the 1950s Althea Gibson became the number-one-ranked female tennis player in the world. She won the French Open, Wimbledon, and the U.S. Open Singles titles in 1957 and 1958, the first African American to do so. The Associated Press named her Female Athlete of the Year in 1957 and 1958. She was the first black woman to appear on the cover of *Sports Illustrated*. After retiring from tennis, she took up professional golf and became the first black woman to hold a Ladies Professional Golf Association (LPGA) Players Card when she finished in the top 80 percent in three tournaments.

In the early forties, black hopes, the kind that Lorraine Hansberry wrote about in *Raisin in the Sun,* were thwarted in every direction. When the young Gibson began training in earnest, the notion of an African American playing tennis at Wimbledon and at Forest Hills, America's Wimbledon equivalent, seemed illusory at best. Ralph Bunche would become the first African American to win the Nobel Peace Prize in 1950, but when Gibson was dreaming of championships, black people in the South still sat in the back of the bus. The landmark case *Brown* v. *Board of*

Education, in which the U.S. Supreme Court declared racial segregation unconstitutional, would not be decided until 1954.

Althea Gibson was born to a family of sharecroppers in South Carolina in 1927. In the 1930s the family moved to Harlem in New York City in search of a better life. The young Gibson showed no interest in academic subjects, devoting much of her time instead to athletics. She played paddle tennis on a court that the Police Athletic League (PAL) had set up near her house on West 143rd Street. Observing her progress with paddle tennis, Buddy Walker, the PAL supervisor, bought Gibson a secondhand tennis racket and took her to the Harlem River Courts, where she became a match for considerably older players.

These local successes led to an offer of lessons from the Cosmopolitan, a prestigious black tennis club. Gibson won her first tournament, sponsored by the all-black American Tennis Association (ATA), and in 1944 and 1945 she won the ATA Girls' Division title. At age eighteen she moved to the Women's Division of the ATA competition. Two ATA officials were crucial in promoting and encouraging her career: Dr. Hubert Eaton and Dr. Robert Johnson assisted Gibson in attending college, and Dr. Eaton invited Gibson to practice on his private court. In 1947, with the encouragement and support of Eaton and Johnson, Gibson won the first of her ten consecutive Women's ATA National Championship titles.

After Gibson played several ATA events, her two benefactors entered her into the U.S. Lawn Tennis Association–sponsored Indoor Championships, in which she reached the quarterfinals. In the winter of 1950 she won first place in the Eastern Indoor Championships and second place in the National Indoor Championships. Yet the USLTA National Tournaments ignored her until July 1950, when *American Lawn Tennis* magazine published a letter by former champion Alice Marble deriding the tennis community for its dismissal of Gibson:

Miss Gibson is over a very cunningly wrought barrel, and I can only hope to loosen a few of its staves with one lone opinion. If tennis is a game for ladies and gentlemen, it's also time we acted a little more like gentlepeople and less like sanctimonious hypocrites. . . . If Althea Gibson represents a challenge to the present crop of women players, it's only fair that they should meet that challenge on the courts.

Marble added that if Gibson were not given the opportunity to play by the wider tennis community, then "there is an ineradicable mark against a game to which I have devoted most of my life, and I would be bitterly ashamed." In the immediate aftermath of the letter's publication, Gibson continued to experience professional rejection on racial grounds, but three months later she was accepted into the national championships at the West Side Tennis Club at Forest Hills. It was not all Marble's doing; in the three months between rebuke and retribution, Gibson had won her match at the important 1950 Eastern Grass Court Championships and had played in the quarter finals at the National Clay Court Championships in Chicago. Gibson's first match against Louise Brough was a fiercely contested one, made even more dramatic by rainstorms, delays, and the press, who camped out on the courts.

In 1951, playing on center court in her first match, Gibson became the first black to play in the All-England Tennis Championships at the All-England Club in Wimbledon. She lost the match. By 1952 Gibson ranked ninth in the USLTA standings. But for some mysterious reason, even after winning the USLTA championships each summer, her play on the tour was declining. Just two years later she was ranked thirteenth. In 1955, at the height of McCarthyism, Gibson was asked by the U.S. State Department to be a goodwill ambassador to Southeast Asia. Following this appointment, she went on to claim the French championships, on May 20, 1956, defeating Britain's Angela Mortimer 6-3, 11-9. Also in 1956, the Associated Press named her Woman Athlete of the Year.

1950–1959

In 1957 Charlie Sifford became the first black to win the Davis Cup in golf, and Gibson defeated the British player Darlene Hard in the final, 6-3, 6-2, becoming the first black player to triumph at Wimbledon. Recognition was no longer withheld. Queen Elizabeth II extended congratulations, and at Gibson's return to New York she was given a ticker-tape parade and escorted to lunch by the mayor. In that same year, Gibson defeated Louise Brough 6-3, 6-2 in the U.S. Open Championship at Forest Hills and received a trophy overflowing with red and white flowers from Vice President Richard Nixon. The *New York Times* recorded that Gibson's remarks to the crowd, including a promise to wear her crown with humility and dignity, "were followed by the longest hand-clapping heard in the stadium in years."

In 1958 Gibson defeated Angela Mortimer at Wimbledon, 8-6, 6-2, and defeated Ann Jones and Darlene Hard at the U.S. Open Championships. In 1959, as champion of the world, Gibson left amateur tennis to play professionally. She signed for one hundred thousand dollars, an unprecedented sum for a woman, to play exhibitions in a six-month tour with the Harlem Globetrotters. In that same year she recorded the album *Althea Sings* and appeared in a film called *The Horse Soldiers.* In 1958 she wrote *I Always Wanted to be Somebody,* and followed this a decade later with the book *So Much to Live For.* She taught in New Jersey school tennis clubs for years and served as athletic commissioner for the state of New Jersey in the mid-1970s. It was Gibson's pioneering turn toward golf, however, that again astonished sports fans around the world. Named to the International Tennis Hall of Fame in 1971, she was inducted into the Women's Sports Hall of Fame in 1980. In 1977 she ran, unsuccessfully, in the Democratic primary election for the New Jersey State Senate. In 1991 she received the Theodore Roosevelt Award, the highest honor bestowed by the National College Athletic Association (NCAA). She continues to inspire us as a woman of grace and bravery—daring to cross the barriers in elite sports such as tennis and golf long before there were successful female athletes such as Chamique Holdsclaw of the WNBA and track star Jackie Joyner-Kersee.

Lorraine Hansberry

The Black Humanist
(1930–1965)

Lorraine Hansberry was one of the greatest African-American playwrights of the twentieth century. Although she is known primarily for her classic work *A Raisin in the Sun* (1959), she was also a prolific writer of essays, film scripts, and a semiautobiographical novel. Her art best exemplifies the fusion of subtle craft and political activism in the African-American intellectual tradition. And she was able to reach this grand achievement before her death on January 12, 1965, at the age of thirty-four.

Hansberry was born in Chicago, on May 19, 1930, to Nannie Perry Hansberry and Carl A. Hansberry. She was a relatively privileged child of middle-class origins with deep roots in the black freedom struggle. Her uncle, William Leo Hansberry, the famous Africanist scholar at Howard University, was a frequent visitor to her family home. In her youth she met Duke Ellington, Paul Robeson, Walter White, and Jesse Owens in her living room. In 1938, her father, who worked closely with the NAACP and the Urban League, ran for Congress and tried to move his family into a white neighborhood near the University of Chicago. Mobs attacked the house and a brick crashed through the window, nearly maiming young Lorraine. In a Supreme Court case the family brought against residential segregation, *Hansberry* v. *Lee,* the NAACP legal team won a victory, yet racist real estate covenants remained in practice. This incident would inspire Hansberry's play about the complexity and suffering of the Younger family, *A Raisin in the Sun.*

Hansberry studied literature at the University of Wisconsin, but left after two years to move to New York City, where she took a job with the radical black newspaper founded by Paul Robeson, *Freedom.* As associate editor of *Freedom,* she became immersed in the political, cultural, and artistic life of New York. She met the progressive Jewish writer Robert Barron Nemiroff in a demonstration and married him in 1953. That year she left *Freedom* to pursue her own writing, which culminated with a play about a struggling black family. *A Raisin in the Sun* opened at the Ethel Barrymore Theatre in New York in 1959.

This extraordinary literary achievement was the first play by a black woman to be produced on Broadway. It won the New York Drama Critics Circle Best Play of the Year Award in competition with Eugene O'Neill's *A Touch of the Poet,* Tennessee Williams's *Sweet Bird of Youth,* and Archibald MacLeish's *JB.* At the age of twenty-nine, Hansberry was—and remains—the youngest American to win this prestigious award. She was also the first woman and first African American to earn the coveted prize. As James Baldwin noted, "Never before, in the entire history of the American theater, had so much of the truth of black people's lives been seen on the stage."

Hansberry's first two screenplays of *Raisin* were rejected by Columbia Pictures as too controversial, as was her powerful television script about American slavery, *The Drinking Gourd.* When her third screenplay of *Raisin* finally was produced as a film with most of the original cast in 1961 it won awards from the Screen Writers' Guild and the Cannes Film Festival.

In the words of Ellen Schiff, Hansberry's second play, *The Sign in Sidney Brustein's Window* (1963), was "one of the most successful characterizations of the Jew on the post-1945 stage." Hansberry's loyal and supportive husband, Robert Nemiroff, notes Hansberry's "tremendous emotional identity with the Jewish radical and intellectual tradition." Though Hansberry and Nemeroff divorced in 1964 (Hansberry was known to be bisexual), he remained her literary executor after her death.

Diagnosed in 1963 with cancer, Hansberry battled onward, moving in and out of hospitals. Six months before her death, she suffered a debilitating stroke, which took her speech and eyesight. Hansberry courageously fought back and regained both. She met with Robert Kennedy, and led a walkout of the meeting when the attorney general failed to comprehend what a group of black intellectuals were saying about civil rights. She managed a fundraiser for the Student Nonviolent Coordinating Committee and continued writing, all the while undergoing heavy chemotherapy and radiation. On January 12, 1965, Lorraine Hansberry died.

The plays left unproduced during Hansberry's life warrant serious attention. Her two fascinating responses to Samuel Beckett's *Waiting for Godot* (1953)—*What Use are Flowers?* and *The Arrival of Todog*—wrestle with the sheer absurdity of life and history. Her uncompleted operatic project on Toussaint L'Ouverture, as well as her nearly completed screenplay based on Jacques Roumain's *Masters of the Dew,* reflect her deep interest in Caribbean history and culture. Nemiroff adapted her writings for the stage as *To Be Young, Gifted and Black,* a show that ran Off-Broadway in 1968–69 and toured college campuses during 1970 and 1971.

For all of the justified prizes heaped on *A Raisin in the Sun,* Hansberry's masterpiece was *Les Blancs* (The Whites). Deliberately modeled on Shakespeare's *Hamlet,* and critically inspired by Jean Genet's *The Blacks,* it is perhaps the most powerful and poignant treatment of European imperialism and African neocolonialism written by an American playwright. Her passionate defense of the dignity of humanity—be it African, European, Asian, or American—is couched in an unrelenting indictment of human injustice. Her command of particular detail is placed, as in all great art, at the service of the universal. In this way, Hansberry was, in the words of Steven R. Carter, "Among the most universal playwrights of her time."

Willie Mays

Say Hey Kid
(1931–)

Willie Mays moved like dancer when he played ball. In 1954, he was the hottest player on the diamond—the leading talent in the National League—making one memorable catch after another. There were "Say Hey Kid" hats (his nickname) for sale, and catchy rhymes eulogized his style. Everyone marveled at his uninhibited and exuberant way of moving on the field—his jumps, leaps, and slides—with his cap lifted from his head by the wind. To top it off, Mays was one of the most exciting center fielders of the day. Red Smith of the *New York Times* once said, "You could get a fat lip in any New York saloon by arguing who was better, Duke Snider, [Mickey] Mantle, or Mays. One point was beyond argument, though. Willie Mays was by all odds the most exciting." He played, according to *Time* magazine, "with a boy's glee, a pro's sureness, and a champion's flair." Willie Mays symbolized the fun of the sport. He transformed playing the game into an art.

For twenty-one years Mays played center field for the Giants in New York, (1951–1952, 1954–1957) and later in San Francisco (1958–1971). In 1972 he was traded to the New York Mets. He retired from the game altogether in 1973. As the Most Valuable Player who helped the Giants to win the World Series in 1954 and who played in every All-Star game from 1954 until 1973, Mays was New York's number one son. Earlier, in the mid-sixties, Mays was the best outfielder in the major leagues, leading the league in stolen bases for four consecutive years. His total home runs were 660. His 660 home runs give him the third-highest all-time record, behind only Henry "Hank" Aaron (755) and Babe Ruth (714).

Twelve Golden Glove awards were awarded to him, for his all-around brilliant playing, and in 1979, the first year in which he was eligible, Mays was inducted into the Baseball Hall of Fame. Between 1954 and 1966 he had 100 or more runs bat-

ted in, and in twenty-two seasons he slugged under .500 only six times. Most significant, black America loved Willie because, as the press made much of it, Mays would do a doubleheader at the New York Polo grounds and then head over to Harlem to play stickball with the kids. No one could move like him. "If you want to know the honest truth," he wrote, "I never got caught up in the competition that so captivated the fans and the press. I never compared myself to Mickey Mantle or Duke Snider or wondered who was a better ballplayer. We all had great respect for one another and never wasted any time comparing batting averages and on–base percentages."

> *I never became a cleaner, or a presser in a laundry. That was the job they trained me for at the Fairfield Industrial High School in Fairfield, Alabama. Don't laugh. That was a big job for most of us young boys then, back in the late 1940s in that part of the South. . . . No, they wound up writing a song about me instead.*
> —Willie Mays

Willie Mays was born in Westfield, a steel mill town in Alabama, in 1931, at the height of the Depression. His parents were divorced and he went to live with an aunt in Fairfield, Alabama. At sixteen he joined his father's semipro baseball team, the Birmingham Black Barons of the Negro National League, sponsored by the steel mill where his father worked. Mays graduated from high school in 1950. Just four years after Jackie Robinson broke the color line, the New York Giants signed Mays and he joined their minor league affiliate. Mays played in Trenton and Minneapolis for one year. In his autobiography, *Say Hey,* Mays reminisces about the fear he had of failing. Leo Durocher, his steady and trustworthy manager, convinced him to stay. Fortunately, by the end of that year, despite the Giants's World Series loss to the Yankees, Mays finished his first season with 20 home runs, 68 runs batted in, and was even named Rookie of the Year.

Between 1951 and 1952 Mays fought in the Korean War, which erupted in 1950. In his absence, the Giants finished second in 1952 and third in 1953. When Mays returned in 1954, the Giants won the pennant, beating the Cleveland Indians in the World Series. That game featured a fantastic catch. Mays caught a ball that sailed off the bat of Cleveland Indian Vic Wertz. His hat fell off in a Chaplinesque whirlwind, his knees spun around on the ground and then he threw it back to center field as though he was just doing his job. The baseball world loved it; he was an American hero. Led by Mays's 41 home runs and .345 batting average, the Giants won the World Series that year, and Mays was named Most Valuable Player, which he was named again in 1965.

1950–1959

In May 1958, the Giants moved to San Francisco, and Willie Mays continued to play for the team until 1972. The Giants won the National League pennant in 1962, but lost the World Series to the Yankees. Mays also had led his league in base stealing, winning the first of his twelve fielding awards for his work in center field. In 1972 he was traded back to New York, this time to the New York Mets, but he only played with them for a year. At the end of the 1973 season, he retired. He had amassed not only 660 home runs, but also 3,283 total hits and a lifetime batting average of .302.

In 1979 Mays was elected into the Hall of Fame, the ninth player in history to get in on his first try. At his ceremony he said, "What can I say? This country is made up of a great many things. You can grow up to be what you want. I chose baseball, and I loved every minute of it. I give you one word—love. It means dedication." But this success was marred by his foray into the casino world. Unsure of what to do after retiring from professional sports, several athletes, such as the boxer Joe Louis, picked up extra and easy money as spokepersons for gambling casinos. Willie Mays decided to work with Ballys in Atlantic City, greeting people and playing a little golf with guests. For this he would be paid one hundred thousand dollars a year. His old rival Mickey Mantle was doing the same thing. In 1979, baseball commissioner Bowie Kuhn forced Mays and Mantle to sever all ties with major league baseball as long as they worked in the casinos, due to the conflict of interest between gambling and holding a position of influence in baseball. Mays chose the casinos, even though he was not involved in gambling. In any case, this ban was later lifted by the new baseball commissioner, Peter Ueberroth. Mays set up a foundation for poor adults and children financed by the golf tournament he ran every year in Briarcliff Manor, New York. Since 1986, he has served as special assistant to the president of the Giants organization.

Mays brought his own distinctive style to baseball—a style that put a premium on being himself at all costs, a genuine down-home sophistication mixed with fun, talent, and irrepressible love. But if you were to focus on a singular event in his career, nothing can hold a candle to that memorable moment when Mays made "the catch" during the 1954 World Series against the Cleveland Indians. It was a moment that would show the world that the black man had a place in that most American of sports.

Rosa Parks

Mother of Civil Rights
(1913–)

Rosa Parks made her historic stand for justice by, famously, sitting down. For simply refusing to move to the back of the Montgomery public bus, she would be remembered as the "Mother of the Civil Rights Movement," but her involvement in the movement went far beyond the moment history has assigned her. Far from an aging, relatively apolitical figure, Parks was at the time of her arrest a seasoned civil rights worker just forty-two years old. The secretary of her local NAACP branch, for years Parks had worked on voter registration drives, legal defenses of unfairly accused African Americans, and efforts to desegregate public transportation.

Born Rosa Louise McCauley on February 4, 1913, she spent her early years in Pine Level, Alabama. Her parents separated soon after the birth of her younger brother, Sylvester, and the children grew up primarily with their mother and her parents. Parks remembers being aware of racial inequality from an early age, watching the abusive treatment her family and other sharecroppers suffered at the hands of white overseers, landowners, and town officials. She attended segregated local schools, later moving to Montgomery for the opportunity to attend junior high school, and then the laboratory school run by the Alabama State Teachers' College for Negroes, where her mother studied teaching. She left before graduating, however, to care for her dying grandmother.

After her grandmother died, Parks went to work in a shirt factory in Montgomery. In 1932, when she was nineteen, she married Raymond Parks, a barber. She would later describe him in her autobiography as the "first real activist" she had ever met. He was a member of the NAACP and had been involved in local efforts to help the defendants in the Scottsboro case, in which eight black men were convicted of raping two white women on a train. Raymond Parks encouraged his wife's

educational dreams, and with his help she finished high school,
graduating in 1933 at the age of twenty.

Even with her diploma, Parks found only semiskilled work,
first in a hospital, then later at an air force base, newly integrated due to President Franklin D. Roosevelt's Executive Order
8002 desegregating the war work effort. The Parkses joined the Montgomery
Voters' League, lead by Edgar Daniel Nixon, a Pullman porter who was one of the
city's most active black citizens. As founding president of Montgomery's branch of
the Brotherhood of Sleeping Car Porters and president of its NAACP chapter,
Nixon was a tireless fighter. He and a black lawyer named Arthur A. Madison organized a voter registration effort beginning in the early 1940s, but most African
Americans in Montgomery continued to be denied their right to the franchise. It
took Rosa Parks two years from the time she first tried to register in 1943 until she
received her voter's card in 1945.

By now she was secretary of the Montgomery NAACP, working closely with
E. D. Nixon and others to record testimony of African Americans who had suffered
harassment, beatings, and lynchings. In 1950 she found a better job, working as a tailor's assistant in a department store, but she continued to work informally for
Nixon, who had left his NAACP post but continued to head the Brotherhood of
Sleeping Car Porters branch. She also worked for a white couple, Virginia and
Clifford Durr, who were liberals and supported desegregation. In 1955 Virginia
Durr encouraged Parks to attend a workshop on implementing the school integration that recently had been ordered by the Supreme Court in its 1954 *Brown* v. *Board
of Education* decision. The workshop was held at the Highlander Folk School in
Monteagle, Tennessee, a radical education center founded by Myles Horton, a white
man, in 1932. At Highlander, Parks met Septima Clark and other black activists, as
well as white people committed to civil rights, and she returned to Montgomery
energized and enthusiastic.

All that optimism met its match when, on December 1, 1955, Rosa Parks, on
her way home from work, refused to move from her seat in the middle of the bus—
the no-man's-land at the front of the "black section" in which blacks were permitted to sit until white people wanted them—when the busdriver asked. As she wrote
in her autobiography:

People always say that I didn't give up my seat because I was tired, but that isn't true. I was not tired physically. . . . I was not old, although some people have an image of me as being old then. . . . No, the only tired I was, was tired of giving in.

She was arrested and charged with breaking the local segregation law. When Nixon and Virginia Durr came to pay her bail, they asked Parks if she would be willing to serve as the test case to end the system of segregation on Montgomery's buses. Above reproach, known for her integrity and hard work, Parks was the perfect defendant to fight segregation; as a member of the NAACP Youth Council said at a rally soon after Parks's release, "They've messed with the wrong one now!"

December 5, the first Monday after her arrest, was slated as both Parks's court date and the first day of a protest by African Americans of all city buses. Black cabs and individual citizens offered their services to provide transportation for boy-

cotters, and despite threatening rain and fears of inadequate publicity, Montgomery's black population stayed off the buses. Parks appeared in court, pleaded "not guilty," was convicted of the charges, and fined fourteen dollars, while her lawyers began planning their appeal. A group of Montgomery's black ministers met and formed the Montgomery Improvement Association, electing as their president a young pastor just twenty-six years old named Martin Luther King, Jr.

All that year, the boycott held. King and Nixon rallied the black population and found ways to get people where they needed to go. Many involved in the boycott faced harassment, and its leaders had to withstand duplicitous offers of negotiation by increasingly angry and defensive whites. In March, King was tried and convicted of leading an illegal boycott, but successfully appealed his conviction. Rosa Parks found herself in demand as a speaker, traveling to New York and San Francisco to address sympathetic meetings. The federal district court ruled in Parks's favor in June 1956, and in November the U.S. Supreme Court did too. Black Montgomery continued the boycott until December 20, when the written order reached city officials. The boycott was over.

Rosa Parks found her own life changed as well. She had lost her job during the boycott, and the racial atmosphere in Montgomery had become oppressive. In 1957 she, her husband, and her mother moved to Detroit. She continued to work as a seamstress, taking on speaking appearances and attending meetings and rallies, marching on Washington in 1963 and Selma in 1965. When a young congressman, John Conyers, asked her to join his staff in 1965 Parks did; she worked for Conyers until retiring in 1988. In 1987, ten years after her husband died, she founded the Rosa and Raymond Parks Institute for Self-Development, which offers youth programs in communication, health, economics, and political skills. In 1989, Cleveland Street in Montgomery (the street that gave its name to the Cleveland Street bus line from which she had been arrested) was renamed Rosa Parks Boulevard. No more dramatic symbol of the courageous resistance that characterized the abolition and civil rights movements exists than Rosa Parks, whose spontaneous courage fueled a movement. Within a decade following her daring act, legal segregation would be struck down by the Civil Rights and Voting Rights Acts of 1964 and 1965. She continues to lend her legendary name to causes of social justice around the world with her unique sense of dignity, humility, and style.

Art Tatum

The Pianist
(1909–1956)

Art Tatum was the greatest jazz pianist of the twentieth century. Everything he played was impossibly perfect. James Lester, his biographer, draws upon one of Tatum's most popular recordings and calls him "too marvelous for words." And it is true. People who knew Tatum talk about him fondly. But when it comes to describing what he did, they are often awed and speechless. Tatum was a master of impeccable technique, a virtuoso in the art of harmony. An old anecdote sums up the matter nicely: His dear friend Fats Waller was playing the piano for an enraptured audience, and someone told Waller that Art Tatum had just entered the club. With great affection, Waller stopped playing and announced, "Ladies and gentleman, *I* may be good, but tonight, *God* is in the house."

Quiet and heavyset, a serious drinker, the modest Tatum was the real thing. After all, it was his generation—Benny Goodman, Artie Shaw, Lionel Hampton, Lester Young, Teddy Wilson, and Coleman Hawkins—that defined American jazz. Many of *their* memories locate Tatum at the pinnacle of their field. After hearing Tatum, Coleman Hawkins experimented with the saxophone and changed its sound to the one that dominates jazz today. His fellow pianists were devastated by Tatum's sheer brilliance. The incomparable Oscar Peterson confessed that he could not play properly when Tatum was in the room. Respect for his dazzling command of the instrument extended to the classical world as well. Itzhak Perlman, the violinist, and Rachmaninoff, the pianist, adored him. His ability to reinvent harmonies, to reinterpret classical songs, and to vary chord progressions in the parameters of a common melody was the stuff of legend. Listening to a recording of Tatum is like having an exquisite conversation with a genius, one that inspires the imagination and delights the heart.

It is all the more remarkable that Art Tatum was the greatest single jazz pianist because he was partially blind. Growing up in Toledo, Ohio, from the age of three his vision was impaired by a series of cataracts that caused him to undergo surgery thirteen times as a child. Though he regained partial sight in his right eye, a blow to the head undid much of the benefit of surgery, and Tatum remained totally blind in his left eye for the rest of his life. Faced with this challenge, Tatum spent his childhood improvising. By the time Tatum reached adulthood, his handicap was undetectable, at least as far as he and his close friends were concerned. He hardly used a cane, and sometimes even willfully endangered himself. As a young boy, his imagination grew more vivid, and his other faculties began to compensate for the absence of sight. Tatum's ears became so perceptive that he could play tunes heard only recently, and he developed a talent for identifying notes from nonmusical sources, like the flushing of a toilet! Tatum's parents, who were themselves musicians, encouraged their son to play not only the piano, but also the accordion, guitar, and violin. Young Tatum was blessed to have as an instructor the visually impaired African-American pianist Overton Rainey. It was the era of ragtime, and from the radio, Tatum learned to master stride piano, as the style was known—the rags and stomps from piano rolls and popular songs. He attended the Cousino School for the Blind in Columbus, Ohio, and the Toledo School of Music. By the time he was sixteen, Tatum also was performing to great acclaim in juke joints all over Toledo.

During the Depression, Tatum won an amateur contest, and soon after landed a job at a Toledo radio station, where he played background music for the intermissions of a shopping show. He was given a fifteen-minute slot in which he could play to his heart's content, and the Blue Network broadcast his sessions. In 1932 the popular singer Adelaide Hall heard him play and asked him to accompany her on the Toledo stop of her tour. He ended up going back to New York with her. He played at the Onyx club on Fifty-second Street, and word soon got around that in the after-hour sessions, where musicians really tested each other, not even the stride kings of the time, Willie the Lion Smith, James P. Johnson, and Fats Waller, could surpass Tatum's dazzling arpeggios and inventive harmonies. He began recording for the Columbia Brunswick label founded by John Hammond soon after his arrival in New York. His earliest recorded solos were "Tea for Two," "Tiger Rag," and Duke Ellington's "Sophisticated Lady."

> Listening to Art Tatum is like going really fast on a bicycle past a Leonardo da Vinci painting.
> —Steve Allen

1950–1959

Tatum traveled frequently on tour. After marrying Ruby Arnold of Cleveland in 1935, he moved to Chicago, where he stayed at the Three Deuces Club and earned a steady income for almost a year. In 1936, the couple moved to Los Angeles, where Tatum made appearances at venues such as the Trocadero, the Melody Grill, and the Paramount Theater. Much in demand at big Hollywood parties, he recorded four sides for Decca in 1937 under the name Art Tatum and the Swingsters. But Tatum was not happily married because he was always on the road. Being absorbed in his music in mysterious ways rendered him inscrutable to most. His second wife, Geraldine, whom he adored, became a widow one short year after the marriage.

Tatum had garnered a distinguished reputation. By the time he toured Europe, although European audiences had never heard him live, they treated him with hushed respect, as they might a classical pianist. When he returned to the United States—white American critics imitated European tastes—Art Tatum was hailed as a virtuoso. Upon his return he found himself playing the Fifty-second Street night clubs and downtown clubs such as Café Society until around 1943. That year he entered the studio with a trio featuring Tiny Grimes and bass player Slam Stewart. The venture was commercially very successful. Two weeks later, Tatum appeared alongside Louis Armstrong for the First Esquire Concert at New York's Metropolitan Opera House, where all the participants were "poll winners" elected by jazz "experts."

In 1956 he appeared in the Hollywood Bowl before an audience of nineteen thousand, in a star-studded performance that included Louis Armstrong and Ella Fitzgerald. Norman Granz initiated an unprecedented project: a marathon recording of Tatum both as soloist and in collaboration with other players. Tatum recorded over two hundred pieces, playing in recordings that were later titled *The Tatum Solo Masterpieces* and *The Tatum Group Masterpieces.* Later that year, Tatum, who complicated a diabetic condition with excessive beer drinking, died from uremia. It was a dreadful loss to the music world, and he was mourned deeply. Ella Fitzgerald and Sarah Vaughan sang at Tatum's funeral at the Rosedale cemetery at Los Angeles. There simply has never been another such piano virtuoso in the history of American music.

Sarah Vaughan

The Divine One
(1924–1990)

She was jazz's only diva. Bille Holiday and Ella Fitzgerald are certainly contenders, but Sarah Vaughan's rich contralto was probably the greatest voice in jazz history. Even when she sang pop and show tunes, she elevated into art their sometimes mediocre words and music. What was her secret? She lacked any musical training. She performed for nearly fifty years, her throat unaffected by two packs of cigarettes a day. Vaughan was a natural. She had perfect pitch, a three-octave range, and an extraordinary ability to make leaps and quick transitions and—the heart of jazz—to improvise. The secret of jazz is that instruments are patterned imitations of the human voice. Sarah Vaughan's secret is that her voice was a jazz instrument.

Sarah Vaughan was born in Newark, New Jersey, on March 27, 1924, into a family of musicians. Her father, Asbury, a carpenter, played guitar and piano, and her mother, Ada, a laundress, sang in the Mount Zion Baptist Church Choir. Sarah began piano lessons at the age of seven and organ lessons the following year. By twelve, she was the church organist and began singing in the choir at Mount Zion. In 1942, at the age of nineteen, Vaughan entered the famous weekly amateur contest at Harlem's Apollo Theater on a dare and won. She sang "Body and Soul" and was awarded ten dollars and a week of performances at the Apollo.

Jazz singer Billy Eckstine heard her sing that week, and recommended her to Earl "Fatha" Hines's big band as a vocalist and second pianist. When Eckstine formed his own big band with a bebop flavor in 1944, it included Dizzy Gillespie and Charlie Parker, and he invited Vaughan to join. With him she cut her first single, "Lover Man," counting Dizzy and Bird among her mentors. Vaughan later said that it was horn players, more than any other musicians, who influenced her vocal style. In 1946 Vaughan left the band to launch a solo career at New York's Café

Society. She met trumpeter George Treadwell, who became her manager and the first of her four husbands. He taught her stage presence and how to dress, turning an unsophisticated young woman into an image to match her talent.

She recorded a highly successful version of "Body and Soul," and over the next few years she consistently won Best Female Singer awards in *Downbeat* and *Metronome* magazines. Fans and critics alike responded to her smoldering and smoky voice; she began to be called "The Divine One," but her friends stayed with "Sassy," the nickname she earned for being honest, blunt, and direct.

In 1949 Vaughan signed a five-year contract with Columbia Records, and continued to record songs for other labels. Some of her best known albums include "The Divine One," "Live in Japan," "Lullaby of Birdland," "Sassy," "Broken-Hearted Melody," "Sassy Swings Again," "I Love Brazil," "The Duke Ellington Songbook," "Brazilian Romance," and the Grammy Award–winning "Gershwin Live!" The diversity of the titles shows something of her versatility and her panoramic musical interests. Her agility and range allowed her to move, apparently without effort, through many genres and styles. In her solo career she experimented with formats as diverse as songs, quartets, and symphonies and in venues as varied as cafés, stadiums, and festivals. She worked with everyone from jazz giants such as Oscar Peterson and Duke Ellington to the Los Angeles Philharmonic and the National Symphony Orchestra.

The music critic and historian Eddie Meadows writes that Vaughan was the "first vocalist to understand and accentuate modern harmonic and rhythmic concepts." For us, Sarah Vaughan lives in her songs, classics like "Misty," "Tenderly," "Send in the Clowns," and "Broken-Hearted Melody." She once said, "I am not a special person. I am a regular person who does special things." What she did made who she was special. But the cigarettes that made her voice rich destroyed her body. Sarah Vaughan died of lung cancer on April 4, 1990—leaving the world a sadder, quieter place.

Muhammad Ali

The Butterfly
(1942–)

Muhammad Ali's voice, his strategic psychological verbal warfare, captured the 1960s' spirit of a defiant black America caught in the turmoil of its own quickened politics. Ali was the preeminent symbol of black America's new self-confidence, its quickness of response, and its sure-footed action. He was the brilliant ring strategist, the furiously fast and playful prodigy who danced circles around his opponents, inviting them to hit him, as he outwitted duller challengers with his fists, his thoughts, and his lip. In the second half of the century, as Norman Mailer ventured in *Existential Errands,* "being a black heavyweight champion [in a period marked by decolonization, antiwar movements, and revolt] was not unlike being Jack Johnson, Malcom X and Frank Costello all in one."

Ali's singular genius was indeed that he was a boxer who embodied and reflected the politics of the times. His assertion of black pride, his conversion to Islam, and his outspoken opposition to the Vietnam War ensured that he could count among his adoring fans peace-loving hippies as well as political militants and vegetarian black Muslims. "He is all that the sixties were," Jimmy Cannon wrote. "It is as though he were created to represent them. In him is the trouble and the wildness and the hysterical gladness and the big nonsense." In a very real sense, Ali, a black nationalist boxing poet who earned more money than all other heavyweight champions before him combined, was the spokesperson of black America's bold new stance against racism at home and colonialist imperialism abroad.

As famous as he was for swift phantom punches, he could also take them. Who can forget the Ali–Foreman fight in Zaire, 1974, where he simply allowed Foreman to wear himself out by punching his body? Like the biblical David, he fought clearly outmatched fights—and won. He stalked his opponents before a fight, psyching them out with astonishingly funny attacks on their person.

The energy and brilliance of his mind were infectious; the couplets entrenched in African-American humor are gems. His record speaks for itself—from his winning an Olympic gold medal, capturing the professional world heavyweight championship on three separate occasions, and successfully defending his title nineteen times—it is no wonder that Ali is rightly considered "the greatest." In 1994 *Sports Illustrated* ranked Ali first on its "40 for the Ages List." In 1987, *The Ring* named him the greatest heavyweight champion of all time. In 2000 he was voted the greatest athlete of the century several times. Every boxing pundit, from Norman Mailer to George Plimpton, has tried to capture the spiritual importance of this strong and handsome David from Louisville, Kentucky. The lessons he taught us as he dominated heavyweight boxing in the 1960s reach far more deeply into the recess of faith and spirituality. Ali often predicted the outcome of his fights, like a prophet of the ring.

Unlike most boxers, Muhammad Ali, né Cassius Marcellus Clay (named for the white Kentucky abolitionist Cassius M. Clay), was not born into a background of poverty. His father Marcellus Clay painted signs, and his mother Odessa (Grady) Clay, worked as a domestic. Ali was not a good student. In fact, when later rejected from the army for scoring at a substandard level, he quipped, "I never said I was the smartest. I said I was the greatest." Yet though he may have graduated 376th in his high school class of 391, he was ferociously intelligent. Ali began boxing at the age of twelve under the tutelage of white Louisville policeman Joe Martin, who helped him to appear in 108 bouts between 1955 and 1960. During this time, he won six Kentucky Golden Gloves titles, his first novice one at age fourteen, two national Amateur Athletic Union (AAU) championships, and two National Golden Gloves crowns. By the time he was eighteen, Ali had won the gold medal in the light heavyweight division in the 1960 Summer Olympic Games in Rome.

Clay turned professional when he signed a promotional contract with a Louisville sponsoring group and met his faithful trainer Angelo Dundee. He made his debut as a heavyweight in October 1960 with a six-round decision over Tunney Hunsaker. Continuing to boast and brag, he won his next eighteen fights, fifteen by knockouts. Ali was not the greatest until he fought Sonny Liston on February 25, 1964, in Miami Beach, Florida; Liston was the reigning heavyweight champion. Liston was his first Goliath. A hardened man, managed by organized crime, Liston had knocked out his last three challengers in the first round. Hardly any of his opponents reached the fifth round. The press—although entertained and annoyed by

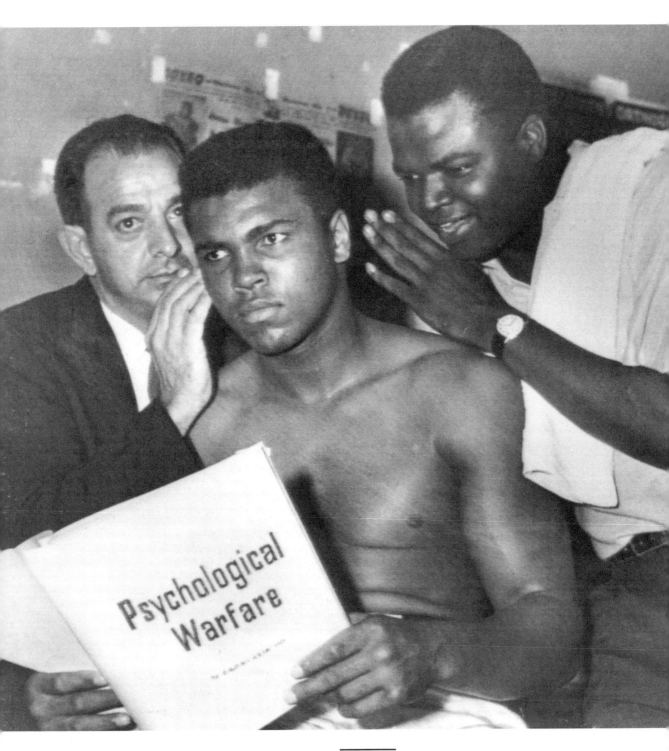

Clay's boasting—predicted that Clay would lose. For weeks before the fight, the twenty-two-year-old Clay bragged to fans and stalked Liston publicly, threatening him with words. To the shock of the world and perhaps himself, Clay defeated Liston when he refused his corner in the sixth round.

Two days afterward, with the sports world reeling in shock, Ali announced his conversion to the Nation of Islam—at the time considered one of the most divisive political black organizations. The country was shocked at his declaration of black nationalism. Malcom X had converted Clay and become his fast friend. The press recoiled from this freshly named Muhammad Ali—the *New York Times* refused to honor this name when writing about him throughout the sixties. In 1965, three months after Malcolm X had been assassinated, the rematch with Sonny Liston was held in Lewiston, Maine. Ali defeated Liston in the first round—on purpose.

Ali defended his title a second time in that same year, against Floyd Patterson. Then, in 1966, the army drafted Ali. He refused to go. When pushed to explain the reasons for his conscientious objector status, he didn't merely say, "I ain't got no quarrel with them Viet Cong." Ali talked about how war was immoral, made digs at the peculiar perversion of justice of black soldiers who went off to war when civil rights were not secure at home, and pointed to the riots to prove it. Consequently, the government overruled the decision of a judge who had granted him conscientious objector status, fined him ten thousand dollars, and sentenced him to five years in prison. They also humiliated him in 1967 by stripping him of his heavyweight title and license to box.

> Since I won't let critics seal my fate
> They keep hollering I'm full of hate.
> But they don't really hurt me none
> 'cause I'm doing good and having fun.
> And fun to me is something bigger
> than what those critics fail to figure.
> Fun to me is lots of things.
> And along with it some good I bring.
> Yet while I'm busy helping my people
> These critics keep writing I'm deceitful.
> But I can take it on the chin
> And that's the honest truth my friend.
> Now from Muhammad you just hear
> The latest and truest word.
> So when they ask you what's the latest.
> Just say, "Ask Ali. He's still the greatest."
> —Muhammad Ali

Ali came back in 1970, scoring knockout victories over Jerry Quarry and Oscar Bonavena. He lost for the first time on March 8, 1971, to soft-spoken Joe Frazier, and would not regain the heavyweight championship until October 30, 1974, when he fought the "Rumble in the Jungle." That fight in Kinshasa, Zaire (now the

Democratic Republic of the Congo) against George Foreman was a classic. Ali, supported by President Mobutu, was loved by the Africans, and in his classic personable antinationalist style, as far as he was concerned, was completely at home in Zaire. Foreman on the other hand, was construed as "the American." The politics of that fight were supremely significant in that Ali became aware of his impact outside of America. He became a truly Pan-African hero.

Among Ali's greatest fights were a fifteen-round victory over Frazier on October 1, 1975, in Manila, Philippines, a fight promoted as the "Thrilla in Manila," and the February 15, 1978, match in Las Vegas, Nevada, when he lost the crown to Olympic champion Leon Spinks in a fifteen-round decision. He regained the crown in 1978, when he became the first fighter to win the heavyweight crown three times, in a rematch at the Superdome in New Orleans, Louisiana. During the late seventies, it became painful to watch Ali fight; he withstood punishing blows to his body, and his reactions inevitably slowed. He retired from boxing in 1979, but came back, to challenge the new heavyweight champion, Larry Holmes, for the crown. On October 2, 1980, in Las Vegas, Holmes dealt Ali the worst loss of his career; he lost again in December 1981 after losing a 10-round decision to Trevor Berbick.

Ali developed Parkinson's disease in the late 1980s. But he still traveled to Iraq to meet President Saddam Hussein in a bid to forestall war in the Persian Gulf in 1990. He acted as a spokesperson for Operation USA in war-torn Rwanda in 1996. He created the Muhammad Ali Community and Economic Development Corporation to teach job skills to low-income public housing residents in Chicago. And that same year at the Olympic Games in Atlanta, a slow-moving and trembling Ali was chosen to light the flame to open the Games. Muhammad Ali gave a new dignity to the black athlete, a dignity determined by his intelligence both inside and outside of the ring, his powerful capacity to articulate his feelings and thoughts, and his moral commitment to justice and equality. He was the greatest boxer and one of the most beloved athletes of the twentieth century.

James Baldwin

Intellectual Activist
(1924–1987)

If Martin Luther King's was the oratorical spoken voice of the civil rights movement, James Baldwin's was its intellectual written voice. It was four decades ago, in 1963, that James Baldwin became *the* voice of black America when he published his prophetic warning *The Fire Next Time*. He made the cover of *Time* magazine; his authority as spokesperson was unimpeachable. He was even spoken of as a candidate for the Nobel Prize. The puzzle was that his arguments, richly nuanced and self-consciously ambivalent, were far too complex to serve the urgent political ends of the day. This, after all, was the man who could argue in his *Notes from a Native Son* that:

[t]he question of color . . . operates to hide the graver question of the self. That is precisely why what we like to call 'the Negro Problem' is so tenacious in American life and so dangerous. But my own experience proves to me that the connection between American whites and blacks is far deeper and more passionate than any of us like to think. . . . The questions which one asks oneself begin, at last, to illuminate the world, and become one's key to the experience of others.

Who was this public intellectual who moved back and forth between social politics and existential subjectivity, who saw that there is no need for racial understanding since we already understand each other all too well, because we have in fact invented each other? James Baldwin was born August 6, 1924, in Harlem Hospital. His deep involvement in human tragedy was not theoretical; it grew from his own experience: His real father was unknown, his preacher stepfather went insane, his own physicality threatened him (his stepfather told him he was the ugliest baby he had ever seen), his homosexuality and his race alienated him from the larger world.

Baldwin's personal lifelong search was for the love that transcends everything, and it is impossible not to see where his social philosophy has its roots. As a youth, Baldwin found pathways leading out, but which also enriched his understanding of where he came from. He read books from the Harlem branches of the New York Public Library. As a child preacher in Mt. Calvary Church under the charismatic Pentecostal ministry of Mother Rosa Horn, he would grow out of the sanctified shouting, but not beyond the gift of the Spirit to witness. In public school he studied under Harlem Renaissance poet Countee Cullen, and he began to write. He graduated from DeWitt Clinton High School in 1942, and knew himself well enough to join the bohemian life of Greenwich Village, where both his sexuality and his writing could be expressed. But Baldwin was still a black man in America. As Josephine Baker and Richard Wright had done before him, on Armistice Day in 1948 Baldwin left for Paris, supported by a Rosenwald Fellowship.

Baldwin emerged as a creative and cosmopolitan intellectual. Despite his discovery of French racism, France became his home. He also discovered a father figure, Beauford Delaney, the troubled expatriate African-American painter, and the person with whom he would make the most permanent and personal partnership, Lucien Happersberger, a married Swiss bisexual. Mostly, Baldwin wrote; his seminal works *Go Tell It on the Mountain, Notes of a Native Son,* and *Giovanni's Room* date from this period. Baldwin continued to struggle with the irony of being an African American. With the dramatic beginning of the civil rights movement, he returned to the States, and made his first visit to the American South. According to one chronicler, Baldwin "saw Southern whites trapped in their own mythology, and blacks made heroic by their struggles. He saw, too, the negative effects of racism on the inner lives of black and white people alike, including the white obsession with black sexuality and the profound connection of sexuality with racism and violence."

One might have hoped that his sense of the vagaries of identity could serve a broader politics, but Baldwin himself eschewed such purposes: He was here to "bear witness," not to be a spokesman. But by the late sixties, Baldwin-bashing was almost a rite of initiation for up-and-coming black intellectuals. Anyone who was aware of the ferment in black America was familiar with the relentless attacks. To Amiri Baraka, star of the black arts movement, Baldwin was "Joan of Arc of the cocktail party," possessed of a "spavined whine and plea" that was "sickening beyond belief." To Ishmael Reed, he was "a hustler who comes on like Job."

In the end, the shift of political climate forced Baldwin to simplify his rhetoric or be shunned. "It is not necessary for a black man to hate a white man, or to have particular feelings about him at all, in order to realize that he must kill him," he wrote in *No Name in the Street.* The old Baldwin would have understood such murder as also suicide.

Did he know what was happening to him? His essays give no clue; increasingly they came to represent his official voice, the carefully crafted expression of the public intellectual James Baldwin. It was left to his fiction to express his growing self-doubt.

In 1968, he published *Tell Me How Long the Train's Been Gone.* Formally, it was his least successful work, but in its protagonist, Leo Proudhammer, Baldwin created a perfectly Baldwinian alter ego, a celebrated black artist who could express the quandaries that came increasingly to trouble his creator. "The day came," Proudhammer reflects at one point, "when I wished to break my silence and found that I could not speak: the actor could no longer be distinguished from his role." Thus did Baldwin, our elder states-man, who knew better than anyone how a mask could deform the face beneath, chafe beneath his own.

James Baldwin and the Freedom Movement met just when each needed the other. The movement needed an intellect that could go beneath the surface of civil rights and see the paradoxical beauty and tragedy of America. Baldwin needed a focus to evoke his intellectual power. He wrote in "Here Be Monsters," an essay published two years before his death, and with which he chose to conclude the nonfiction collection *The Price of the Ticket:* "Each of us, helplessly and forever, con-tains the other—male in female, female in male, white in black, and black in white. We are a part of each other. Many of my countrymen appear to find this fact exceedingly inconvenient and even unfair, and so, very often, do I. But none of us can do anything about it." No author before James Baldwin or since has registered the mutually constitutive nature of white and black American cultures, their funda-mental and inextricable interconnection.

James Baldwin died of cancer on December 1, 1987, in Saint-Paul-de-Vence, his home in France. Baldwin will be remembered, after the vexing social issues about which he wrote have been attenuated or resolved, as a great craftsman of prose. He was a master of our language, and thus of our selves, and for two full decades, he articulated the nuances and complexities of American racial relations as no one has been able to do since.

John Coltrane

The Jazz Prophet
(1926–1967)

John Coltrane made his musical journey solo. Contemplating Coltrane's legacy, what Art Davis, one of Coltrane's favorite bassists, said about him in 1972 comes to mind. John Coltrane was venerated because he possessed that "special something" associated with spiritual and artistic genius. The excitement and unpredictability of his style separated his work from the earlier cool school of Lester Young and Stan Getz. Early critics who later respected the most enigmatic hard bop saxophonist initially despaired of his early "antijazz" trends, his "nihilistic" solo exercises, as they saw them, that rambled on and on past inspiration into "monotony." In the later stages of his career, however, Coltrane won the praise of these same early jazz critics, who had decried these same visionary, artistic explorations as anarchistic and crude. When he died in 1967, avant-garde jazz was robbed of one of the most important saxophonists and stylistic and compositional innovators of the late twentieth century. Now Coltrane's sound is held in awe by jazz musicians—indeed few tenor players remain untouched by his modernist interrogation of tenor harmonies and his improvisatory trademark solos.

Coltrane was indeed a soloist in many senses of the word. He was known by his coterie of devoted listeners as the shy romantic, a paradigmatic angry young man of the 1960s; the saintly aesthete whose passion moved women and men alike; the lyrical nonconformist who challenged acceptable jazz sounds and forms; the skilled practitioner who spent hours working on his craft. Martin Williams, one of the first to examine the life of Coltrane after his death, wrote in *The Jazz Tradition* that Coltrane was one of the most persistent, relentless expanders of possibility—textural, harmonic, and spiritual—in jazz history.

Coltrane was born in Hamlet, North Carolina, in 1926. His family relocated shortly after his birth to a lower-middle-class neighborhood in High Point, North

Carolina. Coltrane's father was a tailor and an amateur musician. His mother, a seamstress, sang and played piano in her father's, the Reverend William Blair's, gospel choir. But despite his parents' lively musical influences, Coltrane's lifelong study of music erupted during a three-year period when death swept through his household. He lost his father in 1939, when Coltrane was thirteen years old, his maternal grandfather a few months later, and then his aunt and uncle. In this formative period marked by adult despair and adolescent insecurity and desire, Coltrane found the alto saxophone, or perhaps it found him, and he began to study the instrument that would be his lifelong partner.

In 1943 Coltrane graduated from high school and immediately set off for Philadelphia. He intended to study music and enrolled in both the Granoff Studios and the Ornstein Conservatory, where he studied saxophone technique and music theory for eight years. His studies were interrupted briefly by a stint in Hawaii, courtesy of the United States Navy, where he played the clarinet in navy bands. The gigs that he managed to get were with the rhythmic big bands, such as King Kolax and Eddie "Cleanhead" Vinson. A lucky break came when he played with the Dizzy Gillespie Big Band (1949–1951) and with Earl Bostic (1952). During this period he switched from alto to tenor saxophone. Other artists who played the tenor saxophone, such as Dexter Gordon, Edward "Sonny" Stitt, Theodore "Sonny" Rollins, and Stan Getz, deeply impressed the young Coltrane. By the early 1950s, Coltrane had developed as a fine saxophonist, but not unlike a few other musicians of his era, he was also teetering on the edge of an abyss of heroin and alcohol addiction.

In 1955 Charlie "Bird" Parker, Coltrane's hero on the alto saxophone, died of alcohol poisoning. In that same year, Coltrane married his first wife Juanita Austin, known as Naima, a newly converted Muslim, who introduced him to broader spiritual themes. Nineteen fifty-five was also the year that Coltrane joined the newly formed Miles Davis Quintet, an ensemble which set the parameters of jazz for the latter half of the decade. Working with the respected and established Davis was an important move for Coltrane. He began to be taken seriously as a cutting edge musician with ambitious ideas about the way to play a saxophone.

During these years, Coltrane's playing attracted critical attention through such recordings as 'Round About Midnight (1956). People began to appreciate Coltrane's idiosyncratic approach; in fact, many concurred that his playing might actually be meaningful, even emblematic, of a personal exploration. Miles Davis, for instance,

distilled the essence of a musical phrase into a few notes. His solos lasted a short time. Coltrane, on the other hand, cramped several notes and series of arpeggios into the smallest harmonic space possible. But his solos were long, so long, in fact, that even Miles Davis became slightly irritated. Davis was once asked by a journalist about the length of Coltrane's solos. He responded, "It takes him all that time to say what he needs to say."

In 1957, Coltrane temporarily departed Davis's band for the opportunity to play with pianist Thelonious Monk, who was making something of a comeback. They played the now famous Five Spot Café engagements. The Five Spot was the premiere club in New York for experimental jazz (Ornette Coleman had played there); it was the perfect sabbatical for Coltrane. He honed his technique of innovative harmonic devices, which critic Ira Gitler coined as "sheets of sound." Gitler later explained that he was attempting to describe the density of textures Coltrane's playing evoked, the multinote improvisations which were so thick and complex that they seemed to be flowing out of the horn by themselves.

Coltrane thought of Monk as a master teacher, "a musical architect of the highest order." He said, "I felt I learned from him in every way—through the senses, theoretically, and technically. I would talk to Monk about musical problems, and he would sit at the piano and show me the answers just by playing them. I could watch him play and find out the things I wanted to know. Also, I could see a lot of things that I didn't know at all." Coltrane returned to Davis's band one year later and recorded some of the most influential jazz recordings, *Milestones* (1958) and *Kind of Blue* (1959).

By all accounts, Coltrane was a spiritual man. Giving up heroin in 1957 must have inspired a sense of self-mastery, for he began to search beyond himself, and to reinvent himself unself-consciously. The spiritualism of India and Africa attracted him, and he studied briefly with Ravi Shankar. Without pretension, he translated musically what he was learning about the decolonized world and how that may have corresponded to being black in America: He played *My Favorite Things* as though it were an Indian raga. He began using a set of pitches, or modes, rather than functional harmony, as in bebop. He also devised a set of harmonic formulas known today as "Coltrane substitutions." Coltrane was also the first to bring back the soprano saxophone as a viable jazz instrument since African-American clarinet and soprano saxophone player Sidney Bechet had done so forty years earlier. Recordings of this period, such as *Blue Train* (1957), *Giant Steps* (1959), and his first hit record, *My Favorite Things* (1960), established him as one of the most innovative musicians in jazz history.

In 1961 Coltrane formed his own band, sometimes called the "classic quartet," that consisted of himself on tenor and soprano saxophones, McCoy Tyner on piano, either Jimmy Garrison or Reggie Workman on bass, and Elvin Jones on drums. Eric Dolphy, Coltrane's close friend, also performed with the group periodically until his death in 1964. The quartet met with acclaim as they toured the United States and Europe. Coltrane's performances during this period are regarded as his finest.

Shortly thereafter, his recording *Alabama* (1963) memorialized four adolescent black girls who were killed in the racist bombing of a Birmingham church. The phrasing and intensity of Martin Luther King's public speech in the wake of this tragic event formed the basis of John Coltrane's composition.

With the possible exception of Charlie "Bird" Parker, no other jazz saxophonist had become so widely appreciated, interpreted, and drawn upon. Throughout much of the 1960s he ranked first among jazz artists in at least one category of the annual *Down Beat* magazine poll. In 1965 he was ushered into the Down Beat Hall of Fame, largely because of his startlingly unique album *A Love Supreme* (1964). The landmark release garnered distinction as Record of the Year by *Down Beat,* and Coltrane was designated Jazz Man of the Year. Coltrane was admired not only for being a musical innovator but for the spiritual qualities of his music and persona. The music of the quartet can be heard on such recordings as *Africa Brass* (1961), *Live at the Village Vanguard* (1961), *Crescent* (1964), *A Love Supreme, First Meditations* (1965), and *Sun Ship* (1965).

Tyner and Jones left the band in 1966 and were replaced by Coltrane's second wife Alice (née Alice McCleod) on piano and Rashied Ali on drums. Pharoah Sanders (né Farrell Sanders) also joined the band on tenor and soprano saxophones. Coltrane was entering an even more avant-garde phase in his artistic development. Unbeknownst to him, however, he was dying from liver cancer. They toured Japan in 1966 but canceled their European dates. He died at the age of forty in 1967. His imprint upon jazz, and the role of the saxophone in it, would remain fundamental.

Angela Davis

Crusader for Social Justice
(1944–)

Angela Davis is old school. She embodies much of the spirit, élan, confidence, and engaged intellectualism that marked the black radicalism of the 1960s. Indeed, while we seem to be living in an era in which many are overcome by a sense of nihilistic hopelessness on the one hand, and a mercenary do-for-self individualism on the other, Davis remains committed to radical politics and social justice. She possesses a fearless vision and optimism, and a rigorous, expansive mind, never retreating from her manner of fighting oppression. This is what we mean by old school.

It was through the politics of the 1960s that Davis became best known. Crowned with a defiant Afro, her image graced the FBI's most-wanted posters. Davis became a black power icon. But her roots in social justice activism go much deeper than the charged events in the 1960s for which she is famously remembered. Davis was one of four children of a pair of schoolteachers (though her father would leave his poorly paid position to buy a gas station) in Birmingham, Alabama. The neighborhood she grew up in was called by the ironic name "Dynamite Hill" because it was a frequent bombing target for white supremacists. She attended segregated public schools where exposure to African-American history early on instilled in her a sense of confidence and pride. Her mother took her to civil rights demonstrations as a young girl. Local police would break up the interracial study groups that the young radical tried to organize with her friends.

Davis attended Elizabeth Irwin High in New York's Greenwich Village, a private school that was a magnet for budding activists. During that time she lived with William Howard Melish, an Episcopalian minister, who was also a friend of the family. The politics of many of its teachers left them unable to find work within the public school system. She graduated in 1961 and attended Brandeis University, where she majored in French literature. She spent a year at the Sorbonne. Her time in Paris introduced her to African students who had grown up under colonial regimes. She found a link between their struggles and her own in the United States; their stories strengthened her resolve for social change. Davis returned to Brandeis, seeking in her academic work a political philosophy that could end the injustice perpetuated against African Americans. She found it in Marxism.

> *We, the black women of today, must accept the full weight of a legacy wrought in blood by our mothers in chains . . . heirs to a tradition to supreme persever-ance and heroic resistance.*
> —Angela Davis

Brandeis professor and philosopher Herbert Marcuse introduced Davis to the political philosophy of Karl Marx. In Marxism, Davis believed that she had found a way to understand and transform the structural conditions of racism in the United States, and of oppressed groups the world over. In 1965, she graduated from Brandeis with highest honors and began graduate work in Germany at the University of Frankfurt, where she studied German and read Kant and Hegel. She soon returned to the United States, however. While her professors encouraged her to stay in Europe, as the racial climate back home rose to a fever pitch in the mid–1960s, she knew she had to return. She completed her master's at the University of California at San Diego, began doctoral work, and became active in the Student Nonviolent Coordinating Committee and the Black Panther party. She also began a long affil-iation with the Communist party that included her running for vice president on the party's ticket in 1980 and 1984.

In 1969, UCLA hired Davis as an assistant professor of philosophy. She quickly became a popular lecturer, but her Communist party membership drew the ire of the university's Board of Regents. Under the leadership of then governor Ronald Reagan, the regents attempted to fire Davis. After protests from students and facul-ty, she was reinstated by court order. Once her contract expired the following year, however, Davis was not rehired.

Davis began working with prisoners and prison activists, a commitment that has remained. She worked with the Soledad Brothers, a Marxist group in California's Soledad prison, offering them support when a guard murdered one of their mem-bers. The killing was ruled "justifiable homicide" by the warden. Soon after the killing, Jonathan Jackson, a young brother of prisoner George Jackson, attempted a high-stakes rescue at California's Marin County Courthouse. The attempt disinte-grated into a shootout that left a judge dead. The weapons used in the rescue attempt were traced to Davis, who had purchased them because of the barrage of death threats she was receiving, and then stored them in the headquarters of the all-black Marxist collective, the Che-Lumumba Club. Davis went underground. The FBI began an intensive search and placed her on its most wanted list. She eventually was captured in New York, extradited to California, and imprisoned for sixteen-months before her case went to trial.

In 1972, Davis was acquitted, though not before she became something of a celebrity within the left's counterculture, her image a ubiquitous symbol of black power. Her high-profile trial drew attention to police abuse of African Americans. With Davis as cochair, her defense committee, renamed the National Alliance

against Racism and Political Repression, has taken on political cases, usually with African-American and Latino defendants.

Davis continued her activism after those turbulent years. She lectures widely—including in the former Soviet Union—on questions of social justice. She maintains a withering critique of notions of the black family and gender relations in the black community, of the prison-industrial complex, and of the very nature of America's capitalist system. Her books include *Angela Davis: An Autobiography; Women, Race and Class; Women, Culture & Politics;* and, most recently, an astute analysis of blues lyrics in *Blues Women.* She currently teaches in the history of consciousness program at UC, Santa Cruz. In the 1960s Angela Davis was the most salient example of the black woman as scholar and activist. Long after the political causes she had embraced lost their faddishness, she has remained a dedicated and consistent radical black activist.

Fannie Lou Hamer

Grassroots Activist
(1917–1977)

She rose and found her voice, and in doing so articulated the aspirations of millions of her fellow black Americans. Fannie Lou Hamer taught America a lesson in democracy. She was born and raised a sharecropper, and became such a powerful political force in her decade that her name became known internationally. She was the twentieth of her parents' children, and her childhood was spent in terrible poverty in the Mississippi Delta. Her family were sharecroppers—farming cotton on land owned by whites, keeping only a small percent of the profits—a system that kept people poor and landless. Hamer began working alongside her older siblings when she was six years old. At twelve, she left school entirely. She married Perry "Pap" Hamer in 1944 and the two moved to nearby Ruleville.

The public aspect of Hamer's life did not begin until 1962, when she began attending meetings sponsored by the Student Nonviolent Coordinating Committee (SNCC). These meetings were designed to educate black people to help them get on the voter registration rolls. In August 1962, Hamer, along with a group organized by SNCC, took a bus to Indianola, the Sunflower County seat, to register to vote. Officials turned away all but Hamer and one other potential voter, then administered a literacy test, which Hamer failed. The test required applicants to copy and interpret complex passages of the Mississippi state constitution. When the group left Indianola, their bus was pulled over because, the police told them, it was the wrong color.

When Hamer returned home she was informed her landlord had dropped by. He left word that Hamer should stop attempting to register or else she and her family would have to leave the property where they had lived and worked for eighteen years. Hamer left that night. She moved in with friends, then went to live with a niece, but she continued to face harassment, including one night shortly thereafter, when somebody opened fire on the house where she was staying. Still, as she would later say, "They kicked me off the plantation, they set me free."

Hamer continued to prepare for voter registration and, now denied her only means of income, began working for SNCC, whose leaders, including James Forman and Robert Moses, held sessions coaching people in constitutional interpretation so that Mississippi blacks—then de facto denied their right to vote—could leap the hurdles crafted by entrenched white power. Hamer took the literacy test again in December 1962 and passed. Working with SNCC and COFO, the Council of Federated Organizations, Hamer recruited and trained others to exercise their voting rights as well, a difficult task since so many poor blacks faced intimidation, economic reprisals, and outright violence for even attempting to register.

On June 3, 1963, Hamer went with other civil rights workers to Winona, Mississippi, for citizenship classes. The group was arrested and taken to jail. While in prison, Hamer and her colleagues were beaten, leaving Hamer, who already limped from childhood polio, bleeding and battered. She suffered permanent damage to her kidneys and eyes. The protection the U.S. Justice

Department had promised SNCC and its field workers came too late; although the police officers later were charged for the beatings, they were acquitted by an all-white jury.

A growing symbol of the hardships endured by grass-roots civil rights workers, Hamer became known for her strong voice, both in speaking and in rallying the weary with her singing. In 1964 Hamer lent her voice to the political arena, helping to found the Mississippi Freedom Democratic party (MFDP), an outgrowth of 1964's Freedom Summer, which brought a flood of black and white volunteers to Mississippi to help educate and empower. Running as the MFDP candidate for the U.S. Senate, Hamer led the fight to open the state's lily-white Democratic party to black voters.

Challenging years of history, Hamer and the MFDP went to Atlantic City, New Jersey, where the nation's Democrats were gathering for their nominating convention. There they hoped to force the party to represent all its people. Facing powerful opposition—and counseled by prominent African-American leaders to tone down her protests—Hamer spoke before the credentials committee, passionately questioning the democratic nature of institutions that systematically excluded the voices of citizens. Although the final compromise seated only two MFDP delegates, Hamer had been heard. The party voted that in future conventions no segregated delegations would be welcomed. The following year, President Lyndon B. Johnson signed the Voting Rights Act.

After the convention, Hamer continued to work for voting rights and, increasingly, economic equality as well. In 1967 she played a fundamental role in founding and leading the National Welfare Rights Organization with George Wiley. In 1969 she founded Freedom Farms, a food cooperative whose purpose Hamer once described as "to produce enough that people just won't know what hunger is." In addition to growing vegetables, Freedom Farms raised pigs and, for a time, provided lots for tenant farmers, black and white, to build their own homes. Four decades after she had to leave school to pick cotton, Hamer was recognized by Howard University and Morehouse College, which granted her honorary degrees, and Delta Sigma Theta sorority inducted her as an honorary member. Hamer died in 1977. She, more than anyone else, registered the voice of the disenfranchised southern African-American working woman as a political force in this country.

1960–1969

Jimi Hendrix

Electric Gypsy
(1942–1970)

Jimi Hendrix took us higher with his guitar. The civil rights movement had morphed into the fight for black power, Elvis joined the army and grew politically conservative, and Beatlemania hit American shores. By the mid-sixties, white America was in the grip of profound culture amnesia, forgetting that the rock and roll music it loved was an appropriation of black cultural forms. Ironically, artists of the wildly popular black Motown label—as well as the Shirelles and Little Richard—contributed to the white-washing of black music. Even British musicians "invading" America, who played in white venues, were indebted to African-American blues music. Long hair and sideburns had come to symbolize a stand for cultural radicalism. Frank Sinatra had infamously growled that rock and roll was sung by "cretinous goons," that it was the martial music for every "sideburned delinquent" on the face of the earth. But to us, early rock and roll was African-American music, and the long-haired Afro signified poetry.

And into this circus of American copycats imitating the Beatles and English bands copying American blacks emerged a serious young rock and roll musician named Jimi Hendrix, an African American from Seattle who people thought was English. He was just twenty-four when he made his national debut at the Monterey Blues Festival in 1967—the summer of love and urban riots. His band, the Experience, was one of the first black-led integrated big-time rock bands: Jimi was backed by his friends Noel Redding on bass and Mitch Mitchell on drums—two skinny white Englishmen with big Afros.

Jimi Hendrix was claimed by all the Age of Aquarius counterculture, and was also claimed by African Americans. He was an icon for late 1960s high school days. His identity may have been claimed by everyone under the sun, but it was what Jimi did with his guitar that will forever define him. He defined his individuality through a complete redefinition of electric guitar. Hendrix's use of feedback, swirling electronic effects, lilting and terrifying riffs changed forever the guitar's musical potential. Hendrix went beyond the fusion of stylistic elements. He was the first to create sound by transforming the electric guitar with blues-derived, socially conscious, beat-driven music. Considered a true virtuoso, left-handed Hendrix played a right-

handed Fender Stratocaster and just turned it upside down. There was symbolism in that.

All too often the seriousness of his music was overlooked in favor of his showmanship. His show was visceral. You didn't have to be a musical expert to see and feel the revolution Jimi made through sound. Hendrix strummed the strings of his guitar with his teeth. He flung it over his head and behind his back, still embroidering the strings with his fingers. Still playing, he made love to it, lying on his back like Big Jay McNeely, a wild musician who had performed that feat with a tenor sax. When he had finished his ode to the electric guitar, he set his instrument of desire alight, so that flames would leap across the stage, obscuring him in smoke. He wore his

Afro wilder than the rest of us and wore slightly brighter shades of clothes. He painted with sound the world of fantasy and freedom.

As a shy young boy growing up in Seattle, Washington, Hendrix's home life was far from ideal. As an infant, his mother left him with relatives and, when his father returned from military service in World War II, the family was so poor that he and his younger brother Leon were placed for a brief time in a foster home. In childhood Hendrix donned a makeshift cape and imagined that he was a sci-fi hero called Mongo who saved the world from Ming the Merciless. In school, he painted pictures of Martian sunsets and summer afternoons on Venus. As he grew older Hendrix devoured the blues, playing air guitar on a plain broomstick. Jimi's father bought him his first guitar when a social worker told him that this sort of fantasy was destructive. Not knowing how to read or write music, he taught himself how to play by listening to recordings of Muddy Waters, B. B. King, and Chuck Berry. He listened avidly to rock and soul and eventually played in a band that performed along the Pacific Interstate-5 corridor. After committing several petty crimes in Seattle, Hendrix joined the airborne paratroopers. Between 1963 and 1965, he worked the Nashville "chitlin circuit" as a backup guitarist for rhythm and blues artists such as Little Richard, Sam Cooke, B. B. King, Wilson Pickett, Ike and Tina Turner, and the Isley Brothers. By 1965 he had relocated to Harlem, where he found work with tenor saxophonist Curtis Knight and his band, the Squires. But with each band, he played backup and, feeling the noose of conformity, he fell into the more experimental Greenwich Village scene with his own band called Jimmy James and the Blue Flames. The band played soul classics, but Hendrix was already demonstrating his talent in long and impressionistic improvisations.

By the mid-sixties, rebellion was in the air, and the signs of black cultural upheaval were everywhere. Hendrix was playing in local New York clubs when John Hammond, Jr., the white blues acoustic artist, booked him for future gigs at clubs frequented by the rich and famous. Chas Chandler, the former bassist for the Animals, heard Hendrix play at Café Wha and convinced him he would become a star if he moved to London. He did, and by 1966 he was indeed famous. While Hendrix thrived in London's rock milieu, he also was opposed to the barbarity of

British racism. "You might think that Jimi Hendrix would appear menacingly swinging from treetops, brandishing a spear, and yelling blood curdling cries of Aargh!" read one newspaper story. "For Jimi, who makes Mick Jagger look as respectable as Edward Heath and as genial as Edward Frost, could pass as a Hottentot on the rampage; looks as if his foot-long hair has been petrified by a thousand shock waves, and is given to playing the guitar with his teeth."

Hendrix formed his band, the Experience, in early 1967. Their first album, *Are You Experienced?,* contained the hits "Hey Joe" and "Purple Haze," which featured Hendrix's famously expansive lyrics ("Scuze me while I kiss the sky"). His second album, *Axis: Bold as Love,* took its inspiration from the black vocal groups of the fifties. *Electric Ladyland* marked Hendrix's mastery of the recording studio, but because the album cover pictured twenty-odd bare-breasted young women, mostly white, it could not be distributed in America.

In 1967 Hendrix returned to America to appear at the Monterey Blues Festival. Jimi Hendrix and the Experience electrified the audience—literally—and almost overnight Hendrix was elevated to the status of rock and roll demigod. In 1969 he established his own lavish studio, *Electric Ladyland,* in New York. However, financial problems, bad management, and the disintegration of his band made for a tumultuous year. In the same year he appeared in the second era-defining concert of the sixties, the Woodstock festival in New York, where he performed his legendary version of "The Star-Spangled Banner."

After Woodstock, Hendrix formed the Band of Gypsies, an all-black band, with Buddy Miles, a friend from the army, on drums, and Billy Cox on bass. They released an album called *Machine Gun* dedicated to all the street fighters waging war in Harlem, Chicago, and Vietnam. Though his art was immersed in American themes, Hendrix remained in London. His increasing financial problems forced him to agree to an Experience reunion in 1970. But the concerts were canceled when one of the musicians who had been slipped a dose of LSD died of a drug overdose. Hendrix found more and more solace in alcohol and drugs.

In 1970, Hendrix died tragically. He mistakenly had taken too many of his girl-friend's sleeping pills, unaware that the European dosage was much stronger. His twenty-seven-year-old barely lived-in body was flown back to Seattle, where he was buried under his own Venus sky.

Martin Luther King, Jr.

Soul Force
(1929–1968)

He is the prophet of the century, and the spoken voice of the civil rights movement. He was a child of the segregated South who insisted that whites were capable of loving their black neighbors. This was all the more remarkable when we remember that he grew up in a world that forced blacks to attend "colored" schools, to use separate water fountains, pools, and restaurants, and to suffer daily abuses and discriminations. His strategy was a gamble in the face of a government and social structure that were controlled by whites, and the intractable power of racist terrorist organizations such as the Ku Klux Klan. Yet, from the day he began to lead the Montgomery bus boycott until his assassination at the age of thirty-nine, Dr. Martin Luther King, Jr., insisted that black Americans could live as their fellow citizens lived. Today, King is a symbol of the triumphs of the civil rights movement, a man celebrated for his dignified, nonviolent approach to fighting for justice against impossible odds.

The son of a Baptist minister, King grew up in a middle-class, religious African-American community in Atlanta, Georgia. Although he lived comfortably, he felt the effects of segregation firsthand. King's parents, strong proponents of civil rights, raised him to follow the laws of segregation, but not to accept them—to view the southern way of life as "a social condition rather than a natural order," and as a social condition that was unjust. King first became aware of the problems created by the social system as a child, when the father of a white friend of his forbade his son from playing with young Martin.

Because he wanted to change the social order, King planned to become a lawyer or a doctor when he entered Morehouse College in 1944. He was not stimulated by the conservative religious views prevalent where he grew up and did not intend to follow his father's footsteps into the pulpit. But at Morehouse, his ideas were challenged by new ways of thinking about morality, religion, and the social problems in the Jim Crow South. Inspired by Henry David Thoreau's "On Civil Disobedience," King began to see noncooperation with injustice as a moral duty. He also learned about the liberal tradition in Christianity, which he found both intellectually and emotionally satisfying.

Eager to learn more about how philosophers deal with social problems, King enrolled at Crozer Theological Seminary in Chester, Pennsylvania. Because King believed that people will lift their souls only after they have raised their social condition, he thought that good ministers had to address both the material and the spiritual needs of their congregations. He wrote: "On the one hand I must attempt to change the soul of individuals so that their societies may be changed. On the other I must attempt to change the societies so that the individual soul will have a chance. Therefore, I must be concerned about unemployment, slums, and economic insecurity." And so he read the works of Aristotle, Rousseau, Hobbes, Mill, Locke, Marx, Rauschenbusch, Niebuhr, and other influential thinkers who addressed these issues. Perhaps most appealing to King was the message of Mohandas Gandhi. Hearing Mordecai Johnson, president of Howard University, speak on Gandhi's trust in the power of love and nonviolent resistance, King was deeply moved. Gandhi's was a philosophy that shaped the way King fought for civil rights.

After graduating from Crozer, King began working toward his Ph.D. at Boston University. There, he continued studying philosophy and religion. His faith in the inherent dignity of individuals grew along with his belief that the most effective way for the downtrodden to gain liberty is through nonviolent resistance. He met and married Coretta Scott while in Boston, and after King graduated from Boston University, the couple moved to Montgomery, Alabama, where King became pastor of the Dexter Avenue Baptist Church in 1954. King encouraged the members of his congregation to seek liberty: "I insisted that every church member become a registered voter and a member of the NAACP and organized within the church a social and political action committee—designed to keep the congregation intelligently informed on the social, political, and economic situations." King himself was involved with the NAACP and with the Alabama Council on Human Relations, an interracial group which elected him its vice president.

His work with civil rights groups and his studies at Morehouse, Crozer, and Boston University prepared King for the Montgomery bus boycott. A perfect example of nonviolent resistance in action, the boycott was a pivotal moment in United States history, a time when black Americans realized the ability of committed and organized groups—even groups of socially and economically oppressed people—to cause change. On December 1, 1955, an African-American woman named Rosa Parks was riding a city bus, tired after a long day, when she was ordered to give up her seat for a white passenger. Her refusal and subsequent arrest inspired Montgomery's black people and their church leaders to protest the laws that required African Americans to ride in the rear of public buses and to give their seats to whites when the buses became full.

King and other black leaders such as E. D. Nixon, Ralph Abernathy, and L. Roy Bennett led the boycott, demanding that bus drivers treat black passengers with courtesy, that passengers sit on a first-come-first-serve basis, and that African Americans be hired as drivers on certain routes. Overseeing such a massive protest was no small accomplishment. King and the other leaders of the Montgomery Improvement Association (MIA) organized the city's black population to find alternate modes of transportation, mostly to white neighborhoods where black women worked as domestics. They set up carpools so that the community could sustain the boycott. Meanwhile, MIA's leaders received threatening phone calls, the police began arresting large numbers of black car drivers for traffic "violations," and homes—including that of MIA president King—were bombed. But finally, after Montgomery's African Americans had spent a year walking and riding in carpools wherever they went, the Supreme Court declared bus segregation laws unconstitutional and blacks began riding the city's buses once again.

> Let us not seek to satisfy our thirst for freedom by drinking from the cup of bitterness and hatred. We must ever conduct our struggle on the high plane of dignity and discipline. We must not allow our creative protest to degenerate into physical violence. Again and again we must rise to the majestic heights of meeting physical force with soul force.
> —Martin Luther King, Jr.

The battle for bus desegregation was victorious, but many other rights were being denied African Americans all over the nation. And so King brought other black ministers together to create the Southern Christian Leadership Conference (SCLC) in 1957. He gained national prominence as he toured the United States speaking about civil rights at rallies and other forums. He visited Ghana to take part in its celebration of independence, a successful battle for freedom carried out by African people that was particularly meaningful to King. He traveled to India the next year to see the country of Gandhi and returned even more committed to the principle of nonviolent resistance. So that he could devote more energy to SCLC, King resigned as pastor of Dexter Avenue Baptist Church and became copastor of his father's church in Atlanta, Ebenezer Baptist.

The next phase in the civil rights movement was initiated by student protesters at the North Carolina Agricultural and Technical College in Greensboro, who started a series of sit-ins at a Woolworth lunch counter. As more and more students across the South became involved, King motivated them with his inspirational rhetoric. He took a key role in the Freedom Rides of the Congress on Racial

1960–1969

Equality (CORE) as well as its voter education program (VEP). The movement focused on Birmingham, Alabama. In 1962, Birmingham, governed by the fierce segregationist Eugene "Bull" Connor, was an excellent stage for the struggle. The public watched their televisions in horror as Connor ordered police dogs and fire hoses on protesters. When King himself was arrested, he wrote his eloquent "Letter from Birmingham Jail" on the merits of nonviolent resistance and the need for civil rights for all Americans.

In 1963, King led the historic March on Washington, where he delivered his well-known and often quoted "I Have a Dream" speech to over 250,000 people. Exhausted from his frequent public appearances, troubled by divisions within the civil rights movement's leadership, and beleaguered by critics, King checked into an Atlanta hospital in 1964. There he was notified that he had won the Nobel Peace Prize. Following his trip to Norway and Sweden, King began to reflect upon the economic nature of racism, and the evil of neocolonialism. King became opposed to the war in Vietnam. A trip to Chicago left him depressed about the insidious nature of racism in the North. His last major operation, the Poor People's Campaign, marked a turn in his thinking about social justice. The great civil rights leader was now agitating for economic rights for indigent Americans of all backgrounds.

On April 4, 1968, King was assassinated as he stood on a balcony at the Lorraine Motel in Memphis. King had spoken in public about the possibility of such an event's taking place, and had said even the night before his assassination: "I may not get there with you. But I want you to know tonight that we as a people will get to the promised land." In his lifetime, student radicals and black power leaders compared King to the black nationalism of Malcolm X. Malcolm himself took issue with the Atlanta preacher's conciliatory stance toward white America. But just as Malcolm's thinking evolved toward the end of his life, King's too took different turns. He was angered by the less obvious white racism he encountered in the North and so deeply concerned about the economic injustices of capitalism that mainstream liberals suspected him of socialism. On the verge of his death, the only African American we celebrate as a hero with a national holiday was deeply depressed and at a low point in his public popularity. Yet Martin Luther King, Jr. was a hero who did more to end segregation than any other single person. He embodied and articulated a complex moral vision that made the struggle of the African American universal.

Thurgood Marshall

The Great Dissenter
(1908–1993)

He was the most important black lawyer of the century, the man who used the law to dismantle Jim Crow. The first African American to sit on the United States Supreme Court, Thurgood Marshall achieved the highest government office ever attained by a black American, and his work on the bench from 1967 to 1991 made him one of the most significant lawyers and judges of the twentieth century. Often called the conscience of the Court, Marshall was a stalwart defender of civil liberties and affirmative action and earned the nickname "the Great Dissenter" for his staunch opposition to the death penalty. Yet his tenure on the Court was only the final phase in a career that spanned half a century and included Marshall's victory as a lawyer in what is widely considered the most important piece of American jurisprudence—1954's *Brown* v. *Board of Education* case—which struck down public school segregation.

Marshall's life as a crusader for equality began in a cradle of relative privilege. Born July 2, 1908, in Baltimore, Marshall grew up in a comfortable home headed by his mother, a schoolteacher, and his father, a waiter and steward at an elegant men's club. Still, Baltimore was a segregated city; the Marshall family faced racism, but did so quietly. His father's advice, which Marshall later recalled, was, "If anyone calls you nigger, you not only have my permission to fight him, you got my orders."

A haphazard student, Marshall nevertheless picked up one critical tool while in high school—a teacher punished him by forcing him to read the U.S. Constitution for each transgression, ensuring that by the time Marshall graduated he knew the document by heart. At Lincoln University in Pennsylvania, a black college taught by an all-white faculty, Marshall abandoned his early plans to study medicine and began to seek a way to fight segregation, a growing determination sparked by Lincoln's referendum on integrating the school's faculty.

When he graduated in 1930, Marshall enrolled at the law school of Howard University. He'd arrived at the perfect place at the perfect time. Howard's law school, for years an unaccredited and uninspiring institution, was undergoing a renaissance, courtesy of its new dean, Charles Hamilton Houston. Houston, who would later become the NAACP's first chief counsel, not only won the school accreditation, he also molded it into a laboratory for civil rights work, believing that black lawyers had to be "social engineers." In and out of the classroom, Marshall would learn from and work with Houston for the next two decades. Defending a black man accused of killing a white man in Loudoun County, Virginia, in 1934, the two saved their client from the death penalty—a tremendous victory in a racist environment.

Although Marshall had established a solo law practice in Baltimore, he continued to work with Houston—who left Howard for the NAACP full-time in 1935—and in 1936 they won an important victory in *Murray* v. *Maryland,* a lawsuit challenging the University of Maryland Law School's discrimination against black applicants. The case had personal resonance for Marshall—his argument questioned not only legal issues but also "moral commitment"—and the ruling brought jubilation in civil rights circles. "He brought us the Constitution," NAACP leader Juanita Jackson Mitchell recalled, "like Moses brought his people the Ten Commandments."

When failing health forced Houston to retire in 1938, Marshall succeeded him as the NAACP's chief counsel, eventually heading its newly formed legal defense fund. He traveled the country defending the precarious legal rights of African Americans for the next twenty years, along the way winning cases that toppled segregated political primaries, restrictive real-estate covenants, and racial payroll inequality for public school teachers. Increasingly, he was invited to act as a roving civil rights ambassador, advising Jackie Robinson as the ballplayer was poised to break baseball's color line, investigating racism in the U.S. Army, and studying race riots for government officials.

Brown v. *Board of Education* was the result of years of planning and effort by both Marshall and his mentor, Houston. Beginning with *Murray,* the two had conducted a campaign of attacking segregation in graduate schools, and victories in that arena had established legal precedent weakening the 1896 *Plessy* v. *Ferguson* decision, with its standard of "separate but equal" accommodations. Five elementary school cases, brought together under the name of one, came before the Supreme Court beginning in 1952; Marshall brought together an argument blending constitutional points and sociological considerations. On May 17, 1954, Chief Justice Earl Warren read the unanimous decision—public school segregation was illegal under the Constitution.

Having won the war, Marshall now found himself fighting the peace—*Brown*'s implementation, hampered by the mandate that desegregation occur "with all deliberate speed," became a battleground that continues to this day. Marshall represented black students attempting to enter previously all-white schools in districts all over the South. Following John F. Kennedy's inauguration as president in 1961, Marshall sought and received appointment to the U.S. Court of Appeals, facing bitter opposition from southern senators but eventually winning confirmation. Of the 112 opinions he issued from that bench, none was overturned on appeal. Four years later, President Lyndon B. Johnson named Marshall solicitor general. When Johnson nominated Marshall for the U.S. Supreme Court in 1967, he faced another confirmation battle, but again he prevailed.

A liberal on an increasingly conservative court, Marshall's independence and integrity found him on the losing side more often than not. Although he crafted important decisions on prisoners' rights, freedom of expression, and other civil liberties cases, Marshall became better known for his blistering dissents in cases that chipped away at affirmative action or that abandoned efforts at making schools equal for all. The historian John Hope Franklin described Marshall as a "great watchdog, insisting that this nation live up to its Constitution." Although he acknowledged that progress had been made, he was outspoken in identifying the continuing racism in American society and did not shy away from criticizing his colleagues for their ignorance of it.

After years of ill health, Marshall stepped down in 1991. When he died in 1993, he became only the second justice to lie in state at the Supreme Court building. A brilliant lawyer, he won twenty-nine of the thirty-two cases he argued before the Court he later joined. A fearless battler, he chose cases that challenged inequality and hypocrisy in all its forms. He used the law of the land to dismantle de jure racism.

Sidney Poitier

The Leading Man
(1927–)

He taught troubled teens, fought racist sheriffs, worked for nuns, and even married a white woman—all in that most mainstream form of entertainment, Hollywood film. Sidney Poitier was everyone's leading man, but he was also *our* leading man, a shining black talent amid the turbulence of the 1960s.

Sidney Poitier's life began in a shoe box. He was born prematurely, weighing only three pounds. His father, fearing the worst, found a shoe box in which to bury his infant son. His mother, grasping for hope that her son would live, visited a soothsayer—a reader of tea leaves—who assured her that the infant would survive.

What other secrets of fate the tea reader revealed to Sidney Poitier's mother that day are lost to history, but she might have imparted to the worried mother some small portent of the illustrious success her tiny infant would have. In a career that has spanned nearly half a century, Poitier has amassed an impressive cinematic resume: fifty-three movies, nine of which he directed; a Best Actor Academy Award for *Lilies of the Field,* the first ever received by a black American; and three books, the most recent of which is a spiritual autobiography entitled *The Measure of a Man.* Along with Harry Belafonte, Poitier created a space for black leading men in Hollywood.

Poitier was born in Miami, Florida, on February 20, 1927, to a tomato farmer father and mother. Raised in Barbados, early on Poitier developed a racial consciousness different from his African-American counterparts. Like his close friend Harry Belafonte, Poitier believes his West Indian upbringing offered something of a psychological advantage when it came time to build a career in the United States. Colonialism aside, growing up in a black majority country meant that most of the doctors, nurses, lawyers, and policemen he encountered were black. "I firmly believe," Poitier has said, "that we both had the opportunity to arrive at the formation of a sense of ourselves without having it f—— with by racism as it existed in the United States." Poitier returned to Miami to live with his brother Cyril before moving to New York City to enlist in the U.S. Army as a physiologist until the end of World War II.

Poitier's early years were marked by challenges: He received only a year and a half of formal education and spent much of his youth "flirting with the reformatory." Acting came about in a rather inauspicious way. As a young man out of work and out of school, Poitier recalls a particular day spent looking for employment in New York. "I was looking in the newspaper for a job," he recalls. "On one side it said 'Dishwasher Wanted.' And on the other it said 'Actor Wanted.' I thought, 'Wait a minute.'" While his first audition was something short of a success—he flubbed his lines and was summarily dismissed ("He led me by the back of the trousers to the door"), this setback only fueled his budding interest in acting. Six months later he won his first part—yet again, something short of promising—as a mime. It was a start.

After achieving some success in the theatre, as a student at the American Negro Theatre in New York City, Poitier made his move to Hollywood films in 1950. After a series of supporting roles in which he earned some distinction—most notably in *Blackboard Jungle* (1955), a film widely censored for its interracial content, and Stanley Kramer's *The Defiant Ones* (1958)—Poitier made his breakthrough playing a role that his friend Belafonte turned down. *Lilies of the Field* (1963) cast Poitier in a kinder light than his often defiant, youthful early roles. The phenomenal success of the film made him the biggest black American movie star of his generation. As the noble, selfless, and saintly Homer Smith, Poitier established his presence in the postwar American cinema. He also became the first African American to win an Academy Award.

In 1967 Poitier was the highest grossing American film star. In this one year, he starred in three box office hits: *To Sir With Love, Guess Who's Coming to Dinner,* and *In the Heat of the Night.* Unlike Belafonte, whose political stances eventually alienated him from the Hollywood mainstream, Poitier was content to work within the constraints of his roles in order to render black characters as fully as possible. Yet his screen persona was always dignified, self-reliant, and strong. Beginning in the 1970s Poitier began to direct, producing a number of lowbrow comedies such as *Stir Crazy*

(1980) and *Ghost Dad* (1990). He returned to acting after a ten-year absence to appear in *Shoot to Kill* (1988), *Little Nikita* (1988), and *Sneakers* (1992).

Poitier's legacy lives on in the success of a new breed of black leading men, including Denzel Washington, Morgan Freeman, Laurence Fishburne, and many others. Just as Bill Cosby did for the medium of television, Sidney Poitier's grace reversed a century of racist stereotyping of black male actors, and created possibilities for performers scarcely conceived before 1960. He is the film industry's living embodiment of the progress generated by the civil rights movement.

1960–1969

Malcolm X

Black Nationalist Prophet
(1925–1965)

Malcolm X was a prophet. Like Martin Luther King, Jr., he foresaw his own untimely demise at the hands of an assassin's bullet, but this did not keep him from telling the truth about the black condition in America and the corrosive influence of white supremacy on the American democratic ideal. In the course of his life, he was many things: a petty crook and a public moralist, a convict and a devout Muslim, a black nationalist and a Pan-Africanist, an ideologue and an icon. His life, as he describes it in his autobiography, was a "chronology of changes."

Following his assassination, allegedly at the hands of black men associated with the Nation of Islam and its leader, Elijah Muhammad, Malcolm has emerged as a black cultural hero of grand proportions. He was portrayed in his lifetime as a hate monger for his militant stance of black resistance. But it is his assertions of black worth, beauty, and strength that were instrumental in forming the black power movement that would follow in the wake of his death. For black college students in the 1960s, for black nationalists now, his words are deeply inspiring.

In the last years of his life, Malcolm X experienced a reevaluation of his political values. Fresh from a hajj to Mecca, he returned invigorated by the potentialities for cross-racial alliance. While this certainly should not be misinterpreted as a facile move toward integrationism—Malcolm was still insistent on black political and economic self-sufficiency—it signaled a shift toward the more traditional Muslim tenets. His potential as a leader was clearly reaching its peak. And while his death was a tragic truncation of this potential, in the words of poet Robert Hayden, he was nonetheless "much more than there was time for him to be."

Malcolm X was born Malcolm Little in Omaha, Nebraska, on May 19, 1925, to Louise and Earl Little. His father, whom he idealizes in his autobiography, was a Baptist preacher active in Marcus Garvey's Universal Negro Improvement

Association. He was killed under mysterious circumstances, though Malcolm imputes that it was because of his militancy. While many have questioned the veracity of the particulars that Malcolm recalls of his early life in his autobiography ("as told to Alex Haley"), it is clear that his father offered him a vision of political activism, resistance to white supremacy, and black separatism influenced by Garvey.

Malcolm's youth was one of fractured bonds. His mother was committed to a mental institution, and Malcolm and his siblings were split up by welfare agencies. By the time he was in the eighth grade, he left school and moved to Boston to live with his half-sister Ella. Here he began the first phase of his life: the hipster and hustler. Like others of the time, Malcolm donned zoot suits, conked his hair, and lindy hopped to the music of the swing jazz orchestras. Malcolm's life was markedly apolitical in these early years in Boston, and later in Harlem. "Detroit Red" and then "Big Red," as he was called, often found himself on the wrong side of the law. He derived his income from dealing drugs, pimping, gambling, and stealing. "I loved the devil," he writes. "I was trying as hard as I could to be white." But in 1946 this phase of his life came to an abrupt close when he was arrested for burglary and sentenced to ten years in prison.

Malcolm found redemption through a religious conversion. While in prison, he was exposed to the ministry of Elijah Muhammad and his Lost-Found Nation of Islam in the Wilderness of North America, the nationalist group usually referred to as Black Muslims. Submitting to the discipline of the Nation, and immersing himself in the Bible and the Quran, Malcolm found new directions for his energies.

> *Anything I do today, I regard as urgent. No man is given but so much time to accomplish whatever is his life's work. My life in particular never has stayed fixed in one position very long. . . . I am only facing the facts when I know that any moment of any day, or any night, could bring my death.*
> —Malcolm X

He began to read voraciously, and he cultivated his oratory skills in prison debates. In fact, a group of prisoners, led by Malcolm, defeated a debate team from the Massachusetts Institute of Technology.

At his release in 1952, Malcolm had transformed himself, renaming himself Malcolm X as a symbolic repudiation of the "white man's name." Malcolm emerged as the preeminent spokesman for the Nation, serving as the most eloquent voice to communicate Elijah Muhammad's message. As a minister, his role was to preach the gospel of Islam, but it was as a racial spokesman—a prophet of rage—that he was most notable. During the peak of his influence, he had more speaking engagements than any other public figure with the exception of Barry Goldwater. While his stardom began to overshadow his organizational allegiance, he was scrupulous in acknowledging his debt to Muhammad. He praised Elijah Muhammad as second only to Allah.

Malcolm's charisma, combined with his burgeoning independent political vision, finally proved too much for Muhammad and the Nation. In the media, he was often presented as the polar opposite of Martin Luther King, Jr. And while King's doctrine of love stands in stark contrast to Malcolm's rage and righteous indignation, by the sixties their visions seemed less incompatible with one another, partially because King moved leftward. In 1963 Elijah Muhammad placed an order of silence on Malcolm, ostensibly in response to his comment that President John F. Kennedy's assassination was an example of "chickens coming home to roost." A more plausible explanation for the ban, though, is Muhammad's growing fear of Malcolm's influence and tensions between the two. Malcolm became disillusioned with his spiritual father after discovering that Muhammad had committed a number of sexual and economic improprieties. The split was finalized after Malcolm discovered that Muhammad had planned to assassinate him.

On March 8, 1964, Malcolm announced his resignation from the Nation and his formation of the Muslim Mosque, Inc. This marks the final phase in Malcolm's life. That same year he made his pilgrimage to Mecca, and renamed himself El-Hajj Malik El-Shabazz. He also had embraced a more orthodox Islam, becoming a Sunni Muslim, and acknowledging the "true brotherhood" of man. Whites, he said, were not devils, as Elijah Muhammad had taught. Nonetheless, Malcolm did not abandon his black nationalist stance. The pilgrimage, he recalled, "broadened my scope probably more in twelve days than my previous experience during my thirty-nine years on this earth." His vision had evolved from that of a street corner black nationalist to a more subtle mix of orthodox Islam, anticolonialism, socialism, and the doctrine of racial solidarity known as black power. In the summer of 1964, Malcolm formed the Organization for Afro-American Unity (OAAU), a black advocacy network based upon the Organization of African Unity. At base, Malcolm saw the importance for building a black infrastructure within America. The institution did not outlive its founder.

Malcolm X was assassinated while speaking at the Audubon Ballroom in New York on February 21, 1965, by gunmen supposedly affiliated with the Nation of Islam. While controversy still surrounds his death—including implications of involvement from the Federal Bureau of Investigation—more controversy has followed his legacy. Malcolm often is portrayed in simplistic terms that boil his message down to a few catchphrases, such as: "By any means necessary." But his influence has proved much more varied than that. While Malcolm left no institutional legacy, he inspired such 1960s groups as the Congress of Racial Equality (CORE) and the Student Nonviolent Coordinating Committee (SNCC), the younger generation of civil rights activists. His most palpable impact, though, came with the black power movement, whose agenda included community control, black pride, and African liberation. His autobiography was required reading among its members.

After the dissolution of black nationalist organizations in the mid-1970s, it seemed as if Malcolm's influence might pass as well. But in the late eighties and early nineties, his legacy was resuscitated, largely by members of the hip-hop generation for whom he was a cult hero. Following the release of Spike Lee's cinematic adaptation of his autobiography in 1992, Malcolm had become the stuff of "Afro-Chic" fashion. "X" hats and other paraphernalia and clothes emblazoned with his name and visage became popular, even with those for whom his message was dim.

While the fad has died down, Malcolm X's prophetic critique of America's original sin—racism and slavery—and its potential redemption is all the more insistent. He was the embodiment of the evolution of black political consciousness, from separatism to coalition-building. Perhaps the latter will be his greatest gift to the twenty-first century.

Hank Aaron

The Hammer
(1934–)

Hank Aaron mastered the difficult technique of the home run. Running down fly balls, stealing bases, swinging the bat high and powerfully, Aaron was an artist when it came to hitting: Three times he had 200 or more hits; four other times he had more than 190. To see him hit was to see elegance at work in the way he sought to anticipate what the pitchers might throw him, pulling his long large legs back, and then to see his powerful wrists hammer the small white ball so that it sailed all the way into the outfield. Aaron's career, spanning twenty-three years in the majors, was record-breaking and precedent-setting at the plate as well as in the field. His total for runs batted in (RBI or "ribbies") is 2,297. For three years in succession (1958, 1959, and 1960) he was a Gold Glove Winner. "Trying to slip a pitch past Aaron is like trying to slip a sunrise past a rooster," Hank Aaron's teammate Joe Adcock once said.

On April 8, 1974, at the age of forty, Hammering Hank, as he was nicknamed, made a 385-foot home run against the Los Angeles Dodgers, surpassing Babe Ruth's record of 714 career home runs. Aaron finished with 755 lifetime, setting a new world record. Despite being one of American baseball's most accomplished players, some even say its greatest player, his challenge to Babe Ruth was taken seriously by white racial supremacists. Aaron lived with all the emotional discontent his record provoked between 1972 and 1974, as he neared Ruth's total. Aaron knew he could be lynched for even trying. But Aaron neither held back nor backed down from his dream, despite the vicious intolerance, the hate mail, and, especially, the death threats that ultimately necessitated FBI involvement. In 1974, as he surpassed all the home run records in the world, he said "I don't want them to forget Babe Ruth. I just want them to remember me."

Aaron began playing ball incessantly in a cleared pecan grove on the other side of his childhood home in a neighborhood called Toulminvile in segregated Mobile, Alabama. Carver Park was the first recreational area for blacks in all of Mobile, and the city initiated a black recreational league, which pulled teams from every black neighborhood. Actually, more black players came from Mobile, Alabama, than anywhere else except Oakland, California. Many in the black world of baseball kept their eyes on Aaron's wondrous batting skills. He first began to play professional baseball in the Negro Leagues, and he moved through the Pritchett Athletics and the Mobile Black Bears until he was signed for two hundred dollars a month to the Indianapolis Clowns.

As a player with the Indianapolis Clowns (who were bought by the Braves in 1952), Aaron, along with Ernie Banks of the K.C. Monarchs, was one of the two finest players in the Negro American League. But he was still a greenhorn, batting cross-handed with the left hand above the right on the handle. Playing shortstop, he led the Negro American League with a .467 average. His playing was excellent, and both the Braves and the Giants wanted to hire him. The Braves offered Aaron $350 a month to play in the minor leagues in the Braves's class C Team in Eau Claire, Wisconsin. At the end of his first year he was selected the league's Rookie of the Year for batting .336 with nine home runs. In 1953, in his second pro season, Aaron was moved to Jacksonville, Florida, to the South Atlantic League, where he played second base and led the league in hitting. Finally, in March 1954, Aaron was signed to play left field for the Milwaukee Braves, first as left-fielder and then as a right-fielder, where he would spend most of his career.

In 1954, a young and skinny Aaron, together with four other black ballplayers, broke the color line in southern baseball, which consisted of the Southern and South Atlantic leagues. It is often forgotten that Jackie Robinson broke the color line only in the northern leagues. He did attempt to play in Jacksonville once, but was escorted off the field by a policeman, and the field was padlocked on the day the Dodgers were supposed to play an exhibition game. The only black player who actually got to play in a Southern League game was Nat Peeple, who batted once for the Atlanta Crackers in 1954, but he failed to get a hit, so was not really counted. It was commonly thought madness for a black ballplayer to play in southern baseball. The Southern League ultimately closed down in 1961, but in the mid-fifties the South Atlantic League, nicknamed the Sally League and made up of Montgomery,

Alabama; Columbus, Augustus, and Savannah, Georgia; Columbia and Charleston, South Carolina; and Jacksonville, Florida, was still strong.

In 1954, five black ballplayers entered this league: Hank Aaron, Horace Garner, and Felix Mantilla were signed by the Milwaukee Braves class A farm in Jacksonville, Florida, the same town that Robinson had been turned away from. Savannah also signed a pair of black players, Fleming Reedy and Al Israel. Thus Aaron played in the major leagues in 1954, playing for the Milwaukee Braves (now the Atlanta

Look, I don't have the vision or the voice of Martin Luther King or James Baldwin or Jesse Jackson or even that of Jackie Robinson. I'm just an old ballplayer. But I learned a lot as ballplayer. Among other things, I learned that if you manage to make a name for yourself—and if you're black, believe me, it has to be a big name—then people will start listening to what you have to say. That was why it was so important for me to break the home record. . . . I had to break that record. I had to do it for Jackie and my people and myself and for everybody who ever called me a nigger.
—Hank Aaron

Braves) and helped them to a world championship, hitting .393 and making three home runs in the 1957 series to beat the Yankees. At the time, Willie Mays was at the top of his game and Aaron was constantly measured against him. But Hank Aaron's slow, thoughtful, and constant style made him unique.

The seventies were the most memorable decade of Hank Aaron's career. In 1970 he made his 3,000th career hit and became the first player to combine 3,000 hits with 500 home runs. That same year he set a major league record with his 12th season of 30 or more home runs. Then, he had just hit his 600th home run against Gaylord Perry of San Francisco and the only person who stood between him and Babe Ruth's record was Willie Mays. He ended the 1972 season as he hit home run 649, surpassing Mays. The media went mad. In 1974 the Braves returned to Atlanta for the home opener on April 8. The game against Los Angeles began with a forty-five-minute salute to Aaron and national networks interrupted programming to report his batting scores. On his second pitch Aaron hit his 715th ball over the left-field fence. Babe Ruth's record was finally broken. Throughout the whole season he appeared "cool." But Hank Aaron had also accomplished other things than home runs in his long career, between 1954 and 1976.

When Aaron retired he founded the Hank Aaron Rookie League program and returned to the Atlanta Braves as a vice president. He was promoted to senior vice president in 1989 and served as corporate vice president of community relations for Turner Broadcasting Systems, Inc. (TBS). He was a member of the Sterling Committee of Morehouse College. In 1982 Aaron was inducted into the National Baseball Hall of Fame. Yet, he still has never received the popular recognition he deserves for toppling the record of the great white icon—Babe Ruth—and going about his business as if he was destined to do it.

1970–1979

Maya Angelou

The Voice
(1928–)

Maya Angelou found a voice for all of us. As a poet, writer, playwright, civil rights activist, producer, and director, she has been a pioneer in fields that were choked by oppression. Angelou has worked as a dancer, a cook, a waitress, and a madam for two prostitutes, all the while raising her son and cultivating her craft. In all its complexity, hers has been a life suited for the stuff of fiction, but all the more compelling for its hard-won truths. She is one of the few figures in American culture who can transcend any category or label. She is simply Maya Angelou and she is our voice.

Author of five autobiographies so far, seven volumes of poetry, two collections of occasional essays, four children's books, and a screenplay, Angelou would seem to have lived her life out on the page. Yet, her life outside of writing is equally compelling. From her years working odd jobs to make ends meet, to her activism during the civil rights movement, Angelou has never remained at a safe distance from the stuff of her art. It comes as little surprise then that her most successful work has come in autobiography—the most self-conscious of genres.

Indeed, whether one considers Angelou's works as autobiography or autobiographical fiction, it is tempting to read them as her act of self-fashioning. But for Angelou, writing autobiography is also something of a collective action. Speaking to black feminist literary critic Claudia Tate in 1983, she said, "When I wrote *I Know Why the Caged Bird Sings,* I wasn't thinking so much about my own life or identity. I was thinking about a particular time in which I lived and the influences of that time on a number of people. I used the central figure—myself—as a focus to show how one person can make it through those times."

Angelou was born Marguerite Johnson in St. Louis, Missouri, on April 4, 1928. She was given the name "Maya" by her younger brother Bailey when he could not pronounce "my sister," and Angelou is a slight alteration of her first husband's name, Angelos. Her early life is well known to readers of the extremely popular first volume of her autobiography, *I Know Why the Caged Bird Sings,* named after Paul Laurence Dunbar's canonical poem. Shortly after her birth, Angelou's family moved to California, but her parents divorced when she was three. Maya and her brother moved in with their paternal grandmother in Stamps, Arkansas. These early years culminated in crisis when the seven-year-old Angelou, in St. Louis visiting her mother, was raped by her mother's boyfriend. Not long after Angelou confided in her brother, the man was mysteriously murdered.

Angelou, in response to the rape, became mute for five years. She began to read voraciously. She "saved her young passion," she tells us, "for Paul Laurence Dunbar, Langston Hughes, James Weldon Johnson, and W. E. B. Du Bois." It was, in part, this same love of literature that helped her emerge from silence. The drive to give voice to the poetry that she could only read silently spurred her to speak. Finally, under the tutelage of a woman named Mrs. Flowers, coupled with her love of literature, she regained her voice.

During high school Angelou returned to California, where she immersed herself in drama, dance, and literature. To support herself she worked as a streetcar conductor in San Francisco, the first-ever female conductor. At sixteen she gave birth to her only child, Clyde (later known as Guy) Johnson. Her second autobiography, *Gather Together in My Name,* chronicles this time in her life. This story begins at the end of World War II and culminates with the end of Angelou's personal war against prostitution, drugs, and dependency.

In 1952 Angelou married her first husband, a Greek sailor named Tosh Angelos. The marriage only lasted two years. Again she was left to support herself and her son by any means necessary. She took a job as a bar girl and dancer at a strip club, which led to a performing gig at a popular San Francisco nightspot called the Purple Onion. This, in turn, led to a job as a professional dancer in 1954 with the international touring production of *Porgy and Bess.*

At her return, Angelou relocated to New York, where she sang at various clubs, and at the acclaimed Apollo Theatre in Harlem. She began to hone her writing skills. As a member of the Harlem Writers Guild she made the connections that would lead to her producing, directing, and performing in *Cabaret for Freedom,* an Off-Broadway revue to benefit the Southern Christian Leadership Conference

(SCLC). She tells of this tumultuous time in *The Heart of a Woman.*

Thus began, too, her life as a civil rights activist. In 1960 she was asked to succeed Bayard Rustin as the northern coordinator for the SCLC. Under the leadership of Martin Luther King, Jr., SCLC was deeply involved in the fight for racial equality. After a year in this capacity, Angelou moved to Africa. In 1961 she met and married Vusumzi Make, a South African freedom fighter. They moved to Cairo where, despite her husband's restrictions, Angelou took the post of associate editor of the *Arab Observer.* In 1963, her marriage to Make ended. Determined to stay in Africa, Angelou relocated to Ghana, where she worked as an administrator for the school of music and drama at the University of Ghana and as features editor of the *African Review.* She recalls this time as the first in her life in which she truly felt at home.

After returning to the United States, Angelou continued her association with the Harlem Writers Guild. James Baldwin, admiring her poetry and intrigued by her life story, suggested that Angelou write her autobiography. The result was *I Know Why the Caged Bird Sings* (1970), a critically acclaimed best-seller. The following year she published her first book of poetry, *Just Give Me a Cool Drink of Water 'fore I Diiie* (1971). She has since published five other volumes of poetry. Her autobiography has grown to include four sequels: *Gather Together in My Name* (1974), *Singin' and Swingin' and Gettin' Merry Like Christmas* (1976), *The Heart of a Woman* (1981), and *All God's Children Need Traveling Shoes* (1986).

In 1971 she produced *Georgia, Georgia,* the first film screenplay by a black woman ever to make it to the screen. She appeared as an actress in Alex Haley's acclaimed series *Roots,* for which she won an Emmy in 1977. On the stage, she performed in *Look Away,* for which she won a Tony in 1973. More recently, Angelou directed the box office hit *Down in the Delta* (1997). In addition to these cinematic and theatrical ventures, Angelou is still very much invested in education. She is Reynolds Professor of American Studies at Wake Forest University in Winston-Salem, North Carolina, and she lectures and gives readings throughout the world. In 1993 she was commissioned by president-elect Bill Clinton to compose a poem to be delivered at his inauguration, in the tradition of Robert Frost's "Provide,

Provide" for John F. Kennedy's inauguration in the 1960s. "On The Pulse of the Morning" attempted to capture something of the American national character—the oneness within many—and the efficacy of individual action. The poem became a best-seller. She was the only woman to speak at the 1996 Million Man March. *I Know Why the Caged Bird Sings* inaugurated a tradition of black female self-revelation in 1970 that would give rise to the sophisticated fiction of Alice Walker and Toni Morrison. And, luckily for us, Angelou keeps singing.

Romare Bearden

Experiential Artist
(1912–1988)

His paintings caught the quickened cadence of black life. Drawing upon a wide variety of influences—Flemish painting, French Cubism, Italian Renaissance painters, African surrealism, jazz, and Zen art—Bearden harnessed a kind of lush American tropicalism, an erotic bricolage of shapes and planes populated by black figural abstractions that evoke allusions to the past. Bearden's achievement was to create a jazz aesthetic in art. He was a cosmopolitan rooted in the history of peoples of African descent.

Although Bearden began painting in the 1930s, he found his form in the heightened radical aesthetic milieu of Harlem in the 1960s and 1970s. Contemporaneous with the black arts movement, Bearden joined Spiral, a group of black artists who would meet to discuss aesthetics and politics. After the group debated many proposals, including one to work only in black and white—something black artist Kara Walker would take up in the nineties—Bearden suggested a group collage, where paintings incorporated ripped and cut art from magazines. No one seemed particularly interested in this idea, and many actively disagreed, so Bearden pursued this path alone. He would become a master of the form.

Bearden was born in Charlotte, North Carolina, in 1912, to Howard Bearden, a local sanitation inspector and steward for the Canadian railroad, and Bessye Bearden, an editor. Shortly after his birth, his family moved to New York. As a boy, he spent summers in North Carolina with southern relatives, and for a period was enrolled in high school in Pittsburgh. But New York would always be his home. Bearden lived in a thriving artistic and intellectual milieu thanks in part to his cousin, Charles Alston, the painter, and his mother, who was the New York–based editor for the African-American newspaper the *Chicago Defender*. The Bearden home was a cultural center: Duke Ellington, Aaron Douglas, or even W. E. B. Du Bois would drop by. As a boy, Bearden was immersed in a creative cauldron of jazz players, writers, and visual artists whom he embraced wholeheartedly.

Bearden was a mathematics major at New York University but wrote thoughtfully about art. One of his first articles, "The Negro Artist and Modern Art," published in *Opportunity* magazine in December 1934, criticized African-American art and artists for their lack of a common aesthetic, and railed against their lack of self-criticism. Influenced by the black cartoonist Elmer Simms Campbell and Miguel Covarrubias, Bearden had begun to try his hand at illustration, contributing cartoons to the campus publication, the NYU *Medley.* The *Baltimore Afro-American, Collier's,* and the *Saturday Evening Post* eventually accepted his work. After graduating with a B.S. in 1935, he began to experiment full-time with tempera, gouache, watercolors, and oils. He rejected the WPA artist programs, thinking them too confining, but became involved with the Harlem scene, sharing a studio with Jacob Lawrence and the writer Claude McKay. He joined the Harlem Artists' Guild, and the 306 group that met at 306 W. 141st Street, an exhibition space. In 1936, he studied with Eastman Campbell and German artist George Grosz at the Art Students League in New York City. Under Grosz's influence, Bearden studied the work of international artists such as Goya, Daumier, Kollowitz, Breughel, Ingres, Durer, Holbein, Pouissin, and the Dutch masters. These formal influences would remain central to his style.

As did Jacob Lawrence during the early forties, Bearden painted genre scenes, but he shifted from social realism to flat geometric abstractions resembling stained-glass windows inspired by cubism. After three years in the army, Bearden's work came to be represented by the Samuel Kootz Gallery in New York, along with other abstract expressionists. Unlike their large-scale works, however, Bearden was creating small-scale, cubist-inspired transparent and opaque oil paintings based on biblical, historical and literary themes. He read and reread Homer and the Bible. He eventually rejected abstract expressionism because of its lack of social concern. He moved to France, where, on the G.I. bill he studied philosophy at the Sorbonne. The writer James Baldwin befriended the young artist, and his acquaintance with artists such as Braque, Brancusi, and Léger exposed him to some of the most exciting artistic debates of the time. But in the mid-1950s, having not much to show for himself artistically, Bearden suffered a nervous breakdown due to the constant pressure he placed on himself to create something new. Returning to America, he met Nanette Rohan. They married, and with her encouragement, he began to paint again in 1954.

Stuart Davis, an American painter, encouraged Bearden to incorporate a jazz sensibility into his work. The suggestion would tranform Bearden's career. Albert Murray has told how Bearden was skeptical at first when he heard Davis talk-

ing about jazz and its possibilities for visual art. But when Bearden heard him describe the way Earl Hines, the pianist, used space as a statement in building structures of sound on the piano, and how Hines's style had profoundly influenced his own color intervals, Bearden was sold. He was impressed further when Davis was able to demonstrate to him the role jazz played in shaping an analogous dynamic in visual design. Bearden suddenly understood that he had been seeking this connection. "From then on," Bearden said, "I was on my way. I don't mean to imply that I knew where I was going. But the more I just played around with visual notions as if I were improvising like a jazz musician, the more I realized what I wanted to do as a painter, and how I wanted to do it. I had gone to him to find about the avant garde and he kept trying to make me appreciate the fact that so far as he was concerned the aesthetic conventions of Harlem musicians to which so many of my habitual responses were geared were just as avant garde as Picasso, Braque, Matisse, Mondrian, and all the rest."

During the sixties Bearden began to make collages using a jazz aesthetic—*Chicago Jazz* (1964) is dedicated to just this,

as is *Seabreeze,* a musical composition that became a hit after Dizzy Gillespie, Billy Eckstein, and Oscar Pettiford recorded it. Composing with paint, transposing with shapes, Bearden enlarged his creations and reproduced them photographically. In October 1964, he had an exhibition at the Cordier & Ekstrom Gallery called *Projections.* It jolted the art world with its conceptual intelligence, and was followed in 1965 by a second show with the same name at the Corcoran Gallery in Washington, his first major exhibition at a major museum. Several collages followed, starring the black subject engaged in myriad versions of real life, juxtaposed with fragmented allusions to history and visual metaphors of black existential concerns. Bearden had arrived as a truly modern artist who used the contemporary sounds of jazz—but also the ways of seeing of modern masters—to interpret color and shape and the disjunctive minor chords of the black experience. By the end of the sixties, Bearden described his own technique quite cogently as combining the painting methods of the Old Masters with the surface and structure of cubism.

Bearden devoted his final years to work on the female nude, jazz, and the Caribbean. He was awarded the National Medal of Arts in 1987. He wrote several articles and books, including the acclaimed and influential *Six Black Masters of American Art* (1972). He died in New York on March 12, 1988.

Bearden's work forms part of a triad of influence and expression that also includes the works of Duke Ellington and Ralph Ellison. Theirs is a shared jazz aesthetic, one rooted in the blues of Bessie Smith but also, in Bearden's case, the blues of the modernists. Bearden is rare in his capacity both to create visual art and articulate the history and theory behind it. More than any other artist, Romare Bearden embodied the African-American subject in modernism and modernism in the African-American tradition.

1970–1979

James Brown

The Godfather of Funk
(1933–)

James Brown—"soul brother number one"—was the master of black funk for over two decades. Playing his music was a ritual at every black dance party during the 1960s and 1970s. Turn on the music of James Brown at one of these affairs, and people would start finger popping. Some dancers tried to imitate (if you can imagine) Brown's pirouettes, his jumps and splits; others, too cool for too much movement, grooved in recognition of the godfather's bass, even as Brown pushed the frontier of musical expression. People cared only about the coolness of his sound. Mr. Brown, as he likes to be known, rapped and crooned before his time, used vibrant horn, raunchy rock and roll guitar, and driving bass overlaid with a grunting, familiar voice like the sound of a moving train. His persona prefigured the flamboyance of the disco years, of techno-funk humor, of the era of his royal highness known as Prince. The leaps and splits, the shoulder-length straightened hair that looked like a wig at the best of times, the gold rings, the ass-twitching legs, and the tight suits—it all set the pace. He was the godfather of soul, profoundly affecting the course of African-American music in the 1960s and '70s. He was the progenitor of funk, building on a solid reputation that began back in the fifties when he fused soul and R & B, and influenced the innovator of techno-funk, George Clinton's Funkadelic and Parliament.

James Joe Brown, Jr., was born on May 3, 1933, near Barnwell, South Carolina. His mother left him when he was four years old and his father took him to live with his aunt who owned a brothel in Augusta, Georgia. As an adolescent, James Brown stole cars and learned to play music. For stealing he earned a prison sentence of eight to sixteen years at a Georgia juvenile training institute; his term ended with parole after three years. Learning to play an instrument, however, enabled Brown to form a gospel soul quartet that included Johnny Terry, who would later become a member of the cool James Brown and the Famous Flames. The Flames began when Terry and Bobby Byrd joined with James Brown upon their release to form a band called the 3 Swanees. They moved to Macon, Georgia, and broke into the local music scene by performing impromptu during the intermission of a Little Richard concert.

Ladies and gentleman. From the man who sang 'Try Me," "Black and Proud!" "Let a Man Come In!" "Ain't It Funky Now," "It's a New Day"! So Let the Brother Rapp! . . . While we do the sex machine! . . . I said, while we do the sex machine! 'Cos' we got soul power! . . . We get up, get into it and involved! . . . Ladies and gentleman, here he is. The greatest entertainer in the world. Mr. Please, Please himself. Hardest working Jaaames Brown!
—Bobby Byrd, introducing James Brown

Clint Branley, Little Richard's manager, renamed them the Flames and signed them. In 1956 the Flames cut their first record, "Please, Please, Please." "Please," later revised, became James Brown's trademark. At the end of every show he sang "Please Please, Please," falling to his knees onstage in mock exhaustion, until a lone helper from backstage covered his royal funkiness with a cape and led him away. Just when you thought he had gone, Brown threw the cape to the floor and returned screeching to the mike. James Brown and the Famous Flames in the fifties consisted of a massive entourage. The band itself grew to twenty people; there were four warm-up soloists, two vocal groups, a troupe of dancers, and a court jester or comedian. Brown could exhibit some crazy autocratic behavior, actually fining his staff for infractions such as lateness or wearing crinkled clothes. He could also be a whirlwind of violence, as future police records would attest.

Despite the political activism of the 1960s, Afro-American musicians were surprisingly quiescent. There were the specific anthems in circulation, such as James Brown's "Say It Loud I am Black and Proud" and "Funky President (People It's Bad)." Those influential recordings were joined by the Temptations's "Ball of Confusion," the Chi-lites "Give More Power to the People," the Isley Brothers' "Fight the Power." The 1970s, on the other hand, marked by the intensification of the Vietnam War and the spreading drug culture, opened with Marvin Gaye's "What's Going On." The 1970s were about funk, new forms of kinetic orality and physicality that were being transformed to meet the new patterns of African-American life and struggle. James Brown was at the forefront of this phenomenon. Funk had begun with his release of "Out of Sight" in 1963. "Live From the Apollo"—arguably the best live album ever made—was followed by classic funk tracks—such as "Poppa's Got a Brand New Bag," his first single in the top ten charts, "Cold Sweat," and "Lickin Stick, Lickin Stick." Brown managed to capture the spirit of working-class black people in urban and agrarian areas. Only black radio stations would play his music, but the extent to which James Brown had become a national black icon was clear when he appeared on television to help cool the riots after the death of Martin Luther King, Jr.

In 1969, Brown released "Mother Popcorn: You've Got To Have a Mother for Me." It launched a dance craze known as the popcorn. But blissful as the seventies were, blessed with rich music—Roberta Flack, Sly and the Family Stone, Al Green, Bill Withers, the Temptations, George Clinton and Bootsy Collins, Jimi Hendrix, Curtis Mayfield, Barry White, the Isley Brothers—this decade was restive racially. Black music reflected this tension, particularly in the new dominance of the base line and heightened spirituality of the lyric. James Brown was an emissary of this growing racially self-conscious assertion even while he could be quite politically equivocal and naïve: He endorsed Richard Nixon at the height of the black power movement and declared himself a Republican.

In 1971 Brown disbanded James Brown and the Flames and formed his new group, the JBS. They began the decade joyously, with an ode to the miniskirt of the seventies—"Hot Pants." Brown's personal life had deteriorated by the mid-seventies with the news of his son's death in 1973 in a car accident. Bobby Byrd, his erstwhile longest bandmember and friend, left the band to pursue a solo career. Financial problems plagued Brown, deleteriously affecting his new record company, Polydor. The business empire that he had built during the sixties consisting of radio stations, a booking agency, seventeen publishing companies, a record label, a production company, and a Lear jet was steadily eroded by the IRS. The financial demise of the godfather culminated in his arrest while on stage at the Apollo Theater. His drug addiction worsened; he was arrested twice and imprisoned once during the eighties for driving high on PCP.

Nevertheless, Brown made a comeback in the 1980s. He was discovered by white Americans and Europeans seeing him for the first time in the movie *The Blues Brothers* or hearing his music from the theme tune for the movie *Rocky IV.* And his music was appropriated, canonized, and sampled by black brothers all over the word on hip-hop records. In 1986, James Brown was inducted into the Rock and Roll Hall of Fame. Imagine one single dance party without him. And the hip-hop generation—with its creative forms of rap music—pays him the greatest compliment by sampling his records to foreground their linguistic virtuosity. In this way, his funky beat will go on forever.

1970-1979

Marvin Gaye

Soul Man
(1939–1984)

More than a pop star, Marvin Gaye was the artistic witness of his generation. He would become the brightest star in the Motown constellation, producing a string of chart-topping hits in the 1960s and '70s and into the '80s. His 1971 album, *What's Going On,* remains one of the handful of classic albums in the history of American music, and while his image is often remembered as the rakishly handsome sex symbol—the sensitive, sensual seducer—he never wanted the limelight. "I didn't want to shake my ass," he told his biographer, David Ritz. "I didn't want to dance, but I'd wind up dancing with the rest of them. In spite of my fears about becoming a sex symbol, I'm afraid I became one."

Gaye's illustrious and tumultuous career spanned the history of rhythm and blues, from doo-wop in the fifties to soul in the eighties. While much is known about his musical triumphs and his personal tragedies—his drug abuse and his violent death at the hands of his own father—the truths of his career remain largely obscured. Above all, Gaye was a Christian artist, and one of the most gifted performers the black church has ever produced. From his early years singing in his father's Pentecostal church, to the final recorded lyrics from his 1982 album *Midnight Love* ("I still love Jesus, all praises to the Heavenly Father"), the Christian faith remained the wellspring of his artistic vision and the resting place of his deeply tortured soul.

Marvin Gaye was born Marvin Pentz Gaye, Jr., on April 2, 1939, in Washington, D.C. Raised in his father's church in the East Capitol projects, Gaye was nurtured on a Christ-centered ethic of love. Early on, he found music as the expression of this emotion. Gaye began as an instrumentalist, playing piano, organ, and drums. Outside of the church, he sang in a doo-wop group named the Rainbows ("Mary Lee," 1955). In 1957, he formed his own group, the Marquees, and recorded "Wyatt Earp" on the Okeh label with Bo Diddley. But it was his 1958 meeting with Harvey

Fuqua, which led to a spot singing first tenor in Fuqua's smooth-harmony rhythm and blues group the Moonglows, that launched Gaye's musical career.

With this exposure, Gaye moved in 1960 to Detroit. This was a time in which Motown Records, headed by impresario Berry Gordy, was emerging as a dominant force in popular music. After Gordy heard Gaye in a local club the following year, he signed him to his new Motown Tamla label on the spot. As it had done, and would do, with so many black performers of the sixties, seventies, and eighties, Motown offered Gaye a public platform for his private passion. Gordy packaged black artists and the sounds of R & B in a format that was not just palatable but seductive to white America. Motown sucessfully broke through the color line that formerly separated "race records" from mainstream releases, and sold black music for what it was: *the* American popular music. Though Gaye would make use of the formidable production prowess and promotional clout of Motown Records, he remained doggedly attached to his roots in the church and the nightclub.

Gaye's early work with Motown amounted to session drumming on hits such as the Marvelettes's "Please Mr. Postman." But after marrying Gordy's sister, Gaye obtained the opportunity he desired: a chance to record an album of standards in the vein of Frank Sinatra and Nat "King" Cole. *The Soulful Moods of Marvin Gaye* was a popular failure, but it offered a portent of the musical genius that would later emerge. Gordy continued to cajole Gaye into recording more material with the characteristic Motown sound; the lead crooning, the close harmony backups, and the strong backbeat. In 1962 Gordy succeeded in getting Gaye to release "Stubborn Kind of Fellow," a song written specifically with him (and his temperament) in mind. The record was a hit, and ushered in a decade in which Gaye worked with nearly every major Motown producer, from Holland-Dozier-Holland to Smokey Robinson. He followed up "Stubborn Kind of Fellow" with "Hitch Hike," his first top forty pop hit. In 1965, he topped the R & B charts twice with "I'll be Doggone" and "Ain't That Peculiar" and, three years later, he ruled the pop charts for seven weeks with his classic "I Heard It Through the Grapevine."

Gaye had over twenty hits to his name by the early seventies, but none greater than the incomparable love songs he recorded with Tammi Terrell. Their musical association began in 1967 and produced a string of hits. Classics such as "Your Precious Love," "Ain't Nothing Like the Real Thing," "Ain't No Mountain High

1970–1979

Enough," and "You're All I Need to Get By" reflect the powerful nuances and cadences of a gospel sound with secular lyrics. But the partnership ended tragically: in 1967 Terrell collapsed in Gaye's arms while performing on stage, the first signs of the brain tumor that took her life three years later. Terrell's death in 1970 sent Gaye into hiding. Despite his success as a solo performer, the loss of his musical soulmate sent him into a period of deep despair. He would not perform in public for five years.

Out of this tragic period, compounded by his brother's firsthand account of the atrocities in Vietnam, the rise of the black power movement, and the invasion of drugs in America's chocolate cities, Gaye found strength to produce the greatest album in African-American popular music: *What's Going On* (1971). This was his first album conceived with complete artistic autonomy, and it was perhaps the first concept album to hang together by means of a set of sociopolitical themes. It was an artistic triumph and profound statement on (and of) the times. Gone were the traditional love songs, and in their place were unabashedly Christian songs such as "God Is Love" and "Wholly Holy" that evoked the love ethic of Jesus as the basis of social change. Gaye's social critique was unstinting; songs such as "Inner City Blues" and "Mercy, Mercy Me (The Ecology)" are the testimony of an artist who has somehow found a way to keep hope alive in the face of radical suffering.

What's Going On marks the peak of Gaye's career. In addition, it was the best-selling album in Motown history up to that point. In the next few years, Gaye followed with a number of popular hits. It seemed that he had resigned himself to his role as a sex symbol—even embraced it—with such smoldering hits as "Let's Get It On" (1972) and "I Want You" (1976). But even amid this success, Gaye's personal demons continued to haunt him. His tumultuous marriage with Gordy's sister ended after fourteen years, and Gaye filed for bankruptcy soon after. His life seemed to take a turn for the better with his marriage to his second wife, Janice, in 1977. They had two children, including Nona, who followed her father into music. And Gaye released his number one single "Got to Give It Up, Part 1," an infectious disco-inflected dance hit. Pressures from the Internal Revenue Service, though, forced Gaye to move to Europe. He released *In Our Lifetimes* in 1981, an album that explored his personal philosophies on love, art, and mortality. It was only a moderate success.

Nineteen eighty-two would prove to be Gaye's most successful musical year in nearly a decade, but it was the final flourish of his life. Early that year, he broke his

longtime relationship with Gordy and Motown Records and released *Midnight Love* on Columbia. The album, behind the strength of the smash single "Sexual Healing," went double platinum and earned Gaye two Grammys. His performance at the Grammy Awards telecast, followed by his memorable appearance on the Motown twenty-fifth anniversary television special, were his last public performances.

Spiraling further and further into a cycle of depression and cocaine dependency, Gaye sought solace in his parents' home. It was not long before Gaye resumed his longtime conflict with his father, who had been at odds with his son since Gaye was a teenager. The particulars leading up to Gaye's death at his father's hands are still unclear. After a Sunday morning shouting match, in which Gaye threatened several times to commit suicide, his father took out a gun and shot his son to death.

But Gaye's music has outlasted his shockingly tragic life. Soon after his death, Columbia and Motown collaborated to release *Dream of a Lifetime* and *Romantically Yours,* both culled from unreleased tapes from the *Midnight Love* sessions. In 1987 he was inducted into the Rock and Roll Hall of Fame. His pure genius and troubled life bespeak the tensions of a man sensitive to the sufferings and shaken by the truths of himself, his society, and the world.

Barbara Harris

The Bishop
(1930–)

She reached for heaven. When Barbara Clementine Harris was consecrated a bishop in the Episcopal Church, she became the first woman in nearly two thousand years to achieve that status in the group of historic churches governed by apostolic succession. Those churches understand apostolic succession as the religious authority that extends in an unbroken line down from Christ himself through the apostles. Over the centuries, the Roman Catholic, Eastern Orthodox, Oriental Orthodox, and Anglican churches have all defined themselves as standing in that line and deriving their legitimacy from it. These churches include most Christians who have ever lived, and their governing overseers or bishops for twenty centuries have all been men. Of course, Harris is not the first American or the first person of African descent to break through that barrier, but she is the first woman bishop in history, and she is an African-American woman.

Barbara Harris's life and ministry is characterized by a commitment to breaking barriers, to social action, and to focusing on what she calls "justice work." This means involvement on behalf of the poor, gays and lesbians, women, those with AIDS, blacks, and prisoners, along with criticism of bombers of abortion clinics and opposition to the death penalty. Widely known as an effective preacher, Harris's sermons articulate these beliefs. Speaking about another African-American "first," Absolom Jones, the earliest African-American Episcopal priest, she said, "He knew that you cannot temporize with oppression or compromise with injustice in any form." She compares Jones with the prophet Isaiah, whose "message was for the afflicted, the underprivileged, the broken-hearted, the captives and the bound—not those in prison or captivity per se, but those caught in a confining and oppressive social condition. Physically and spiritually wretched, frustrated by unfulfilled hopes, they desperately needed some good news."

Speaking out for the marginalized and invisible, Harris's prophetic preaching is rooted in the good news of the gospel: "Jesus is freedom in the face of captivity; Jesus is justice in the face of oppression; Jesus is forgiveness in the face of guilt; Jesus is brotherhood and sisterhood in the face of prejudice, discrimination, racism, classism, and elitism. And that love, in the face of hatred, begins and ends in him." Harris came by her faith growing up in inner-city Philadelphia, where she was born in 1930 to Walter Harris, a steelworker, and Beatrice Price Harris, a church organist. She was baptized and confirmed in St. Barnabas Episcopal Church, but, when she saw it as being too moderate, she moved to North Philadelphia's Church of the

Advent. She joined the Union of Black Episcopalians and the bitter struggle for women's ordination. She participated in Martin Luther King, Jr.'s Selma march, as well as voter registration drives in Mississippi.

Harris experienced a call to the ministry, by which she says she believed herself "directed" and "urged to come forward and offer such gifts as I felt God had given me." She was ordained in 1980. She served as rector of St. Augustine of Hippo Church in Norristown, and she became chaplain of the Philadelphia Prison System. In 1984 Harris accepted the position of executive director of the Episcopal Church Publishing Company, where she published *The Witness,* a left-of-center magazine. She wrote a regular column entitled, not surprisingly, "*A Luta Continua:* The Struggle Continues." Nine years after her ordination she was elected suffragan bishop of Massachusetts, assistant bishop in a wealthy but progressive Episcopal diocese of over one hundred thousand members with a tradition of innovation. Harris was consecrated on February 12, 1989, in Boston's Hynes Convention Center before a crowd of eight thousand people. The long processional threw off the musical schedule, and a gospel choir broke into "Ride On, King Jesus, No Man Can Hinder Me" as Harris started down the aisle.

The uniqueness and historic significance of Harris's consecration was nearly lost in controversy. There was still patriarchal opposition to women's ordination (despite the fact that, as Harris says, "It was time"), and some fellow bishops threatened not to recognize her authority. There was criticism of the fact that she did not have a college or seminary degree, although she had studied privately, as the church permits. She points out that her experience in business, public relations, and advertising was a unique kind of education not available to seminarians. She was divorced, but so was her male predecessor, about whom no one had raised objections. Harris believes the underlying issue was, in fact, the question of who is going to run the church: "The old boys' network was losing its power," she says.

Over ten years after the fact, the controversy over Harris's consecration has faded. During her bishopric, Barbara Harris has not been quite the public figure some people feared, and some people hoped, she would be. Her name is rarely in the paper or on the TV news. Her daily work is primarily the routine tasks of the church overseer: visiting parishes, confirming young people, presiding at meetings. But the church's message has always been communicated primarily through preaching, and in a denomination hardly noted for its eloquence or oratory, Bishop Harris is a stellar preacher. Slight of stature and with a gravelly voice, attired in rich Episcopal vestments, Bishop Barbara Clementine Harris in the pulpit proclaims the prophetic message that led her to the ministry:

No one expects us to eliminate all of the evils of the world, nor to liberate all those who are oppressed, nor to feed all who are hungry, or to house the millions who are homeless. But when the oppressed see one who fights for liberation, their burden is lightened because they know that somebody stands with them. . . . For it is in solidarity with those in pain that true community finds its realization.

Harris plunged deep into the mysterious depths of the Christian gospel and came up at the top of an ancient Christian church with her black female self intact.

Dorothy Height

The Club Woman
(1912–)

In the old days, it was the club women who got the job done. White-gloved, wearing hats and pearls, these women cut an exemplary no-nonsense figure for the community. Through their organizations, they could provide for the sick and the destitute, care for orphaned children, establish beneficiary societies when no one else could. Dorothy I. Height epitomizes that tradition. Bringing upward of ten million black families together in the 1980s in a series of National Council of Negro Women's Black Family Reunion Celebrations was the culmination of Height's vision and hard work.

Height organized black women for over fifty years. She worked hard to fight black female labor invisibility, and she championed the needs of their families when mainstream media demonized them. Her commitment and her breadth of involvement in women's groups remains unsurpassed, but in particular she was critical to the success of three influential women's organizations: the National Council of Negro Women, Delta Sigma Theta, and the YWCA. Since 1957, Height led the largest black women's umbrella organization—the National Council of Negro Women, which consists of 4 million members, 240 local groups, and 31 national organizations. Now the NCNW is headed by Dr. Jane E. Smith, but the eighty-eight-year-old Height continues to serve as chair and president emerita. Height presided over the national black women's sorority, Delta Sigma Theta, from 1947 to 1957, and she has worked vigilantly with the Young Women's Christian Association since the thirties.

Height was in a sense handpicked by the grand dame of organizational politics, Mary McLeod Bethune, who first spied the young Height at the 1938 World Youth Congress held at Vassar College. At the time, Height was a sole representative of the

Harlem Youth Council and was one of ten American youngsters asked to help Eleanor Roosevelt plan a national youth congress from 1937 to 1938. Bethune, president and founder of the NCNW, wasted no time in asking Height to come and join her. Thus began their long relationship. Bethune saw in Height a successor. Bethune's urgency and mature activism inspired Height in return. "Faced with grim realties of absence of power and exclusion from opportunity," Height said about her mentor, "[Bethune] *really* understood the need for collective power of black women on behalf of themselves and their families."

Anyone who follows Height's work, however, realizes that although a protegée of Bethune, her outstanding record of accomplishment for women's groups is hers alone. The work has been broad and deep—ranging from fair wage and union issues in the 1930s and 1940s, to civil rights and labor improvements in the 1960s and 1970s, to black self-help programs for the extended family through the 1980s and 1990s. While Height worked for the NCNW, or Delta Sigma Theta, or the YWCA, she headed or sat on important policy-making boards such as the U.S. Department of Defense Advisory Committee on Women, 1952–1955; the New York Welfare State Board, 1958–1968; the Office of Emergency Planning's Presidential Committee on the Status of Women; and the President's Committee for Equal Employment Opportunity. Height is a club woman, a sorority sister, an international civil rights leader. That tradition of devoted service to the community that Height has perfected so well, she attributes to her mother, Fannie Height, a devoted participant in the local Baptist church and member of its organizations, who instilled in her daughter the pursuit of meaning and service in her life and others.

Height was born in 1912 in Richmond, Virginia. As a child, she migrated with her family to the small mining town of Rankin, Pennsylvania, where her father, a building contractor, and her mother, a private nurse, quietly rose to a middle-class existence. Height was an A student throughout her school years, an avid basketball player (she is five feet eleven), and, even as a teenager, an admirable orator. Cutting an imposing figure at that early age and eloquent enough to win an oratory competition (the Elks Fraternal Society National Oratorical Contest), Height was able to pay to attend New York University for her college years. This acceptance came at a crucial time, for Barnard, her first choice, had delayed her entrance because of a racial quota. She graduated from New York University with a bachelor's and a master's degree in psychology in 1933.

In the thirties, Height thrilled to the excitement of New York. In addition to meeting some of the leading African Americans of the day, she also was exposed to the poor black migrants from the South who labored without recourse. Suddenly, Height was forced to confront the problems that plagued low-income areas, and she did so passionately. She became actively involved in municipal politics and found a job with the New York City Welfare Department as a caseworker in 1935. She also studied part-time at the New York School of Social Work to strengthen her background in a new and challenging area. The young Height took as her cause the substandard conditions of female black domestic workers, who essentially stood on streets all over Brooklyn and the Bronx while people in cars bargained for their housekeeping services. Height likened what she saw daily to a modern slave market. Thoroughly without protection, except for the employers who exploited them, and without adequate unionization, the domestic workers were poorly paid and even more poorly treated. She took the issue of fair and equal payment further, testifying on workers' behalf before the New York City Council. Gradually, before she knew it, the middle-class Height had become a labor union organizer.

Height was also involved with the newly formed Christian Youth Association, eventually becoming one of its leaders. She represented the organization at the International Church Youth Conference in Oxford, England, and served as youth delegate in Amsterdam, Holland, in 1938. The same year, she accepted a position at the Young Women's Christian Association (YWCA) in New York, working also as an assistant director at the Harlem home for black women—the YWCA's Emma Ransom House.

The YWCA changed Height's life as much as she would affect its future. The "Y" was not an interracial organization before Height, among others, actively steered it away from its practice of internal segregation. When she moved in 1939 to Washington, D.C., to be executive director of the Phillis Wheatley YWCA, she also became active in the national planning levels of the YWCA. To this end, she helped coordinate the YWCA's 1946 convention—one that chartered a policy of integrating YWCA facilities nationwide, and she was duly elected the organization's national interracial education secretary. Moreover, throughout the years of the civil rights movement, Height busily organized and engineered white and black involvement for voter registration drives and for campaigns against racism. She served on the national staff of the YWCA USA from 1944 to 1977, where she was active in developing its interracial and ecumenical education programs. In 1965, she would inaugurate the Center for Racial Justice—still a major initiative of the National YWCA.

In the mid-1940s, Height's reputation broadened because of her work on behalf of domestics and the YWCA. Those who knew her commented on her organizational prowess. Here was an organizer who got things done and she could do them well. When Delta Sigma Theta asked her to serve as president in 1947, the sorority embarked on a national job analysis program that would analyze black women's labor conditions, with the goal of furthering employment opportunities for them. Until 1956, Height charted Delta's first international chapters with black women in the Caribbean and Africa. In fact, she initiated the sole African-American private voluntary organization working in Africa. The Delta chapters assisted their Haitian sisters during Hurricane Hazel in 1957 and started a bookmobile for poor black people in Georgia.

After the death of Mary McLeod Bethune in 1957, Height assumed the presidency of the National Council of Negro Women. Buoyed by the turmoil of the sixties, the NCNW began to focus on voter registration drives in the South and voter education programs in the North. Height herself became one of the few visible mainstream female civil rights leaders. She worked closely with Martin Luther King, Jr., Roy Wilkins, Whitney Young, A. Philip Randolph, and others. Virtually all the principal civil and human rights events in the 1950s and 1960s were attended by Height, a remarkable record by any standard. Projects such as Operation Women Power and its push toward rural food cooperatives reflected the NCNW's subtle shift toward more radical politics in this decade and the next. It also showed that the NCNW, with its national planning board and its administrative staff of more than ninety members, had become a serious contender for foundation grants, which they continue to receive today for programs in business expertise and vocational training.

As a self-help advocate (because she has simply dismissed the portrayal of the black community as dependent and welfare-oriented), Height has initiated successful NCNW–sponsored food, child care, housing, and career educational programs. President Reagan presented her the Citizens Medal Award for distinguished service in 1989, the year she also received the Franklin Delano Roosevelt Freedom Medal from the Franklin and Eleanor Roosevelt Institute. But most fitting, for her work with women Height was inducted into the International Women's Forum Hall of Fame in 1991 along with feminist leader Betty Friedan and the Norwegian prime minister, Gro Harlem Brundtland. Since 1986, the multicultural Black Family Reunion Celebration has encouraged families to work together. She is often spotted in African garb now, appealing to young people to get involved, to be participants in their destiny, to organize and confront issues of drugs, poverty, and family disintegration. And the formula must work, because historically the club women have never failed as a community. Dorothy Height—the best-known club woman in the twentieth century, following in the tradition of Bethune, Burroughs, and Terrell—still does the job.

Barbara Jordan

The Nation's Conscience
(1936–1996)

Barbara Charlaine Jordan was one of the world's great wordsmiths. A reporter once asked her whether she was nervous being black and female in a legislature that teemed with racists and sexists. "You must understand," she replied. "I have a tremendous amount of faith in my own capacity. I know how to read and write and think, so I have no fear." The U.S. Congress was alternately caressed and castigated by her eloquence while she was alive, and her voice of intelligence is sorely missed in her death.

A lawyer, scholar, author, and presidential adviser, Jordan followed in the tradition of Justice Thurgood Marshall. Throughout her political career she attempted to wrest integrity from politics, and she was not deterred or diminished by the inevitable disappointments. She invigorated the national debate wherever it touched upon the neglected questions of social justice and constitutional integrity. She spoke boldly on a range of difficult issues, from the Watergate scandal to the North American Free Trade Agreement (NAFTA). She was an elected official in the Texas Senate and U.S. House of Representatives and was appointed chair of the U.S. Commission on Immigration Reform by President Bill Clinton in 1993. She combined the eloquence of the black preaching tradition with the prudence of the American political tradition. Her deep sense of conscience was providential for the country in the 1970s.

Barbara Jordan was not the only African American in the House during the 1970s, nor was she the first. The latter honor belonged to Shirley Chisholm, who was elected in 1964. The growing number of black representatives during Jordan's time included Andrew Young, Yvonne Braithwaite Burke, Cardiss Collins, Walter E. Fauntroy, Parren J. Mitchell, John Conyers, Jr., and Ronald V. Dellums. In 1967, Carl

Stokes of Cleveland, Ohio, and Richard Hatcher of Gary, Indiana, were the nation's first black elected mayors of major cities. The Congressional Black Caucus was formed in 1971 by the African-American members of the House of Representatives to strengthen black representation on Capitol Hill. In 1996 Charles B. Rangel, who had been one of the caucus chairs, explained what Barbara Jordan meant to them: "Barbara Jordan has been to the Congressional Black Caucus what Hubert Humphrey was to the Democratic Farmer Labor Party in Minnesota; what Susan B. Anthony was to the suffrage movement; what Jackie Robinson was to baseball; and what Sojourner Truth was to early freedom fighters." However, Jordan has been criticized by more than a few African Americans for her adoption of a centrist approach in Congress. But this centrism was actually what enabled her to sucessfully cultivate and maintain relationships that helped push her legislation through the Senate, bills that dealt with blacks, minorities, women, and the poor. She once said that she did not believe in black or white racism, a statement that belied her belief in an American diversity that most Americans, black or white, do not contemplate. Certainly it was a maverick position to take at the height of the black power movement and later, when Jesse Jackson was making a bid for power from the center left, it caused consternation and celebration among her listeners.

Jordan was born in Texas on February 21, 1936, to Benjamin and Arlyne Patton Jordan. The Reverend Benjamin Jordan worked full-time in a warehouse and full-time as a Baptist minister. Barbara Jordan's own passion and talents for debating marked her childhood and adolescence. By 1952, she had a collection of honors, including the Girl of the Year Award presented by the Zeta Phi Beta Sorority from Phillis Wheatley High School. She went on to do undergraduate work at Texas State University from 1952 to 1956, where Professor Thomas Freeman mentored her. She joined his debating team, and as a member of the first debate team from a black university to compete in the forensic tournament held annually at Baylor University in Texas, Jordan won first place in junior oratory. She graduated magna cum laude from Texas Southern University in 1956 and received a law degree from Boston University in 1959.

After qualifying for the bar in both Massachusetts and Texas, Jordan moved back to her home state and set up a law practice in her mother's kitchen. The civil rights movement was underway, however, and as the country exploded in marches and demonstrations, politics increasingly became more appealing to her. She launched her first political campaign and ran for the Texas State House of Representatives in 1962. She was unsuccessful. That same year, however, she was appointed as the administrative assistant to Judge William Elliot of the Harris County Court. Her political ambition was checked again in 1964 when she ran a second time and lost.

But the Voting Rights Act of 1965, signed by President Lyndon Johnson in response to successful protest from voting rights groups, inspired her to run again. Since Reconstruction the political life of blacks had been constrained by poll taxes and other discriminatory devices. In 1966 Jordan, using grassroots tactics, ran and won the Democratic primary with more than 60 percent of the vote. She won the election by a margin of two to one over J. C. Whitfield, a former state representative, making herself and Curtis Graves the only two blacks in the Texas state legislature. Jordan became the first black woman to be elected and the first African

American since 1883 to serve in the Texas Senate; the first to chair the labor and management relations committee, or any large committee, and the first freshman senator named to the Texas Legislative Council.

During her six-year tenure as a senator in the Texas state legislature, Jordan focused on ensuring fair employment practices. She gave firemen college credits and devised programs for the education and training of the handicapped. The Texas Department of Community Affairs was established by her, and she rejected as restrictive a voter registration law that would have hit hardest at Mexican Americans and blacks. The *Houston Press,* previously anti-Jordan, suddenly began to praise her after President Johnson deferred to her publicly on a race question at a conference that he had organized for a briefing on his proposed fair housing initiative. The press characterized her as the next black spokesperson, which of course Jordan did not claim to be. She was famous for interpreting the Constitution for all persons in her state, which meant not only blacks, but also the Native, Asian, Mexican, and white Americans. She wrote laws to improve workmen's compensation, to create a Texas Fair Employment Practices Commission, and to set a minimum wage for the truly poor and the Texan farm workers.

In the 1972 election she became at thirty-six the first black woman elected to Congress from the South. In the House she became a junior member of the judiciary committee. It was in this committee that she participated in confirmation hearings for two vice presidents and in the impeachment hearings for Richard Nixon.

Thirty-five people were charged with determining the fate of President Richard Milhous Nixon during the summer of 1974. Barbara Jordan was one. The Watergate scandal, uncovered by Bob Woodward and Carl Bernstein, reporters for the *Washington Post,* exposed the president's involvement in the break-in, and subsequent cover-up, of the Democratic National Committee (DNC) headquarters at the

1970–1979

Watergate complex. Evidence showed that Nixon and his advisers had authorized the installation of eavesdropping devices inside the DNC headquarters and had silenced Watergate defendants with copious amounts of money. An enemies list had been compiled that included Congressman John Conyers (D-Michigan), CBS newsman Daniel Schorr, actress Carol Channing, and comedian Bill Cosby. Richard Nixon fired independent prosecutor Archibald Cox, because he had requested tapes that Nixon had installed in the White House.

Jordan spoke forcefully against Nixon, both in open and closed sessions, and at the same time managed to be entirely nonpartisan about the whole affair. The issue remained the U.S. Constitution, and it has often been noted that she was one of Congress's most learned authorities on the document. The nation was impressed with the way she pressed for Nixon's impeachment on well-argued grounds. After her reelection in 1974 over Republican Robbins Mitchell, where she received 80 percent of the vote, Speaker of the House Carl Albert named her to the policy and steering committee and its task force. They were to make up an action agenda for the ninety-fourth Congress. One of Jordan's key achievments was the broadening of the Voting Rights Act of 1965 to include Mexican, Native, and Asian Americans. She was also the author of the Consumer Goods Pricing Act of 1975.

In 1976, at the national Democratic convention, Jimmy Carter was nominated for president and Barbara Jordan was the keynote speaker. She was appointed to his advisory board on ambassadorial appointments, but she was not given a position of real influence and power. In 1978 she announced her retirement from politics. She was stricken with multiple sclerosis, and the pressures of Congress were exhausting. Jordan was appointed as distinguished professor at the Lyndon B. Johnson School of Public Affairs at the University of Texas at Austin, where she developed great enthusiasm for teaching. In 1992 she returned briefly again to the spotlight as the keynote speaker at the Democratic national convention that nominated President Bill Clinton. He bestowed on her the Presidential Medal of Freedom in 1994. It was fitting. She was a treasured Democrat, in the most noble sense of the word. Jordan believed in America's Constitution, and the fact that she was not included in its first two hundred years of implementation did not deter her love for the ideals and principles of democracy. It only strengthened her resolve to correct it.

Leontyne Price

Stradivarius Among Singers
(1927–)

Leontyne Price is a diva. Although there have been famous African-American opera singers, prior to the mid–1960s black classical vocalists were limited almost exclusively to concert recitals, whether in the church or concert hall. Along with Robert McFerrin and Janet Collins, Marian Anderson broke that tradition briefly when she sang, backed by a full symphonic orchestra, at the Metropolitan Opera House. But Leontyne Price defied race and class and region to pursue a life in the world of opera. Everyone it seems, who was privileged to meet Price encouraged her on her way, and her soprano voice was rightfully likened to the finest of violins.

Leontyne Price first entered the popular imagination in 1955 in NBC's dramatic and unprecedented broadcast production of Giacomo Puccini's tragic melodrama *Tosca*. It was the middle of the 1950s and there was Price singing opera on national television—the first black woman ever to do so. She gave such a sensual, graceful rendition of Floria Tosca, the principal character who eventually jumps to her death, that her performance is counted as a historic moment.

After her stunning television debut, Price appeared in major works, both here and in Europe. A number of brilliant African-American opera singers, such as Shirley Verrett, Grace Bumbry, Mattiwilda Dobbs, Gwendolyn Simms, and Leonora Lafayette, performed during this period. But too often, we lost them to Europe, which recognized their talents beyond the color line. African-American opera companies, such as Opera/South and the National Ebony Opera, began to open, creating opportunities for African-American vocalists working in the operatic field. Price's entrance on the national stage coincided with the years of heightened civil rights activism in the South. With the political stakes so high, her dignified presence was especially beloved. During that period she memorialized Verdi's beautiful story of the Ethiopian slave, *Aida,* and performed the wily Bess in George Gershwin's American classic, *Porgy and Bess.* She sang the leads in opera classics as varied as *Madama Butterfly, La Bohème, Il Trovatore, Don Giovanni* and *Antony and Cleopatra,* which was written especially for her by her admirer Samuel Barber. Having conquered stages at the Metropolitan, the San Francisco Opera Company, the Lyric Opera of Chicago, and the major European opera venues, Price could afford to be more experimental in the 1970s. During the seventies she did fewer grand performances and concentrated on concert recitals and recordings, exposing larger, more popular audiences to the gravity and grace of opera. Hearing her exquisite vocal powers, black people sat up and took note of that world—many of them for the first time.

Leontyne Price grew up in Laurel, Mississippi—named for the region's overgrowth of laurel shrubs. James Price, a carpenter, and Katherine Baker Price, a midwife and a soprano in their church choir, gave birth to Mary Violet Leontyne Price in 1927. They had a son, George, two years later. Price showed musical talent as an infant, and she started piano lessons when she was only three years old. As a girl, she sang in the church choir and often accompanied her mother on the piano. She also made a little pocket money singing at local funerals and weddings. Price gave her first recital—on the piano—at Oak Park High during National Music Week in 1943. She played selections from Rachmaninoff, I. J. Paderewski, and Tchaikovsky as well as "Bugle Boy Boogie" and her own arrangement of "Deep River."

In 1944, Price enrolled in Wilberforce University, the black college in Ohio. The faculty nurtured her talent, and she was encouraged to perform as much as possible by Charles H. Wesley, the distinguished historian, and Catherine Van Buren, her first formal voice teacher. They advised her to change her major from music and education to voice. In 1948, Price's senior year, she was asked to sing on the same program as Paul Robeson, who was visiting nearby Antioch College. Robeson was so impressed with her that he immediately offered Price any assistance she needed to pursue a career in music. Her professors, knowing she could not afford any of the best music schools, established a Leontyne Price Fund for which Robeson gave a fundraising concert. Altogether, they raised one thousand dollars, and Price was bound for the Juilliard School in New York.

New York was wildly exciting and liberating for the novice talent. She saw her first live operatic performance, Puccini's *Turandot,* at the City Center. After a standing-room viewing of *Salome* at the Metropolitan Opera House, she made the decision to dedicate her life to opera. Florence Page Kimball, a former concert singer, coached Price in voice, diction, and German lieder. She supplemented her school work with singing in the Riverside Church choir. When Frederic Cohen, the director of Juilliard's opera department, first heard her he was convinced they had found the voice of the century. Soon she was singing in many Juilliard productions; her first role was Aunt Nella in *Gianni Schicchi.*

In 1952, musical directors Robert Breen, Blevins Davis, and Virgil Thomson saw her perform at Juilliard. Davis and Breen were casting for the role of Bess for a production of Gershwin's *Porgy and Bess,* while Virgil Thomson was engaged in mounting a Paris revival of his and Gertrude Stein's opera *Four Saints in Three Acts* for the 1952 International Arts Festival. Price bowled them over with her voice; it was the break she needed. She was immediately offered the roles of Saint Cecelia and of Bess, which she per-

formed to acclaim. During the production of *Porgy and Bess* she married the opera celebrity William Warfield, who had been cast as Porgy. *Porgy and Bess* was a huge success and ran in New York, London, and Paris to massive acclaim. Her talent now roundly established, she was asked to perform Floria Tosca in the NBC television production of *Tosca* two years later. NBC also asked her to star in *The Magic Flute* in 1956.

After appearing in Handel's *Julius Caesar* in 1956 at the American Opera Society, she made her opera-house debut in 1957 as Madame Lidoine in *Dialogues des Carmélites* by French composer Francis Poulenc at the San Francisco Opera House. These performances were followed by roles in *Aida* (1957), *Il Trovatore* (1958), *The Wise Maiden* (1958), *Don Giovanni* (1959), *La Forza del Destino* (1963), *Un Ballo in Maschera* (1965), *Il Tabarro* (1970), *Thaïs* (1959), and *Turandot* (1959). Price was triumphant in Verdi's *Aida* at La Scala in Milan and *Madama Butterfly* in Vienna, both performed in 1960. From 1961 to 1969, she was a fixture at New York's Metropolitan Opera House, speaking out against injustice while thrilling audiences with over 118 performances. Her debut at the Met in *Aida* (1961) evoked a forty-two-minute ovation, certainly the longest in the history of opera. Price was of such stature that she was asked to open the new Metropolitan Opera House at Lincoln Center in 1966, in the premiere of Samuel Barber's *Antony and Cleopatra*.

Certainly by the 1970s Price was one of the most admired and influential women in America. In 1971, *Ladies Home Journal* recognized her with its One of America's Most Important Women Award, while *Harpers Bazaar* conferred on her the American Women of Accomplishment Award. But Price already had been honored with awards: the Presidential Medal of Freedom in 1964, the NAACP's Spingarn Medal in 1965, and over the years she has received twenty Grammy Awards for her contributions to opera and classical music. Yet beyond these prizes and awards, Leontyne Price has received the high judgment of the best music critics and the high praise of opera lovers as one of the century's greatest artists. She claimed one of the highest art traditions of Europe for her own, and opened opera to all of us in the process.

Richard Pryor

The Comedian
(1940–)

Richard Pryor forced us to laugh at ourselves, black and white alike. He was the inspiration for our own one-liners. We practiced his jokes, to our adolescent delight, and we waited eagerly for each new record. He was the quintessential satirist, in the finest humanist tradition, and an accomplished mime of our vibrant sixties, downbeat seventies, and greedy eighties. An utterly gentle, tragic figure, Pryor belonged to a prophetic tradition that used laughter borne from the comedic part of the soul to show the moral hypocrisy of society. At his height, the brother personified unending social commentary, vulnerable and volatile, outrageous and obscene. His soliloquies and one-man skits often dealt with the injustices and hardships of African Americans subjected to a litany of abuses, along with their courageous and irreverent responses, from institutionalized racism to poverty.

Pryor spoke candidly about the everyday interactions between people, celebrating at times the cultural gulf between black and white, lamenting the horrors of racial bigotry to be found on both sides. He rescued the demeaning, but powerful word "nigger" from those who did not know how to use it. And, after his trip to Africa and the fire which almost killed him, he even rescued himself from the word's corrosive influence. His comedy was not entirely political. Pryor played with existential issues, from the primordial fluids of love and excrement to our confused quest for love and sex. All of it was fodder for his act. A comedian adored by all America, Pryor's humanist heart was always striving, revealing his pride, hope, and compassion for black people, and indeed, at the end of the day, all people.

Pryor's life was difficult, hard to digest at times. Many a true word is spoken in jest, the saying goes, and if one thinks about the places that Pryor took us to in the name of a laugh—the vibrant brothels of his childhood, the seedy clubs owned by mobsters, the "real side" of the police station, the tragedy of the hospitals—they were all places he knew intimately. Clearly, one of his achievements was translating the stressful and intolerable situations in his own life into jokes so we could laugh as well as cry and complain at all the unvoiced resentments and social tensions we cannot deny. His intimacy and frankness about his life redeemed him and all who watched him.

Pryor would get up on stage and show us how unenlightened, turbulent, and brutal he could be. This redeemed his comedy from artifice and vulgarity and placed him squarely in the tradition of serious satirists such as Mark Twain and the sardonic, tragicomic Lenny Bruce, who told "it" like it was. In the black world, Pryor followed the tradition of Bert Williams, the comedian who called his act, with great underestimated irony, the "Real Coon"—as opposed to the white fake one. Pryor was also influenced by Dick Gregory, Bill Cosby, and the inimitable Redd Foxx, an idol of Pryor's, who starred in the number one hit seventies family TV show *Sanford and Son* but who also kept his act "real" by doing nightclub gigs in Hollywood. Foxx's material was so real it was X-rated.

Pryor, from Peoria, Illinois, was born in 1940 to Gertrude Thomas and Leroy Pryor. His mother was a prostitute in his grandmother's brothel; his father was her son and his mother's sometime pimp. The young Pryor was raised in the brothel primarily by his grandmother, Marie Carter, and, by all accounts, he gravitated to humor early in order to cope with the chaos of his early life. Pryor was expelled from his Catholic school in the seventh grade when the religious order discovered what his folks did for a living. At age fourteen he joined a community drama group, which he has said influenced him positively, but he left after two years. He worked as a janitor, truck driver, packinghouse laborer, boxer, and petty thief before joining the army at seventeen, which sent him to Frankfurt, Germany. After an honorable discharge, he began a stand-up comedy career. First performing successfully in Peoria nightclubs, he gained the confidence to try the more competitive nightclub scene in New York, where he arrived in 1963 with two dollars in his pocket.

> "We're celebrating two hundred years of white folks kickin ass. . . . You all probably have forgotten it. Well, I ain't never gonna forget it."
> —Richard Pryor

Pryor came on the heels of a group of black comics such as Dick Gregory and Bill Cosby who, although funny, were of a different ilk. The two were among the first to play to interracial audiences, and they had a style suited for family audiences. Cosby and Gregory, for instance, did not talk about sex nor did they use the word "nigger," and unlike Pryor's shows, white people in their audiences were not fodder for their jokes. Pryor imitated elements of these two giants when he first arrived in New York. In fact, he remembers thinking to himself about Cosby, "Goddamn it. This nigger's doin' what I'm fixin' to do. I want to be the only nigger. Ain't room for two niggers." But by the late 1960s, even though his managers and friends advised him against it, Pryor decided to present his "real side" by plumbing the bottomless reserve of folk humor in the black community. He found characters such as Mudbone, winos, pimps, and holy women. As time went on and he recorded his stand-up routines, appreciation of what he was doing grew.

The year 1974 was important for black people in media and entertainment. Beverly Johnson appeared on the cover of *Vogue* magazine, the first black woman to do so. Stevie Wonder released the pathbreaking album *Fulfillingness' First Finale*. And Pryor won his first Emmy for his writing for the Lily Tomlin special *Lily*. He also released the successful album *That Nigger's Crazy*, which became a gold record and got him on the cover of *Rolling Stone* magazine. His success continued to grow. On television Pryor headlined two series, *The Richard Pryor Show* (1977) and *Pryor's Place* (1984). He made guest star appearances on dramatic shows such as *The Wild, Wild West* and *The Mod Squad*. Beginning in the 1970s, he had major roles in several famous films, including *Lady Sings the Blues* and *Uptown Saturday Night*, and Pryor appeared in more than forty other movies, including *Stir Crazy, Silver Streak, Jo-Jo Dancer*, and *The Bingo Long Traveling All-Stars & Motor Kings*. He recorded almost twenty albums, and appeared on countless television programs, mostly between the mid-seventies and mid-eighties. Despite his overwhelming success, Pryor was

1970–1979

plagued with financial and drug problems, "I snorted so much cocaine that I could have snorted up Peru. Could have bought myself some property instead," announced Pryor in one skit. By 1980 his cocaine use reached record highs, and, after freebasing, Pyror accidentally set himself on fire on June 9 that year. He suffered burns all over his body and nearly died. During months in the hospital, he had three skin grafts, plastic surgery, suffered from kidney complications and pneumonia. His friend Jim Brown, the actor and football player, stayed by his side. Redd Foxx sent him a card that said, "I knew you were looking for me, but I didn't expect you to send up smoke signals."

Pryor gradually recovered. In 1982 he made his directorial debut in *Richard Pryor Here and Now.* In the eighties he continued to be antiestablishment and abrasive, but something clearly had changed. He was clean and seemed to be entering a new stage of life. He had moved to Hawaii with his wife, Jennifer Lee, and he was calmer. The fire had changed his life. Just eight years later, Pryor developed multiple sclerosis, the chronic, debilitating disease of the central nervous system. Despite obvious frailty Pryor returned to live performing in 1992 at the Comedy Store in West Hollywood. He was presented with the American Comedy Awards Lifetime Achievement honor that same year. But by January 1993 Pryor found it difficult to sustain a performance.

It was hard watching Pryor struggle courageously with his illness. It was difficult for him to live with it, because he is such a physical person. On stage, he contorted his body and face, prancing up and down, ranting and raving. He was a master of the vernacular, delivering his skits and stories like a preacher, like a brother on the corner, weaving in and out of the white, black, and Asian accents that dot our America. Yet, in October 1998, when Pryor was honored with the Kennedy Center Celebration of American Humor Mark Twain Prize he was barely able to whisper "Thank you."

Richard Pryor is important because he is a different kind of comedian. He articulated to the world the wit and humor of black folk: the irony of being black in America, the pain for which laughter is the only medicine, the craziness of racism, both personal and institutional, the subtleties of black words and speech. Pryor pushed the limits. He was neither predictable nor safe. He knew that telling the truth is the deepest level of humor, because he knew that black life in America is so often absurd.

Alvin Ailey

The Dancer
(1931–1989)

Alvin Ailey lived large. He was a tall man: six feet tall, huge hands, big-boned, and surprisingly burly—not what we usually expect in the lithe, tucked bodies of dancers. His physical size and presence were metaphors for how he saw dance. His own productions, though hardly lacking in subtlety or technical precision, tended toward expansive, grandiloquent movements. They also had something of the sensibility of popular theater. Ailey did not believe that modern dance had to be geared to a rarified, specialist audience. He believed it could be appreciated—and claimed as the tradition—of all people. With that in mind, and without lowering the standards of his productions, he set out to entertain on a grand scale. Plans for his *Celebration of Duke Ellington,* held at the New York State Theater in 1976, originally included dances by almost all of America's major choreographers. Although many of them bowed out, Ailey simply made more of the dances himself, instead of scaling down the project.

Ailey was born in Rogers, Texas, a small town about sixty miles northeast of Austin, in 1931. He would first move with his family the eighty miles to Navasota, in the valley of the Brazos River, and later, at the age of twelve, to Los Angeles. LA was booming during the years Ailey spent there. It thrived on the industry brought in by World War II and it was blossoming as an entertainment capital. During his adolescent years in Los Angeles, Ailey was first exposed to dance, theater, performance, and the showmanship of the entertainment industry. While still in high school, one of Ailey's teachers dragged his disinterested class to a downtown theater to see the Ballet Russe de Monte Carlo perform. Ailey was hooked. He began making the trip downtown by himself practically every week to see performances. On one of his sojourns, he was surprised to see an advertisement for a troupe containing black dancers. It was the company of choreographer, dancer, and ethnologist

Katherine Dunham. Ailey made daily trips to see Dunham's dancers. He would repay her for the inspiration later on in his career by inviting her to stage her *Choros* for his company.

Still, despite this growing passion for dance, Ailey did not plan to pursue it as a career. He had planned to study Romance languages at UCLA. It was only an introduction to Lester Horton in 1949 that changed his mind, providing a fortuitous turn in the history of American dance. Horton, the founder of the first racially mixed dance company in the United States, offered Ailey a dance scholarship. Over the next two years he provided the foundation from which Ailey's genius could emerge. Not only did Horton teach Ailey the foundations of his vocabulary, technique, and method, but his sense of showmanship, of the possibility that dance—the rarefied and elitist art—could have a wider, popular audience. Horton also drew on Japanese and Native American dance traditions, providing Ailey with the possibility for the multicultural influence on his own choreography, and the possibility that the body, through the kinetic spectacle of movements, could be an allegorized narrative of human community.

In this sense, while black vernacular traditions provide the obvious idiomatic gel for Ailey's choreography, they were not his sole inspiration. Ailey himself has admitted the profound influence his early years in black communities in the South would have on his work. In celebrated works such as *Blues Suite* and *Revelations*, Ailey relied on the black folk culture of a somewhat romanticized and idyllic portrait of a cloistered and unsullied rural Texas. "The first desire," he said, "came from the early soul experience, the fields and honky-tonks of the Brazos Valley. The people in *Blues Suite* were people I actually knew—I could say, 'This is the man who lived around the corner.' 'The Processional' and 'Wade in the Water' in *Revelations* came from images of my own baptism. . . . And of course there were the churches; there is something poetic about the service in a black church, and something very dramatic."

In many senses, however, Ailey's work was animated by the larger cultural consequences of the great epic narrative of African-American migrations from a rural, agrarian South to an urban, industrialized North. His work contained a dialogue between rural and urban and between black vernacular tradition and the international traditions of avant-garde and modern dance. In what is perhaps a characteristically American move, he employed dancers of various races, sizes, and body types; he believed in the importance of individuals firing the company through their own experience. "I've always felt that I wanted to celebrate the differences in people," Ailey said. "I didn't want all the same bodies, or all the same color, in my company."

When Horton died unexpectedly in 1953, Ailey took over the company, but it soon disbanded. Ailey and his partner, Carmen de Lavallade, were invited in 1954

1980–1989

to dance in a Truman Capote production. While in New York, they danced in television productions and Broadway musicals, and Ailey tried his hand at acting. He also studied with some of the contemporary masters of modern dance: Martha Graham, Doris Humphrey, and Anna Sokolow, adopting some of their theories of movement and space.

In 1958, Ailey formed the Alvin Ailey American Dance Theater, premiering *Blues Suite* and *Revelations* at the Ninety-second Street Y that year. Despite its popularity and success, the company would struggle financially for its first few years, with dancers working for little pay. In the mid-1960s, the U.S. State Department sponsored Ailey for tours of Australia, Southeast Asia, Senegal, North Africa, and the USSR, where their work received long, thunderous ovations from normally staid, polite audiences. These tours would make Ailey's company one of the best known in the world, and they would never fail to excite audiences with their brash and intelligent spectacles of movement.

Ailey himself stopped dancing in 1965, but he continued producing. He choreographed work for his own company, as well as for the Joffrey Ballet and the Harkness Ballet. Dances were commissioned for the openings of the Metropolitan Opera House at Lincoln Center and the opera house of the Kennedy Center in Washington. In 1971 alone he produced nine works, including *The River* for the American Ballet Theater, working to a score by Duke Ellington. By the time of his death, he had seventy-nine original works to his credit, many of them still in the repertoires of such companies as the American Ballet Theatre, the Dance Theatre of Harlem, Paris Opera Ballet, and La Scala Ballet.

Ailey also recognized the importance of a dance company acting as an archive of tradition. He began to build a repertory dance theater that would preserve the major works of American dance by such figures as Talley Beatty, May O'Donnell, Pearl Primus, José Limón, and his mentor, Lester Horton. "Modern dancers should do repertory as classical companies do," Ailey once said. "We've lost too many works over the years. The idea of presenting important pieces still needs to be dealt with in a serious way in American dance, and it's important to keep the ballets alive. They are part of our cultural heritage as Americans." Ailey brought the unique heritage of African America into the living tradition of American dance. In doing so, he also celebrated the beauty of the black body as no one has done before or since.

Bill Cosby

The Father
(1937–)

Bill Cosby was the first African-American comedian to construct his routines around the ironies and foibles of the human condition rather than simply on race or race relations. He made us visible in that most American of media—the television series, from the adventures of *I Spy* to the home comforts of the Huxtables. Through his Emmy Award–winning 1980s' television series, *The Cosby Show,* which focused on the lives of a doctor, his lawyer wife, and their children, he fundamentally changed the way blacks are represented in America's living rooms on television.

William Henry Cosby grew up in a poor neighborhood in North Philadelphia. The oldest of Ana and William Cosby's three sons, he grew up in a neighborhood full of eccentric characters, many of whom he later brought to life in the animated series *Fat Albert*. A bright but underachieving student, Cosby dropped out of high school to join the U.S. Navy in 1956. After working in the medical corps, he received his high school diploma before leaving the service in 1960.

That same year, an athletic scholarship brought Cosby to Temple University, where he studied psychology and was on the football and track teams. While in college Cosby made his professional comedy debut—years after his fifth-grade teacher asked him to perform before the class—and before long he had left school to work full-time in show business. His stand-up routine was a quick success, leading to bookings in New York clubs and, before long, an album titled *Bill Cosby Is a Very Funny Fellow, Right!* The record was nominated for a Grammy Award in 1963, beginning a string of successful albums that won Cosby six Grammy Awards from 1964 to 1970; his twenty-four records have sold more copies than any other comedian's.

Tapped in 1965 to costar opposite Robert Culp in the television action series *I*

Spy, Cosby was an instant sensation. He won three straight Emmy Awards for his performance as the dapper, erudite Alexander Scott—the first black role on television that eschewed racial stereotyping and highlighted its character's intelligence and charm. After leaving *I Spy* in 1969, Cosby went on to star in two of his own, less successful, shows: *The Bill Cosby Show* (1969–1971), a comedy series in which he played a high-school basketball coach, and *The New Bill Cosby Show* (1972-1973), a variety program.

The early cancellation of both shows didn't deter Cosby, but it helped set him on a new course. He returned to his studies, earning a B.A., master's, and doctorate in education from the University of Massachusetts. His interest in children and their growth, along with their comic side, dovetailed in *Fat Albert and the Cosby Kids,* an animated CBS hit from 1972 to 1979. Cosby was its writer, host, and actor. *Fat Albert,* Cosby has said, was a showcase for the child-rearing and educational studies he had taken in graduate school. The show crystallized Cosby's appeal, broadly blending comic storytelling, affectionate exaggerations of characters from his own life, and a humane, positive outlook.

Throughout the 1970s, Cosby also acted in movies, including the Sidney Poitier–directed *Uptown Saturday Night* (1974) and *Let's Do It Again* (1975), but his film career, culminating in 1990's *Ghost Dad,* has never approached the success of his television and recording work. Married in 1964 to Camille Hanks, Cosby's family grew to include five children by 1977. His children, Erika, Erinn, Ennis, Ensa, and Evin all bear names beginning with the letter "E" to stand, Cosby has said, for "excellence." Family life began to dominate Cosby's comedy work, including frequent guest appearances on the PBS series *The Electric Company;* it was the comic possibilities of parents and children that would bring Cosby his greatest success.

First aired in 1984, *The Cosby Show* came along at a time when network situation comedy was presumed to be a dying genre. The show, which starred Cosby as Cliff Huxtable, an obstetrician and father of five, and Phylicia Rashad as his wife, Claire, a lawyer, not only resurrected the situation comedy, it became one of the most popular and beloved series in television history. Cosby oversaw all aspects of the show's production, scrutinizing scripts for possible negative images of family life in general and African Americans in particular. His insistence on a positive portrayal of strong parents and wholesome children struck some as heavy-handed, but audiences embraced the show, as did many African-American leaders, who were thrilled to see a normal, healthy, and highly successful black family on television. The show, which ran until 1992, also featured many previously underappreciated black actors and highlighted black achievement through its understated inclusion of such details as African-American paintings on the Huxtable walls and Huxtable children going off to historically black institutions for college. Cosby, who has long served as a spokesperson for products ranging from Jell-O to Coca-Cola to Kodak, reaped enormous financial benefits from the syndication of *The Cosby Show* (the deal was estimated at $600 million). He and his wife, Camille, have been active in charity

work, giving financial support to a variety of causes, including the NAACP, the United Negro College Fund, and the National Sickle-Cell Foundation. In 1998 the couple donated $20 million to Spelman College, the largest gift ever received by a historically black college. In addition, he has written two best-selling books for adults, 1986's *Fatherhood* and 1989's *Love and Marriage,* along with several books for children. His *Little Bill* books moved to television in 2000 in an animated series. In January, 1997, Cosby's only son, Ennis, was killed by a would-be robber; in the wake of the tragedy the Cosby family established the Ennis William Cosby Foundation to help children and young adults struggling with dyslexia, which Ennis had overcome. He was working on a doctorate in education at the time of his murder.

Despite tribulations, Cosby has stayed active in television, starring in a new series, named simply *Cosby,* in which Phylicia Rashad again plays his wife. In 1998 Cosby was honored at the Kennedy Center's annual celebration on America's cultural and artistic treasures. No single black actor has affected the medium of television more profoundly in its representation of black people as the social and intellectual equals of white Americans than Bill Cosby. He reversed a century of racism in the visual representation of African Americans in American popular culture.

John Hope Franklin

The Academic
(1915–)

John Hope Franklin told the story of our people. He made it inexcusable for any history of America ever again to omit the history of African Americans. The recipient of more than one hundred honorary degrees and author of universally respected scholarly studies on black America, John Hope Franklin is the best-known and most influential black academic of his generation.

Born on January 2, 1915, Franklin grew up in the predominantly black town of Rentiesville, Oklahoma, the son of a lawyer and a schoolteacher. As a child, he heard firsthand accounts of the rioting that killed at least one hundred blacks in Tulsa in 1921. His father, who was working in Tulsa at the time, survived, but it was a lesson in racism that haunted the younger Franklin's childhood.

Franklin attended Fisk University, where he earned high honors and a bachelor's degree in history in 1935. Encouraged by his history professor, Theodore Currier, to apply to Harvard University for graduate school, he earned his master's degree there in 1936 and a doctorate in 1941. He was rejected by the local army recruiter when he tried to sign up for service in World War II. His brother, Buck, a high school principal, suffered a breakdown after serving in the then-segregated army. "The Army wrecked him," Franklin said of his brother, who died in 1947.

After spending his first years in academia teaching at black institutions, including Fisk and Howard universities, in 1956 Franklin was appointed chair of the history department at Brooklyn College. Although this was an extraordinary breakthrough, he found the ostensibly less racist North just as inhospitable as the Jim Crow South. "You could vote," he later recalled, "but that was about all." Despite his position as head of the all-white fifty-two-person department, Franklin faced entrenched racism, and visited more than one hundred real estate agents before he found one who was willing to sell him a house.

Franklin spent eight years at Brooklyn, then eighteen at the University of Chicago, again as chair of the history faculty. His work, notably his sweeping *From Slavery to Freedom: A History of American Negroes,* first published in 1947, earned him a reputation as the successor to historians W. E. B. Du Bois and Carter G. Woodson (both Harvard Ph.D.s in history). Even more than his predecessors, though, Franklin was the person responsible for conferring academic legitimacy on the study of black history. "John Hope Franklin is an uncommon historian," NAACP chairman Roy Wilkins wrote, "who has consistently corrected in eloquent language the misrecording of this country's rich heritage."

From Slavery to Freedom has sold more than three million copies and continues to be used widely. Written in 1943, another of Franklin's groundbreaking works, *The Free Negro in North Carolina, 1790–1860,* was one of the first books to uncover the history of black Americans outside the institution of slavery. Other projects furthered research on the birth of Jim Crow and other aspects of American racial inequality. In addition to his scholarly work, Franklin early on lent his efforts to the fight for civil rights. He conducted research for Thurgood Marshall during the 1954 landmark case *Brown* v. *Board of Education,* which ended legal segregation in public schools, and he marched with Martin Luther King, Jr., in Washington, D.C., in 1963 and in Selma in 1965.

In 1982 Franklin returned to the South, to Duke University, from which he retired as James B. Duke Professor of History Emeritus in 1992. Still busy in retirement, Franklin took on new projects, including *The Color Line: Legacy for the Twenty-First Century* (1993), which the *New York Review of Books* praised for its "almost heroic" tone of restraint in the face of disappointment and anger. Describing himself as "cautiously optimistic" about the state of race relations at the end of the century, Franklin nevertheless admits to "some restrictions and a lot of caveats."

When President Bill Clinton tapped Franklin in 1997 to chair his advisory board on race and reconciliation, he laid aside an uncompleted history of escaped slaves, tentatively titled *Dissidents on the Plantation,* and accepted the position. The board, which reported in 1998, was criticized for not doing enough, but Franklin said he hoped its work would prove a watershed, with its focus on educational and economic equality.

Franklin was awarded the Presidential Medal of Freedom in 1996. He has served as past president of Phi Beta Kappa, the Organization of American Historians, the American Historical Association, and the American Studies Association. The John Hope Franklin Research Center, a repository for African and African-American studies documentation and an educational outreach division of the Rare Book, Manuscript, and Special Collections Library, was founded at Duke in 1995 in his honor. Without him, the eager young scholars of our generation would never have had the chance to focus their energies on the history, philosophy, and literature of the African-American experience. Franklin's work established a solid foundation for the growth of the field of African-American studies as a serious subject of scholarly inquiry. He was the first African-American historian to establish the field without the backing of a mainstream department of history. Today, when so many of our colleges and universities support lively programs and departments of African-American Studies, it is impossible to imagine the world of learning without the influence of John Hope Franklin.

Jesse Jackson

The Rainbow Man
(1941–)

He is the most visible and articulate successor to Dr. King. Jesse Jackson has spent his lifetime fighting for recognition and equality on multiple fronts. He marched next to Martin Luther King, Jr. in the 1960s. He ran for the presidency in the 1980s, and he battled for an increased black presence on Wall Street in the 1990s. Jackson has long been a voice for empowerment. Not surprisingly, as his public profile has grown Jackson also has confronted criticism from several quarters. The recipient of more than forty honorary degrees, arguably the most powerful African American in political and economic terms, Jackson continues to head Operation Rainbow/PUSH, a national organization that reflects its founder's most cherished goals in promoting financial equality, educational improvements, voter registration, and self-esteem.

The man who would later exhort crowds to repeat "I am somebody" grew up in a situation that encouraged him to believe he was a nobody. Born October 8, 1941, in Greensville, South Carolina, Jesse Louis Jackson is the son of the former Helen Burns (she later married Charles H. Jackson), a teenager when she gave birth, and Noah Robinson, one of the richest black men in Greensville. Although Jackson visited Robinson as a boy, his biological father refused to acknowledge his paternity publicly for most of Jackson's childhood; his attention increased, however, as Jackson developed into a star athlete and student in high school.

After graduating in 1959, Jackson entered the University of Illinois on a football scholarship, but he left soon, after being denied the quarterback position he wanted. He enrolled in North Carolina Agricultural and Technical State College, a historically black school, where he became both starting quarterback and president of the student body. Jackson's leadership abilities blossomed in college, where he joined students protesting discrimination in local restaurants, libraries, and other public spaces. In his early civil rights work, he also found his future career: He decided he would become a minister.

Newly married to the former Jacqueline Brown, in 1964 Jackson returned to Illinois to attend Chicago Theological Seminary. He would not finish his degree there until thirty-five years later. In 1965 Jackson traveled with a group of fellow seminarians to march with Martin Luther King, Jr., in Selma, Alabama; Jackson's real career was just beginning. After Selma, Jackson went to work for King's Southern Christian Leadership Conference (SCLC); in 1966 he assumed leadership of the Chicago branch of Operation Breadbasket, an SCLC-founded organization devoted to bottom-line economic equality and justice. By 1967 he was its national chairman. Coming from a childhood of poverty, Jackson brought uncommon vigor and energy to the fight for steady jobs, ample food, and common dignity.

During his climb to ever-increasing status within the equality movement, Jackson found himself at odds with SCLC leadership, even falling out with King himself. Witnesses recall that the two had just begun to reconcile in April 1968, when King was assassinated while standing on the balcony of the Lorraine Motel in Memphis, Tennessee. Accused of grandstanding in the wake of King's death, Jackson was passed over for the role as King's SCLC successor, that job going instead to King's friend and partner, the longtime civil rights activist Ralph David Abernathy. Jackson stayed on to help the SCLC's failed antipoverty effort—which culminated in Resurrection City, a tent community of protesters who camped in the nation's capital to publicize the problems of the poor—but left in 1971 to form his own organization, Operation PUSH.

Standing for People United to Serve Humanity, Operation PUSH became Jackson's forum for launching a variety of programs, ranging from job training to voter registration. Jackson's use of the call-and-response ritual so prevalent in the black church had crowds chanting "I am somebody," and the message of self-empowerment and positive energy brought Jackson a national audience. He began appearing on television talk shows, speaking at union rallies, and campaigning for political candidates; by the end of the 1970s he was America's best-known black leader. Although he had never held elective office, Jackson ran for the Democratic nomination for the presidency in 1984 and 1988. Despite some extraordinary victories he lost both times in the primaries, and was further disappointed when the rumor that nominee Michael Dukakis was going to ask him to join the ticket fizzled in 1988.

> *Future leaders, those who lead the nation, must know that the flag is red, white and blue, but the nation is not red, white and blue. It is red and yellow and brown and black and white.*
> —Jesse Jackson

Jackson's candidacies, though failing to win him a nomination, brought liberal issues to national attention; at Democratic conventions he delivered what were considered among the best political speeches ever given. In addition, his runs for the White House energized the black electorate, increasing voter registration among African Americans. But the negative baggage he had accrued—including Jackson's out-of-character reference, in 1984, to New York as "Hymietown"—proved too much. As his career as a candidate ended, Jackson became a powerful behind-the-scenes presence in international politics, helping to broker the release of hostages from Iraq in 1991, Bosnia in 1999, and Sierra Leone in 2000.

Continuing his work with Operation PUSH and the Rainbow Coalition, a political advocacy group he founded in 1986, Jackson has continued to be a force in the domestic arena. Whether working for statehood for the District of Columbia, speaking on behalf of expelled high school students in Decatur, Illinois, or launching an initiative to increase black power on Wall Street, Jackson has scarcely slowed his pace. In 2000 Jackson, who has five children, collaborated with his son, Jesse Jackson, Jr., a congressperson representing a district in Illinois, to write *It's About the Money*, a book of financial advice for African Americans. Like his mentor near the end of his life, Jackson has redefined the nature of the civil rights struggle to embrace economic relationships as the underlying cause of discrimination.

1980–1989

Michael Jackson

Moonwalker
(1957–)

Michael Jackson is one of the most popular musical entertainers of the twentieth century. He sold over a hundred million records in the 1980s, including the biggest-selling album in music industry history, *Thriller.* The importance of Michael Jackson is to be found not simply in his astonishing moonwalk dance or the frenzied tabloid coverage of his undeniable eccentricity or his place in postmodern pop culture. More significant is the way in which he has assembled, reinvented, and imagined for himself and a worldwide audience an amalgam of elements from the American popular musical and cultural imagination to assume an iconic, near mythic status.

In 1982, before fifty million viewers, Michael Jackson performed his number one single "Billy Jean" on the TV special *Motown 25: Yesterday, Today and Forever.* He lip-synched to a recorded track and electrified the world with his performance of the moonwalk. His costume echoed the attire of other great black performers: a Jimi Hendrix–style military jacket with tasseled epaulets and a rhinestoned glove on just one hand à la Little Richard. The king of pop had arrived, speaking a language that embodied the "show" phenomenon in black culture. People were dumbstruck. Audiences cheered on this young man whom we had known as a little boy.

Everyone knew Michael Jackson as the former lead of the Jackson Five, a Motown singing group made up of the five Jackson brothers. The youngest member of the group, Michael was so small when he started dancing and singing that he doesn't remember much from the earliest days. He does remember singing at the top of his voice, dancing with real joy, and working too hard for a child. He has said that his father, who controlled him with an iron fist, mentally abused him. By the time Michael was eight years old, the Jackson Five was performing five sets a night, six nights a week, in strip clubs, gambling joints, and nightclubs. His imitation of

James Brown's fancy footwork, and his sophisticated rendition of lovelorn adolescent lyrics, in songs like "I Want You Back," made him the focus of the entertainment.

Jackson was the first black child to be marketed and publicized in a way that precluded a personal life. A cultural phenomenon, his persona was used to sell T-shirts, comics, and an animated television series. Berry ("Magic Man") Gordy, founder of Motown records, already had made Diana Ross and the Supremes, Gladys Knight and the Pips, Stevie Wonder, and Marvin Gaye famous, among many others. In 1971 he decided to launch solo careers for Michael, Jermaine, and Jackie. Michael's debut album was *Got to Be There,* rich in hits such as "Rockin' Robin," a funky revival of Bobby Day's song. The following year he made it to the British top ten with his remake of Bill Wither's "Ain't No Sunshine." At the same time, he became the youngest performer to score an American number one hit with "Ben," the film theme about a boy and his pet rat. He learned to emulate the styles of James Brown, Jackie Wilson, Sammy Davis, Jr., and Diana Ross.

In 1976 Jackson costarred as the scarecrow with Diana Ross in *The Wiz,* a Motown-produced remake of *The Wizard of Oz.* Composer Quincy Jones wrote the soundtrack. Jones and Jackson became friends, and in 1979 Jackson left Motown for Epic Records to collaborate with Jones on *Off the Wall.* Capping the disco era, this somewhat soulful album, funky in places and enhanced with string orchestration and horn arrangements, sold more than seven million copies and included the number one hits "Don't Stop 'Til You Get Enough" and "Rock With You." *Off the Wall* revived Jackson's career; he was now represented as the self-assured disco dancer, complete with a handsome Afro and a tuxedo.

In 1982, the year that Julius "Dr. J." Erving electrified NBA crowds with his slam dunks, Jackson released *Thriller,* also produced by Quincy Jones. At the same time that *Thriller* was released, Jones won five Grammy Awards for *Dude,* including producer of the year. Jackson and Jones had become a show-stopping combination. On Grammy night in 1984, Jackson received more than twelve nominations for *Thriller.* Over forty million people bought the album, whose seven chart-topping singles included the number one hits "The Girl Is Mine," "Billie Jean," and "Beat It." "Billie Jean," with its somber preoccupations, was an especially big hit, and Jones, who wrote and produced it, spent three weeks on the bass licks alone.

Thriller was heralded as a black landmark in the white-dominated market. Six of the album's songs were top hits, and Jackson's videos of these songs were the first by an African American to receive regularly scheduled rotation on MTV. Still a new phenomenon, the series of videos that accompanied the album made Jackson the first music-video superstar. Directed by Jon Landis, the seventeen-minute *Thriller* minimovie was acclaimed as the most successful music video ever made. Because of its unforeseen success, mainstream popular musical acts rode heavily on the dramatics of the music video, rather than on the lyrics, and only a full-fledged visual story, complete with plot, would suffice.

In the making of *Thriller* and in its aftermath, Jackson mirrored trends of the 1980s and set new ones. Middle-aged viewers were skeptical, but the young and the old alike were captivated. Few young American teenagers remained untouched by the ubiquitous Michael mania, and older blacks always supported him through the vicissitudes of his physical appearance, because despite his youthfulness, they identified with his art. A phenomenal dancer whose steps have been described as defying gravity, he had drawn inspiration from the Hollywood screen and the dancing superstars of an earlier era, and his choreography played deeply on American mythology and sentimentality.

Jackson also captured the momentum of the 1980s in his business deals. He signed a multimillion-dollar contract to advertise Pepsi-Cola, which sponsored the reunited Jackson Brothers Victory tour. In 1985 he spent $47.5 million to purchase ATV Music, which held the rights to most of the Beatles's songs. When Jackson married Lisa Marie Presley, Elvis Presley's daughter, he acquired the copyrights to the Presley collection of hits. A deal in the fall of 1995 with Sony Records added more assets to his repertoire, including the *Three Stooges* movies. *Bad* (1987), his follow-up coproduction with Jones, led to his first solo tour. *Moonwalk* (1988), his biography, was named after the floating dance step that he had perfected from its urban dance roots. Jackson released two more albums in the 1990s: *Dangerous* (1991) and *HIStory—Past, Present and Future, Book I,* which anthologized old hits with new material; both these albums fell short of his earlier successes.

Jackson's personal difficulties in the late 1980s and the 1990s were highly publicized, though close friends stood by him. His two marriages, first to Lisa Marie Presley and then to Debbie Rowe, both ended in divorce. After being badly burned during a Pepsi commercial, his skin color became progressively lighter, another subject that created adverse publicity for him. In a televised interview with Barbara Walters he attempted to overcome the reputation for eccentricity that had begun to swirl around him.

Jackson's mastery of the dance and the lyric defined popular culture in the 1980s around the world. At the end of the century, his career appeared to be a slow fade, but Michael Jackson's story is not over. The sources of his artistic and personal power remain to be fully understood. The cultural and social allegories of his life have yet to be seriously evaluated and will still evolve. Both shrewd and vulnerable, he is perhaps the best and the least known star of our time.

1980–1989

Carl Lewis

The Victor
(1961–)

He ran the fastest and he jumped the furthest even when he was older than anyone else in the field. As a ten-year-old, Carl Lewis stood for a photograph next to his hero, Jesse Owens. What exactly does a legend say to a legend-in-the-making? Lewis recalls that it was along the lines of "have fun." Like Owens, Lewis's achievements have become the stuff of legend: four gold medals in the 1984 Olympics in Los Angeles, matching the mark set by Owens in Berlin in 1936; nine gold medals in all, as many as any other single athlete in the history of Olympic competition; numerous world championship medals; multiple world-record setting victories in both the 100 meter and the long jump. But these accomplishments, remarkable as they are, only tell part of the story.

So much of Lewis's career, like the races he ran, can be captured in moments—fleeting instances that define his competitive drive and that have assured him a permanent place in the pantheon of stars of track and field. Recall Lewis as a thirty-five-year-old man (already an ancient in his sport) returning once again to the Olympics in 1996, the site of his past glory, and capturing the gold in the long jump with a leap of 27 feet, 10¾ inches, his longest jump at sea level in four years. Or picture Lewis at his coming-out party to world stardom, the 1984 Olympics, winning the 100 meters by the largest margin in the history of Olympic competition—he was clocked at an astonishing twenty-eight mph at the finish.

While Lewis has indisputably established himself as one of the greatest individual athletes in all sports (in a list of the top one hundred athletes of the century, ESPN ranked him number twelve), popularity and cross-over stardom have eluded him, at least in the United States. Some see him as brash, even arrogant. Even his peers often interpreted his distance and haughtiness and confidence as arrogance. "He rubs it in too much," said Edwin Moses, two-time Olympic gold medalist in the 400 hurdles. "A little humility is in order. That's what Carl lacks."

Frederick Carlton Lewis was born in Birmingham, Alabama, on July 1, 1961, and raised in suburban Willingboro, New Jersey. He and his three siblings (including sister Carol, also a track star) grew up around the track; their parents, Bill and Evelyn, were actively involved in local track clubs. But Lewis was not an immediate sensation. A diminutive child, it wasn't until a growth spurt at fifteen (in which he grew two and one-half inches in a month, requiring crutches to walk until his body adjusted to the change) that he began to show promise as an athlete.

If you don't have confidence you will always find a way not to win.
—Carl Lewis

By high school, he had gained a national reputation, breaking the prep school long jump record with a leap of 26 feet, 8 inches. Now grown to his full stature, the six-foot two-inch, 173-pound Lewis committed to the University of Houston over Tennessee or the hometown track power, Villanova. As a freshman, he qualified for the 1980 Olympics in the long jump, placing second at the trials, only to have his Olympic dream deferred due to a U.S. boycott of the Moscow games. A year later, he was the number one ranked athlete in the world in both the 100 meters and the long jump. Passing on his final two years of college eligibility, Lewis set his sights on the Olympics by training with the Santa Monica Track Club. In Los Angeles in 1984, Lewis found the world stage on which to showcase his abilities, winning the gold in his four events—the 100 meter, the 200 meter, the long jump, and the 4 x 100-meter relay.

For all his achievements, one would assume that Lewis would have emerged as a highly visible ambassador of his sport, like Magic Johnson, Larry Bird, and Michael Jordan were to the NBA, or like Wayne Gretzky was to the NHL. Lewis would seem to be the perfect spokesperson for a sport that has often been marginalized in the athletics-obsessed American consciousness. While Lewis certainly did much to raise the profile of track and field, his success did not translate to well-deserved endorsement deals or public appearances. After 1984, Lewis had every reason to think that the endorsement offers would come, that his gold would turn to green. But the flood of offers never came.

In the years since Lewis's first trip to the games, his career has played itself out in much the same schizophrenic fashion: athletic excellence, coupled with commercial disappointment. He returned to the Olympics in 1988 and defended his golds in the 100 meter and the long jump, a feat never before achieved in Olympic competition. Even this, though, was marred by controversy. In the 100-meter final,

Lewis got off to a good start, but in the final fifty meters he was overtaken by the Canadian sprinter Ben Johnson, who shattered the world record in a time of 9.79 seconds. Lewis, it seemed, would have to settle for silver (as he had done by losing in the 200-meter final, breaking a two-year winning streak in that race). But soon it was revealed that Johnson had tested positive for steroids; he was stripped of his medal and the gold belonged to Lewis.

Perhaps Lewis's single greatest moment came at the 1991 world championships in Tokyo. As a thirty-year-old, he was largely discounted by the media. A younger group of athletes had begun their ascent, including Dennis Mitchell and Leroy Burrell (who trained with Lewis at the Santa Monica Track Club). Many in the media were saying, not without some relish, that Lewis's time had passed. He would prove them wrong.

In perhaps the greatest race in the history of the 100 meters, a total of six runners broke the ten-second mark, with Lewis leading the pack in world record time—9.86 seconds. "He passed us like we were standing still," said the second-place Burrell. Surprisingly, this marked the first time in Lewis's life that he could claim an untainted, unshared world record. "The best race of my life," Lewis would say. "The best technique, the fastest. And I did it at thirty."

Lewis had little time to savor his victory, however, when only five days later he came up short in the long jump against Mike Powell, ending Lewis's decade-long unbeaten streak in the event. Even in defeat, Lewis's performance was nothing short of spectacular; three times he reached 29 feet, a distance he had never before topped. But this personal record was overshadowed by Powell, who unleashed a leap of 29 feet, 4¼ inches, the longest jump in history. Lewis would take revenge on Powell the next year in the Barcelona Olympics, edging him out by 1¼ inches to win his seventh gold. His eighth would come later that week, as he anchored the record-setting 4 x 100 meter relay team.

Our final image of Lewis in competition is a fitting one: a record ninth gold medal draped around his neck, before an American crowd. For a moment, at least, adulation was his. "Lewis beat age, gravity, history, logic and the world at a rocking Olympic Stadium in Atlanta to win the Olympic gold medal in the long jump," *Sports Illustrated* columnist Rick Reilly wrote. "It was quite possibly his most impossible moment in an impossibly brilliant career." We will always see him suspended in the air, his long legs stretched impossibly far, making a jump so high he seems to be flying.

Jessye Norman

Diva
(1945–)

Jessye Norman is the diva of our people. Picture 1989, the bicentennial of the French Revolution. Jessye Norman, draped with the tricolor, is singing *La Marseillaise* in flawless French. The crowds cheer, riveted by this black American who somehow embodies France's most celebrated day. Or go back to 1969—when Norman has just signed a three-year contract with the Deutsche Opera in West Berlin. Her debut role is Elizabeth in Richard Wagner's *Tannhäuser*. The role calls for a blonde Nordic person, but Norman transforms her audience's preconceptions. She draws from a vast ocean of ability, voice, and dignity to elevate us with her rich soprano voice. Director Jean Jacques Beineix had Norman in mind when he invented a character based on her in his 1982 film, *Diva*.

Norman was born and raised in an educated family in Augusta, Georgia. She sang throughout her childhood and adolescence, urged on by the piano playing of her mother and her father's singing in the family's Baptist church. At age seven, she entered her first vocal competition, singing "God Will Take Care of You." As a child she was introduced to opera via the New York Metropolitan Opera's weekly live broadcasts on the radio and later performed arias for Girl Scout and PTA meetings. The first aria she mastered was "My Heart at Thy Sweet Voice," from French composer Camille Saint-Saëns's *Samson and Delilah*. When she was sixteen she visited the music department at Howard University and sang for voice instructor Carolyn Grant, who later became her vocal coach. Norman attended Howard and graduated with honors in 1967, completing a summer of postgraduate study at the Peabody Conservatory in Baltimore, before going on for her master's degree at the University of Michigan. At Michigan, French baritone Pierre Bernac and soprano Elizabeth Mannion coached her in voice. In 1968, she received a scholarship from the Institute of International Education, which allowed her to enter Bavarian Radio's international music competition in Munich, Germany. The following year, she won. In 1969, Norman sailed to Europe to begin work with the Deutsche Opera Berlin. She made her Italian debut in Florence in George Frideric Handel's *Deborah* in 1970, and the following year she performed in Mozart's *Idomeneo* in Rome, Giacomo Meyerbeer's *L'Africaine* in Florence, and Mozart's *Marriage of Figaro* at the Berlin Festival. The BBC broadcast her recording in 1971, introducing her to British audiences. That recording became a finalist for the Montreux International Record Award competition.

Norman's professional American debut took place at the Hollywood Bowl in Los Angeles in *Aida* in 1972. A long-awaited east coast debut occurred in the Great

The African-American Century

Performers series at Lincoln Center in 1973, where she thrilled audiences with selections from Brahms, Wolf, Strauss, Mahler, Wagner, and Satie. Several opera houses and theaters hosted her, including the Kennedy Center for the Performing Arts in Washington, Carnegie Hall, and the Los Angeles Philharmonic Orchestra.

Norman's 1983 debut at the Metropolitan Opera in the one-hundredth production of *Les Troyens* was broadcast nationally on public television, ensuring her a devoted coterie of American opera aficionados. She invigorated African-American attention for the opera. As a veteran Wagernian, Norman astounded her audiences in roles such as that of Sieglinde in *Die Walküre* in the Met productions that followed *Les Troyens.* Her *Liebestod* from Wagner's *Tristan und Isolde* again was broadcast live from Lincoln Center, when she performed at the 148th opening of the New York Philharmonic.

Norman has expanded her repertoire into many different areas. In 1988, she sang a concert performance of Francis-Jean Marcel Poulenc's one-act opera *La Voix Humaine,* based on Jean Cocteau's 1930 play. She has interpreted songs from films and musical comedies by such composers as George Gershwin, Cole Porter, and Harold Arlen, performed with dancer Bill T. Jones, and sung African-American spirituals in an acclaimed concert with fellow black soprano Kathleen Battle at Carnegie Hall. Norman has won three Grammys, *Musical America*'s Outstanding Musician of the Year Award, the *Commandeur de l'ordre des Arts et des Lettres,* the Paris *Grand Prix National du Disque,* London's Gramophone Award, and the Edison Prize.

Norman has said that she draws on the lamentation of the black woman as well as spirituals in her interpretation of classical opera. To her, the African drum is a complex voice, and that the African-American epic experience has been nothing if not musical. Norman is part of that epic drama. She enacts with technical brilliance the passion of those quotidian ancient dramas. Her majestic voice and aesthetic sensibility elevate them in turn.

Martin Puryear

The Sculptor
(1941–)

He is a poet of massive forms. He sculpted *Self* in 1977, out of wood. A dark magisterial cedar and mahogany form that evokes the heaviness of stone emerging from the bowels of the earth, *Self* is completely hollow within, playing on the contrast between its contour and the void. In August of that same year, Puryear made a yurt, modeled after the dwellings of Central Asian nomadic peoples, entitled *Where the Heart Is Sleeping.* Enclosing functional objects and a small bronze West African chair, and surrounded by carved falcons, it is a metaphor for cultural adaptability and personal mobility—where the perceived boundaries of self are transcended.

Puryear is a poet who works with organic material rather than words—a master sculptor and craftsman. His contribution to the plastic arts is as profound as Romare Bearden's and Jacob Lawrence's are to the visual arts. To stand near a Puryear piece, near his suspended circles or his compact monoliths and his eccentric shapes, is to be close to one of the best sculptors of the twentieth century. His quiet, exquisitely handcrafted work is broadly derived from modernist abstraction, and often hints of his experiences in Africa, Scandinavia, and Japan.

Puryear was born in Washington, D.C. His father worked with the postal service and his mother taught elementary school. The eldest of four boys and two girls, he entered Catholic University in Washington, D.C., in the fall of 1959. As a biology major, he hoped to fulfill a youthful ambition to become a bird-life illustrator. He switched to art in his junior year, where he began to concentrate on painting and philosophy with Nell B. Sonneman. In 1962 he participated in a group exhibition at the Adams Morgan Gallery in Washington. One year later, the same year of his graduation, he won his first award, for one of his entries in the Maryland Regional Exhibition held at the Baltimore Museum of Art.

Puryear's African and Scandinavian journeys in the next stage of his life are considered wellsprings of training and inspiration. Etched, joined, and carefully carved into the grain of his pieces are the numerous cultural and formal influences he experienced in his fieldwork. In 1964, at a time of rising black consciousness in the arts, Puryear joined the Peace Corps and traveled to Sierra Leone in West Africa to teach biology, English, and French. While there, he studied informally but intensively with sophisticated master woodworkers and with potters, cloth dyers, and carpenters. In the village of Segbwema, he developed a sense of craftsmanship and learned how to downplay his own ego. Craftsmanship in America was something most sculptors seemed to shun, having their pieces fabricated for them.

By the end of his two-year term in the Peace Corps, Puryear had decided to apply to the Swedish Royal Academy of Art in Stockholm. Receiving a Scandinavian-American Foundation study grant, he studied printmaking and explored Scandinavian furniture-making. He was introduced to James Krenow, the most esteemed furniture maker in Sweden at the time. Krenow taught him how not to dominate the wood, but to bring out its natural beauty, even if achieving this effect involved far more tinkering and finishing than the layman realized. Like the Russian constructivists, Krenow also taught him the merits of labor unfettered by the demands of the marketplace. Although Puryear, for the most part, eschews politics, he sensed an affinity with workers, particularly African-American workers: "Their hands were always busy, their backs always bent. It would be very hard for me to turn into the kind of person who is giving orders for the work to be realized by somebody else. I guess I don't trust that." Integral to Puryear's approach is the intense effort and time that he puts into every piece of work, leaving each one with the imprint of his own hands. In Sweden, Puryear's work appeared in the 1967 and 1968 annual exhibitions of the Swedish Royal Academy of Art, while he also worked briefly as a designer for SCAN, a Scandinavian furniture company. He is a great admirer of the rugged outdoors, and especially of Arctic landscape, and is well versed in the stories of Matthew Henson and Jim Beckwourth, other pioneers, counting them both as people he admires. Puryear traveled widely in Scandinavia. Although the landscape was "incredible and expansive," he felt undernourished as an artist and constrained by Europe, so he returned home.

The late sixties' art world had been influenced by minimalist sculpture—primarily an attempt to shape the spectator's experience of space through basic geometric forms and a rejection of emotive expression. Puryear flirted with its style but retained a deep emotional intensity in all his works. He studied with Richard van Bruen, Al Held, and James Rosati at Yale University, earning an MFA in 1971. He subsequently taught at Fisk University as an assistant professor of art and had his first U.S. individual exhibition in 1972 in Washington. Through 1978, he taught as an assistant professor of art at the University of Maryland, traveling back and forth to his studio in Brooklyn. His first commissioned outdoor sculpture, completed in 1977 for Art Park in Lewiston, New York, dealt with his recurring theme of how to bridge the distance among formal, aesthetic, and contextual or environmental concerns.

I enjoy and need to work with my hands. They give you a measure of the extensions of mind and body. . . . As I work on a particular piece, it evolves slowly into its own unique statement of invention.
—Martin Puryear

Also in 1977, Puryear faced a profound loss. A fire ravaged his Brooklyn studio, damaging much of his work. He found a new studio for one year at the Institute for Art and Urban Resources in Chicago. Rather than wallow in depression, he became more prolific than ever, the fire galvanizing him to delve even deeper than before. He concentrated on a large body of wall-mounted sculptures and a number of outdoor projects while teaching at the University of Illinois at Chicago. His work appeared both in the 1979 and 1981 biennial exhibitions at the Whitney, and he was commissioned to create both the famous *Bodark* arc, for the Nathan Manilow Sculpture Park at Governors State University in University Park, Illinois, and *Sentinel,* for Gettysburg College in Pennsylvania. His studio work at this time was known by forty rings—wall-mounted sculptures—most made up of strips of wood laminated into roughly circular configurations. From 1982 to 1984 he traveled to Japan, where he studied Japanese domestic architecture and gardens.

Puryear was forty-six years old when he had his first New York solo exhibition, at the David McKee Gallery in 1987, but four major Manhattan museums already had shown his work, and he was the recipient of many honors. His work was included in the 1989 biennial at the Whitney Museum of American Art. He received the Frances J. Greenberger Foundation Award. In 1990 he received the Skowhegan Prize for sculpture. He is a winner of a McArthur "genius" grant and was among the winners of the thirty-third annual creative arts awards for sculpture at Brandeis University. He won first prize as the sole U.S. representative in the 1989 São Paulo biennial. One of the few African-American artists to receive this degree

1980–1989

of national and international acclaim, he is regularly commissioned to make pieces for public places and is known for his architectural work as well.

Just as his work reflects diverse craft and fine art traditions from around the world, Puryear always has resisted categories and boundaries of identity. For this reason, he prefers to be represented in our volume not by a photograph of a man, but by a photograph of his sculpture, *For Buckworth*. In this, he remains the quintessential Puryear—the genius who defies us to know him as anything other than "artist."

Alice Walker

Womanist Embracing the Color Purple
(1944–)

Alice Walker has dedicated her life to writing and to social change. Her sustained exploration of these sometimes disparate worlds has created an intersecting space for her literature, scholarship, and activism—a space that was best described by fellow writer-activist Toni Cade Bambara as one of "cultural work." Among her many contributions, Walker introduced the term "womanist" into feminist vocabulary and has led fights against the sexual and genital abuse of women's bodies. Her best-selling novel, *The Color Purple* (1983), is widely credited with founding a revolution in black women's studies.

Alice Walker was born on February 9, 1944, in Eatonton, Georgia. She was the eighth and youngest child of Minnie Tallulah Grant Walker and Willie Lee Walker. Her parents were poor sharecroppers whose lives inspired both Walker's own political activism and her art. As a young man, her father was a tireless community activist, beaten down physically and spiritually by the social injustice of the American South. Her mother worked the fields, sewed clothes, canned vegetables and fruits, made quilts, and cultivated and preserved flowers. The commitment, energy, inner strength, and beauty that Walker saw in her parents' lives are found in her fictional characters.

In the summer of 1952, when Walker was eight years old, her brother accidentally shot her in the right eye with his BB gun. Suddenly disfigured, Walker became withdrawn and alienated and found herself alone in a world of the poetic imagination and literature. When she was fourteen years old, her older brother paid for an operation to remove the scar tissue from the damaged eye, an event that allowed Walker to feel more confident about her physical and intellectual attributes. She began to perform better academically and she eventually became her high school valedictorian and prom queen. In her collection of essays *In Search of Our Mothers'*

Gardens (1983), Walker says she resolved her conflict about the injury when her baby daughter, Rebecca, looked at her and asked, "Mommy, where did you get that world in your eye?"

In her high school years, Walker received three gifts from her mother that she believes shaped the contours of her life: a sewing machine that gave her permission to make her own clothes; a suitcase that gave her permission to leave home; and a typewriter that gave her permission to write. When she left for Spelman College in Atlanta, she became involved in politics. She picketed the White House during the Cuban missile crisis in 1962, attended the World Youth Festival in Finland, demonstrated in SNCC protests in Atlanta, and attended the March on Washington in 1963. Walker transferred to Sarah Lawrence, a women's liberal arts college in Bronxville, New York, where she completed her B.A. in 1965. Graduating from Sarah Lawrence, she moved back to the South and volunteered with voter registration drives. She saw her trip to Mississippi as essential to her well-being: "That summer marked the beginning of the realization that I could never live happily in Africa or anywhere else until I could live freely in Mississippi." She traveled and taught throughout the South and began teaching at Jackson State in 1968. In 1970 she was appointed writer-in-residence at Tougaloo College. That same year, Walker's first novel, *The Third Life of Grange Copeland,* was published. Believed by many critics to be her most sophisticated novel, it centers on family violence, sharecropping poverty, and the metaphorical reincarnation of the main character.

As a teacher at Wellesley College in 1972, Walker lectured on the writings of Zora Neale Hurston, a then marginalized figure from the Harlem Renaissance. She later edited an anthology of Hurston's work, *I Love Myself When I'm Laughing . . . and Then Again When I Am Looking Mean and Impressive.* In 1973 Walker found Hurston's grave and placed a headstone there. It reads: ZORA NEALE HURSTON A GENIUS OF THE SOUTH. In the same year Walker published a collection of short stories, *In Love and Trouble: Stories of Black Women.* In 1976 she published her second novel, *Meridian,* which details the complex lives of community activists in the South during the civil rights movement.

In 1982 Walker began to write *The Color Purple,* which she has said was inspired by the idea of "two women who felt married to the same man." Convinced it would take her five years to complete the book, she finished it in a year. Charles Johnson called the publication of the book "a cultural event." It was instrumental in giving voice to black women and their experience. Walker received a great deal of criticism for her portrayal of black men in the story, specifically the character Mister, but she pointed out that all her characters, including Mister, had "the courage to change." Walker received the 1983 Pulitzer Prize for fiction and the American Book Award for *The Color Purple.* The movie version of the book, produced and directed by Steven Spielberg, garnered eleven Academy Award nominations, though it too generated controversy over its depiction of black men.

1980–1989

In 1983 Walker published *In Search of Our Mothers' Gardens: Womanist Prose,* which explores her life and relationship to politics and art as a black feminist. She continued her political activism and was arrested blocking a gate at the Concord Naval Weapons laboratory in 1987. She published *The Temple of My Familiar* in 1989, a novel that took her eight years to write. In 1992 Walker published *Possessing the Secret of Joy,* a novel that criticizes the practice of female circumcision. Her interest in female genital mutilation took her on a journey to Africa with filmmaker Pratibha Parmar to make the documentary *Warrior Marks: Female Genital Mutilation and the Sexual Binding of Women. The Same River Twice: Honoring the Difficult* and *Anything We Love Can Be Saved: A Writer's Activism* deals with the death of her mother, the breakup of her thirteen-year relationship with *Black Scholar* editor Robert Allen, and her depression and awakening bisexuality. In 1998 she published *By the Light of My Father's Smile,* a multinarrated story that explores the relationship between fathers and daughters as well as spirituality and sexuality.

Walker once confessed how stunned she was by her success as a writer: "You know, I just kind of found myself doing it. I remember wanting to be a scientist, wanting to be a pianist, wanting to be a painter. But all the while I was wanting to be these other things, I was writing. We were really poor, and writing was about the cheapest thing to do. You know, I feel amazed that I have been able to do exactly what I wanted to do." Alice Walker—through her own vibrant writing and her rediscovery of Zora Neale Hurston—has done more than any other author to articulate the contours of an African-American women's literary tradition.

August Wilson

The Dramatist
(1945–)

August Wilson brings black lives to the stage. He has established himself as the preeminent figure in African-American theater, both for his individual aesthetic triumphs and his sustained creativity. In commenting on Wilson's proposed ten-play cycle chronicling the black American experience in the United States, theater critic Lawrence Bommer said, "Wilson has created the most complete cultural chronicle since Balzac wrote his vast *Human Comedy,* an artistic whole that has grown even greater than its prize-winning parts." Wilson, himself, has a far more humble and pragmatic vision of his art: "All I want is for most people to get to see [my plays]."

Throughout his career, Wilson has negotiated the grandness of his aesthetic vision with the often recalcitrant theater business, in which serious black playwrights have had a notoriously difficult time getting produced. To Wilson, his art is inseparable from the political action of expanding black possibilities in this country. "Those who would deny Black Americans their culture," he has said, "would also deny them their history and the inherent values that are part of all human life." Since gaining critical recognition with *Ma Rainey's Black Bottom* in the early 1980s, Wilson has established himself as one of the most prolific and profound voices in American theater. Unabashedly, he has confronted the tensions of American racial and sexual politics. Most dramatically, perhaps, he has dealt with the effects of racism on intraracial black communities rather than within a constrictive white-black racial dynamic.

August Wilson was born Frederick August Kittel in Pittsburgh, Pennsylvania, to a white father and a black mother. After his father, a German baker, left the family, Wilson's mother took on cleaning jobs and welfare payments to support her six children. After his mother remarried, Wilson and his siblings moved to a mostly white middle-class neighborhood in which the racial tensions were high. Over the

next few years, Wilson held a succession of odd jobs, even serving a brief tour in the army. Most of all, he began to see himself as a writer—more specifically, as a poet. Heavily influenced by the Welsh poet Dylan

Thomas, and later by black nationalist poet Amiri Baraka, Wilson brought a heightened race consciousness to his verse.

In 1968 Wilson and a friend, Robert Penny, founded Black Horizons Theater Company in their old Pittsburgh neighborhood known as the Hill. Wilson had little previous experience in theater, but his work producing minor plays for Black Horizons inspired him to begin writing his own plays. In 1972 he began writing *Jitney,* about a gypsy cab station. It was produced in 1978 at Black Horizons and in 1982 at the Eugene O'Neill Center's National Playwright Conference. *Jitney* was revived in 1997 for a national touring performance. By 1977 he had written *Black Bart and the Sacred Hills,* a satiric musical about a black outlaw of the Old West.

But it was *Ma Rainey's Black Bottom* (1982) that brought Wilson national attention. Lloyd Richards, then the dean of the Yale Drama School, liked the play and had it produced, first at the Yale Repertory Theater and then on Broadway. Richards and Wilson formed a collaboration that has seen them through a number of subsequent productions. *Ma Rainey* traces a day in the life of the real-life blues singer Gertrude "Ma" Rainey as she confronts exploitation from racist white record executives and her own exploitation of her fellow black musicians. The play received immediate critical acclaim—the *New York Times* hailed Wilson as "a major find for the American theater," and remarked on his ability to write "with compassion, raucous humor and penetrating wisdom." The play had a run of 275 performances on Broadway and earned Wilson the New York Drama Critics Circle Award.

Ma Rainey was also the first installment of Wilson's grand vision of a cycle of ten plays—one for each decade of the century—capturing the stories of African Americans in the United States. Wilson followed this play with *Fences,* his 1987 Pulitzer Prize–winning play set in the later 1950s. The play focuses upon Troy Maxson, a garbage collector and former Negro Leagues ballplayer, who builds figurative fences between himself and his family. His next play, *Joe Turner's Come and Gone* (1986) debuted on Broadway while *Fences* was still playing. Set in a Pittsburgh boardinghouse in 1911, Joe Turner delves into the persistent memory of slavery in

1980–1989

the context of freedom. The play offers a tragicomic rendering of black American experience that is sensitized to racial brutality and to transcendence.

Wilson's next play, *The Piano Lesson,* won him his second Pulitzer Prize and a Tony Award in 1990. This drama pits brother against sister in the Depression 1930s as they decide on the future of a treasured heirloom—a piano carved by their father (a former slave carpenter) with Africanist portraits. While the play is dominated by Wilson's vaunted realism, it culminates in a supernatural incident. Some critics were uncomfortable with the melding of the realist and magic-realist elements of this and other Wilson plays. But Wilson staunchly defends his aesthetic as demonstrating the fluidity of black expressive culture.

Wilson produced *Two Trains Running* on Broadway in 1992. Set in a rundown diner on the verge of being sold, the play chronicles the responses of its regular patrons. The play received only limited critical approbation, but his next play, *Seven Guitars* (1995), proved more successful. This play tells the tragic story of the last week in the life of a blues guitarist named Floyd Barton. Theater critic Jack Kroll described it as "a kind of jazz cantata for actors" with "a gritty, lyrical polyphony of voices that evokes the character of destiny of these men and women who can't help singing the blues even when they are just talking." The play draws upon Wilson's longtime fascination with the blues idiom and its potentialities as a dramatic form.

In his years since first striking out as a poet and playwright, Wilson has garnered his share of awards, prizes, and other forms of recognition. He has seen his work performed on the stage, adapted for film and television, and read widely. Far from being seduced by his commercial success and crossover appeal, Wilson's vision of theater returns to the four fundamentals defined by W. E. B. Du Bois in the 1920s: his plays are by, for, about, and near black people.

Louis Farrakhan

The Charmer
(1933–)

1990–1999

He inspires, he enrages, he preaches, he inflames. He is the most recent—and most powerful—advocate for black self-reliance in a long tradition of black nationalists. The career of Louis Farrakhan is an unlikely one.

Born Louis Eugene Walcott in Roxbury, Massachusetts, in 1933, Farrakhan was for a long time a devout Episcopalian. His mother came from Barbados; his father was Jamaican. Farrakhan was, for the most part, raised by his mother, who stressed education and music in raising him and his older brother. Early in life he began to devour books; by high school he was an honor student studying, among other subjects, Latin, German, calculus, and medieval history. He was also a star on the track team.

Farrakhan hoped to attend Juilliard School of Music after high school owing to his tremendous talent as a classical violinist; instead, in 1950 he went off to a teachers college for blacks in North Carolina on an athletic scholarship. It was in the South that Farrakhan first experienced the full impact of racism. There were many incidents, to be sure, but one he remembers with particular force involved being refused entrance to a movie theater in Washington, D.C. "A very close friend of mine had just been killed in Korea, and I walked down the street with a twenty-dollar bill in one hand, and my wallet in the other, and at that point I was very, very angry with America," he said. "I started writing a calypso song called 'Why America Is No Democracy.'"

In another life, Gene Walcott could just as easily have become a professional musician; indeed, he did drop out of college after a few years to become a singer, styling himself "The Charmer." It is tempting to imagine him writing calypso-inflected protest songs—Belafonte meets Ochs—but his musical career seems mostly to have involved fending off female fans in nightclubs. During that time,

Farrakhan seems to have had little interest in politics, racial or otherwise. Malcolm X was beginning to make waves as a black Muslim preacher in Boston, but Farrakhan would have nothing to do with him. Still, he was growing more distant from the Episcopal church: "I couldn't understand why Jesus would preach so much love and why there was so much hate demonstrated by white Christians against black Christians."

In 1955, Walcott was playing a club in Chicago when he ran into some old friends who had become involved with the Nation of Islam. He agreed to go hear Nation leader Elijah Muhammad speak at the mosque, and when he did he liked what he heard. That night he filled out the form to register as a Muslim, though he did not receive a reply. It was not until hearing Malcolm X in person that he was convinced: "I'd never heard a man talk like that."

Before long, Walcott had become Minister Louis X of the Boston mosque. He had been trained well by Malcolm in public speaking; he also brought his own gifts to the task. He recorded a song entitled "A White Man's Heaven is a Black Man's Hell," which was something of a hit in black Muslim circles, and he swiftly established himself as one of the more promising members of the leadership. He wrote a play entitled *The Trial,* in which a black prosecutor (usually played by Louis) tries the White Man for his myriad sins; at the conclusion, a black jury finds the defendant guilty and sentences him to death. Audiences responded with clamorous ovations.

During these years, Malcolm X was the public face of the Nation of Islam, while Louis, eight years his junior, was his best student. In 1964, however, Malcolm broke with the Nation of Islam, telling reporters that he had been disillusioned by discovering that Elijah Muhammad had fathered several children with his young secretaries. Since Elijah's philanderings had long been an open secret among the Muslim elite, Malcolm's claim to have been shocked struck the other ministers as unlikely and vengeful, aimed solely at causing embarrassment. Louis stood against Malcolm, remaining loyal to the Nation in the crisis.

In a column that appeared in December of that year, Louis X wrote what are now notorious words: "The die is set, and Malcolm shall not escape. . . . Such a man as Malcolm is worthy of death." Malcolm, of course, was assassinated a few months later in Harlem; Farrakhan has been dogged since by speculation that he was somehow involved in the killing. One of the men convicted of the murder said that once Malcolm had been denounced as a traitor, he simply understood it to be his duty to kill him. In recent years, Farrakhan has made conciliatory moves to Malcolm X's widow, Betty Shabazz, and her daughters, as well as Elijah Muhammad's son, Wallace Muhammad. Farrakhan has admitted his responsibility in helping to create the poisonous atmosphere in which Malcolm's assassination took place, but he denies any more direct involvement. In February 2000 he and Imam Warith D. Mohammed reconciled.

Farrakhan was now left to fill the void left by Malcolm. By the end of 1965, he had assumed Malcolm's old position as minister of Harlem Mosque No. 7 and as Elijah Muhammad's national representative. Most people believed that he was being groomed as Muhammad's successor. Farrakhan himself seems to have believed this, waiting patiently for the better part of a decade as Muhammad's health declined. And yet in 1975 when the moment came, Muhammad chose his own son, Wallace Deen Muhammad, to lead the Nation of Islam. It was an odd choice: Wallace had sided with Malcolm X against his own father and been excommunicated for several years; he had seriously studied Sunni Islam and believed the teachings of his father to be heresy; he had even renounced the racial doctrines so dear to his father.

By 1977, Louis Farrakhan had had enough. He announced that he was splitting from Wallace in order to reestablish the Nation of Islam according to its original tenets. He reintroduced the racial myths of Elijah Muhammad, although in attenuated form. Through the late seventies into the early eighties he was busy shoring up the Nation both economically and ideologically, but the country at large took little notice.

All that changed in 1984 when Jesse Jackson ran for president; Farrakhan, in a break with Elijah Muhammad's principled abstention from politics, decided to vote. He went so far as to volunteer the Nation's Fruit of Islam to provide security for Jackson during the campaign. Many Jews, already concerned about Jackson's position on Israel and his referral to New York as "Hymietown," were outraged at comments by Farrakhan to the effect that Hitler was wickedly great. That the context indicated he meant "great" in the same way *Time* named Hitler "Man of the Year" for 1938 mattered not at all in the stir that followed. All of a sudden, Farrakhan was infamous as a Hitler-lover and anti-Semite.

For better or worse, the public reaction greatly magnified his importance. Before the brouhaha, Farrakhan's speeches drew a handful of listeners; afterward, he spoke routinely to audiences of ten thousand. He became a national figure, and his worldview known to all. For many, he became the only black man standing up to white America. His beliefs that a centuries-old conspiracy of international bankers ran the world, inciting wars for profit, might have gone over well with an inner-city audience hungry for secret histories of how things went wrong, but he had little sensitivity to how his theories played to mainstream audiences.

Louis Farrakhan remains enormously popular among black Americans—an appeal never more clearly demonstrated than by the 1995 Million Man March, an event only he could have orchestrated. Obviously, much of that appeal is due to the lack of radical black leadership. But it is telling that the march made no specific political point; it was utterly divorced from public policy. Whereas the 1963 March on Washington was made to protest public accommodations—and resulted in the signing of the Civil Rights Act the following year—the Million Man March, while a symbol of concern and unity, ignored critical welfare and Medicare legislation being voted on at the time.

The hold Farrakhan has on black America has little to do with politics or legislation; it's both more vague and powerful than either. His power stems from his appeal to blackness. While much has been made of his ability to strike fear into the hearts of whites (What do blacks really think of me?), what is critical is the fear he inspires in blacks. The truth is that black Americans of all backgrounds often feel vulnerable to charges of inauthenticity, of disloyalty to the race. Farrakhan's sway over blacks—the response his call finds—attests to the enduring strength of our own feelings of guilt, our own anxieties of having been false to our people, of having sinned against our innermost identity.

Farrakhan is a man of fixations, but the reciprocal fixation on Farrakhan found in the so-called mainstream (black and white) is a sign of our own impoverished political culture. Thirteen decades have passed since emancipation and half our black men between twenty-four and thirty-five are without full-time employment. One black man graduates from college for every hundred who go to jail. People say that Farrakhan is now the leading voice of black rage in America. We admire his radical spirit, while we still look to the next generation of black leaders who will offer transformative radical solutions.

Michael Jordan

Superman
(1963–)

He always sinks the ball. More than bookends for an unparalleled basketball career, the college days and final pro games remind us of something that we are liable to forget at a time when Jordan is icon, Jordan is Jumpman, Jordan is general manager of the Washington Wizards: Above all, Jordan was (and, no doubt, still is) an athlete of sublime gifts. He has been called by the misguided a "genetic freak" for his combination of strength, speed, and power, but such a term obscures Jordan's greatest virtues: his grace and intelligence on the court. Whether you imagine him soaring through the air, silhouetted like his iconic Nike image, or simply walking through the airport in an elegantly cut suit, it is impossible to deny the powerful physical presence that is Michael Jordan, the one who always makes the clutch play with grace under pressure.

It is all the more remarkable that in a nation that has done such violence to the black body, in a nation still bifurcated along racial lines, the undeniably black, proudly masculine Jordan could become perhaps the single most respected and beloved person in America, if not the world. Try boiling it down to a simple syllogism: *Young black men are white America's greatest fear. Michael Jordan is the überblack man. Therefore, Jordan should be the most feared man in America.* The fact that he is not attests to the complex alchemy of race and identity that is American social existence. Perhaps Spike Lee had it right in *Do The Right Thing,* when he had his Italian-American character say to Mookie (played by Lee): "But Prince, Michael Jackson, Michael Jordan—they aren't black!" Jordan's agent, David Falk, echoes this sentiment. "People don't look at Michael as being black," he says. "They accept that he's different because he's a celebrity."

The bitter irony of this is not lost on black Americans—that race somehow doesn't "count" when it comes to individual black achievement, but it does when it comes to black transgression. This is not, by any means, to implicate Jordan himself. He has never tried to be anything other than what he is: a black brother from Wilmington, North Carolina. But this black brother has come to signify much more. He has become a basketball icon, an international corporate spokesman—a corporation unto himself—and yet something of him remains undeniably genuine. He is, in the words of NBA commissioner David Stern, "at once credible and incredible."

Perhaps this seeming paradox is the best way to describe the ineffable force that is Michael Jordan. "What has made Michael Jordan the First Celebrity of the World is not merely his athletic talent," *Sports Illustrated* wrote, "but also a unique confluence of artistry, dignity, and history." And certainly one should add to that, "marketing." Simply put, Michael Jordan is the greatest corporate pitchman of all time. Edible cake decorations, golf-club covers, shower curtains, pot holders, aprons, rulers, kitchen towels, sleeping bags, canteens, insulated travel mugs, napkins, tablecloths, popcorn tins. These are but a fraction of the many commodities to which Jordan has loaned his name, likeness, and image. *Fortune* magazine recently estimated that he has generated a staggering $10 billion in revenue and counting. Just how far has the marketing of his persona gone? A recent advertising campaign for Brand Jordan shows the faces of New York Yankee shortstop Derek Jeter and Milwaukee Bucks All-Star Ray Allen, with the word "Jordan" stamped across their faces in block print. Talk about branding. Recently, he directed some of this clout for Bill Bradley's campaign for the Democratic presidential nomination.

Jordan-the-man was born on February 17, 1963, in Brooklyn, New York, but soon moved with his parents and four siblings to Wilmington. So much of his story after this point is the stuff of legend. Cut from the varsity team as a high school sophomore, he came back the next year bigger and more determined.

"It was embarrassing not making that team," Jordan recalls. "They posted the roster and it was there for a long, long time without my name on it." He used the setback as motivation. "Whenever I was working out and got tired and figured I ought to stop, I'd close my eyes and see that list in the locker room without my name on it," Jordan said, "and that usually got me going again."

After two standout years on the Laney High School varsity squad, Jordan earned a scholarship to the University of North Carolina. There, under the stewardship of the coaching legend Dean Smith, Jordan quickly became a force to reckon with.

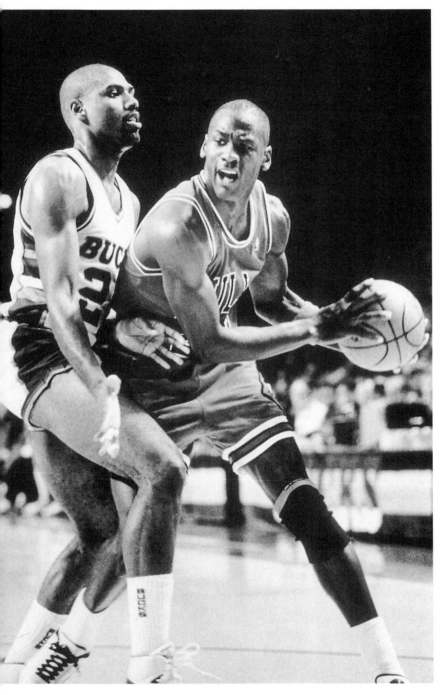

Starting as a freshman, a rarity with Smith's Tar Heels, Jordan hit the winning shot in the 1982 title game against the Georgetown Hoyas. Over the next two years, he was named first-team All American, also earning College Player of the Year honors as a junior. That summer, he entered the NBA draft and was selected third behind Akeem (later Hakeem) Olajuwon and, in a pick that will forever go down in infamy, behind *Sam Bowie.*

It became abundantly clear to Chicago, and soon the rest of the sports world, that Jordan was something special. Perhaps the crowning moment of his early career came not during an NBA game, but during the 1988 slam-dunk contest. Tearing a page from Julius Erving's book of moves, Jordan took flight at the free-throw line, hovering in the air for what seemed like an eternity, and coming down with a forceful dunk. The image was destined to hang in countless bedrooms of boys and girls wanting to be like Mike. Despite such flashes of brilliance, Jordan's early career was plagued by doubt. Many said that while he was undeniably a great individual player, he would never bring his team to greatness. No matter how many scoring titles he would win, they said, he would never achieve the stature of Magic Johnson, Bill Russell, or Larry Bird—players who transcended *themselves* in the name of collective glory. We may look back and wonder, six titles later, what we were thinking; pausing to mention that we, of course, never doubted he could achieve this.

15 seconds left. A lanky North Carolina freshman named Michael Jordan, legs splayed, wrist cocked, and tongue jutting out of his mouth, sinks a fadeaway seventeen-footer to clinch the national championship.

5.2 seconds left. In what would be his final game, playing for the NBA championship against the Utah Jazz, Jordan takes the ball at the top of the key, jab steps, drawing his defender off balance, and raises up for the winning jumper as the buzzer sounds.
—Sports broadcaster

Change was in the wings. Before the start of the 1989–1990 season, Jordan's fifth year in the league, Phil Jackson was promoted from assistant to head coach of the Chicago Bulls. Along with basketball mastermind Tex Winter, Jackson instituted the triangle offense—what was destined to become the signature playing style of the Bulls dynasty. Over the next year, the Bulls made moves to surround Jordan with complementary, if not stellar, players. A nucleus of Scottie Pippen, Horace Grant, Bill Cartwright, B. J. Armstrong, and John Paxon made the Bulls competitive in Jackson's first season as coach. They pushed the Detroit Pistons to the seventh game of the Eastern Conference finals. But it was the subsequent year that marked the beginning of the dynasty. Jordan led the Bulls past Magic Johnson and the Los Angeles Lakers, garnering the finals Most Valuable Player award. This first championship would lead to a "three-peat" (one of two in the nineties).

It is conceivable that Jordan and the Bulls could have won as many as eight titles in the nineties, but life and baseball got in the way. On the eve of the 1993–1994 season Jordan announced his retirement from basketball. While he claimed he was leaving the sport because he no longer enjoyed it, and the sense that he had done all that was possible on the boards, many believed it was a direct result of the trauma of his father's murder in the summer of 1993. Combined with his well-publicized gambling troubles, this shock may have been enough to push him away from basketball. His competitive nature yearned for outlet, and it wasn't long before

1990-1999

he had traded in his high-tops for cleats, signing a minor league contract with the Chicago White Sox. This, too, may have been a tribute to his father—a longtime baseball fan. While playing for the Birmingham Barons of the Class AA Southern league, Jordan batted a modest .202 with three home runs and fifty-one RBIs, with a dubious glove in centerfield. And while he improved significantly in the Fall League while playing for the Scottsdale Scorpions (batting .252), basketball beckoned him once again.

Jordan may well be the only player ever to play in his retired jersey. After an abbreviated 1994–1995 season in which he performed in only seventeen regular season games, and the Bulls made an abrupt exit from the play-offs in the Eastern Conference semifinals against the Orlando Magic, Jordan returned triumphant in his first full season back. In 1995–1996, Jordan led the Bulls to an astounding 72-10 record—the best in the history of the league—and recaptured the championship trophy. Two more championships later, both at the expense of the Utah Jazz, and the Bulls had earned their second three-peat.

The numbers that are Jordan's career tell only part of the story, but they became more dazzling still. Playing eleven full seasons, he led the league in scoring a record ten times, and in 1986–1987 became the only player besides Wilt Chamberlain to score more than 3,000 points in a single season, netting 3,041. His 31.5 scoring average is the highest in NBA history and his 29,277 points rank an all-time fourth behind Kareem Abdul-Jabbar, Chamberlain, and Karl Malone. He won the regular season MVP five times and the finals MVP six times. In 1991 and 1992, he became the only player to win back-to-back regular season and finals MVP awards, and in 1993 he became the first to win the finals MVP for three consecutive years, a feat he repeated from 1996–1998. He also earned two Olympic gold medals.

When he announced in 1995, and again in 1999, that "I know from a career standpoint I have accomplished everything that I could as an individual" who could deny him? How rare this holds for anyone—yet Jordan's artistic and athletic gifts justify such a grand claim, and we were blessed to see him do them from the grandstands, the auditoriums, or in our homes.

Spike Lee

The Director
(1957–)

$\mathbf{S}$pike Lee is the most visible and influential black filmmaker of this past century. He has made more commercial films about black people than any other African American except independent filmmaker Charles Burnett. Since emerging from the ranks of independent film in 1986 with the acclaimed *She's Gotta Have It,* Lee has repeatedly challenged audiences to question their easy assumptions about race, class, gender, and their many intersections. He has become a fixture in American popular culture through his own brand of black nationalism— he hires and works with fellow African Americans as much as possible—and his savvy for marketing and merchandising, whether it is his production company 40 Acres and a Mule or the ubiquitous X-hats inspired by his *Malcolm X* in the early nineties. Although too often overlooked by mainstream Hollywood—he has yet to receive an Academy Award nomination for best picture or best director—the consistency of his output has made him a formidable force in the film industry. During a recent airing of HBO's *The Chris Rock Show,* Rock asked guest Spike Lee to 'fess up: "Spike, you make more movies than everybody else, you got courtside seats to the Knicks, you got the beautiful wife, the kids . . . Why are you so mad? You the maddest black man in America!" For once Spike Lee was speechless.

Where Lee goes, controversy follows. Whether it is the furor surrounding the inflammatory riot scene in *Do the Right Thing* or Lee's chastisement of white director Quentin Tarrantino for his use of the word "nigger" on film, Lee has been a lightening rod for the electric tensions of race in America.

Born Shelton Jackson Lee in Atlanta, Georgia, on March 20, 1957, and raised in the Fort Greene section of Brooklyn, New York, Spike was surrounded by music and art—his father is jazz musician Bill Lee and his mother was an art teacher. After graduating from the black institution Morehouse College, he went on to study film at New York University's renowned Tisch School of the Arts. His master's thesis project, "Joe's Bed-Stuy Barber shop: We Cut Heads" (1983), won him the Student Director Oscar from the Academy of Motion Pictures in 1986.

At the age of twenty-nine, Lee seemed poised for a major studio deal. "I thought that now that I had this plaque on top of my television that Columbia, Warner Brothers, Fox, Universal, Spielberg, Lucas, they would call me," Lee recalls. "So I just sat by the phone and sat by the phone some more. Then the phone got turned off. That's when I decided, I have to try to do it more independently."

Lee's independent route consisted of securing the scant $125,000 needed to produce his first feature film script. Filmed in black and white during a furious twelve-day shooting schedule, *She's Gotta Have It,* with its independent black heroine and its mix of style, sex, and shock value, propelled Lee into the international spotlight. The film grossed a surprising $8.5 million domestically and was awarded the Prix de Jeunesse at Cannes. Lee followed this up with another financially successful effort, the 1988 feature *School Daze,* which raucously dramatized the politics of skin color within an all-black college such as Morehouse.

But it was *Do the Right Thing,* Lee's 1989 film chronicling the cataclysmic events of a single summer day in Brooklyn, that established him as America's foremost black cinematic voice—and one of its most controversial cultural figures. *Jungle Fever* (1991) explored the conflicts that can doom interracial romance. The epic *Malcolm X* (1992), which starred Denzel Washington in the title role, created a surge of renewed popular interest in the slain leader among black and other Americans. These and his following films—*Crooklyn* (1994) and *4 Little Girls* (1997) on the Birmingham church bombing—are the realization of Lee's commitment to bringing fully conceived black stories, black characters, and black actors to the screen. "So many of our stories are yet to be told," Lee wrote in his 1991 foreword to *Five for Five: The Films of Spike Lee,* "and I am getting a shot to tell the ones I know in films."

Over the past fourteen years Lee has directed a startling fifteen films, engaging everything from jazz musicians (*Mo' Betta Blues*) to phone sex (*Girl 6*) to blue-chip basketball (*He Got Game*) to street hustling (*Clockers*). His most recent project, *Bamboozeled* (2000), takes on blackface minstrelsy in a contemporary context, promising more controversy to come.

Perhaps Lee's most significant legacy is the model he has established for success as an African American in the film industry. "Make Black film by any means necessary!" Lee would say, riffing off of Malcolm X's black nationalist call. It became Lee's catchphrase, and also his calling. Indeed, Lee has led the charge of black directors, producers, and actors into mainstream Hollywood. His movies have not only offered a model for circumnavigating the seemingly impassible barriers of the white-dominated studio system, but have also helped launch the careers of a number of prominent black actors, including Denzel Washington, Laurence Fishburne, Angela Bassett, and Samuel L. Jackson.

With all of this, Lee is hopeful, if not optimistic, about the future of black filmmaking. "You got to put this in historical perspective," Lee said in a recent interview. "Films, until recently, have cost a lot of money, and so because of that we have not produced our Toni Morrisons, our James Baldwins, our John Coltranes, our Louis Armstrongs—it didn't cost anything to have an instrument. But it's gonna come. It's gonna come." We believe him.

1990–1999

Wynton Marsalis

Brother Swing
(1961–)

Wynton Marsalis keeps the music swinging. From his gut-bucket New Orleans blues playing to his baroque classical trumpet recitals at symphonies around the world, Marsalis has demonstrated a technical virtuosity and an elasticity of musical form that have established him as one of America's foremost musicians. In addition, through his Peabody Award–winning PBS series, *Marsalis on Music,* and his work on National Public Radio, Marsalis has led a personal crusade for music education. As the musical director of Jazz at Lincoln Center in New York—a post held since 1987—Marsalis has institutionalized a musical idiom that has thrived upon its insurgency.

Throughout, he has honed his own playing, establishing a unique voice inflected with disparate influences, ranging from Louis Armstrong to Miles Davis. Blending postbop harmonies with the melodic sensitivity of trumpeter Louis Armstrong and the penchant for mutes and "freak" effects of cornet players Joe Oliver and Bubber Miley, Marsalis fashioned a mature style that is distinctly his own. During his rise to prominence in the 1980s, Marsalis was alternately praised and disparaged for his neo-traditionalist insistence on the primacy of swing. Stepping over his immediate musical predecessors, leapfrogging the fusion and electronic jazz movements of the 1970s, Marsalis cast a wise eye to the roots of the jazz tradition. Some saw this move as a sign of disrespect for his musical elders (and perhaps there is something to this), but Marsalis seems to have remained unperturbed by such criticisms.

Since he debuted as a member of Art Blakey's renowned Jazz Messengers, Marsalis has become one of the most prolific artists in all of music. He has released several albums that represent a broad sweep of musical expression, from his recent jazz oratorio, *Blood on the Fields,* to his interpretations of classical concertos. Since his years with Blakey's ensemble, Marsalis has worked with a host of prominent musicians of all generations, and helped break in a new group of "young lions," including Marcus Roberts, Roy Hargrove, and Christian McBride. Marsalis's work places him at the center of a rapidly expanding constellation of young black jazz artists who, bucking popular musical trends toward hip-hop and R & B, are carrying a rich tradition of musical excellence into the twenty-first century.

Wynton Marsalis was born on October 18, 1961, in New Orleans, Louisiana, the birthplace of jazz. The son of jazz pianist Ellis Marsalis, and the namesake of late jazz great Wynton Kelley, Marsalis grew up in a jazz milieu. The Marsalises are perhaps the first family of contemporary jazz: In addition to pianist father Ellis (b. 1934), they include Wynton's older brother, saxophonist Branford (b. 1960) and younger brothers Delfeayo (b. 1965) and Jason (b. 1976). At the age of six, Marsalis received his first trumpet from Al Hirt, then his father's bandleader. By the age of twelve, inspired by the legendary trumpeter Clifford Brown, Marsalis began his study in earnest.

As a teenager, Marsalis divided his time among a number of musical ensembles, playing in New Orleans marching bands, performing solo recitals at the New Orleans Philharmonic, and doing gigs with his older brother in their funk band, the Creators. At age eighteen he enrolled at New York's prestigious Juilliard School of Music, where he continued his formal training. But the majesty of the blues called him, and he left Juilliard in 1980 to tour with Art Blakey's Jazz Messengers, the renowned collective that had launched so many careers over the decades.

After a stint the following year with Herbie Hancock and his V.S.O.P. unit, Marsalis signed an unprecedented contract with Columbia Records to record both jazz and classical albums. Marsalis soon assembled a quintet that included his brother Branford. The group recorded several albums, most notably the grand *Black Codes from the Underground* (1985), before splitting up that same year. By 1986, Marsalis had organized the Wynton Marsalis Quartet, featuring pianist Marcus Roberts. Since the mid-1980s he has retained the core members of this group, while supplementing it with other musicians to release albums and tour as a septet or as an orchestra.

Perhaps Marsalis's most significant contribution to the jazz world has come in his role as cofounder and artistic director of Jazz at Lincoln Center, an ongoing project of New York's prestigious Lincoln Center for the Performing Arts. From this post, Marsalis has expanded his influence in shaping the critical and popular appreciation for jazz. He has brought back to the spotlight the music of past jazz greats such as

Louis Armstrong, Sidney Bechet, and perhaps most notably, Duke Ellington. Such influence has also garnered criticism from those who see Marsalis's traditionalism as a slavish allegiance to the past. Jazz, they say, always has been about tradition, yes, but also about *change*. Marsalis's vision of jazz, while certainly steeped in a rich musical history, is his own. Unlike his brother Branford, who has pushed the limits of the jazz idiom into more contemporary (and commercial) musical genres with his work with pop star Sting and his hip-hop group Buckshot LeFonque, Marsalis's sensibilities are unabashedly focused on keeping the tradition visible and vibrant.

> [Wynton] Marsalis is interested in the entirety of music from the place far below decks where the coal that fuels the engines is lifted shovel by shovel and thrown into the flame, all the way up to the most luxurious quarters, where even room service is luminous with grace.
> —Stanley Crouch

Furthermore, Marsalis is one of the few jazz musicians to have won almost equal praise for his classical solo work and for his jazz performances. In 1984 he won a Grammy for his classical debut, *Trumpet Concertos* (1983), and another for his second jazz album, *Think of One* (1983), marking the first time in the history of the awards that an artist won in two different musical categories in the same year. Since then he has won six more Grammys.

Marsalis's recent compositions, many of them commissioned by Lincoln Center, have reflected this hybridization of the classical and the jazz genres. In the classical realm, Marsalis debuted his first string quartet, *(At the) Octoroon Balls* in 1995. The following year he collaborated with Anthony Newman (on harpsichord and organ) to release *In Gabriel's Garden,* recorded with the English Chamber Orchestra. His jazz compositions increasingly have suggested the influence of Ellington. *In This House, On This Morning,* released in 1993, evoked the spirit of the black church. The following year's *Blood on the Fields,* an oratorio for three singers and a fourteen-piece orchestra and a kind of operatic slave narrative, tells the story of two Africans—Leona and Jesse—who find love after being sold into slavery, then escaping to freedom. In 1997 *Blood on the Fields* earned Marsalis a Pulitzer Prize for music, the first time a nonclassical composition won this award. In 1999, he issued no less than an incredible ten CDs. England's Royal Academy of Music named him an honorary member; the United States Congress awarded him a citation for his contribution to music education. In 1996, *Time* magazine named him one of America's twenty-five most influential people. And while some may disagree with his aesthetic stance, few can argue with the remarkable influence he has had in keeping the music alive.

Toni Morrison

Laureate
(1931–)

Toni Morrison is the first African American to receive the Nobel Prize, in 1993, for literature. Her work is analogous to that of Sarah Vaughan: It is characterized by lyrical, poetic realism. She is an epic storyteller who compels us to remember those "unspeakable" terrors that have shaped American and African-American culture, and she is a deeply spiritual writer, concerned with the perennial questions of love and death, the will to be free and the forces—both internal and external—that circumscribe that freedom.

She was born Chloe Anthony Wofford to George Wofford and Rahmah Willis Wofford on February 18, 1931, in Lorain, Ohio. For Morrison, both parents were visible sermons of black dignity and determination. She has said that her father distrusted "every word and every gesture of every white man on earth." She graduated with honors from Lorain High School, where she excelled in Latin. She studied English at Howard University (where she changed her name to Toni) and obtained a B.A. degree in English. After receiving an M.A. from Cornell with a thesis on the theme of suicide in the works of William Faulkner and Virginia Woolf, she taught at Texas Southern University and Howard University, where her students included Stokely Carmichael, Houston Baker, Jr., and Claude Brown. During this period she married architect Harold Morrison, and the couple had two sons before their marriage disintegrated. While at Howard, Morrison began to meet informally with a small group of poets and writers. It was during this time that she "dashed off" a story about a black girl who longed for blue eyes, which would become the germ of her first novel, *The Bluest Eye*.

Morrison resigned from Howard in 1964 and took a job as a textbook editor for Random House in Syracuse, New York. The company eventually relocated her to New York City where, until 1985, she continued to work as an editor with such

African-American writers as Toni Cade Bambara, Gayle Jones, Angela Davis, and Muhammad Ali. Her editorship of *The Black Book* (1974)—an experimental collage of African-American history and literature—was a major event in the world of African-American letters. She taught at Yale and the State University of New York at Purchase, and held the prestigious Albert Schweitzer chair in the humanities at the State University of New York at Albany. She is currently the Robert F. Goheen Professor in the Humanities at Princeton University.

Morrison's first novel, *The Bluest Eye* (1969), is an incisive probe into the complex dynamics of black self-hatred. Her second novel, *Sula* (1973), nominated for the National Book Award, is a bold exploration of the conflicted affection between two strong female protagonists. The enormously successful National Book Critic's Circle Award novel, *Song of Solomon* (1977), takes us to a black world of "triumph and risk" in which "without ever leaving the ground, black people could fly" in the face of nothingness and nobodiness. In *Tar Baby* (1981), Morrison investigates the folkloric dimensions of African-American culture that both sustain and stifle black psychic health and creativity. In her last two novels—as well as her work in criticism, *Playing in the Dark* (1992)—Morrison (like James Baldwin) skillfully depicts the profoundly American character of black life and the black content of American culture. Love and betrayal loom large in *Jazz* (1992), while in *Paradise* (1997), the background of the Oklahoma territory is the treacherous terrain for communal strife and struggle. In *Beloved* (1987)—her Pulitzer Prize–winning fifth novel—Morrison undertakes the boldest, and most complex, re-creation of the effects of slavery on the enslaved. Morrison plunged deep into the forbidden waters of American slavery—the impact of which is still denied in our time—and, like Louis Armstrong, unveiled the blue note deep in the core of black American life.

In *Playing in the Dark* Morrison said, "My work requires me to think about how free I can be as an African-American woman writer in my genderized, sexualized, wholly racialized world." It is through her poetic attention to language that Morrison always has sought to liberate language from what she calls "its sometimes sinister, frequently lazy, almost always predictable employment of racially informed and determined chains." When she accepted the Nobel Prize she sounded this theme of the importance of language to our lives and our future: "Word work is sublime . . . because it is generative; it makes meaning that secures our difference, our human difference—the way in which we are like no other life. We die. That may be the meaning of life. But we do have language. That may be the measure of our lives." Her art beckons us to remember, endure, and prevail.

Colin Powell

The General
(1937–)

Colin Powell is the first black person in American history who could actually become the president of the United States. In the 1950s and 1960s black people in America would say, "When a Negro is president . . . " with all the awe and reverence of a born-again Christian saying, "When Gabriel blows his trumpet and Jesus appears." A certain millenarian intonation, combined with the speaker's shining eyes, would force you to pause and marvel at the very idea. Then reality would set in and you would joke away the impossible: "It'll be called the Black House then." But for Colin Powell, courted by both major political parties as well as by independents, the vision is no laughing matter: He could be the first black man to be president.

Ten years ago, before Saddam Hussein sent his Republican Guard into Kuwait, one had to be deeply interested in the goings-on inside the Washington Beltway to even know who Colin Powell was. He was largely unknown to the black community, and to the rest of the nation. After the Gulf War, political conservatives were drawn to him, delighted with his war record, the fact that he had voted for Reagan in 1980, and most important, the prospect of forcing Democrats to run against a black man.

But Powell himself was silent to the point of being a cipher, a blank screen onto which anyone could project his hopes. Some, however, managed to ask where the man had come from and what his politics were. It seemed obvious that he believed in a strong military, but did he stand with George Bush on social issues? With the black community? Did he even have stands on issues? Was he a mugwump or just a professional soldier who had been trained to keep opinions to himself?

Nobody was sure. Still, we did know something of Powell's background. He was born in Harlem in 1937, though his parents soon moved to the Bronx. They were both Jamaicans who had immigrated to this country years before, and Powell owns to the complex bloodlines of many West Indians: African, English, Irish, Scottish, and possibly Arawak ancestry. Never a distinguished student, Powell did immerse himself in his duties as an acolyte at the local Episcopal church. He has commented that in the military he found "a little bit of the ritual and structure of the Episcopal church."

In 1954 Powell entered the City College of New York and its R.O.T.C. program. Rising to the rank of cadet colonel, he was made a second lieutenant in the army upon graduating in 1958. His first post was in Germany, where he served for two years before returning to America. It was then that he met Alma Johnson, whom he married in 1962, and with whom he had three children. A few months after the wedding, Powell was sent to Vietnam.

During his first tour in Vietnam, Powell performed with distinction as an adviser to South Vietnamese troops; he received a Purple Heart when he stepped on a punji stick. It was not long after the injury that Powell returned to America. He was most struck, he wrote in his 1995 autobiography, *My American Journey,* by the conflicts at home. That his wife had been living in Birmingham, Alabama, with her par-

ents at the time of the church bombing that killed four girls made the troubles immediate; that the date of his return, November 22, 1963, coincided with the assassination of President John F.

Kennedy made him despair. It was, he wrote, "a world turned upside down."

Powell's next years would be occupied by climbing the rungs necessary to a military career. Powell excelled in this close world where one mistake, one bad review by a superior, could mean the end of his career. He performed so well at Fort Benning's Infantry School that he was asked to become an instructor. In 1966, he became a major; then he managed to graduate second in his class at the United States Army Command and General Staff College before being sent back to Vietnam in 1968. On this tour he worked on the staff of headquarters in the rear, though he did receive a Purple Heart and a Soldier's Medal when he rescued men from a helicopter crash.

Powell's return to America saw the beginning of his rise from promising young officer to political star. At every turn, Powell succeeded: an MBA from George Washington University in 1971; White House fellow the following year; acceptance to the War College; commands of divisions around the world; senior military assistant to the Reagan administration; National Security Adviser; four-star general; chairman of the Joint Chiefs of Staff (and this is the abridged resume). It is a career to wonder at, and one imposing enough that Powell could probably show respectably in a presidential election simply by referring to it repeatedly; not surprisingly, in his early sallies onto the lecture speaking circuit after retiring from the military he seemed reluctant to venture past the truisms of civic religion. In his speeches he could be counted on to give thanks to a country that had given him such opportunity.

Powell always has been long on uplift, especially when it comes to children and education. In conversations about the crisis in the inner cities, he says, "You've got to start with the families, and then you've got to fix education so these little bright-eyed five-year-olds, who are innocent as the day is long, . . . have all the education they need." Powell continues, "You know, I'm sort of a liberal guy, up to this point, but here's where I become a Republican: Once these kids come out of school, there has got to be a capitalistic entrepreneurial system that is just burning up the place to create the jobs for these kids. And therefore you've got to lower the tax burden off business."

In keeping with his position as a self-proclaimed "fiscal conservative with a social conscience" (this is before anyone had heard of "compassionate conservatism"), Powell came out in favor of a modest form of affirmative action based on qualifications more than quotas, of free enterprise *and* unions, and of a smaller, but more active, government. Of course, in the end, we know that personality and character, not contradictory or compromising positions, will be his selling point; that he is pro-choice, for the death penalty, for moderate gun control, and opposed to school prayer should attract voters, but it is his solidity, strength, and effectiveness that would sway them.

Especially tricky for Powell is the well-established distortive effect of race on polls: Many blacks who soar in public surveys get brought to earth in the voting booth. Look no further than Jesse Jackson: Many whites say they're going to vote for a black candidate, but end up pulling another lever when they're alone in the booth. Not only are a significant number of Powell's supporters still vague on what he believes in, they are also fuzzy on what they might do should they ever actually have the chance to vote for him.

Still, a striking aspect of Powell's prospective run isn't the amount of support he already has, it's how few people think of him negatively. In this, he is somewhat analogous to General Eisenhower, another former military leader who came to politics in a prosperous era. Powell is aware of the similarity: "Eisenhower was a person who could put together very interesting coalitions and be a natural war leader the people would respect. They saw Ike and they felt comfortable and confident."

But a black Eisenhower? That remains to be seen, even if we are closer now than we have ever been. He really could become president of the United States of America; even to come close would change the country forever. He might not succeed, but it would be another step toward that original, wistful vision: "When a black man is president . . . " These days that vision is serious and, because of Colin Powell, is even something we might see in our lifetime.

Tupac Shakur

Hip Hop Existentialist
(1971–1996)

Through his music he reached millions. In his life he epitomized the vitality and the violence of an entire generation of urban black youth. Through his death Tupac entered the pantheon of black talents who have left us before their time.

Rap artist Tupac Shakur was shot outside of the Las Vegas MGM Grand casino following the Mike Tyson and Bruce Seldon heavyweight title fight on September 7, 1996. While the Las Vegas coroner pronounced Shakur dead six days later, some still insist that (like a hip-hop Elvis) he is still alive. They may have a point. With a spate of albums, three movies (*Bullet, Gridlock'd,* and *Gang Related*), and a collection of his poetry all released posthumously, Tupac has been prolific beyond the grave. And of course, from suburban malls to urban street corners, the look and sound of American teenagehood has been transformed forever by the popular culture phenomenon that Tupac and his fellow rap artists created: raw street language, gangsta clothing, rhythm-driven music that uses rhymed spoken words and freely "samples" the hits of earlier pop artists.

Vilified by many, idolized by others, Shakur became in death something that no one could become in life. Harry Allen, venerable hip-hop journalist and "media assassin," explains the ineffable quality of Shakur's posthumous power this way: "The people you miss the most are the people who, in some fashion, made you feel your existence most powerfully; who made you feel most alive." In this way, Shakur serves as a kind of hip-hop existentialist hero—undeniably black, undeniably masculine, undeniably American.

The startling contradictions that marked Shakur's life make him all the more compelling and troubling. Rapper. Poet. Actor. Activist. Alleged sex offender. Somehow all of these describe a man who at twenty-five years of age was still figuring out who he was, and who he might become. Tupac Amaru Shakur ("Tupac Amaru" means "Shining Serpent"—the name of an Incan Chief. "Shakur" means "thankful to god.") was born Lesane Parish Crooks in the Bronx, New York, on June 16, 1971. The son of former Black Panther Afeni Shakur, he was initiated into the world of black nationalism from his earliest days. Always struggling, often destitute, Shakur and his mother moved throughout his youth, finally settling in Marin City, California, in 1988. He had acted on stage while attending the Baltimore School for the Arts, but it wasn't until moving to California that Tupac began to concentrate exclu-

sively on music. Shakur soon left home to join the rap group Strictly Dope. Three years later, with little more than a book of rhymes and a swagger, he rapped his way onto Digital Underground's 1991 hit "Same Song." In the words of DU's Sleuth-Pro, "He blew it up."

Later that year, Shakur released his first solo album, *2Pacalypse Now*, which went gold. Even on this first album, Shakur played out the strange contradictions of his life. The album features both "Brenda's Got a Baby," a keen yet tender portrayal of a teenage mother's fate, and "I Don't Give a F——," a violently defiant anthem against white police officers. When a Texas state trooper was killed by a teenager listening to the album, Vice President Dan Quayle launched his public assault on Hollywood and the music business. Shakur's second album, *Strictly 4 My N.I.G.G.A.Z.*, launched him into the pop charts with singles such as "I Get Around" and "Keep Ya Head Up." His subsequent releases, *Me Against the World* and *All Eyez on Me*, established him as a multi-platinum star in the ever-expanding hip-hop stratosphere. Employing his resonant baritone and a distinctive "flow" (rhyme cadence), Shakur was in complete control of the microphone.

Too often, though, Shakur's life spun out of control. As his music and film career expanded, his private and public life followed a disarmingly similar path. In 1992 he made his cinematic debut as the conflicted young hustler Bishop in Ernest Dickerson's *Juice*. "He blew the audition away," Dickerson says. "He was outstanding." He followed this up with another turn as a charming but troubled postal employee in John Singleton's film *Poetic Justice*. At the same time, he found himself embroiled in a number of legal battles. In October 1993 he was arrested for allegedly shooting two off-duty police officers in Atlanta. Over the next two years, he returned to court on numerous occasions, once for assaulting a film director, and eight months later, for allegedly sodomizing a twenty-year-old woman in a Manhattan hotel suite.

Then in 1995, just days before his conviction on the sexual assault charge and sentencing of one and one-half to four and a half years in prison, Shakur was robbed of forty thousand dollars worth of jewelry and shot twice as he entered a New York City recording studio, barely escaping with his life. The shooting was clouded in accusations that rival East Coast rappers were involved, which fanned the flames of an East Coast–West Coast rivalry. This helped to create the atmosphere of discord and violence that may have contributed to the deaths of both Tupac and, a year later, the Notorious B.I.G.

From behind bars Shakur released his third album, *Me Against the World,* recorded before his prison term, which went double platinum and earned him two Grammy nominations. The album reflects Shakur's sense of his own mortality, with songs such as "If I Die 2Nite" and "Death Around the Corner" foretelling his own violent death. In October 1995, Death Row Records head Marion "Suge" Knight put up $1.4 million in bail for Shakur's release from jail, pending appeal. Shakur recorded his first album for the Death Row label, *All Eyez on Me,* which included tracks with Death Row artists Snoop Doggy Dogg and Dr. Dre. Shakur became Death Row's artistic centerpiece and its strongest mouthpiece in the rivalry with New York–based Bad Boy Entertainment, home to Sean "Puffy" Combs and Christopher Wallace (a.k.a. the Notorious B.I.G.).

> *MISSING*
> *Tupac Amaru Shakur*
> *Last Seen: Sept. 13, 1996*
> *Las Vegas, Nevada*
> *DOB: 6/16/71*
> *Age: 28*
> *Height: 5'10"*
> *Weight: 168*
> *Hair: Black*
> *Eyes: Brown*
> *Numerous Tattoos*
> *$10,000 REWARD for information leading to location and contact*
> *—Tupac Web Site, 1999*

Shakur's increasing sense of mortality proved all too prescient. His murder is still largely shrouded in mystery; rumors implicating rival East Coast rap artists continue to flourish. And even Shakur's estate has been plagued by lawsuits. But beyond the discord, beyond the often opportunistic manipulations of Shakur's legacy, it is his music that remains to bear witness to a promising life and powerful art cut short. To borrow from Robert Haydn's poem about Malcolm X—another African-American figure cut down in his prime—Shakur was "much more than there was time for him to be." His music lives on as a constant reminder that we must always heed the words of our young, no matter how angry they are.

Denzel Washington

(In)visible Man
(1954–)

Denzel Washington has mounted an all-out assault on the limitations of black actors in Hollywood. Having worked his way through the repertory theater ranks and gained exposure on the hit television drama *St. Elsewhere,* Washington has built a body of work comparable to any actor of his generation. He is an actor of incomparable gifts.

Along the way, he has used his imitative skill to capture several complex black historical personalities. "I've had the good fortune to play three interesting men," Washington said in a recent interview, with his usual modesty, "Stephen Biko and Malcolm X, and now Rubin ['Hurricane' Carter]. They all have what I call a 'concentrated dose of life.'" And while Washington's longevity already has insured that the dose of life he offers will be sustained, he nonetheless shares with his characters an intensity and passion for his discipline. Directors and actors who have worked with him marvel at his ability to inhabit his character. "[Denzel] has intellectual weight, spiritual gravity, and a powerful sexual and romantic presence," said Kenneth Branagh, fellow actor and Washington's director in *Much Ado About Nothing.*

Indeed, it has often been this "powerful sexual and romantic presence" that has dominated Washington's public image. He is perennially among *People* magazine's list of the sexiest men alive; grandmothers and schoolgirls alike (of all hues) swoon for him. Washington, though, is leery of accepting the role of sex symbol. "I don't worry about any of that so much anymore," he says. "I'm Denzel, I'm an actor. There's going to come a time when [journalists] say, 'Oh, he used to be this' or 'He's a has-been that,' when I was never that to begin with. I've learned to concentrate on what I do. What I do is the reason that anybody's calling me anything anyway." What Washington does is consistently make critically acclaimed and popular films, a rare combination in Hollywood these days. Looking over his filmography, one is hard-pressed to find a flop or a miscue. All his work has expanded the scope of his craft. Even the more conventional big-budget action films in which he has starred are challenging. *Crimson Tide* (1995) and *The Siege* (1998) are the thinking man's blockbusters, and Washington is the thinking man's movie star.

Washington was born in Mount Vernon, New York, in 1954 with his roots squarely in two centers of black American cultural life: the church and the barbershop. The son of a preacher man and a hairdresser, Washington learned early on about the transformative power of storytelling from both the sacred and profane traditions. After graduating from high school, Washington enrolled at Fordham University, where he began to pursue stage acting. He won the lead in a number of student productions, including a staging of *Othello.*

In 1977, after receiving his B.A. in journalism, Washington moved to San Francisco, where he continued to study acting at the American Conservatory Theatre. It was not long before he won his first television role as Wilma Rudolph's boyfriend in *Wilma* (1977). But it was his work on the stage that caught the attention of major studio executives. He won an Obie award for his portrayal of Private Peterson in *A Soldier's Play* (a role he would reprise in the 1984 film *A Soldier's Story*). His next big break came when he landed the role of Dr. Philip Chandler in *St. Elsewhere,* the popular television medical drama. After a six-year stint on the show, between 1982 and 1988, he made the transition to feature films for good.

More than a decade has passed since Washington left the small screen, and his achievements are nothing short of remarkable. He has received four Academy Award nominations, two for best supporting actor, in *Cry Freedom* (1987) and *Glory,* (1990),

> *I don't like to preach too much.*
> *I like to get quiet, and then I*
> *attack through my work.*
> —Denzel Washington

the latter of which won him an Oscar, and two for best actor (for the title characters in Spike Lee's *Malcolm X,* 1992, and Norman Jewison's *Hurricane,* 1999). Such critical acclaim has cemented his place among Hollywood's A-list and earned Washington a level of influence rarely, if ever, achieved by a black actor. He heads an all-too-short list of black actors who consistently receive work, which includes Wesley Snipes, Laurence Fishburne, Morgan Freeman, and Samuel L. Jackson. And yet by Washington's own estimation he still does not receive many scripts, owing, no doubt, to the industry belief that black actors—even those of Washington's estimable skill—can only play "black" characters.

In response to Hollywood's limitations, Washington has used his clout to help bring to the screen African-American stories for which he feels a commitment and passion: *Malcolm X,* which became a cause célèbre when funding ran out; *Devil in a Blue Dress* (1995), the critically acclaimed adaptation of Walter Mosely's Easy Rawlins detective novel; and *The Preacher's Wife,* a surprise holiday hit that offered a black reinterpretation of an old Cary Grant film. Outside his acting career, Washington has cultivated his privacy, rarely consenting to interviews and shunning the Hollywood social scene. Instead, he has dedicated his time to his wife, Paulette Pearson, and his four children. When Washington does make public appearances, it is usually in support of charities, including the Boys' and Girls' Club of America, the Nelson Mandela Children's Fund, and the Gathering Place (an AIDS hospice). Washington also stays close to his church roots; he is a devout Pentecostal.

Denzel Washington is what novelist Ralph Ellison liked to call an "inside-outsider": a person who would seem to be at the center of American life, yet who somehow also observes it from a remove. He is at once accepted in Hollywood as a proven box office draw and disregarded for certain roles not specified for a black actor, both the most visible of celebrities, and yet an intensely private, even mysterious, figure. But he has fashioned himself, without pretense, into an actor of the highest order. Washington's constant example of dignified artistry is his grand attack on injustice. His inner rage is transfigured into outer beauty.

Oprah Winfrey

Oprah
(1954–)

Oprah Winfrey, the epitome of compassion, is an actress, producer, celebrity, and most important, television talk show host. Winfrey is the most famous and successful African-American woman in history. The *Oprah Winfrey Show,* a perennial ratings powerhouse, has become the stage on which Winfrey preaches self-improvement, empowerment, and compassion. She is known for her easy intimacy and powerful connection with her audience, mostly women, who hug her, cry on her shoulder, share with her their struggles and triumphs. It is a skill Winfrey has parlayed into media superstardom, controlling not only her television show but also a production company, a philanthropic foundation, and her popular and influential book club. Her impact on American culture is immeasurable.

None of this could have been predicted from Winfrey's start in the world. The only child of a twenty-year-old soldier and an eighteen-year-old farm girl, Winfrey has described her parents' courtship as "a one-day fling under an oak tree." Neither Vernon Winfrey nor Vernita Lee was prepared to raise their daughter when she was born. The infant Oprah—her name, misspelled by the county clerk, was meant to have been Orpah, after a Biblical character—was sent soon after her birth to live with her paternal grandmother in Kosciusko, Mississippi, where she would stay until she was six.

Winfrey's early childhood was often harsh and lonely, living in rural poverty with her grandmother, a strict follower of the Faith–United Mississippi Baptist Church, a fundamentalist denomination. A bright and talkative child, Winfrey's only social outlet was the church, in which she gave her first public performance, reciting a theme about Easter. Although she recalls loving the opportunity to speak before an audience, Winfrey also has spoken of the teasing and cruelty of other children toward her: She was dubbed "the preacher" and "little Jesus" for her eager-to-

please, adult–friendly personality. She did not have many friends, and her grand–mother was not a person to show pride or joy in the charming, intelligent child she was raising. In interviews Winfrey has said that the beatings she received from her grandmother "would be called child abuse now."

It would get worse before it got better. At the age of six, Winfrey's mother, who had left for Milwaukee soon after her birth, came to claim her. Moving up north to live with a mother she barely knew, Winfrey entered a chaotic life and became increasingly isolated and unhappy. It was in Milwaukee that she was allegedly victimized sexually by several adult relatives and friends of the family. Although she continued to do well in school (she had skipped two grades in elementary school), and even made friends, she began acting out. Finally, at age fourteen, she was sent to live with her father and stepmother in Nashville. This change, according to Winfrey, saved her from becoming a juvenile delinquent.

Flowering under her father's strict but loving discipline, Winfrey focused on her schoolwork and was popular enough to be elected president of her mostly white class her senior year of high school. In addition, she joined the drama and oratory clubs, and entered her first beauty pageant, winning the title Miss Fire Prevention. Her poise and personality in the pageant attracted the attention of a local radio station that hired Winfrey to read the news on the air several times a day. Winfrey's dream of going away to college became a reality when her beauty competition next earned her a full scholarship to Tennessee State University in Nashville, which she entered in the fall of 1970.

Even though she won another pageant her freshman year—Miss Black Tennessee—Winfrey found college less satisfying than high school. When a local television station offered her a job as news anchor, she took it, working in the evenings while going to class days. In 1976 she left Nashville for an anchor's job in Baltimore's ABC affiliate. It was a disaster. The qualities that made her a success in Nashville—spontaneity, informality, emotional openness—proved a bad fit in the Baltimore job. Depressed, Winfrey began to gain weight, adding some sixty pounds to her pageant-era size. But rather than let Winfrey go, her producers decided to try her in a different role, cohosting a morning talk show. It clicked. Finally, the woman who had dreamed of being either a teacher or an actress got to be both.

> *I come here celebrating every African, every colored, black Negro American everywhere that ever cooked a meal, ever raised a child, ever worked in the fields, ever went to school, ever sang in a choir, ever loved a man or a woman, ever cornrowed, ever Afro'd, every wig-wearing, pigtailed, weave-wearing one of us. I come celebrating the journey, I come celebrating the little passage, the movement of our women people.*
> —Oprah Winfrey

1990–1999

People Are Talking, Winfrey's Baltimore talk show, brought out all her skills. Always more comfortable without a script, Winfrey proved adept at thinking on her feet, asking all the questions her audience was dying to ask, often with outrageous results. After eight years of ever-increasing popularity, in 1984 Winfrey left Baltimore to host *A.M. Chicago,* a morning talk program consistently ranked second after that city's talk-show king, Phil Donahue. Local media played up a duel between the two shows, but there was no real race: Within months Winfrey's ratings were double those of Donahue's show. Oprah Winfrey's status as a national celebrity was confirmed clearly when Mike Wallace came to interview her for *60 Minutes*—CBS network's popular Sunday night magazine.

Winfrey's show, soon renamed *The Oprah Winfrey Show,* went into national syndication in 1986, making its star a very rich woman. The deal netted her an estimated $30 million. But more than that, the show introduced a new kind of television that emphasized women's voices, the appeal of personal stories and the power of sharing them. Although Winfrey had drifted from the strict Christianity of her childhood, she brought a strong spirituality to her show, focusing on her audience's sense of inner strength and well-being. She was warm and personal, hugging guests and audience members, her eyes welling with tears when they spoke of pain or loss. Viewers saw her as a friend, someone they understood; when she publicly revealed her own survival of childhood sexual abuse she forged a powerful bond of sisterhood with other survivors.

Even while achieving television stardom, Winfrey took on new projects. In 1985 she acted in *The Color Purple,* a film adaptation of Alice Walker's novel. Although the Steven Spielberg–produced movie garnered mixed reviews, many critics singled out Winfrey's performance for praise. In 1986 she formed Harpo Productions, becoming the first black woman to own a television and film studio. Harpo releases often mined literature by African-American women, producing *The Women of Brewster Place,* based on a book by Gloria Naylor, in 1988, *The Wedding,* based on a book by Dorothy West, in 1998, and the film version of Toni Morrison's *Beloved,* starring Oprah herself, in 1999. Winfrey's lifelong passion for reading led her to create an on-air book club that has revolutionized the publishing world. This irrepressible and irresistible icon of late-twentieth-century American culture will continue to surprise us in the next century.

Tiger Woods

The Golfer
(1975–)

Golf's first black superstar, Tiger Woods trained for the sports spotlight from an early age. A true prodigy, Woods was demonstrating an already perfect swing on national television by the age of three. Called "the Mozart of his sport" by the *New York Times,* Woods has not only conquered golf's biggest prizes—winning the Master's Cup at twenty-one and the PGA championship at twenty-three—he has broken into the top ranks of sports fame in terms of product endorsements, fan clubs, and public acclaim. Remarkable for any golfer, Woods's accomplishments are made all the more compelling by his having achieved the pinnacle of success in a sport previously inaccessible to African Americans. He is to golf what Arthur Ashe was to tennis—the young man who shattered the racist walls of his sport with style and confidence.

Born December 30, 1975, in Cypress, California, Woods was christened Eldrick, but nicknamed Tiger after a Vietnamese friend and soldier buddy of his father's. His parents, Earl and Kultida, a native of Thailand, knew early on that their son had special talent. At ten months, he climbed out of his high chair to whack a golf ball with a plastic putter; by two he shot with his own, specially shortened, clubs. After appearing on CBS News and the *Mike Douglas Show* at age three, Tiger shot a 48 on a nine-hole course, and he just kept getting better. "It was mind-boggling to see a 4½-year-old swinging like a refined touring pro," his first coach told reporters. "It was like watching a PGA player shrunk to fifty pounds."

Woods soon became a local celebrity, signing autographs at the Cypress Golf Club for adult admirers before he was even tall enough for regular golf clubs. He won his first tournaments at eight and nine, and nearly won again at ten, but his birdies in the last six holes left him two shots back. Coaches and parents noticed his competitive fire and worked to teach him patience and tolerance for the occasion-

> *I don't just want to be the best black player or the best Asian player. I want to be the best golfer ever.*
> —Tiger Woods

al loss. A bright and serious child, Tiger also attracted attention for his generosity—worried at age nine about Ethiopian famine victims, he asked his parents to send the twenty dollars in his piggy bank to Africa.

Meanwhile, the wins continued, and before long the Woods's living room was filled with Tiger's trophies. At fifteen—when *Sports Illustrated* first profiled him—he became the youngest golfer to win the U.S. Junior Amateur Championship, a tournament he won three times in a row. In 1994 he graduated from high school and entered Stanford University on a golf scholarship. In the same year, Woods graduated to the U.S. Amateur tournament, becoming the youngest player in history to win that contest, too. He won again in 1995 and 1996.

NCAA eligibility rules allow golfers to enter a limited number of PGA events per year, and Woods had started playing against adults in 1992 at the age of sixteen. By 1996 the entire golf establishment waited to hear when he would turn pro. Woods was a serious student who, at thirteen had written Stanford's golf coach to discuss his plan "to obtain a quality business education," and had maintained a 3.7 grade point average throughout high school. But he routinely dominated collegiate tournaments, and the NCAA limitations began to chafe. In the summer of 1996, after two years at Stanford, Woods left college and the world of amateur golf.

Already famous among golf enthusiasts and other sports fans (*Golf World* named him man of the year in 1994 and *Sports Illustrated* followed suit in 1996), Woods entered pro golf as a full-fledged media sensation. Focus on his race intensified and made him uncomfortable. Growing up black in an all-white neighborhood, Woods had faced prejudice, and he had received death threats as a teenager playing in tournaments. Describing himself as "Cablinasian"—a combination reflecting his mixed racial background, of black, white, Thai, Chinese, and American Indian ancestry—he refused the mantle of black golfer, preferring recognition for his athletic prowess. Despite the public's mixed reaction to his son's self-definition, Earl Woods simply commented that no matter what Tiger might want, "his race can't be ignored."

Neither could his golf. After his dramatic 1997 win at the Master's, golf's most prestigious tournament, Woods was chosen Male Athlete of the Year by the Associated Press. He had won five major tournaments, earned more than $2 million in PGA events, and reached the sport's number one ranking in June 1997—the youngest player ever to attain that status. In 1998, Woods won three major events, placed in the top ten thirteen times in twenty tournaments, and brought home nearly $3 million in tournament prizes.

His upward trajectory continued in 1999, when Woods won the PGA Championship, along with nearly a dozen other tournaments, earning more than $7 million worldwide. Once again he was named the Associated Press's Male Athlete of the Year and PGA Player of the Year. Endorsement deals from Nike, Titleist, American Express, Wheaties, and Rolex have earned Woods well over $100 million. On June 19, 2000 he won the 100th U.S. Open, with a record-breaking fifteen-shot margin. His extraordinary success has revolutionized the sport and radically changed the attitudes of black people toward golf. In both senses, this great athlete is a cultural icon of the first order, a young man, in reporter Jim McCabe's words, "Whose genius brought the game as close to the edge of perfection as ever witnessed."

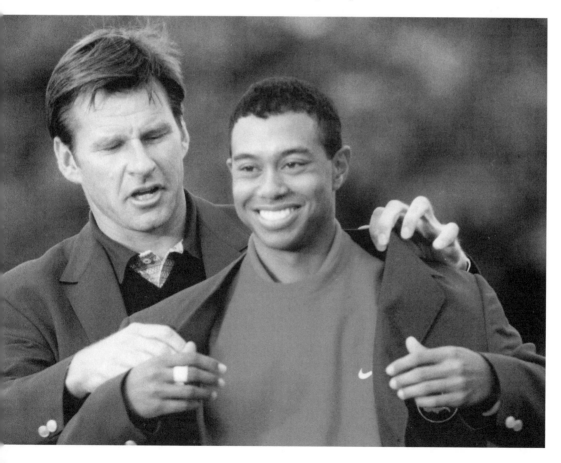

Timeline of the African American Century

1900   Elijah McCoy receives a patent for a self-lubricating device for engines in motion.

1901   William Monroe Trotter founds the militant newspaper *The Boston Guardian.*

1902   Virginia eliminates blacks as voters by imposing a subjective "understanding test."

1903   Maggie Walker is the first black woman to open a bank, St. Luke's Penny Savings.

1904   George Poage wins a bronze medal in the 400-meter hurdles at the St. Louis Olympics.

1905   Police brutality against African Americans in New York evokes public protest.

1906   Alpha Phi Alpha, the first black fraternity, is founded at Cornell University.

1907   Holding a Ph.D. from Harvard, Alain Locke becomes the first black Rhodes Scholar.

1908   Allensworth, an all-black town, is founded in California north of Bakersfield.

1909   Fifty women organize the National Association of Colored Graduate Nurses.

1910   Sixty-seven African Americans are lynched in the United States.

1911   The National Urban League is formed to improve economic conditions for blacks.

1912   Bill Foster creates the first black-directed film, *The Railroad Porter.*

1913   Harriet Tubman, a major participant in the Underground Railroad, dies.

1914   In France, African-American aviator Eugene Bullard wins one thousand dollars from a white man who bet blacks were incapable of learning to fly.

1915   Oklahoma passes a state law requiring the segregation of telephone booths.

1916   Carter G. Woodson publishes the first issue of the *Journal of Negro History.*

1917   Thousands of blacks march silently down Fifth Avenue in New York City to protest lynching.

1918   Segregated units of black American soldiers fight in France during World War I.

1919   Edward Brooke, who will be the first black U.S. Senator since Reconstruction, is born.

1920   The National Negro Baseball League is organized.

1921   *Shuffle Along,* the pathbreaking black jazz musical, opens in New York.

1922   Claude McKay publishes his collection of poetry, *Harlem Shadows.*

1923   Over a half million African Americans leave the South for the promise of jobs and freedom in the North.

1924   DeHart Hubbard, a track and field athlete, wins an Olympic gold medal in Paris.

1925   A. Philip Randolph founds the Brotherhood of Sleeping Car Porters Union.

1926   Arthur Schomburg's black book collection goes to the New York Public Library.

1927   The Supreme Court strikes down laws prohibiting blacks from voting in primaries.

1928   Nella Larsen publishes her Harlem Renaissance novel *Quicksand.*

1929   The Great Depression disproportionately affects "first-fired" African Americans.

1930   In a gesture of respect, the *New York Times* begins capitalizing "Negro."

1931   Elijah Muhammad founds the separatist, and militant, Nation of Islam.

CHRONOLOGY

1932	An African-American team, the New York Rens, defeats the Boston Celtics to win the World Basketball Championship.
1933	Caterina Jarboro sings *Aida* with the Chicago Opera Company.
1934	LeRoi Jones, who will become poet Amiri Baraka, is born in Newark.
1935	Percy Julian develops a drug for the treatment of the eye disease glaucoma.
1936	Jesse Owens wins four gold medals at the Berlin Olympics.
1937	William Edmonson is the first black artist to have a show at the Museum of Modern Art.
1938	Pioneer jazz cornetist Joe "King" Oliver dies in Savannah, Georgia.
1939	Mississippi's U.S. Senator Theodore Bilbo introduces a "Back to Africa" bill.
1940	Hattie McDaniel wins an Oscar for her role as "Mammy" in *Gone With the Wind*.
1941	Navy messman Dorrie Miller shoots down Japanese planes at Pearl Harbor.
1942	Aretha Franklin, the future "Queen of Soul," is born in Detroit.
1943	James A. Porter publishes *Modern Negro Art*.
1944	Harry McAlpin is the first black reporter given White House press credentials.
1945	All branches of the U.S. military remain segregated despite orders to the contrary.
1946	Frank Yerby's novel *The Foxes of Harrow* becomes a national bestseller.
1947	Larry Doby is the first black to play baseball in the American League.
1948	White Southerners form the "Dixiecrat" party to maintain white supremacy.
1949	WERD-AM in Atlanta becomes the first black-owned radio station.
1950	Gwendolyn Brooks receives the Pulitzer Prize for her book of poems *Annie Allen*.
1951	John H. Johnson's *Jet* magazine debuts in Chicago.
1952	For the first time in seventy years no lynchings are reported.
1953	Fisk is the first black college to have a chapter of Phi Beta Kappa.
1954	In the *Brown* v. *Board of Education* decision, the Supreme Court outlaws segregation in public schools.
1955	Chuck Berry releases his rock 'n' roll hit *Maybellene*.
1956	Sammy Davis, Jr., debuts on Broadway in the musical *Mr. Wonderful*.
1957	Fats Domino records *I'm Walkin'*.
1958	Alvin Ailey forms his own American Dance Company.
1959	Paule Marshall publishes her novel *Brown Girl, Brownstones*.
1960	College students in Greensboro, North Carolina, sit in at Woolworth's lunch counter.
1961	The average annual income for white men is $5,287; for black men, $3,015.
1962	Federal troops ensure James Meredith's admission to Ole Miss (the University of Mississippi).
1963	Four girls are killed when Birmingham's Sixteenth Street Baptist Church is bombed.
1964	The Supremes' *Where Did Our Love Go* hits number one on the pop charts.
1965	National Baseball Congress names Satchel Paige all-time outstanding player.
1966	Robert Weaver is the first African American appointed to a cabinet post.

1967	Robert Lawrence is selected by NASA as an astronaut for the space program.
1968	The Poor People's Campaign gathering in Washington, D.C., fails.
1969	Harvard University establishes an Afro-American Studies Department.
1970	Maya Angelou publishes *I Know Why the Caged Bird Sings.*
1971	The Black Caucus boycotts President Nixon's State of the Union address.
1972	*Sanford and Son,* starring comedian Redd Foxx, debuts on TV.
1973	Marion Wright Edelman founds the Children's Defense Fund.
1974	*The Sting* film soundtrack introduces the ragtime music of Scott Joplin to a new, appreciative public.
1975	The media reveal that the FBI and CIA have spied on black civil rights and political leaders.
1976	Alex Haley publishes *Roots,* a saga reflecting blacks' African heritage.
1977	Randall Robinson founds TransAfrica, a lobbying organization.
1978	Fay Wattleton begins her term as president of Planned Parenthood.
1979	Arthur Lewis wins the Nobel Prize for economics.
1980	Levi Watkins, Jr., implants an automatic defibrillator in a human heart.
1981	President Reagan dismantles federal antidiscrimination programs.
1982	Quincy Jones produces Michael Jackson's *Thriller,* which becomes the best-selling record of all time.
1983	Vanessa Williams is the first black Miss America.
1984	Singer Marvin Gaye is shot and killed by his father.
1985	Eddie Robinson of Grambling State University becomes the most successful football coach in history.
1986	The film version of Alice Walker's *The Color Purple* is nominated for eleven Oscars.
1987	Harold Washington, the first African-American mayor of Chicago, dies unexpectedly.
1988	Public Enemy, the rap group, makes the charts with *Bring the Noise.*
1989	Kenneth Chenault becomes president of American Express Financial Services.
1990	President George Bush vetoes the Civil Rights Bill of 1990.
1991	Photographer Gordon Parks publishes his autobiography *The Learning Tree.*
1992	The Whitney Museum exhibits the work of painter Jean-Michel Basquiat.
1993	Rita Dove becomes the nation's poet laureate.
1994	Ralph Ellison, author of *Invisible Man,* dies in New York.
1995	Bernard Harris is the first black astronaut to walk in space.
1996	George Walker receives a Pulitzer for his music in the film *Lilacs.*
1997	Betty Shabazz dies of burns from a fire set by her grandson Malcolm.
1998	David Satcher is confirmed as U.S. Surgeon General.
1999	Amadou Diallo is shot forty-one times by New York City police officers.
2000	The Reverend Vashti McKenzie is elected the first female bishop in the AME Church.

A Guide to Further Reading

Space does not permit us to list every important book that illuminates or narrates aspects of the African-American Century. A complete bibliography of twentieth-century African-American history and culture would fill a volume as long as the one we've written. Obviously, many of our one hundred figures are writers themselves—W. E. B. Du Bois, Richard Wright, Ralph Ellison, Alice Walker, James Baldwin, Toni Morrison, to name a few—and their works should be read by every thinking person. But there are many other scholars, journalists, and writers who have made inestimable contributions to our understanding of central African-American subjects; we think of Gunther Schuller on the history of jazz and swing, C. Vann Woodward on the Jim Crow South, Leon Higginbotham on race and the law, or Taylor Branch on the history of the civil rights movement, to name a few. Every year a host of young writers and scholars bring new voices and insights to our experience. And of course websites such as www.netnoir.com and www.Africana.com offer a wholly modern way to navigate the world of knowledge about the African-American world. The following list is intended simply to suggest useful points of entry for any reader who wants to journey further into the magnificent history of the African-American Century.

General works

Appiah, Kwame Anthony, and Henry Louis Gates, Jr., eds. *Africana 2000: An Encyclopedia.* CD-ROM. Redmond: Microsoft, 1999.

Appiah, Kwame Anthony, and Henry Louis Gates, Jr., eds. *Africana 2000: The Encyclopedia of the African and African American Experience.* N.Y.: Basic Books, 1999.

Bennett, Lerone, Jr. *Before the Mayflower: A History of Black Americans.* N.Y.: Penguin, 1982.

Christian, Charles M. *Black Saga; The African-American Experience: A Chronology.* Boston: Houghton Mifflin, 1995.

Franklin, John Hope, and Alfred A. Moss. *From Slavery to Freedom: A History of Negro America.* N.Y.: McGraw Hill, 1994.

Harding, Vincent. *There Is a River: The Black Struggle for Freedom in America*. N.Y.: Vintage, 1983.

Hine, Darlene Clark, et al., eds. *Black Women in America: An Historical Encyclopedia.* 2 volumes. Brooklyn, N.Y.: Carlson Publishing, 1993.

Logan, Rayford W. and Michael R. Winston, eds. *Dictionary of American Negro Biography*. N.Y.: W.W. Norton, 1982.

Salzman, Jack, David Lionel Smith, and Cornel West., eds. *Encyclopedia of African-American Culture and History*. 5 volumes. N.Y.: Simon & Schuster, 1996.

Smith, Jessie Carney, ed. *Notable Black American Women*. 2 volumes. Detroit: Gale Research, 1992, 1996.

Biographies of the One Hundred Figures in *The African-American Century*

1900–1909

W. E. B. Du Bois
Lewis, David Levering. *W. E. B. Du Bois: Biography of a Race, 1868-1919*. N.Y: Henry Holt, 1993.
———. *The Fight for Equality and the American Century, 1919–1963*. N.Y.: Henry Holt, 2000.

T. Thomas Fortune
Thornbrough, Emma Lou. *T. Thomas Fortune, Militant Journalist*. Chicago: University of Chicago Press, 1972.

Matthew Henson
Counter, S. Allen. *North Pole Legacy: Black, White, and Eskimo*. Amherst: University of Massachusetts Press, 1991.

Jack Johnson
Gilmore, Al-Tony. *Bad Nigger: The National Impact of Jack Johnson*. Port Washington, N.Y.: Kennikat Press, 1975.

Scott Joplin
Berlin, Edward A. *King of Ragtime: Scott Joplin and His Era*. N.Y.: Oxford University Press, 1994.

Henry Ossawa Tanner

Henry Ossawa Tanner. Philadelphia: Philadelphia Museum of Art, 1991.

Madame C. J. Walker

Bundles, A'Lelia. *On Her Own Ground: The Life and Times of Madame C. J. Walker*. N.Y.: Scribner, 2001.

Booker T. Washington

Washington, Booker T. *Up from Slavery*. William L. Andrews, ed. N.Y.: Oxford University Press, 1995.

Ida B. Wells Barnett

McMurray, Linda O. *To Keep the Waters Troubled: The Life of Ida B. Wells*. N.Y.: Oxford University Press, 1998.

Bert Williams

Smith, Eric Ledell. *Bert Williams: A Biography of the Pioneer Black Comedian*. Jefferson, N.C.: Mc Farland, 1992.

1910–1919

Mary McLeod Bethune

Holt, Rackham. *Mary McLeod Bethune, A Biography*. Garden City, N.Y.: Doubleday, 1964.

George Washington Carver

McMurry, Linda O. *George Washington Carver, Scientist and Symbol*. N.Y.: Oxford University Press, 1982.

Benjamin O. Davis, Sr.

Fletcher, Marvin. *America's First Black General: Benjamin O. Davis, Sr., 1880–1970*. Lawrence, KS: University Press of Kansas, 1989.

Thomas A. Dorsey

Harris, Michael W. *The Rise of Gospel Blues: The Music of Thomas Andrew Dorsey in the Urban Church*. N.Y.: Oxford University Press, 1994.

W. C. Handy

Handy, W. C. *Father of the Blues: An Autobiography*. N.Y.: DaCapo Press, 1991.

James Weldon Johnson

Johnson, James Weldon. *Along This Way: The Autobiography of James Weldon Johnson.* N.Y.: DaCapo, 1999.

Jelly Roll Morton

Lomax, Alan. *Mr. Jelly Roll*, Berkeley: University of California Press, 1973.

Charles Henry Turner

"Dr. Turner Named to Hall of Fame." *New York Amsterdam News* (June 3, 1975), p. A-5.

Jimmy Winkfield

Hotaling, Edward. *The Great Black Jockeys: The Lives and Times of the Men Who Dominated America's First National Sport.* Rockland, CA: Forum, 1999.

Carter Goodwin Woodson

Goggin, Jacqueline. *Carter Goodwin Woodson: A Life in Black History.* Baton Rouge: Louisiana State University Press, 1993.

1920–1929

Louis Armstrong

Giddins, Gary. *Satchmo.* N.Y.: Doubleday, 1988.

Junius Austin

Burkett, Randall K. *Black Redemption: Churchmen Speak for the Garvey Movement.* Philadelphia: Temple University Press, 1978.

Josephine Baker

Baker, Jean-Claude, and Chris Chase. *Josephine: The Hungry Heart.* N.Y.: Random House, 1993.

Bessie Coleman

Rich, Doris L. *Queen Bess: Daredevil Aviator.* Washington, D.C.: Smithsonian Institution Press, 1993.

Marcus Garvey

Hill, Robert A., and Barbara Bair. *Marcus Garvey: Life and Lessons.* Berkeley: University of California Press, 1987.

Langston Hughes

Rampersad, Arnold. *The Life of Langston Hughes: 1902–1941: I, Too, Sing America; The Life of Langston Hughes 1941–1967: I Dream a World.* N.Y.: Oxford University Press, 1986, 1988.

Ernest Everett Just

Manning, Kenneth. *Black Apollo of Science: The Life of Ernest Everett Just.* N.Y.: Oxford University Press, 1984.

Oscar Micheaux

Green, J. Ronald, and R. Ronald Green. *Straight Lick: The Cinema of Oscar Micheaux.* Bloomington: Indiana University Press, 2000.

Bessie Smith

Albertson, Chris. *Bessie.* N.Y.: Stein and Day, 1972.

Jean Toomer

McKay, Nellie. *Jean Toomer: Artist.* Chapel Hill: University of North Carolina Press, 1984.

1930–1939

Marian Anderson

Keiler, Allan. *Marian Anderson: A Singer's Journey.* N.Y.: Scribner, 2000.

Sterling A. Brown

Gabbin, Joanne V. *Sterling Brown: Building the Black Aesthetic Tradition.* Westport, CT: Greenwood, 1985.

Father Divine

Watts, Jill M. *God, Harlem U.S.A.: The Father Divine Story.* Berkeley: University of California Press, 1992.

Charles Hamilton Houston

McNeil, Genna Ray. *Groundwork: Charles Hamilton Houston and the Struggle for Civil Rights.* Philadelphia: University of Pennsylvania Press, 1983.

Zora Neale Hurston

Hemenway, Robert. *Zora Neale Hurston.* Urbana: University of Illinois Press, 1980.

Robert Johnson

Guralnick, Peter. *Searching for Robert Johnson*. N.Y.: E.P. Dutton, 1989.

Joe Louis

Mead, Chris. *Champion: Joe Louis, Black Hero in White America*. N.Y.: Scribner's Sons, 1985.

Jesse Owens

Baker, William Joseph. *Jesse Owens: An American Life*. N.Y.: Simon & Schuster, 1988.

Paul Robeson

Duberman, Martin Bruml. *Paul Robeson*. N.Y.: Alfred A. Knopf, 1988.

Bill "Bojangles" Robinson

McKelway, St. Clair. "Profiles–Bojangles." *The New Yorker* (Oct. 6 and 13, 1934).

1940–1949

Charles Drew

Hardwick, Richard. *Charles Richard Drew, Pioneer in Blood Research*. N.Y.: Scribner, 1967.

Katherine Dunham

Dunham, Katherine. *A Touch of Innocence: Memories of Childhood*. Chicago: University of Chicago Press, reprinted 1994.

Duke Ellington

Hasse, John Edward. *Beyond Category: The Life and Genius of Duke Ellington*. N.Y.: DaCapo Press, 1995.

Billie Holiday

O'Meally, Robert G. *Lady Day: The Many Faces of Billie Holiday*. N.Y.: DaCapo Press, 2000.

Lena Horne

Buckley, Gail Lumet. *The Hornes: An American Family*. N.Y.: Alfred A. Knopf, 1986.

Jacob Lawrence

Wheat, Ellen. *Jacob Lawrence: American Painter.* Seattle: University of Washington Press, 1986.

Adam Clayton Powell, Jr.

Hamilton, Charles V. *The Political Biography of An American Dilemma.* N.Y.: Atheneum, 1991.

A. Philip Randolph

Pfeffer, Paula F. *A. Philip Randolph: Pioneer of the Civil Rights Movement.* Baton Rouge: Louisiana State University Press, 1996.

Jackie Robinson

Rampersad, Arnold. *Jackie Robinson: A Biography.* N.Y.: Alfred A. Knopf, 1997.

Richard Wright

Fabre, Michael. *The Unfinished Quest of Richard Wright.* Urbana: University of Illinois Press, 1993.

1950–1959

Ralph Bunche

Henry, Charles P. *Ralph Bunche: Model Negro or American Other?* N.Y.: New York University Press, 1999.

Nat "King" Cole

Epstein, Daniel Mark. *Nat King Cole.* N.Y.: Farrar, Straus, and Giroux, 1999.

Miles Davis

Davis, Miles, and Quincy Troupe. *Miles: The Autobiography.* N.Y.: Simon & Schuster, 1990.

Ralph Ellison

Watts, Jerry. *Heroism and the Black Intellectual: Ralph Ellison, Politics, and Afro-American Intellectual Life.* Chapel Hill: University of North Carolina Press, 1994.

Althea Gibson

Gibson, Althea. *I Always Wanted to Be Somebody.* N.Y.: Pyramid, 1960.

Lorraine Hansberry

Carter, Steven R. *Hansberry's Drama: Commitment Amid Complexity*. Urbana: University of Illinois Press, 1991.

Willie Mays

Mays, Willie, and Lou Sahadi. *Say Hey: The Autobiography of Willie Mays*. N.Y.: Simon & Schuster, 1988.

Rosa Parks

Brinkley, Douglas. *Rosa Parks*. N.Y.: Penguin, 2000.

Art Tatum

Lester, James. *Too Marvelous for Words: The Life and Genius of Art Tatum*. N.Y.: Oxford University Press, 1995.

Sarah Vaughan

Gourse, Leslie. *Sassy: The Life of Sarah Vaughan*. N.Y.: Scribners, 1993.

1960–1969

Muhammad Ali

Remnick, David. *King of the World. Muhammad Ali and the Rise of an American Hero*. N.Y.: Alfred A. Knopf, 1999.

James Baldwin

Leeming, David. *James Baldwin: A Biography*. N.Y.: Alfred A. Knopf, 1994.

John Coltrane

Porter Lewis. *John Coltrane: His Life and Music*. Ann Arbor: University of Michigan Press, 1998.

Angela Davis

Aptheker, Bettina. *The Morning Breaks: The Trial of Angela Davis*. Ithaca, N.Y.: Cornell University Press, 1999.

Fannie Lou Hamer

Mills, Kay. *This Little Light of Mine: The Life of Fannie Lou Hamer*. N.Y.: Dutton, 1993.

Jimi Hendrix

Black, Johnny. *Jimi Hendrix: The Ultimate Experience*. N.Y.: Avalon, 1999.

Martin Luther King, Jr.

Garrow, David J. *Bearing the Cross: Martin Luther King, Jr., and the Southern Christian Leadership Conference*. N.Y.: William Morrow, 1986.

Thurgood Marshall

Davis, Michael D., and Hunter R. Clark. *Thurgood Marshall: Warrior at the Bar, Rebel on the Bench*. N.Y.: Citadel Press, 1994.

Sidney Poitier

Poitier, Sidney. *The Measure of a Man: A Spiritual Autobiography*. San Francisco: Harper, 2000.

Malcolm X

The Autobiography of Malcolm X. N.Y.: Grove Press, 1964.

1970–1979

Hank Aaron

Aaron, Hank, and Lonnie Wheeler. *I Had a Hammer: The Hank Aaron Story*. N.Y.: HarperCollins, 1992.

Maya Angelou

Angelou, Maya. *I Know Why the Caged Bird Sings*. N.Y.: Bantam, 1997.

Romare Bearden

Schwartzman, Myron. *Romare Bearden: His Life and Art*. N.Y.: Harry N. Abrams, 1990.

James Brown

Brown, Geoff. *James Brown: Doin' It to Death*. London: Omnibus Press, 1996.

Marvin Gaye

Ritz, David. *Divided Soul: The Life of Marvin Gaye*. N.Y.: DaCapo, 1991.

Barbara Harris

"Harris, Barbara." *Current Biography* 5 (June 1989), pp. 24–28.

Dorothy Height

"A Quiet Crusader for Civil Rights." *New York Times* (Aug. 13, 1979), p. C15.

Barbara Jordan

Rogers, Mary Beth. *Barbara Jordan: American Hero*. N.Y.: Doubleday, 1998.

Leontyne Price

Hill, Ruth Edmonds, and Patricia Miller King, eds. *The Black Women Oral History Project*. Westport, CT: Greenwood, 1990.

Richard Pryor

Williams, John A., and Dennis A. *If I Don't Stop I'll Die: The Comedy and Tragedy of Richard Pryor*. N.Y.: Avalon, 1993.

1980–1989

Alvin Ailey

Dunning, Jennifer. *Alvin Ailey: A Life in Dance*. N.Y.: DaCapo Press, 1998.

Bill Cosby

Smith, Ronald L. *Cosby*. N.Y.: St. Martin's Press, 1986.

John Hope Franklin

Franklin, John Hope. *Race and History: Selected Essays, 1938–1988*. Baton Rouge: Louisiana Sate University Press, 1989.

Jesse Jackson

Hatch, Roger D., and Frank E. Watkins. *Reverend Jesse Jackson: Straight from the Heart*. Philadelphia: 1987.

Michael Jackson

George, Nelson. *The Michael Jackson Story*. N.Y.: Dell, 1984.

Carl Lewis

Lewis, Carl, and Jeffrey Marx. *Carl Lewis: One More Victory Lap*. San Antonio, TX: Aum Publications, 1996.

Jessye Norman

"Norman, Jessye." *The New Grove Dictionary of American Music*. H. Wiley Hitchcock, ed. Stockton Press, 1986.

Martin Puryear

Benezra, Neal. *Martin Puryear*. N.Y.: Thames and Hudson, 1993.

Alice Walker

Lauret, Maria. *Alice Walker*. N.Y.: St. Martin's Press, 1999.

August Wilson

Wolfe, Peter. *August Wilson*. N.Y.: Macmillan, 1999.

1990–1999

Louis Farrakhan

Gardell, Mattias. *In the Name of Elijah Muhammad: Louis Farrakhan and the Nation of Islam*. Durham: Duke University Press, 1996.

Michael Jordan

Jordan, Michael, and Mark Vancil. *For the Love of the Game: My Story*. N.Y.: Crown, 1998.

Spike Lee

Lee, Spike, and Lisa Jones. *Do the Right Thing: A Spike Lee Joint*. N.Y.: Fireside, 1989.

Wynton Marsalis

Gourse, Leslie. *Wynton Marsalis: Skain's Domains, A Biography*. N.Y.: Music Sales, 1999.

Toni Morrison

Patrick Wexler, Diane. *Toni Morrison*. Orlando: Raintree Steck Vaughn, 1997.

Colin Powell

Powell, Colin, and Joseph E. Persico. *My American Journey*. N.Y.: Random House, 1995.

Tupac Shakur

White, Armond. *Rebel for the Hell of It: The Life of Tupac Shakur*. N.Y.: Thunder's Mouth Press, 1997.

Denzel Washington

Davis, Thulani. "Denzel in the Swing." *American Film* (Aug. 1990), pp. 26–31.

Oprah Winfrey

Winfrey, Oprah, and Robert Waldron. *Oprah*. N.Y.: St. Martin's Press, 1988.

Tiger Woods

Strege, John. *Tiger: A Biography of Tiger Woods*. N.Y.: Broadway Books, 1998.

Index

INDEX

INDEX

INDEX

(Illustrations listed in order of appearance)

1900–1909

W. E. B. Du Bois   *Photographs and Prints Division, Schomburg Center for Research in Black Culture, The New York Public Library/Astor, Lenox and Tilden Foundations*

T. Thomas Fortune   *Photographs and Prints Division, Schomburg Center for Research in Black Culture, The New York Public Library/Astor, Lenox and Tilden Foundations*

Matthew Henson   *Courtesy of The Explorers Club*

Jack Johnson   *Collections of the Library of Congress*

Scott Joplin   *Archive Photos*

Henry O. Tanner   *Henry Ossawa Tanner in his Paris Studio. Henry Ossawa Tanner Papers, Archives of American Art, Smithsonian Institute*

Madame C. J. Walker   *Photographs and Prints Division, Schomburg Center for Research in Black Culture, The New York Public Library/Astor, Lenox and Tilden Foundations*

Booker T. Washington   *Archive Photos*

Ida B. Wells-Barnett   *University of Chicago Library Collection*

Bert Williams   *Photographs and Prints Division, Schomburg Center for Research in Black Culture, The New York Public Library/Astor, Lenox and Tilden Foundations*

1910–1919

Mary McLeod Bethune   *Photographs and Prints Division, Schomburg Center for Research in Black Culture, The New York Public Library/Astor, Lenox and Tilden Foundations*

George Washington Carver   *Archive Photos*

Benjamin O. Davis, Sr. © *Bettmann/CORBIS*

Thomas Dorsey   *Archive Photos*

W. C. Handy   *Photographs and Prints Division, Schomburg Center for Research in Black Culture, The New York Public Library/Astor, Lenox and Tilden Foundations*

James Weldon Johnson © *CORBIS*

Jelly Roll Morton   *Archive Photos*

Charles Turner   *Princeton University Library Collection*

Jimmy Winkfield   *Churchill Downs Inc./Kinetic Corporation/Louisville, Kentucky. Ann S. Tatum— Curator Kentucky Derby Photo Archives*

Carter G. Woodson   *Photographs and Prints Division, Schomburg Center for Research in Black Culture, The New York Public Library/Astor, Lenox and Tilden Foundations*

1920–1929

Louis Armstrong *Photographs and Prints Division, Schomburg Center for Research in Black Culture, The New York Public Library/Astor, Lenox and Tilden Foundations*

Junius C. Austin *Randall K. Burkett, Private Collection*

Josephine Baker *The Shubert Archive*

Bessie Coleman *Photographs and Prints Division, Schomburg Center for Research in Black Culture, The New York Public Library/Astor, Lenox and Tilden Foundations*

Marcus Garvey *© Bettmann/CORBIS*

Langston Hughes *Carl Van Vechten by permission of Van Vechten Trust/Yale Collection of American Literature, Beinecke Rare Book and Manuscript Library*

Ernest Everett Just *Princeton University Library Collection*

Oscar Micheaux *Photo courtesy of South Dakota State Historical Society*

Bessie Smith *Frank Driggs/Archive Photos*

Jean Toomer *© Bettmann/CORBIS*

1930–1939

Marian Anderson *© CORBIS*

Sterling Brown *Moorland-Spingarn Research Center/Howard University*

Father Divine *AP Wideworld Photo*

Charles H. Houston *© Bettmann/CORBIS*

Zora Neale Hurston *Collections of the Library of Congress*

Robert Johnson *Robert Johnson Studio Portrait. Hooks Bros., Memphis, 1935. © 1989 Delta Haze Corporation. All Rights Reserved. Used by Permission.*

Joe Louis *© CORBIS*

Jesse Owens *Hulton-Deutsch Collections/CORBIS*

Paul Robeson *Courtesy of Paul Robeson, Jr.*

Bill "Bojangles" Robinson *Metronome/Archives Photo*

1940–1949

Charles Drew *Photographs and Prints Division, Schomburg Center for Research in Black Culture, The New York Public Library/Astor, Lenox and Tilden Foundations*

Katherine Dunham *© Bettmann/CORBIS*

Duke Ellington *© Bettmann/CORBIS*

Billie Holiday *© Bettmann/CORBIS*

Lena Horne *Metronome/Archive Photos*

Jacob Lawrence *© Bettmann/CORBIS*

Adam Clayton Powell, Jr. *Bob Henriques/Magnum Photos Inc.*

A. Philip Randolph *Photographs and Prints Division, Schomburg Center for Research in Black Culture, The New York Public Library/Astor, Lenox and Tilden Foundations*

Jackie Robinson *Pittsburgh Courier/Archive Photos*

Richard Wright *Carl Van Vechten by permission of Van Vechten Trust*

1950–1959

Ralph Bunche *Carl Van Vechten by permission of Van Vechten Trust*

Nat King Cole *© Bettmann/CORBIS*

Miles Davis *Stone/Hulton Getty Collection*

Ralph Ellison *Frank Driggs/Archive Photos*

Althea Gibson *Althea Gibson Foundation*

Lorraine Hansberry *David Attie, Lorraine Hansberry, 1959 Courtesy* Vogue. *Copyright © 1959 (renewed 1987, Condé Nast Publications Inc.)*

Willie Mays *© Bettmann/CORBIS*

Rosa Parks *© Bettmann/CORBIS*

Art Tatum *Frank Driggs/Archive Photos*

Sarah Vaughan *Breitenbach/Archive Photos*

1960–1969

Muhammad Ali *© Bettmann/CORBIS*

James Baldwin *Bob Parent/Archive Photos*

John Coltrane *© Mosaic Images/CORBIS*

Angela Davis *© Miroslav Zajíc/CORBIS*

Fannie Lou Hamer *© Bettmann/CORBIS*

Jimi Hendrix *Michael Ochs Archive/Venice, California*

Martin Luther King, Jr. *© Bettmann/CORBIS*

Thurgood Marshall *Stone/Hulton Getty Collection*

Sidney Poitier *© Bettmann/CORBIS*

Malcolm X *Archive Photos*

1970–1979

Hank Aaron *Archive Photos*

Maya Angelou *Wayne Miller/Magnum Photos*

Romare Bearden *© Frank Stewart*

James Brown *© David Corio*

PHOTO CREDITS

Marvin Gaye *Stone/Hulton Getty Collection*

Barbara Harris *Mikki Ansin/The Liaison Agency*

Dorothy Height *Photographs and Prints Division, Schomburg Center for Research in Black Culture, The New York Public Library/Astor, Lenox and Tilden Foundations*

Barbara Jordan *Texas Senate Media*

Leontyne Price *Photographs and Prints Division, Schomburg Center for Research in Black Culture, The New York Public Library/Astor, Lenox and Tilden Foundations*

Richard Pryor © *Bettmann/CORBIS*

1980–1989

Alvin Ailey *Eric N. Hong*

Bill Cosby © *Lynn Goldsmith/CORBIS*

John Hope Franklin *Duke University Photography*

Jesse Jackson © *Bettmann/CORBIS*

Michael Jackson © *Lynn Goldsmith/CORBIS*

Carl Lewis © *Bettmann/CORBIS*

Jessye Norman *Courtesy of Jessye Norman*

Martin Puryear *Courtesy of Donald Young Gallery*

Alice Walker *Stone/Hulton Getty Collection*

August Wilson *AP/Wide World Photos*

1990–1999

Louis Farrakhan *Jim Bourg/The Liaison Agency*

Michael Jordan *Sporting News/Archive Photos*

Spike Lee *Lara Jo Regan/The Liaison Agency*

Wynton Marsalis © *Frank Stewart*

Toni Morrison *AP/Wide World Photos*

Colin Powell *Reuters/Stephen Jaffee/Archive Photos*

Tupac Shakur © *Steven Wolf/CORBIS*

Denzel Washington *Bob Grant/Fotos International/Archive Photos*

Oprah Winfrey © *1998 HARPO Productions, Inc./Photographer: Timothy White*

Tiger Woods *Reuters/Mike Blake/Archive Photos*